How States Shaped Postwar America

How States Shaped Postwar America

State Government and Urban Power

NICHOLAS DAGEN BLOOM

University of Chicago Press
Chicago and London

The University of Chicago Press, Chicago 60637
The University of Chicago Press, Ltd., London

Published 2019
Printed in the United States of America

28 27 26 25 24 23 22 21 20 19 1 2 3 4 5

ISBN-13: 978-0-226-49831-7 (cloth)
ISBN-13: 978-0-226-49845-4 (e-book)
DOI: https://doi.org/10.7208/chicago/9780226498454.001.0001

Library of Congress Cataloging-in-Publication Data

Names: Bloom, Nicholas Dagen, 1969– author.
Title: How states shaped postwar America : state government and urban power / Nicholas Dagen Bloom.
Description: Chicago : University of Chicago Press, 2019. | Includes bibliographical references and index.
Identifiers: LCCN 2018041637 | ISBN 9780226498317 (cloth : alk. paper) | ISBN 9780226498454 (ebook)
Subjects: LCSH: Urban policy—New York (State)—History—20th century. | Urban renewal—New York (State)—History—20th century. | Rockefeller, Nelson A. (Nelson Aldrich), 1908–1979. | Urban policy—United States—History—20th century. | Urban renewal—United States—History—20th century.
Classification: LCC HT176.N7 B56 2019 | DDC 307.3/4160974709044—dc23
LC record available at https://lccn.loc.gov/2018041637

♾ This paper meets the requirements of ANSI/NISO Z39.48–1992 (Permanence of Paper).

For Brenna Roxie Bloom, the writer

Contents

The Urban Challenge

1

Planning for Prosperity

The unprecedented improvement in American living standards during the 1950s and 1960s was a welcome change from years of economic troubles and a second global war. Breadwinners drove powerful cars to steady work in a booming industrial sector, sleek center-city high-rises, and luxuriant suburban office parks. Comfy suburban subdivisions to which they returned in the evening boasted green lawns, government-insured mortgages, and residential zoning. More high school graduates than ever before had hopes of attending colleges and universities. The prosperity of this era, despite a wide gap between the prospects of white and black families, echoes today as a reference point for the American way of life.[1] Americans achieved this high standard of living because of the astonishing productive capacity of the nation's powerful metropolitan areas. Even sleepy southern states, once far behind the North in the percentage of city dwellers, urbanized rapidly in the postwar years thanks to highways, air-conditioning, relocation of industry, and federal spending.

America's growing urban majority was not randomly distributed across the nation's many states. By 1960, 62.8 percent of the national population inhabited sprawling Standard Metropolitan Statistical Areas, of which there were 212 by 1960, an increase of 24 in 10 years. These metropolitan areas—constellations of interconnected cities, suburbs, and towns—dominated the nation's culture, demographic trends, and private and public sectors.[2] The rise of metropolitan America raised a fundamental question: Would the tiered American political system of local, state, and federal governments competently manage such complex urban systems? The mounting social and environmental costs of postwar urban consumer society offered a grim answer.

The drawbacks of rapid, large-scale urbanization, often related to fractured or incompetent public leadership, became a target of postwar media and academic critics. John Kenneth Galbraith's 1958 best seller, *The Affluent Society*, offered an unflattering portrait of a society so consumed with production that it had lost any sense of what he called *social balance*: "The family which takes its mauve and cerise, air-conditioned, power-steered and power-braked automobile out for a tour passes through cities that are badly paved, made hideous by litter, blighted buildings, billboards and posts. . . . They pass on into a countryside that that has been rendered largely invisible by commercial art. . . . They picnic on exquisitely packaged food from a portable icebox by a polluted stream and go on to spend the night at a park which is a menace to public health and morals." Newspapers and media outlets highlighted the "shortages and shortcomings in the elementary municipal and metropolitan services," including overcrowded schools, unsafe neighborhoods, riots, threadbare parks, litter, dirty air and water, and collapsing mass transit.[3] Widely read articles in *Fortune* magazine by sociologist William H. Whyte expanded into popular books in the 1960s, questioned the environmental toll of sprawling cities and suburbs. Mostly unflattering portraits of suburban life, including Whyte's *The Organization Man* (1956) and John Keats's *The Crack in the Picture Window* (1956), dissected the pros and cons of the new affluence to individuals, families, and communities. Studies criticizing the new urban order sold briskly in this era, including *The Death and Life of Great American Cities* (1961), *Megalopolis* (1961), *The Highway and the City* (1963), and *God's Own Junkyard* (1964).[4]

The prominent New York intellectuals writing many of these books and articles were sensitive to the trend lines as they experienced firsthand the most complex, vexing, and advanced urban problems close to home. New York City had entered a new kind of urban crisis, not just a temporary economic downturn. The city's five boroughs collectively lost about 100,000 residents during the otherwise booming 1950s, even as the suburbs and the distant Sunbelt cities thrived, indicating that a century and a half of stunning growth had come to a disturbing end. During the 1960s and 1970s, urban crime across New York City skyrocketed, factories closed or moved to the suburbs or out of state, and private housing abandonment accelerated. A racial dimension complicated the declining urban situation as "thousands of unskilled poor, drawn by the legendary opportunities of the northern cities, have come from the south and Puerto Rico to swell already massive ghettos." Their frustration mounted in the crummy tenements or grim public housing projects, second-class schools, poorly kept neighborhoods, and dead-end jobs. Cut off from the American good life, but aware of suburban bounty, they were getting impatient.[5] The frustration over urban conditions even inflected life for Manhattan's white elite. Many "executives looked around them and noted an appalling lack of housing for their middle-income executives, the snarled transit system . . . higher personal income tax in the city, strife-ridden public schools, unsafe streets, [and] faltering public utilities." A slow stream of major companies and their employees shifted to suburban campuses or pulled up stakes from the region entirely.[6]

The urban crisis documented in Rust Belt cities like New York and Detroit was a factor even in emerging Sunbelt metropolises such as Miami and Los Angeles. Central cities across the nation were entering a period of sustained decline and racial change as their prosperous citizens, then mostly white, decamped for the suburbs. The bulldozing of center-city districts for private-sector redevelopment and highways from Los Angeles to Miami raised questions about displacement, equity, and the quality of new environments, usually without delivering on the utopian landscapes promised in public relation campaigns. The nation's urban mass transit systems, once extensive in both the North and the South, were collapsing.

The suburban edge also revealed distinct shortcomings, coast to coast, due to rapid growth. Subdivisions often required a level of urban services borne either by unsuspecting home buyers or neighboring taxpayers. Many developers openly cut corners on water treatment, parks, and other public services. Most suburban colleges and universities, if they existed at all in fast-developing areas, had trouble meeting the surging demand for excellent, low-cost higher education. Highways that brought suburbanites to the edge quickly crowded with commuters; aging rail lines barely sufficed to maintain commutes to good center-city jobs. Holidaying suburbanites discovered that existing state parks failed to deliver a quality natural experience.

Americans today may look on the postwar decades as a lost golden age, but opinion on the achievement was decidedly mixed at the time—and not just among elite critics. The American urban standard had, after all, revealed severe and numerous flaws. New York City, as the nation's media capital, was the most frequent face of urban decline, but this was a matter of editorial choice and accessibility for reporters rather than a unique situation. Almost all of America's big cities were on the brink because the same economic and social forces were in play. Riots from Newark to Cleveland to Los Angeles in the 1960s confirmed trends documented years, and sometimes decades, before. If urbanized regions were the future of America, something dramatic would need to be done.

What Do States Owe Cities?

The first states to grapple with urban policy in the postwar era were the most beset by urban issues (traffic, pollution, poverty, etc.), such as New York, Michigan, California, Massachusetts, and Illinois. Many of these had been majority urban for decades and, as a result, leaders there had been grappling with municipal issues at the state level, including laws addressing housing, water quality, roads, etc. Here originated what political scientists Robert Connery and Gerald Benjamin called "urban governorship," an expectation that governors would "help solve problems that were spilling over urban borders into the hinterland."[7]

The first wave of activist postwar governorships, including Thomas Dewey (R-NY), Earl Warren (R-CA), and G. Mennan "Soapy" Williams (D-MI), set the stage for broader expansion in the 1960s. Governor Dewey, a northern Republican with a long-standing interest in good government, was recognized for an aggressive highway program, mass transit preservation, state housing projects, civil rights laws, and the creation of the State University of New York. Earl Warren of California laid the groundwork for the state's postwar supremacy in higher education. "Soapy" Williams during his twelve-year run in Michigan worked with Walter Reuther and other labor leaders to make major advances on "civil rights, compulsory health insurance, training programs for the unemployed, public recreation, [and] education" in order "to make Michigan a laboratory for social democracy."[8] A second generation of prominent state governors built on this strong start, including Edmund "Pat" Brown (D-CA) and Nelson Rockefeller (R-NY), who enjoyed unprecedented and sustained support for urban-oriented policies by their state legislatures.

As urbanization became characteristic of life in growing cities within traditionally rural states such as Georgia, North Carolina, Texas, Florida, Oregon, and Arizona, state governments began to address needs generated by growing metropolitan areas. Residents shared concerns about disinvestment, racial conflict, and poverty, quality housing shortages, clogged roads, and polluted waterways. The changing landscapes and lifestyles generated southern and western state leadership with an urban accent. In North Carolina, Governor Luther Hodges (D-NC) led the development of North Carolina's Research Triangle Park. His successor, James Terry Sanford (D-NC), invigorated the state's universities. Among the new players were Tom McCall (R-OR), keen on conservation and land-use issues, and segregationist Governor C. Farris Bryant (D-FL), a pioneering force on highways, state university expansion, urban representation in state government, and conservation. Legislative creativity ensued across the nation. Sunbelt metropolitan areas in states like

Florida, Texas, Arizona, and California were big winners from postwar state investments as they sprawled in tandem with the new highways, colleges, stadiums, parks, transit systems, and more.

American states initiated urban policy on an unprecedented scale in the postwar years, but they had always possessed the power to shape urban life, even if they had been reluctant to exercise that control directly. State governments had created all local governments, and states had progressively granted municipalities growing powers in land use, nuisance control, and public infrastructure. Governor Rockefeller, who positioned himself as a spokesman for activist governors during his long service as New York's governor (1959–1973), reminded his peers many times that in American governance, "the State is the ultimate authority. . . . It gave a portion of its sovereignty to the Federal government. . . . But it reserved a share of the sovereignty, and local government is a creature of it."[9] While those on the right laid the loudest claim to "states' rights" as a justification for defying federal power, many postwar governors demonstrated that federalism could be equally useful as a source for urban-oriented progressive state planning. States' rights cuts both ways on the political spectrum. Activist states could be inventive and, if necessary, boldly extend the scale and scope of state-funded and state-controlled urban policy.

State-level power, many governors believed, would have to be affirmed in an era of intrusive federal actions.[10] Successful federal programs in social insurance, highways, and aviation overshadowed the mixed record of most other national domestic programs. Federal programs were, as a rule, generally smaller and less generous than those desired by most governors and mayors. Many federal initiatives, such as mortgage insurance, urban interstates, defense contracting, and urban renewal frequently worsened conditions in older city centers. The massive shift to suburbs, aided by other federal programs, put stresses on schools, sewers, and local government. Compounding the problem further was an open bias in federal spending to the emerging Sunbelt. The State Urban Relations Committee of the National Governors Conference in 1968, led by Governor Richard Hughes (D-NJ) argued that well-funded states needed to temper the trend to "one size fits all" policies: "Indeed, the States are the necessary 'middle ground' between the rigidity of centralization and the limited capacity and resources which are characteristic of highly decentralized local government."[11]

The postwar gaps in urban policy and the faltering outlook for so many cities created an opportunity for states. American state governments possessed a wide range of latent powers that could be used for new initiatives. Most federal policies and grants required permission, grant of powers, and even implementation through state offices. This screening process created opportunities for governors and state legislatures to adapt and control the application of federal grants and laws. Courts also endorsed state supremacy over claims of local home rule that allowed them to create powerful new policies and institutions, such as regional transportation authorities and metropolitan planning agencies that ignored municipal boundaries. The Supreme Court's *Baker v. Carr* (1962) and *Reynolds v. Sims* (1964) decisions requiring redistricting finally gave urban voters a stronger (although rarely dominant) voice against rural interests, the "tyranny of the small town," in state legislatures.[12]

States usually possessed comparatively robust institutional health that aided implementation. Most American states enjoyed more stable revenue sources than cities and could more easily create new ones that they used for ambitious programs in transit or higher education. Governors had the advantage of not having to deal, as mayors often did, with crippling municipal problems of white flight, ghettoization, declining revenues, entrenched labor unions, and disinvestment. States employed a growing civil-service-screened bureaucracy that contrasted sharply with their city-based counterparts, who often secured jobs thanks to political machines or ethnic niches. The rise of centralized state government divisions and agencies "with broad functional responsibilities" frequently replaced a fragmented system of agencies, thus calling forth "an executive structure which is manageable and capable of coordinated planning and implementation." There were many reasons for optimism.[13]

Paying for Urban Policy

Governors who succeeded in policy did so by convincing the metropolitan public and their colleagues in state legislatures that careful and sustained effort to achieve ambitious goals would enhance postwar prosperity. Families and individuals would benefit from new state parks, tighter environmental regulations, publicly operated mass transportation, new university and hospital campuses, mixed-income housing programs, and speedy urban highways and interstates. Indeed, middle-class families gave their political support to state initiatives, at least for several decades, because they saw room for improvement in their tap water, the state parks they visited, and their children's crowded grade schools and colleges. African American families—a growing, vocal, and increasingly visible part of the electorate—welcomed new services, housing programs, educational opportunities, and legal protections in states that would aid in social mobility.

Governors spent most of their political capital, and engaged in planning, as part of selling specific public goods and services such as college campuses and parks to voters, business interests, labor unions, and state legislators. One polling expert concluded that while Americans were still generally conservative politically, in practice, they were "operational liberals" who could be coaxed to support specific, even expensive, environmental, infrastructure, or social programs.[14] As a result, promoters avoided overly intellectual justifications when speaking to the public. Jon C. Teaford in *The Rise of the States* (2002) makes a strong case that in the postwar era "the states were alive and well, and beyond the glare of the public's attention, they were molding the nation's future" in areas like transportation and higher education.[15] State governments rarely granted urban leaders all the "home rule" powers that they demanded, and in many cases reserved the final say on crucial local policy and tax decisions, but this reservation of power often translated into new state-run urban enterprises (mass transit, urban higher education, and redevelopment agencies) rather than the absence or elimination of crucial programs. So much state-sponsored public action inevitably required an unprecedented scale of planning and governance.[16]

A reinforcing loop developed as many programs, entrusted to new agencies and authorities, rolled out of statehouses, bringing cleaner air and water, statewide conservation plans, expanded college campuses, redeveloped downtowns, subsidized housing programs, new hospitals and mental health facilities, and regional economic development. Almost all these benefits flowed to fast-growing urbanized regions.[17] Developers, landowners, contractors, engineers, planners, and architects (components of the urban growth machine) won lucrative, low-risk contracts. In time, many became successful players at the state level with organizations and power bases that produced a steady flow of innovative programs. Ideology often mattered less than interests. A steady uptick in spending on state government lobbying was just one indication of the growing role of states in urban affairs.

The cumulative cost of state programs reflects the transformed role of states in American life. From 1950 to 1966 state spending increased 247 percent, a rate of increase higher than that for federal spending on domestic programs and roughly equal to the increase in local expenditures.[18] In 1958, state aid to local government averaged just $47 ($404 in 2017 dollars) per capita.[19] By 1978 aid to localities had reached $300 ($1,145 in 2017 dollars) per capita, with much higher levels for the most urbanized states. These figures do not include the massive amounts of debt states issued for programs with significant urban impacts such as campus development, highways, mass transit, housing, and more.[20] By 1978 states provided approximately $50 billion

($191 billion in 2017 dollars) in direct state aid to local government (the majority for schools and the rest for general support, highways, welfare, etc.) out of a national total of $85 billion ($324 billion in 2017 dollars) in intergovernmental support. States today (2018) still provide significant funding to many local governments, primarily in the form of school aid, but the amount varies widely due to the degree of urban home rule, the extent of local taxation, and the level of local debt permitted by state legislatures.[21]

State/Federal Partnership

The level of state aid to city regions was unprecedented. Rarely, however, did state sources of revenue (taxes, fees, bonds, etc.) suffice to meet the challenge of providing quality services on a regional urban scale. State officials, often in partnership with city leaders, thus spent a growing portion of their time and energy fighting to initiate and sustain federal contributions to state and local government. The federal role in urban interstates is a familiar touchstone for urbanists and was transformative in ways that most federal aid to states and cities was not, but the state/federal partnership ran deeper than roads.

The rolling out of nearly every state initiative either responded to or was closely followed by a federal program or subsidy. State officials for decades could count on a sympathetic ear from many federal officials, in both parties, who believed in the constructive role that government could play in the lives of ordinary Americans. Elements of the New Deal order were quietly sustained after World War II through federal/state partnerships in housing, urban infrastructure, housing, parks, and social services. Hundreds of millions and sometimes billions of dollars in federal aid flowed into states for interstates, completion of expensive waste treatment plants, mass transit modernization and expansion, medical and mental health services, university research facilities and federal student aid, and new housing programs. Some of these programs developed independently of state lobbying, but others were direct responses to new state-level needs.[22]

Nelson Rockefeller's successful public campaign in the late 1960s for federal revenue sharing with states and local governments has been dismissed by some as an act of desperation. Many state and federal leaders supported his effort, however, and accepted shared federal revenues in practice, because he had a solid point that the federal government could have done much more to address the needs of urbanized states. States were expected to spend unprecedented sums even though the federal government still collected 64 percent of all taxes in 1969, compared with just 19 percent collected by states and 17 percent by cities. New York was particularly shortchanged, receiving from the federal government just $1.4 billion ($9.4 billion in 2017 dollars) for the state and $1.7 billion ($11.5 billion in 2017 dollars) for the city of the $22 billion ($149 billion in 2017 dollars) in federal taxes collected statewide.[23] Without revenue sharing, Rockefeller warned of "a wave of bankruptcies" in state and city governments nationally.[24]

Rockefeller received bipartisan support, including that of 32 governors, and together they convinced the Nixon administration to prioritize the proposal. Revenue sharing had enemies on the left and right but also demonstrable benefits: immediate help for stressed states, flexible dollars for local priorities, and streamlined federalism for conservatives. The Nixon administration's revenue sharing program, less than hoped for but still crucial, passed in 1972.[25] The combination of revenue sharing, underlying federal subsidy programs, and grants had a cumulative impact on state and local finances. By 1975, federal funds counted for between 15 and 20 percent of state and local revenue in the nation's 10 largest states: California, Florida, Illinois, Indiana, Massachusetts, Michigan, New Jersey, New York, Ohio, and Texas. By 1973, New York State alone received $3.45 billion ($19.3 billion in 2017 dollars) in various federal nonappropriated subsidies, a ninefold increase from 1958. The federal government, despite successfully sharing approximately $85 billion over the life of the program, and the program's demonstrated efficiency, terminated revenue sharing in 1986.[26]

The robust postwar federal/state partnership faltered in the 1980s on many fronts and has remained, to the present, strained by cutbacks and ideological differences. The declining state/federal partnership has hurt ambitious and expensive state programs in higher education, urban highways, mass transit, affordable housing, and more. Representatives of state and metropolitan interests have, however, have fought hard in Washington, DC, and state capitals to sustain and update programs or find funding alternatives. Except for extreme cuts in the most antigovernment states and successful attacks on the most liberal agendas (like public housing and mass transit), the state/federal partnership has survived. The source of that persistence is the mainstream popularity and success of so many different state activities—even when the public does not fully recognize them as subsidized government services.

The State-Sponsored American Urban Landscape

The growing influence of state government on American urban life has been underappreciated in urban history, public policy, and contemporary culture. The result of this nearsightedness is an incomplete picture of the forces and personalities that shaped and continues to influence our modern city regions where most Americans now live. *How States Shaped Postwar America* demonstrates this massive and enduring impact by reexamining the urban landscape from the perspective of how state government has reshaped cities since the 1940s. State efforts, usually in the background of urban policy, are foregrounded and highlighted in the chapters that follow.

This book is shaped around five crucial aspects of American urban form: *urban planning and development* (urban redevelopment, state office development, and regional planning), *transportation* (mass transit and highways), *higher education* (small city/suburban and center-city campuses), *metropolitan housing* (subsidized mixed-income housing, fair housing laws, and deinstitutionalization), and the *environment* (water quality, state parks, and regional conservation).

Governor Nelson Rockefeller's New York projects are featured in the book as primary examples of the new spirit of state government because New York had dramatic urban problems, developed many widely imitated programs, and spent the most to address urban issues. Yet New York's experience, as the stories that follow demonstrate, was distinct mostly in the size and number of its programs. New York's leaders grappled with typical issues for state urban policymakers across the country: the split between rural/urban and urban/suburban interests in state legislatures; the tensions among federal, state, and local officials over responsibility and costs; the enormous expense of meeting the infrastructure needs of the modern metropolis; the mixed outcomes of idealistic programs; and the clash between liberal and conservative ideologies. Each chapter thus weaves together New York examples with those from other states to illustrate, as best as is possible in a decentralized federal structure, the complex national pattern.

The accumulated case studies in this book, and many more not included, illustrate both the perils and promise of different types of urban-related state policies. Many state programs succeeded and were widely imitated, others underperformed, some landed in the middle of expectations, and some generated significant political backlash as attitudes and budgets shifted. In total and over time, however, these programs profoundly changed American metropolitan life. The public developed new expectations about government service (i.e., public transit, public higher education, and environmental regulations) that for most of American history had been ignored or considered primarily private responsibilities. Metros looked different and operated differently because of state action. Without the intervention of states, large public systems in fields like education, transportation, housing, tourism, and the environment might not exist or would be unrecognizable.

This book focuses on a detailed, manageable set of high-profile initiatives with a significant and enduring physical presence in metropolitan areas. There remain many opportunities for additional research on states and urban affairs. A similar analysis of state influence on urban policy and metropolitan life could be applied to K–12 funding, prisons, airports, and more. Would the suburbs, for instance, have been desirable without new K–12 school buildings often deeply underwritten by states? This question and others of a similar nature deserve attention. My aim in writing this book is to open new areas of research by making a strong case for a selected set of state government topics.

Urban Planning and Development

States played an important role in *urban planning and development* at different scales. State leadership in the 1940s included enabling legislation created for cities to utilize eminent domain and participate in local downtown redevelopment programs. The federal Housing Act of 1949 accelerated the number and scale of programs by state-authorized authorities and agencies. Illinois, however, pioneered a broader planning approach to urban renewal that helped shape revisions in the federal Housing Act of 1954. By 1960 46 states "had given the go ahead on legislation authorizing either public housing, slum clearance for redevelopment, or neighborhood conservation and rehabilitation." A few of these redevelopment projects succeeded, like Pittsburgh's famed Golden Triangle and Baltimore's Charles Center, yet many failed to attract promised downtown reinvestment.[27]

Even after the retreat from urban renewal as an overt public policy during the 1960s and 1970s, most states retained or added influential economic development agencies and authorities that in the succeeding decades gave rise to stadium districts, industrial and research parks, retention packages for corporations, and breathtaking convention centers. The cumulative impact of these "bread and butter" urban development projects have often been profound, helping to reshape the image and economic vitality of large cities like Chicago, New Orleans, and Las Vegas. Some of the outcomes have been more debatable, with deep subsidies going to private companies that have not repaid their debt in terms of jobs or other investments.

State government as a force for redevelopment is also evident around most of America's 50 state capitals. The growing number of bureaucrats and state programs required more office buildings in and around the historic capitol buildings. Capital malls and other collections of state administrative buildings began to reshape the downtowns of state capitals from Texas to California. New York's Brasilia-styled Nelson A. Rockefeller Empire State Plaza was the most ambitious and expensive state office complex, but the scale of

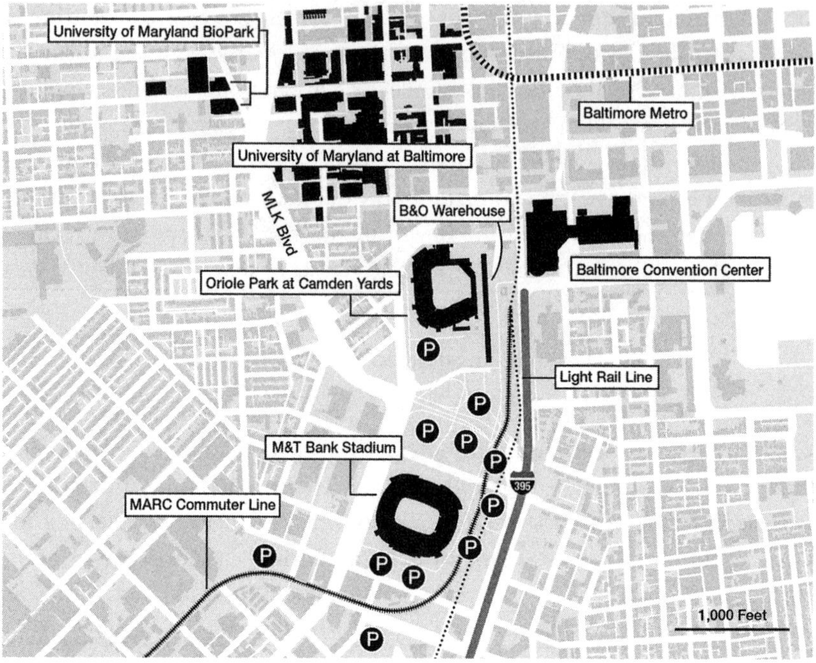

FIGURE 1. Highlighted projects and transit lines indicate the crucial role of state investments in downtown Baltimore. Map by Minna Ninova, 2018.

the offices there shared much in common with new state office complexes across the country. The large number of state capitals means that states have had a cumulatively impressive amount of office-related / campus initiatives. The expansion of state government often had significant spillover effects on other cities. States thus played a quiet but essential role in real estate markets in many noncapital cities because they rent, develop, or own large office or other administrative buildings.

State government was during the postwar period a fertile source of *regional plans*, most of which aimed to establish a better balance between nature and urbanization around American cities. Growth was already undermining the pastoral beauty sought by most suburbanites. States had delegated land-use decisions to local government, but their actions seemed irresponsible or weak in the face of development pressure. As local governments faltered, many states stepped up the pressure for planned growth. Many plans spilled out of state offices, some of excellent quality, but few were very effective in the face of an established system of local control and powerful market forces. Some state planning efforts simply encouraged managed sprawl. A select few of these ambitious initiatives, however, like Oregon's SB 100, requiring urban growth boundaries, dramatically limited development around cities. State plans like these remain lodestones for today's planners, although they are not without detractors who have waged political battles against them.[28]

Transportation

The entrance of states into the field of urban *mass transit* was revolutionary. Private companies dominated urban mass transit in American cities before the 1950s. The automobile and airplane boom of the twentieth century bankrupted nearly all American private transit and rail companies, effectively eliminating or hobbling transit networks in almost every American city by the 1960s. The few cities, like New York, that operated transit systems, struggled to maintain quality service in an era of urban crisis. With billions already invested in traditional downtowns, an aggressive urban renewal program under way, a small but vocal suburban rail commuter constituency, and many city residents either unable or too poor to drive, transit advocates across the nation realized that systems, or portions of those routes, could only be saved with additional state support.

Early pioneers in state-authorized urban mass transit included New York, California, Maryland, Massachusetts, and Pennsylvania. Some states, including Maryland, Illinois, Georgia, and California, eventually helped urban mass transit systems modestly expand with a mix of local, state, and federal aid. By the 1970s *every state* but Virginia had added mass transit under the responsibilities of their state departments of transportation, and most cities had regional mass transit systems authorized, managed, and usually subsidized by states. Compared to New York's sprawling Metropolitan Transportation Authority (MTA), most other state systems were small, but they were also proportional to residual or expected transit demand in auto-oriented regions. Administrators met the operating and capital needs through a complex and unstable combination of fares, new taxes, direct state aid, state-secured transit bonds, and federal grants secured through aggressive state lobbying efforts in Washington, DC.

State governments were, however, generally reluctant to commit the resources required to develop first-class mass transit systems. Even in America's most transit-dependent regions like New York and Boston, most citizens traveled by cars rather than rail, thus limiting political support for deep subsidies of mass transit. The automobile-associated lobbies were also far more organized in state capitals and Washington than transit riders, operators, or manufacturers. Much of the funding for modern improvements or expansion therefore focused upon fraying central business district / suburban connections to maintain broader political support for otherwise unpopular mass transit funding bonds or bills. This focus on the prosperous often led the main body of city riders—usually minority and working class—on buses or undermaintained residual subway or trolley systems.[29]

The same conservatism in planning and spending was absent as state governments took new responsibility for regional highway systems. When scholars think of highways today, they mostly focus upon federal interstates and their impact on cities and suburbs. State highway divisions, however, were the first pioneers of high-speed turnpikes and parkways such as Connecticut's verdant Merritt Parkway. The creation of new state highways, a growing number of which were in and around cities, augmented the early twentieth-century auto boom. States created robust, dedicated funding streams, such as gas taxes, to fund road development and maintenance. When necessary, states did not hesitate to divert general revenues into highway development and maintenance. The high standards and public demand for driving at the state level contributed to federal support for highways and interstates when it became clear that even more funding was needed to create a network at the scale and quality required for an entirely auto-oriented, urbanized society.

Once bankrolled by the federal government, with dedicated and sustained revenues, states reshaped urban landscapes, plowing urban interstates through neighborhoods and expanding rural state highways into regional arteries. Many scholars have justifiably celebrated the "freeway revolt" of the 1960s, when local citizens opposed highway expansion, but the urban highway programs also constituted an unprecedented planning role for states in shaping the growth of cities, delimiting neighborhood boundaries, and expanding the use of eminent domain. The steadfast support for highway growth, even as costs rose, contrasted sharply with the short leash states maintained for mass transit. The willingness to match road capacity with peripheral growth significantly contributed to suburban sprawl and helped drain the middle class, and eventually just about everyone else, out of traditional center cities.

State highways in fast-growing states continue to expand both in width and length, particularly in areas like Texas and North Carolina where suburban growth is strong. State departments of transportation (DOTs) remain the dominant force for metropolitan-scale road expansion, sustain large staffs, lobby for federal funds, and spend billions annually on road expansion and maintenance. State highway divisions provide hidden subsidies that help underwrite the suburban good life.

Higher Education

The creation of a massive system of *state-supported higher education* campuses was a direct response to the growing affluence and expectations of families in growing city regions. In 1945–1946 there were just 624 state-controlled and supported institutions and 1,144 private colleges, with only 800,000 students on each side of the private/public divide. Total state spending on public higher education nationwide in 1949 was just $213 million ($2.2 billion in 2017 dollars).[30] State appropriations for higher education nationally had already quadrupled to $891 million in 1955–1956 ($8.2 billion in 2017 dollars) in response to the veteran initiatives and broader demand. The expansion of the California system (universities, state colleges, and community colleges) under Governors Earl Warren and Pat Brown inspired the national planning of campuses both to educate the baby boomers and as engines of regional economic development. Many states aggressively expanded their systems in the succeeding years. Between 1959 and 1969, annual state tax funds for public institutions nationally increased from $1.4 billion ($11.9 billion in 2017 dollars) to $6.1 billion ($41.3 billion in 2017 dollars).[31]

Spending in the 1960s looked moderate a few years later. By 1977 total state spending for public higher education institutions topped $31 billion ($127 billion in 2017 dollars), of which $19 billion ($78 billion in 2017 dollars) derived from state taxes rather than tuition. Despite a recession, retrenchment, and new tuition charges, state spending on higher education grew a respectable 200 percent from 1969 to 1979. The total number of public higher education institutions by 1979 reached 1,478, leading to a campus building boom.[32]

Campuses can be counted as hundreds of new postwar planned communities, expanded to include sufficient living and teaching space to serve millions of additional students. State campus administrators, mostly exempt from local zoning laws and blessed with large parcels of land and extensive bond capability, developed innovative plans that included central pedestrian districts, experimental architecture, vast parking lots, and ring roads feeding into regional highway networks. The rise of the state college campus often encouraged suburban social, economic, and cultural independence from traditional center-city anchor institutions. States did not, however, ignore center cities. State-sponsored downtown academic campuses like the University of Maryland at Baltimore or Cleveland State University eventually made significant contributions to central-city economies, workforce quality, and broader redevelopment programs.

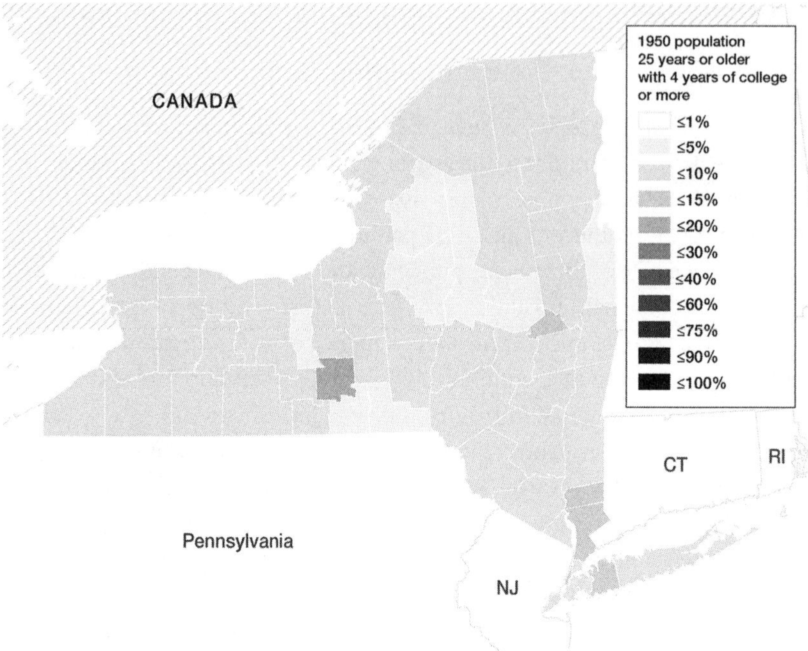

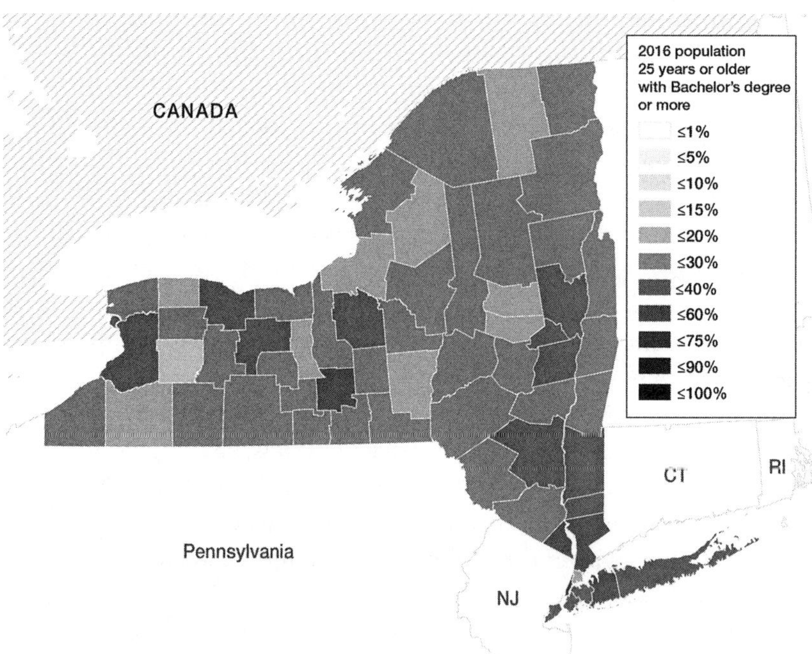

FIGURES 2 AND 3. The growing percentage of college graduates around metropolitan areas in New York, and in other states, is the result of sustained state investment in public higher education. Maps by Minna Ninova, 2018.

Metropolitan Housing

Subsidized urban housing was a new frontier for most states in the 1960s and 1970s. Most governors and state legislators, even in the North, remained skeptical about center-city public housing for low-income residents. By 1960, for instance, the results of state low-income housing programs were modest compared to potential need: New York had financed thousands of public housing apartments; Massachusetts had developed subsidized housing for veterans and the elderly; Connecticut had sponsored nearly 10,000 moderate-cost rental units; and Pennsylvania had its own moderate-cost rental program.[33] Widespread problems in many dimensions of public housing by the 1950s and 1960s confirmed suspicions about the perils of publicly managed housing.

The subsidized housing that governors and state legislators approved during the 1960s and 1970s relied on public/private partnerships and mixed-income tenanting, foretelling the contemporary American affordable housing approach. Rockefeller's Housing Finance Agency (HFA, 1960) pioneered the selling of bonds to finance loans for developers of middle-income and, later, mixed-income housing projects. During the late 1960s and early 1970s states moved aggressively into the creation of similar state housing finance agencies, and by 1972 there were already 16. State leaders took advantage of the tax-exempt bond market, the talents of private developers and managers, and more flexible federal housing programs such as Section 236 and project-based Section 8 to enter the housing field. These new approaches mostly succeeded in avoiding the "projectitis" and concentration of towers so unpopular in the postwar public housing programs.[34]

The housing finance model invented by New York was so widely imitated that by 1980 over 37 states had established similar agencies. HFAs became reliable partners with the federal government and by 1980 had laid the groundwork for the construction of approximately one-third of the nation's Section 8 project-based units.[35] HFAs are arguably even more critical today. By 2004, the 56 American HFAs had "issued a cumulative total of $192 billion in mortgage revenue bonds to service 2.4 million home loans, and over $55 billion in multifamily bonds to fund 687,000 apartment units. They have also supported the development of over 1.7 million rental units as administrators of the Low-Income Housing Tax Credit (LIHTC) since its inception in 1987." HFAs are well regarded for their role in developing supportive housing developments for targeted groups such as veterans, homeless families, and the disabled. Such a large and growing portfolio, more decentralized than public housing and designed to blend in, has mostly escaped analysis by those

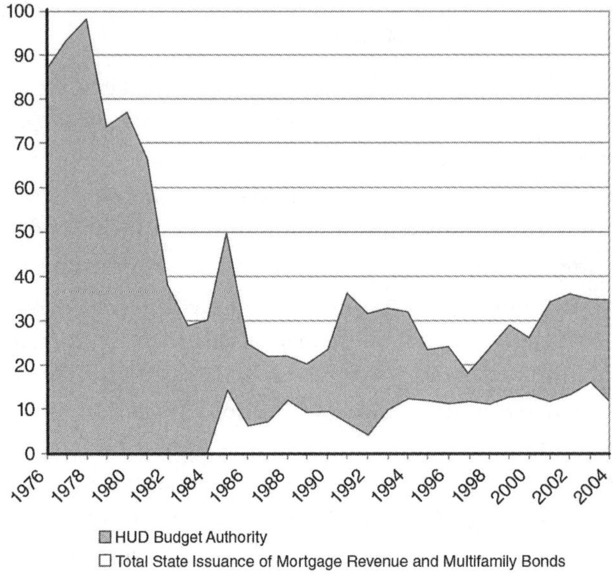

FIGURE 4. State Housing Finance Agency cumulative bond offerings, 1976–2004. Reproduced with permission from Corianne Payton Scally, "States, Housing and Innovation: The Role of State Housing Finance Agencies" (PhD diss., Rutgers University, 2017).

in urban history. The flowering of HFAs is recent, and the partnerships are complex. Public housing, FHA policy, and other controversial federal efforts also make for a much more dramatic story of government intervention in housing markets.[36]

State government agencies played a growing role in *policing housing discrimination.* A few states planned, built, and subsidized housing designed to break down suburban economic and racial segregation, with generally disappointing results. A few of these "fair share" state-led programs remain in place, including in New Jersey, California, and Florida. States during this same era showed greater interest in legal levers, *fair housing laws,* to integrate the existing private housing market, including in the suburbs. A few states had laws banning discrimination in subsidized housing by 1960 (Massachusetts, New Jersey, New York, Oregon, and Washington), but five states (California, Colorado, Connecticut, Massachusetts, and Oregon) had already pioneered stronger laws banning discrimination in the selling and renting of private housing. Stronger state antidiscrimination laws multiplied during the 1960s in states like New York and California. These pioneering state laws put federal officials on notice, pioneered crucial if imperfect legal strategies, and would be complemented and superseded by the Fair Housing Act of 1968. Housing discrimination has survived both state and federal laws, but the various housing activities in sum reflected a new and controversial role for states that crossed city and suburban lines.[37]

State governments played a crucial role in *deinstitutionalization* that dramatically impacted urban housing conditions. In the mid-twentieth century, states stepped back from their dominant position running rural, residential facilities for the mentally ill. Most of these facilities were of a poor standard, and mistreatment was common. As part of a broad revolution in mental health treatment, with federal encouragement, states in the 1950s and 1960s began switching out residential care with urban-based community mental health systems. The initial rollout was optimistic, but the long-term impacts were mixed. For most of the formerly institutionalized patients, the improvements were beneficial. Most states failed to follow through, however, on the provision of high-quality, decentralized, urban-based residential care. As a result, city governments by the 1970s and 1980s faced a growing population of mentally ill homeless people with limited housing options. States have, in recent years, played essential roles in the rise of supportive housing, which represents a significant middle ground between the institution and independent living.

The Environment

Cities had ignored or unsuccessfully wrestled with water pollution since the nineteen century; state legislatures deferred to the antiregulation stance of corporations. The damage to urban property and health became a public concern after the Second World War in the context of an improving standard of living: "The widespread use of private septic tanks and individual wells in new densely populated suburban areas since World War II has caused concern among state and local health agencies because of associated hazardous chemical and bacterial pollution." By 1960, six million homes in American metropolitan areas were pumping human waste into often leaky or undercapacity septic systems, threatening the groundwater and surface water nearby. Another five million metropolitan residents were still pulling water from their own wells.[38]

Many states imposed pioneering new rules and regulations focusing on *water treatment*. By most accounts, states lacked the funds to make good on their promises because of limited funds and local resistance. Many states also refused to stall the development of new suburbs lacking proper sewer hookups, magnifying a growing problem of groundwater contamination that remains with us today. The limits of state aid to water treatment led to powerful new federal grants and regulations in the 1970s and 1980s. State agencies, however, still played a crucial role in the enforcement of both state and federal clean water laws.

States had some success balancing urban demand and natural landscapes through park development and planning. Many governors increased the number and size of *state parks*, with an emphasis on active recreation such as camping and fishing for urbanites out for a weekend or day's drive. Federal lands (650 million acres) dwarfed state holdings (about four million acres), but state governments densely programmed state parks for urban recreation. State parks were usually more accessible to urbanites than the vast and often inaccessible federal lands in the West.

Many state leaders eventually came to believe that preserving these parks and treasured landscapes would require unprecedented controls over private neighbors. State governments in Hawaii and Vermont inspired what was called a "land use revolution" by setting unprecedented limits on private lands. These rules, in turn, inspired Governor Rockefeller's restrictive zoning system for managing the Adirondack Park's six million public and private acres and California's coastal protections in the 1970s. The public, governors, and state legislatures successfully created land-use regulations for areas of high scenic and recreational value.[39]

2

Nelson Rockefeller: America's Urbanist Governor

The expansion of New York state government under the leadership of Governor Nelson A. Rockefeller tested to the limit the potential of state government in urban affairs. Rockefeller stood out in the 1960s as the American governor most profoundly and earnestly engaged in urban policy, was widely recognized at the time for his creative initiatives, and frequently served as the unofficial spokesman of America's urban-oriented state officials.[1] By the time the governor stepped down in New York, he had campaigned for, and mostly won, massive increases in voter-approved bonds, tapped every possible federal subsidy (and lobbied for many more), invented unprecedented new powers for state authorities and agencies, pioneered riskier "moral obligation" bonds to pay for his grand plans, and multiplied annual state funding to cover state government's activist role. These efforts were many, but they were unified by an overarching goal of building better metropolitan areas.

Governor Rockefeller was a giant on the urban scene in no small measure because he brought to New York State policy his family's grandiose vision for urban social and physical transformation. With much more money at their disposal than other philanthropists, the family had already planned or influenced entire urban environments. Many of their large projects in urban transformation required master plans and slum clearance to scrape away the nineteenth-century city for either an idealized past, as at Colonial Williamsburg, or the streamlined, modern, rationalized order of the Rockefeller and Lincoln Centers. When necessary, the family bought up vast acreage that formed the core of priceless public parks, designed for the pleasure of mobile city dwellers, such as the Palisades and the Grand Teton and Acadia National Parks. The Rockefeller family underwrote the Regional Plan Association, doing much to popularize a modern vision for New York that, in turn, influenced progressive planners concerned about metropolitan social equity, employment trends, and environmental quality. Nelson Rockefeller demonstrated his interest in urban planning as part of private programs he underwrote in the 1940s and 1950s for modern housing, industrialized agricultural production, and infrastructure development in Latin America.[2]

How the family vision would play out in state government, with a Republican descendent in charge, was uncertain. Governor Rockefeller and his team incrementally unfolded their grand planning approach to suit the changing needs and moods of the 1960s public. In 1959, for instance, Rockefeller already lamented "the demand for additional park and recreational space; retrograding city areas; traffic jams; highway carnage; drainage problems; dry faucets; smog; double session schools; police, fire protection and health measures as the character of both city and suburbs change; crime; vandalism; rising frustrations; and soaring costs." It may have been "crystal clear that the demand for planning comes from the facts of contemporary life," but the next steps were murky for a governor who had promised a "pay as you go" fiscal solvency platform.[3] The early years of Rockefeller's tenure were in fact characterized by a reluctance to jump full in on government direction or assumption of formerly private functions in urban areas.

Rockefeller initially believed, in fact, that limited grants or new regulations on private interests might just do the trick. Tax breaks for commuter railroads, tax breaks and low-interest loans for urban housing developers, antidiscrimination rules for suburbs, and conservation purchase schemes for open space seemed initially sufficient to attract high-minded private interests so that government could remain the subordinate partner. As the years passed, however, Rockefeller and his team discovered that to make a greener, more equitable, better-educated, and more dynamic state, the government would have to invest financially and extend its powers in new ways, at a far more significant level than anticipated. The notion of public/private partnerships remained, and in some instances thrived, but the public planning, management, and financing expanded much more than would have been predicted from Rockefeller's early years in government. The same frustration with limited government inspired governors to take dramatic actions in other American states.

The Rockefeller Method

The many dimensions of the Rockefeller planning effort can seem overwhelming at first. The diverse efforts were unified, however, by an underlying vision that viewed state government as the key to a prosperous, growing, and greener metropolitan landscape.

During the Rockefeller years, a new generation of planned college campuses across the state rose both to serve as guarantors of social mobility for the mostly suburban baby boom generation and as incubators of postindustrial economic development for aging upstate metropolitan areas. Rockefeller's assertion of control over New York City's regional rail and subways had as its primary goal the preservation of the nation's most crucial white-collar business centers in Manhattan—and thus the health of the downstate region. His housing administrators planned vast middle-income towers and urban renewal programs to shore up the tax base and social diversity of the state's declining city centers. Billions in bonds for clean water that Rockefeller endorsed aimed to balance quality-of-life improvements with urban growth. The plans for preservation of the Adirondacks the governor commissioned stabilized the Northeast's most celebrated natural preserve for the enjoyment of urbanites, often at the expense of extractive industries and long-treasured local property rights. The scale of intervention in state government at so many levels was new, even for New York, but also ideologically coherent: state government would help create and sustain a more prosperous urban order.

During his many reelection campaigns, lavishly funded out of his fortune, brochures distributed to potential voters featured the massive state programs in transportation, the environment, education, and housing—the Rockefeller Republican Record—as demonstrations of his effectiveness to targeted metropolitan constituencies. Planned infrastructure and institutional development had plenty of natural allies. Politicians in big cities and fast-growing suburbs, labor unions, and other interest groups lobbied hard in Albany for the new programs. Republican and Democratic leaders in the state legislature, at least until the early 1970s, fell into line for reasons mixing need, idealism, and patronage. Elected officials representing upstate suburban and urban districts, some otherwise conservative, responded to constituent pressure and made sure they got a piece of these generous new programs in transportation and higher education.[4]

Rockefeller, in the scientific, philanthropic style of his father and grandfather, hired seasoned and forward-looking professionals to oversee this transformation. Rockefeller Republicanism was a team effort, greased by Rockefeller's willingness to provide salary supplements to professionals eager to test out new ideas, including housing expert James Gaynor, Anthony Adinolfi of the State University Construction Fund, political scientist William Ronan (who served as Rockefeller's powerful secretary and then head of the

MTA), environmental lawyer Henry Diamond, and urban renewal impresario Edward Logue. These professionals played key roles in unprecedented, large state-controlled organizations such as the Urban Development Corporation (UDC), the New York State Housing Finance Agency, the State University Construction Fund, the Adirondack Park Agency, the MTA, and the Department of Environmental Conservation. These state agencies, some with the ability to fund billions of dollars' worth of projects, and often possessing extensive regulatory functions, provided resources for operations on a metropolitan and regional scale. The creation of powerful authorities and agencies like these, with the force and funds to make changes on a metropolitan scale, was a typical strategy in American postwar states.[5]

Rockefeller backed up these officials in the media and legislature by creating robust intellectual justifications for their new powers and programs. Joseph Persico, a Rockefeller speechwriter, believes that the governor created "Potemkin villages of objectivity. He appointed committees, commissions, boards, panels, and task forces, heavy with respected names and recognized authorities. By his eleventh year in office, he had appointed eighty-one such bodies." Persico believed, with some justification, that many of these committees existed "to give the appearance of detached judgment to what he had already decided to do." The best of the reports, like the powerful Heald Report on the State University of New York's (SUNY's) future or the report of the Temporary Commission on the Future of the Adirondacks, analyzed problems in the context of data, best practices, and verified needs. The commissions, filled with respected allies and academics, produced widely endorsed blueprints for aggressive agencies and authorities that would have been more easily rebuffed as merely the personal political agenda of the Governor.[6]

Looking back on over a decade of planning, Rockefeller in 1970 remembered that "when I took office as Governor of New York State, it was evident that government was living from year to year, responding mainly to immediate urgencies." His ambitious goal over the years that followed was to extend planning processes to "all areas of organized human activity, social and economic as well as the physical environment." This statement was not an exaggeration, either. Those within the Republican Party eventually came to recognize, with much horror, that Rockefeller was serious about planning, social integration, and costly spending. Many Democrats were even more confounded, left to vote for Rockefeller (as many did), propose even more extensive programs, or criticize from the sidelines the financing methods for social planning initiatives they otherwise supported.[7]

The broad popularity of the governor attests to his success in delivering the goods to voters across the state. Rockefeller usually collected dependable

Republican votes upstate and in the suburbs but confounded his opponents by doing surprisingly well in New York City. In 1966, for instance, 36 percent of voters in mostly liberal Jewish neighborhoods pulled the lever for him. In 1970, despite his rightward turn and an excellent Jewish opponent on the Democratic side, Rockefeller still collected 32 percent of the vote in Jewish neighborhoods. He lost the city that year by just 17,041 votes not only because of a turn among white ethnic Democrats to the Republican Party but also because of his progressive record of using government to address social needs.[8]

The Political Price of Urbanism

The notion that New York State, or any other, enjoyed a golden age of urban policy should not be mistaken as a claim that such planning emerged smoothly or even achieved all its lofty goals. From a political and financial perspective, Rockefeller and his team paid dearly. The 1960s and 1970s criticism of planning and architectural dogmas was accompanied by an even more widely held skepticism of postwar society developed by the counterculture, grassroots activists, environmentalists, and many conservatives. Rising expectations, fluid social patterns, and urban unrest often frustrated the best intentions of state administrators. Many citizens took to streets, campuses, meetings, and editorial pages to make their case against Rockefeller and various plans and policies.[9]

In New York City residents continued to criticize relocation required for state-sponsored urban renewal; affluent residents of Westchester bitterly fought subsidized housing; whites fled from urban middle-income housing complexes built to keep them in New York City; many Adirondack residents despised tighter environmental regulations; New York metropolitan residents rejected a number of important bridge, airport, and highway proposals; fiscal conservatives questioned Rockefeller's reliance on risky bonds; city residents felt shortchanged by the tremendous expansion of SUNY; statewide voters rejected many bond proposals for housing and mass transit; local politicians ignored pleas for regional and intergovernmental cooperation; federal officials resisted numerous calls for funds to bail out transit; and commuters remained deeply dissatisfied with service on the new MTA and subways. Conflict, resistance, and delays filled the pages of the era's newspapers and magazines. This book devotes many of its pages to this friction and the many unexpected outcomes as well as the achievement. The resistance and complexity experienced in New York parallels similar skepticism about large-scale government programs in other states.

In response to controversy, intransigence, and potential resistance, Rockefeller's team, like peers in state government elsewhere, took a pragmatic approach that counted both wins and losses. Many projects from their inception responded directly to expected criticism by offering a revised version of planning in the first place. State-sponsored subsidized housing in the 1960s and 1970s, for instance, wherever possible minimized relocation, included a range of income groups, and showed considerable attention to design or the surrounding context than had typical tower block housing projects. Environmental regulation intentionally responded to the growing public support for clean air and water, wilderness, and outdoor recreation.

Where resistance was vocal and dangerous politically, because Rockefeller and his team faced well-financed and sophisticated opponents, the administration grudgingly canceled or delayed the most controversial projects, such as the energy facility planned at Storm King on the Hudson, subsidized housing projects in affluent sections of Westchester County, many highway links, and the proposed bridges across the Long Island Sound. Other times, however, the administration canceled only the most controversial aspect of a program or made essential concessions to placate the opposition, such as successful negotiations leading to the Adirondack Park rezoning. Rockefeller and his team grew accustomed to a certain amount of static, and where opposition was weak, and their local partners strong, they sallied forth with few meaningful compromises on increasingly controversial programs such as urban renewal plans for Albany and many ultimately destructive highway projects. When we look beyond New York, we see a similar mix of state government compromises and steamrolling.

Costly Urbanism

Almost every physical project of the Rockefeller era, like those in most other states, exceeded estimated costs because of factors such as the scale of statewide systems (impacting multiple cities and towns), increased public expectations, higher than expected construction costs, site complexity, endemic local corruption, escalating operating costs, various delays, and rising inflation.

In New York, for instance, regular state capital expenditures for needs like highways and pollution control increased from $312 million 1959 ($2.6 billion in 2017 dollars) to $631 million ($4.2 billion in 2017 dollars) in 1969,[10] funds derived from a mixture of tax revenues, voter-approved bonds, and first-instance appropriations.[11] By the time Rockefeller left office in 1973, he had increased voter-approved state debt from $912 million (1959) to $3.4 billion ($19 billion in 2017 dollars).[12] "Moral obligation" debts, issued by agencies like the Housing Finance Agency and the Urban Development Corporation,

Cumulative Record of Financing and Repayment

Year Ended October 31		Short-and Long-Term Financing Secured	Short-and Long-Term Financing Repaid	Interest Paid on Short-and Long-Term Financing
1961	$	63,863,00	12,000,000	32,000
1962		93,013,000	20,575,000	1,829,000
1963		467,883,000	35,943,000	4,555,000
1964		960,197,000	337,282,000	17,664,000
1965		1,369,540,000	523,536,000	38,777,000
1966		1,750,030,000	811,202,000	67,116,000
1967		2,262,268,000	1,046,313,000	103,754,000
1968		3,189,585,000	1,512,189,000	150,228,000
1969		3,960,314,000	2,059,288,000	216,329,000
1970		4,981,104,000	2,668,564,000	305,106,000
1971		6,510,812,000	3,419,299,000	421,187,000
1972		8,690,570,000	4,637,510,000	570,775,00
1973		10,687,411,000	5,987,711,000	764,384,000
1974		12,581,918,000	7,539,650,000	1,019,406,000
1975		14,021,835,000	8,776,123,000	1,304,719,000
1976		15,919,107,000	10,683,573,000	1,644,715,000
1977		17,527,727,000	12,088,995,000	1,981,309,000
1978		18,763,312,000	13,245,653,000	2,312,128,000
1979		19,896,307,000	14,197,357,000	2,655,232,000
1980		20,936,852,000	15,178,773,000	3,020,047,000
1981		21,074,502,000	15,372,542,000	3,395,394,000
1982		21,267,082,000	15,491,724,000	3,777,104,000

FIGURE 5. Cumulative loans and the interest costs of the HFA. Chart by Minna Ninova, 2018.

added billions more to the totals. Much of this debt was sold at relatively high interest rates, generally higher than more conventional state-secured bonds.[13] "First instance appropriations" from the state government, to be reimbursed by agencies and authorities like the MTA, counted by 1973 for $3.466 billion ($19.4 billion in 2017 dollars). Total New York state debt, long and short term, by 1973 reached $11.8 billion ($66.1 billion in 2017 dollars), which was 20 percent of all state debt nationally. Debt service was eating 6 percent of general fund expenditures by 1973. Tax breaks to housing projects can be counted as billions in lost revenues for state and local governments over the decades.[14]

The governor found that he had to boost not only capital spending and related debt but annual state operating spending on various services. This he did, and then some—a feat made possible by a state that for most of his terms was affluent by national standards in family income and economic production. The number of New York State employees on the payroll, needed to staff an expanding infrastructure, drove the growth. During the 15 years of Rockefeller's service as governor, annual state budgets rose from $2 billion in 1959 ($17 billion in 2017 dollars) to $8.75 billion in 1973 ($49 billion in 2017 dollars). The greatest portion of this money was directly returned to cities and towns as school or other aid (62 cents of every dollar ca. 1971), and the state's expensive welfare rolls hit 1.7 million recipients in 1971, but there was no mistaking a more expansive, and costly, state enterprise in nearly every dimension.[15] New SUNY and mental health / hospital employees, most notably, accounted for 60 percent of the increase in state workers between 1959 and 1969.[16] The total employees on the state payrolls during Rockefeller's terms in office jumped from 100,000 in 1959 to 183,000 in 1973.[17] Urbanized areas, both cities and suburbs, were big winners on state aid compared to rural areas during the Rockefeller years. State aid accounted for an average of 29 percent of budgets for New York's Big Six cities (Syracuse, Buffalo, Rochester, Albany, New York City, and Yonkers) in 1973, an increase of roughly 10 percent from 1959.[18]

To cover these high operating capital, debt financing, and operating costs Rockefeller imposed the state's first sales tax and separately taxed gasoline and cigarettes. The rich paid heavily, as maximum top rates increased from 7 to 15 percent of income. Rockefeller increased various taxes in 1959, 1963, 1965, 1966, 1968, 1971, and 1972. By the early 1970s, New York had become the highest-taxed state, combining local and state charges, per capita. Corporate taxes, however, declined as a share of tax collected during these years to meet Rockefeller's goal of maintaining a business-friendly environment (a questionable but widely endorsed strategy in many American states then and now). Fees to cover the costs of many services also rose rapidly during these years and after, including SUNY and City University of New York (CUNY) tuition charges, park facility charges, and MTA transit fare increases.[19] The legislature had, of course, signed off on this aggressive taxing and spending. A state Democratic leader from Brooklyn acknowledged, "We're just as much to blame as Rockefeller and the Republicans."[20]

Governor Rockefeller understandably became more conservative in his approach to governance in the 1970s, in part to assuage the right wing of his party, which regularly chopped his budget requests in the state legislature, but also to reign in spiraling government costs that threatened the competitiveness of the state. For a decade "Rockefeller the activist" discussed how "the state university must be built, school aid increased, slums eradicated . . . mass transit modernized," but by 1970 he was "talking about the bare cupboard of state resources, the state losing industry" and "spiraling taxes."[21] Rockefeller had already pushed the limit on state debt of all kind, and he could not simply print money like his counterparts in the federal government. Like many American governors, he was forced to make difficult choices to balance budgets; in any case, the state legislature consistently cut his budget requests from 1966 to 1973.[22]

He and the legislature in the early 1970s cut state employee numbers by the thousands and made major cuts to the state's generous Medicaid coverage, welfare benefits, state aid to K–12 education, mental health, SUNY, and youth programs. Many on the left who might have grudgingly admired his programs never forgave him for this later fiscal conservatism. His loosening of New York City's rent control laws, the imposition of the Rockefeller Drug

Laws, support for President Richard Nixon, the Attica disaster, and his reluctance to aid the city of New York more generously as its economic conditions declined in the early 1970s permanently tarnished his legacy among the New York City elite.[23] Much of the existing Rockefeller research, written by a generation shaken to its core by the city of New York and the state's financial crisis during the 1970s, tended to dismiss him as financially imprudent. Many of the crucial deals he orchestrated have also broken down or frayed over the years in areas such as education, mass transit, and housing.

Rockefeller's gubernatorial successors, however, pulled the state back from the brink thanks to New York City's global financial renaissance. Massive profits generated in Manhattan from the 1980s to today, some related to Rockefeller investments (mass transit and redevelopment projects), improved the state's outlook further.[24] Robust tax collection, debt refinancing, belt tightening, additional federal funds (federal student aid, Medicare, federal environmental grants), and massive new bond issues by later state administrations (for the MTA, for instance) sustained most of Rockefeller's initiatives. The Hugh Carey (1975–1982) and then Mario Cuomo (1982–1994) administrations maintained Rockefeller's programs while steering a more fiscally conservative path into the 1990s. The nation's largest regional rail system survived and modernized, all the SUNY and CUNY campuses remained open, not a single housing project was demolished or abandoned, parks expanded, and environmental programs continued. State government support for programs with a primarily urban constituency, despite some contraction due to economic and political cycles, was repeated across the nation in the postwar years.

The Forgotten Power Broker?

The case studies of significant state programs in the chapters that follow contribute to revisionist approaches to modern New York City history by writing Governor Rockefeller and New York state government into the city's urban history.[25] Nelson Rockefeller as urbanist has been given a more modest role in the story of the modern city than Robert Moses, John Lindsay, Jane Jacobs, Edward Koch, and other figures now familiar from books, films, and exhibitions. Yet Rockefeller was at heart a New Yorker with a bold vision for the city and its suburbs.

Rockefeller may have lived and governed from Albany during legislative sessions, but he spent more time in suburban Westchester County or his offices and living quarters in Manhattan's midtown. His strategic use of the mass media, including hundreds of addresses in the city, paid television shows,

FIGURE 6. Quality urban housing for the urban middle classes. New York State Division of Housing and Community Renewal, "Programs for People," courtesy of the Rockefeller Archive Center.

polling, and modern campaign advertising, marked him as a savvy executive on par with other CEOs of his time. He relied heavily on the New York City region for professionals in public administration, architecture, planning, and graphic design. His policies, while necessarily pitched as statewide initiatives, proved in the long term to be indispensable to the New York City region.

The enduring legacy of Rockefeller-era planning can be seen today in New York City. There are still tens of thousands of New Yorkers living in Mitchell-Lama and Urban Development Corporation housing projects. The apartments that have not converted to market prices remain some of the best values in the state; those that have shifted to market rates now make significant annual tax contributions to municipal bottom lines.[26] Massive and sustained state contributions to CUNY, both in capital and operating support, have helped transform the system into one of the nation's largest and most respected networks of urban higher education. The Metropolitan Transit Authority, including the Long Island Rail Road, Metro-North Railroad, and New York City Transit, has in the long term improved and updated service in the New York region from its lowest point in the 1960s. The city's waterways are cleaner, a process that started in the Rockefeller era. City dwellers are major consumers of state park service, including beaches, in the region. The Urban Development Corporation (UDC), and its successor, the Empire State Development Corporation, has played a key role in the Times Square redevelopment, Javits Convention Center, Hudson Yards, Columbia's Manhattanville Campus, and Atlantic Yards. The UDC and the state's Battery Park City Authority collaborated to bring forth the popular residential community, commercial center, and stunning park space along the Hudson. These redevelopment projects are vital to creating the kinds of urban enclaves of the type favored by global corporations, talented workers, and travelers.

Even though the state's urban areas during the 1960s and 1970s enjoyed the lion's share of benefits from state planning, the state is an easy target for frustrated local politicians, particularly those running the city of New York. Mayors Robert Wagner and John Lindsay, like mayors ever since, believed that Albany stiffed New York, set unreasonable limits on local finances, and often micromanaged city affairs, but this sense of foul play conveniently overlooks the massive investment the state has made. By 1970–1971, for instance, the city of New York was getting more back, on an annual basis, from the state than it was contributing to Albany in tax revenues.[27] In 1973, the city received $2.5 billion in state aid, one-quarter of the city's budget. Additional billions in debt guarantees in areas such as housing and mass transit reflected an even more profound commitment. The city of New York was also a primary beneficiary of federal revenue sharing championed by Rockefeller. The state's Municipal Assistance Corporation made many local enemies in the city for its program of austerity after 1975, but it also restored solvency and brought investors back to the city's bond offerings.[28] As part of the plan for solvency, state leaders also gave the city of New York the power to levy personal and corporate taxes "at a rate set by the state." Today, after multiple extensions of the legislation, these "personal and corporate income taxes represent nearly one-third of its tax receipts."[29]

The state and city remain financially intertwined today, if not to the satisfaction of either upstate or downstate factions. In 2011, a Rockefeller Institute study found that the city contributes 45 percent of all state revenues and receives back 40 percent of the state's revenues—not including debt issued on behalf of city services like transit.[30] The city is shortchanged, but not by that much, and far less by New York State than by the federal government. The city's massive operating budget ($85 billion in 2017) is composed of 15 percent state grants; CUNY is largely dependent on state aid, and the MTA benefits from both operating subsidies and vast debt issued by New York State.[31]

Rockefeller's governorship was, in retrospect, as crucial to the New York City region's future as the economic bonds forged by Mayor Fiorello LaGuardia, Robert Moses, and President Roosevelt during the New Deal. Thus the state with the most prominent hand in urban policy had the most significant impact on its populous downstate region. New York City, its suburbs, and the state government became financially and administratively involved at an unprecedented level, and these political partners have remained intertwined ever since. Rockefeller and his lieutenants even developed new ways to tap the federal government for needed funds. New York City's leaders will probably always feel angry about being shortchanged on spending, and they have some legitimate criticisms, but it is a mistake to think that this tug-of-war is more than the typical process of negotiation between two powerful and intimate entities. Rockefeller, like many governors of his time, drew state government deeply into urban affairs.

Urban Planning and Redevelopment

3

State Urban Redevelopment Policy

State government held the promise of a new era of urban planning. It was from states that growing towns and cities had first derived their charters and powers to regulate daily life and urban form. In the late nineteenth century, "though state legislatures were potentially masters of the city, throughout much of the United States they were compliant servants of urban spokesmen" who delivered the growing powers city leaders needed to control nuisances, secure adequate water resources, and develop streets and transit in an orderly manner.[1] State leadership remained responsive in the twentieth century. States in the 1920s dutifully adopted federal enabling legislation for local zoning laws that radically curtailed the rights and traditions of American urban property owners. In the 1930s, many states granted local public housing authorities the right to clear slums, borrow money, accept federal funds, and build projects. The ability of state legislatures and governors to add new powers for cities and suburbs, and the extent to which the courts stood behind them, indicated that states possessed enormous potential in the emerging field of urban planning.[2]

State intervention in urban planning accelerated in the postwar era. In the 1940s and 1950s, responding to local concerns about dramatic downtown decline, states showed unprecedented enthusiasm for programs that promised to redevelop central business districts and neighborhoods. Northern elites in the nation's older cities pushed states to enable large-scale, planned, center-city redevelopment. As early as 1945, New York, Illinois, Maryland, Michigan, Minnesota, and Pennsylvania had adopted state legislation authorizing local authorities or redevelopment agencies to use eminent domain to clear and assemble property for private commercial and residential redevelopment. Pittsburgh's pioneering Golden Triangle project moved forward thanks to the 1945 Pennsylvania Urban Redevelopment Law provisions allowing the use of eminent domain in "blighted" sections of cities. By 1948, 25 states had authorized similar redevelopment programs—downtown rebuilding had become a national state-sanctioned program even without a federal partner. Center-city interests, North and South, believed that their core districts were vulnerable to decline.[3]

The federal government's Housing Act of 1949, a compromise measure that took years of stormy negotiation between housing and real estate interests, built on the growing state/local redevelopment partnership. The act promised public housing to liberals, while its famous Title I subsidized land clearance for "primarily residential" programs of private-sector reconstruction desired by local political and business elites. But in practice, the act disappointed almost everyone. The public housing was delayed and/or unattractive, and most developers outside New York City were reluctant to commit resources to luxury or middle-class housing in or near dying downtowns without an equally aggressive program of commercial reconstruction. The Title I projects that did move ahead, many of them in New York under the guidance of Robert Moses, indiscriminately cleared neighborhoods without a broader plan for neighborhood stabilization or tenant relocation.

State governments, sensitive to local pressures, led the way on national policy redesign in the early 1950s. Experts recognized Illinois in the early 1950s for the Urban Community Conservation Act (1953). The law responded, in part, to the concerns of University of Chicago administrators who sought to stabilize their Hyde Park environs. The Conservation Act was also a first step toward mitigating the most destructive aspects of slum clearance on neighborhoods. Illinois's Urban Conservation Boards created plans that "could include proposals for the use of land, needed alterations and improvements in the street system, suggestions for additional public areas and public buildings, recommended demolition of specified structures and the rehabilitation of others."[4]

The Housing Act of 1954 brought together multiple strands of this emerging reform and reaction: the neighborhood conservation model from Illinois, private-sector pressure for subsidized commercial redevelopment, and citizen renovation and code enforcement of the famous "Baltimore Plan." The 1954 act's call for "urban renewal" included requirements for "workable plans" that would include renovation or cleanup programs of neighborhoods rather than slum clearance alone. The act's allowance for subsidies of commercial redevelopment projects and a modest public housing program reflected the consistently business-friendly approach that won over supporters.[5] By 1961, all but five states had authorized various types of redevelopment agencies to engage in broader planning to meet the new standards of the federal legislation. The Housing Act of 1954 proved to be a boon for commercial interests; the workable plans often served as a cover for continued destruction, and delays remained chronic nationally in the federal program because of declining center-city market power, red tape, developer incompetence, and lack of available investors. President Eisenhower in 1960 "reported that of 647 urban development projects planned in 385 communities since the program started 10 years previously, only 26 projects had been completed and that progress 'has been slow' on many of the 355 currently under way."[6]

Some states, like New York, recognized that funding was an important factor in the delays. Elected leaders realized in the 1950s and 1960s that cities were frequently too poor to move acquisition, clearance, and planning projects along at a decent clip. To help cover the local share of federal urban renewal, New Jersey offered tax breaks for private redevelopment, Oregon sold revenue bonds, and Pennsylvania, Massachusetts, and Connecticut provided capital grants.[7] In 1970, seven states (California, Connecticut, Delaware, Massachusetts, New Jersey, New York, and Pennsylvania) still directly subsidized urban renewal through loans or grants. The total number of states in the subsidy business was small, but the notion of states underwriting center-city redevelopment projects at any level was a radical change in state/local relations.[8]

New York Exemplar

New York's program of urban redevelopment, both in the city of New York and in other cities statewide, *was* pioneering, more extensive, and more deeply subsidized by the state government than most, but the differences in scale are misleading. New York was moving in step with a growing postwar state/federal/local partnership that aimed to rebuild city centers along modern lines. The vast number of acres cleared and new towers in the park erected in New York were different primarily in quantity rather than quality.

New York City, on the surface, seemed to be the rare healthy postwar metropolis that would defy the signs of urban decay apparent across the nation. New York City's development community, for instance, added 145 square million feet of office space between 1947 and 1980. Market forces drove most of this commercial redevelopment, with comparatively little direct financial help from a government agency in thriving Midtown areas such as Park, Third, Sixth, and Madison Avenues.[9]

Outside Manhattan's major commercial districts, however, city, state, and federal subsidies were needed to stimulate the creation of a new urban environment. Construction coordinator Robert Moses, through his leadership of the Slum Clearance Committee (1948), transformed neighborhoods like the Lower East Side and Harlem through blends of federal, state, and city funds to cover the cost of assembling and clearing properties in redevelopment zones; federal, state, and city road and highway funds to make space for cars and trucks; federal, state, and city public housing programs to create hygienic apartments for the poor and working class; and federal, state, and city subsidized housing programs to anchor the middle class within the city limits. Combined urban redevelopment projects rolled over neighborhoods not only because of Moses's forceful personality but also because of broad agreement among the elite that thousands of city acres needed to be cleared to make way for modern housing, highways, cultural centers, expanded universities, and more.

Redevelopment of so many different kinds and in so many areas caused tremendous disruption. Many communities in the 1950s and 1960s in New York City rebelled against city planners and urban renewal plans. Eventually, many redevelopment projects stalled, were transformed, or occasionally were canceled. Yet even outspoken critics of Moses's bulldozer approach who preferred renovation of old buildings, like chairman of the City Planning Commission James Felt and Mayor John Lindsay, still supported redevelopment in areas where the market was too weak. City leaders felt they were in such a desperate situation, with decentralization sucking out middle-class population and businesses, that to reject redevelopment entirely was impractical. The result was that urban redevelopment, with renovation added as a key element, continued to be an essential element of city policy.

Upstate leaders, facing even more dramatic decline than their peers in Manhattan, clung to disruptive redevelopment and highway plans as their last, best hope. Albany, Buffalo, Syracuse, Schenectady, and Rochester—like so many industrial and commercial powerhouses across the Rust Belt—were losing vitality. Healthy metropolitan employment statistics often masked inner-city decline; middle-class residents, corporate headquarters, department stores, and many industries pulled up stakes.

New York State aided in the clearance of downtown districts both upstate and downstate throughout the 1960s despite a growing chorus of urban renewal doubters. Between 1959 and 1969 the state supplied $167.5 million to 52 municipalities to help clear and assemble 4,018 acres of "substandard property." The program, approved by voters in 1958, used the proceeds from the sale of state-secured bonds to help local governments cover the cost of up to half of the cost of an urban renewal program (the federal government provided much of the rest). State urban renewal also helped pay for the "work-

FIGURE 7. Justifying slum clearance with photographs. New York State Division of Housing and Community Renewal, Annual Report 1960/61. New York State Archives, courtesy of the Rockefeller Archive Center.

able" plans required in federal urban renewal associated with the more progressive aspects of the Housing Act of 1954. So many acres assembled and cleared reflect the depth to which urban land values had sunk in numerous New York cities and towns. The city of New York was the largest single recipient of state grants, indicating continuing interest of local leaders in redevelopment, but the participation in the program was broad.[10]

Hundreds of thousands of units, mostly older center-city apartments, were lost statewide without replacement by housing or anything else. Many stores were wiped out, and the remaining commercial concentration drained from towns large and small because of large gaps in the older urban fabric. Carving out downtown space for cars often made the situation worse as many cities "in their central areas, are losing the aspect of cities and seem almost to be gutted, in a disorderly mess of buildings and of parking areas."[11] Many small cities, like Schenectady, started with grand modernist plans, lost developers, and ended up with surface parking, disjointed shopping facilities, a hotel, a few office buildings, and not much else. One accounting of the fate of 2,471 acres in the urban renewal program found that just 198 sprouted new development between 1949 and 1967.[12] Rockefeller's 1968 summary of the program's failure in one upstate city can stand in for many:

> There is one community that shall be nameless, in which the process has taken so long that all of the corporations that were either going to build office build-

> ings or other facilities in the area have now already relocated in the peripheral area of the community. Therefore, the land stands vacant in this important city in our State; and now there are no prospective tenants because they couldn't wait for the process of government to work.[13]

There were many contributing factors beyond government failure. The lack of developer, corporate, and investor interest in dying downtowns and neighborhoods was undoubtedly crucial. Government red tape and bureaucracy were, however, contributing factors. The average time to develop new projects was a glacial 13 years in New York City and 8 years statewide.[14]

The UDC and Urban Redevelopment

State officials, who had entrusted redevelopment to local business and civic interests with dismal results, began looking for alternatives. One solution, with many variants nationally, was the creation of state authorities with the power to develop projects from start to finish, rather than just clear land, in urban areas. A prominent exemplar in this bold extension of state power was the Urban Development Corporation (1968). Rockefeller turned to Charles Urstadt, a veteran of the once mighty Zeckendorf urban renewal team, to design the UDC legislation with a broad mandate in housing, urban renewal, regional planning, industrial development, and more. The Rockefeller administration gained passage of the laws to create this innovative public benefit corporation in the state legislature by rallying potential supporters of urban redevelopment and strong-arming opponents during the troubled days following the King assassination.

The UDC housing program became large and controversial and has received widespread attention, but the UDC's urban renewal program proved far more enduring, remains in partial force today, and is arguably even more influential and representative nationally. At one level, the UDC was a political down payment by Rockefeller to encourage the federal government to make a $150 billion investment in urban areas and housing—and help get him elected president—neither of which happened. At another level, however, the UDC was a force to redevelop cities on a radical, state-led basis that flowed from both the failings in the existing state/federal renewal program and a growing realization of the tools that states could craft to address defects.[15]

Planners in the United States had only dreamed of a powerful organization like the UDC that included in its arsenal the integrated powers of planning, zoning, financing (revenue bonds on a vast scale), design, and construction. It could also create local subcorporations, with similar powers, to undertake its various projects. Rockefeller predicted as much as $6 billion in total investments to include $1 billion of state-secured "moral obligation" bonds and $5 billion in private financing. The UDC could even act as an initial sponsor and developer for housing or other projects if no private party could be found, turning projects over at the end of the development process to the private sector. The agency condemned properties it wanted, built recreational and other facilities as part of wider neighborhood planning, and could even override local zoning. This total planning power would be used to create "a new atmosphere" within cities that "would attract people back into the cities on a mixed-basis, mixed-income basis and an integrated basis." The UDC's language and goals contrasted sharply with the public housing program that had intentionally concentrated poor people in "second ghettos" constructed on top of cleared slums. The UDC aimed to spread prosperity within cities rather than serving poor people primarily.[16]

Ed Logue, whom Rockefeller enticed from the powerful Boston Redevelopment Authority to lead the UDC, took credit for demanding the power to override zoning. Logue remembered telling Rockefeller in a consultation phase that the UDC concept was "the greatest development bill that I've ever

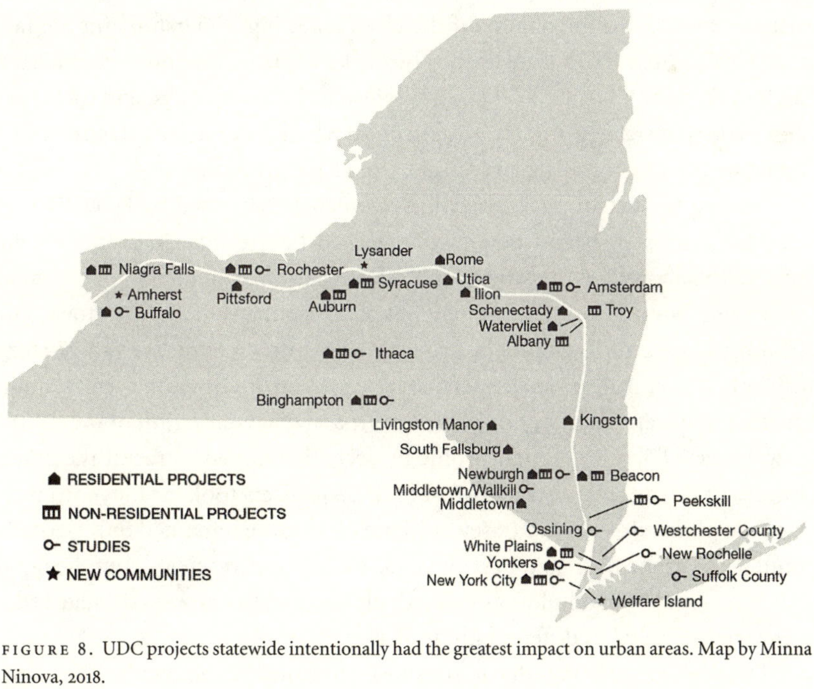

FIGURE 8. UDC projects statewide intentionally had the greatest impact on urban areas. Map by Minna Ninova, 2018.

seen. You can build new towns with this; you can put housing all over the state, you can do industrial development. . . . But it won't work." The only hope was to bypass local control, particularly Mayor "Lindsay's zoning and planning operation." Rockefeller agreed, and the bill passed with the UDC's enhanced powers despite Urstadt's justified fear that the UDC would pay a high political cost for overruling local governments.[17]

Rockefeller initially faced resistance from civic leaders in New York City.[18] Mayor John Lindsay and many other New Yorkers considered the UDC concept a brazen attempt to destroy local control and citizen participation. Rockefeller did not help the situation by referring to Ed Logue as being "successful in Boston the same way Bob Moses was successful in New York: because of a tremendous personality and drive and the ability to break through red tape."[19] Donald Elliott, head of the City Planning Commission, worried that the UDC "could return us to the day when massive construction programs simply shifted the locations of our slums and did not solve the fundamental problems." Rockefeller, however, received crucial support from Mayor Lindsay's opposition, including Bronx Borough president Herman Badillo, who said, "It's laughable for the mayor to talk about home rule" because he believed the city government ignored local opinion anyway.[20] *New York Times* columnist Ada Louise Huxtable worried that the UDC "could plunge the city right back into the bulldozer age," but she was willing to take a "wait and see" attitude because of the quality of the city's planning leadership and the fact that UDC would be "a state agency headed by one of the most experienced men in the urban business."[21] Lindsay, New York City officials, and most big-city leaders upstate eventually came around when they realized that the UDC could be used to complete large-scale, expensive projects.

Among the urban renewal projects created or launched by UDC by 1975 was the Roosevelt Island new town (delayed before the UDC entered the scene), the Shoreline Apartments in Buffalo (part of a planned 10,000-person waterfront community), urban renewal plans for the Buffalo downtown, the Clinton Square redevelopment project in downtown Syracuse (an 18-story office tower and new department store), and an international convention center in Niagara Falls, key to a "plan for massive revitalization of the downtown area." These were high-profile projects that aimed to recast the entire images of downtown districts. Most of these projects took far longer to realize than planned (such as Roosevelt Island) and some remained only partially built (such as the Buffalo waterfront) due to the 1970s recession, but the rapid launching and many buildings rising demonstrated the power of a state redevelopment agency in different kinds of sites.[22]

Despite a crisis in 1975 due to subsidized housing financing, the UDC con-

FIGURE 9. The UDC included a range of urban activities. Urban Development Corporation, *UDC in 72*. New York State Archives, courtesy of the Rockefeller Archive Center.

tinued to play a crucial role in center-city economic development in New York State's cities. Mayor Ed Koch, for instance, agreed to a leading UDC role on the Times Square project because the UDC staff "have the expertise and they know how to move fast." Real estate historian Lynne Sagalyn agrees that at the time, "no other state agency had as seasoned a team of in-house development professionals." The UDC brought to the table expedited tax agreements, eminent domain, and exemption from local land reviews and zoning needed to clear the low-rent businesses in place, develop ambitious plans, and attract new investors. The relationship between city and state required extensive negotiation between Mayor Koch and Governor Mario Cuomo, but the collaboration worked so well in the long term that many today consider Times Square too successful as a tourist destination. The UDC was also the force behind the glass-enclosed Jacob K. Javits Convention Center (1986) on what was then the moribund far West Side. The 1.8-million-square-foot facility has contributed billions in economic impact to the city, including 17,000 related jobs, two million annual visitors, and 480,000 annual hotel rooms rented (all figures as of 2015).[23]

The iconic 92-acre Battery Park City mixed-use district downtown also benefited from long-term support from state government, including the UDC, without which it would have failed. Envisioned by the Rockefeller brothers (David and Nelson), Mayors Wagner and Lindsay, and other civic leaders as a supplement for redevelopment of the Lower Manhattan business district, it was much debated in form and content in the 1960s. Governor Rockefeller and the state legislature, after coming to terms with the city, created the Battery Park City Authority (BPCA) in 1968 with the power to plan, finance (issue bonds), and develop the project. Continuing battles over social mixture, design, and interagency fighting combined with the 1970s recession to delay the development. The BPCA restarted the development process in the late 1970s with the pioneering New Urbanist plan by Cooper, Ekstut Associates (1979), additional state financial support, and UDC control of the land to break the "tight zoning district controls" of the city. The BPCA also won city tax abatements, attracted commercial and residential developments (with UDC assistance), and hired top landscape firms for the waterfront esplanade and public spaces. Billions of dollars in subsequent real estate development created an elite residential and commercial enclave.[24] According to Sagalyn, the combined force of the Port Authority, Battery Park City Authority, and UDC meant that "the state's presence dominated the West Side of Manhattan, almost continuously, from the Battery to Times Square."[25]

The merger of the UDC with the state's Department of Economic Development in 1995 to create the Empire State Development Corporation (ESDC) spawned powerful corporate subsidiaries that play a crucial role in large-scale, long-term urban redevelopment projects across the state. In New York City, important initiatives like Atlantic Yards, Harlem Community Development, Queens West, Brooklyn Bridge Park, Columbia Manhattanville expansion, and Moynihan Station all benefit from powerful state-enabled ESDC development corporations. These corporations expedite complex projects by engaging in activities such as site planning, zoning, and environmental review (including overriding local zoning); developer selection; financial support; land assembly through purchase and eminent domain; site remediation; and park/open space design and creation.

Upstate, the ESDC and its subsidiaries are engaged in the large-scale "Buffalo Billion" program to diversify the Buffalo region after decades of decline. Among the projects aided or planned are downtown public space enhancements to attract business, neighborhood revitalization programs, enhanced waterfront and park spaces, a planned light rail extension to the State University of New York at Buffalo Amherst campus, and deeply subsidized technology and biotech hubs associated with major educational institutions.[26] The ESDC underwrites similar, if more modest, urban redevelopment efforts in Rochester and Syracuse.[27] These programs have moved forward despite corruption investigations and mixed results because Governor Andrew Cuomo believes that they are crucial to maintaining his political base in struggling upstate metropolitan areas. It is no exaggeration to say that much of the force for upstate city planning is coming from New York State via the ESDC. The reports generated by the state reflect best practices in contemporary planning. Because the ESDC is identified as a state economic development agency rather than an urban planning agency, there is limited recognition of how deeply the state has remained in the downtown redevelopment field.

The Persistence of Urban Redevelopment

The critical role the UDC and ESDC have played in urban redevelopment —on various levels and in multiple cities—has echoes in state authorities and agencies across the nation. Many of the powers possessed by the UDC are subdivided into focused agencies with specific responsibilities in areas such as redevelopment, tourism, and economic development. State agencies provide support to long-term, expensive, and often controversial planning initiatives that would be difficult to sustain politically or economically within city government.

The collapse of urban renewal as a stated policy goal did not mean the end of state engagement in urban redevelopment authorities and agencies. With the loss of most federal urban renewal dollars in the 1970s, and with public resistance to slum clearance, these authorities found alternative activities (such as commercial revitalization, economic development, brownfield remediation, housing stabilization, etc.) through a mix of state, local, and federal funds. Modern urban redevelopment agencies are staffed with planners who came up through the ranks long after the worst sins of the postwar urban renewal program, so they tend to be imbued with "best practices" derived from advocacy planning and the New Urbanism. Redevelopment authorities are still active and influential in cities and towns in states such as Massachusetts, Pennsylvania, Minnesota, Wisconsin, Virginia, Louisiana, and New Jersey.

The New Orleans Redevelopment Authority, tracing its roots back to a community improvement agency created by the Louisiana State Legislature in 1968, has spent decades engaged in housing rehabilitation and affordable housing development, infrastructure and park improvements, land banking of vacant property, and reenergizing of commercial corridors. Pittsburgh's Urban Redevelopment Authority (1946), which created the pioneering Gateway Center, is still active in housing rehabilitation, brownfield remediation, and business development. The Boston Redevelopment Authority (1957), now the Boston Planning and Redevelopment Agency (1993), made its name with controversial 1960s clearance projects such as the Government Center and the West End project, but since the 1970s has been a key force behind popular additions to the city, including Quincy Market (1976), Charlestown Navy Yard redesign (1974–), Central Artery Plan (1991), Columbia Point Master Plan (2009), and much more. The state's Massachusetts Turnpike Authority also controlled Boston's transformative Big Dig highway tunnel and redevelopment project.[28]

Urban redevelopment agencies with broad responsibilities retain importance in many states but have often been supplemented, and sometimes eclipsed, by state-sponsored stadium and convention center authorities or agencies. The focus of these state investments, paired to various private and city partnerships, is the creation of facilities serving a regional, relatively prosperous audience of concertgoers and conventioneers able to pay high ticket and convention prices. In some cases, states were early postwar facility sponsors, but in most cases, city officials turned to state authorities as the scale of projects exceeded the financial or political capabilities of local government.

Specialized state sporting authorities are now crucial anchors and players in center cities and booming suburbs. Until the late 1970s team owners favored suburban sites "close to major highways and with plenty of land for parking," but since then their emphasis (and that of city and state officials) has shifted to underutilized sites adjacent to downtown.[29] The cost of these facilities has skyrocketed into the many hundreds of millions and sometimes over a billion dollars each. The various authorities developed the facilities with private partners (sports teams, hotels, etc.) supplemented by revenue bond offerings and taxes on hotels or other tourism-related interests. They are frequently renovated or rebuilt to suit escalating standards of visitors, team owners, and convention sponsors. State investments in light rail frequently serve these stadiums to reduce game-day crowding. Doubts about the wisdom of investing so much public money in these facilities, even when the demonstrated benefits are limited, are usually brushed aside. The cumulative investments in downtown urban space count for significant sections of center cities, require vast parking areas (most patrons arriving by car on state highways), and support affiliated nightlife and entertainment. Most authorities maintain a community-relations branch to mitigate the impact of traffic, which may include extra neighborhood security, place marketing, and other community benefits.

Examples from around the country indicate the scale and urban impact of these efforts. The Illinois Sports Facility Authority (1987) built a stadium for the White Sox, renovated Soldier Field for NFL football, and looks after 97 acres of Chicago waterfront parks. Guaranteed Rate Field (1991), home of the White Sox, is a typical state/local/franchise project. The governor and state legislature pushed for a replacement of the aging Comiskey Park, authorized the issuance of hundreds of millions in debt to fund its construction (and a massive renovation not long after it was built), agreed to an annual state payment of $5 million (the city also kicks in $5 million annually), and offered easy terms for extra profits to the White Sox. Debt issued to underwrite construction and renovation, totaling approximately $400 million, will not be retired until 2036.[30] Similar sweet deals are visible a few hundred miles east. The state-enabled Pittsburgh Sports and Exhibition Authority (1998) has combined over a billion dollars in hotel, sales, and parking revenues, private investments, and state funds ($338 million) for projects related to two stadiums, a convention center, and related infrastructure.[31]

The Maryland Stadium Authority (1986) stands out for a growing role in Baltimore's broader urban redevelopment since the 1980s. The authority first earned national recognition with the vast Camden Yards stadium development project (1992, 85 acres), which spread tourism beyond the city's famous Inner Harbor. Camden Yards became an architectural and planning model because of its neotraditional appearance and adaptive reuse of historic buildings. The authority next invested in a vast football stadium (1998) adjoining Camden Yards. The combined projects, promoted by Governor William Donald Schaefer (1987–1995) and former long-time mayor of Baltimore, revitalized a former industrial/rail area and are vibrant on game days. Many have, however, criticized the authority for creating an isolated suburban-style enclave of parking lots and stadiums in an otherwise rundown and impoverished city. The complex is part of a downtown district with deep roots in Maryland state government: downtown state office buildings, the state's light

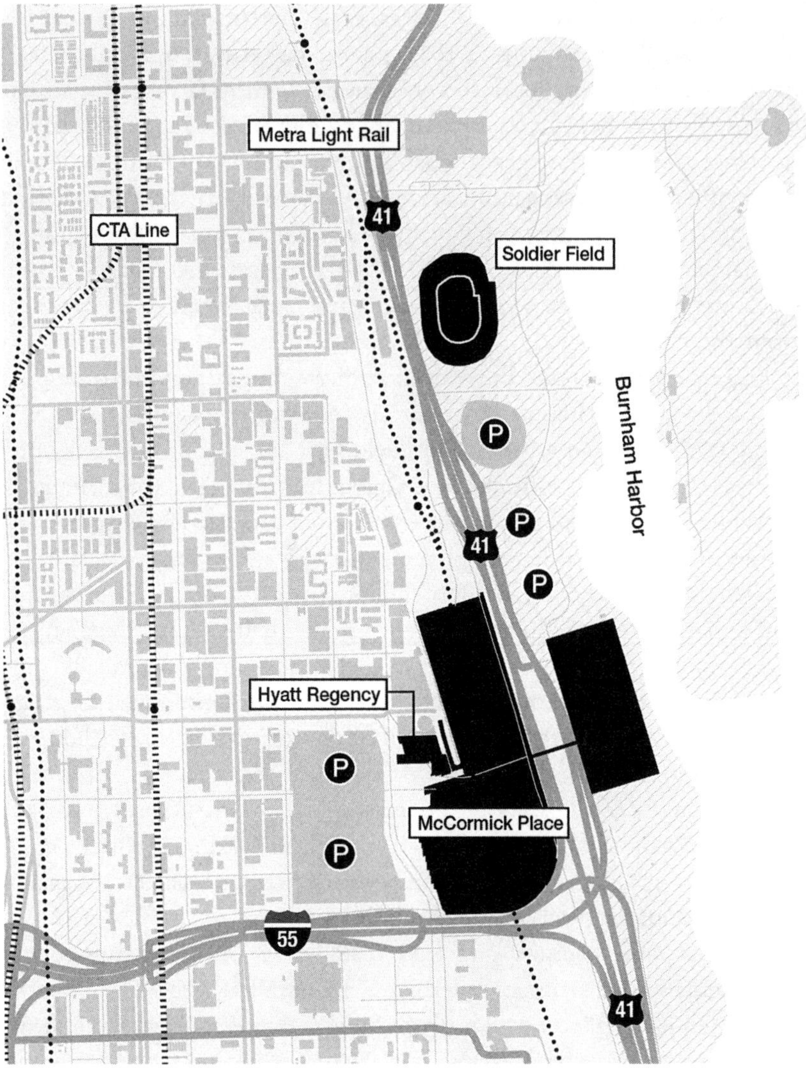

FIGURE 10. McCormick Place convention center, state highways, mass transit, and stadium in Chicago's center city are typical of state downtown investments in the postwar era. Map by Minna Ninova, 2018.

rail network, the Baltimore Convention Center (financed with $136 million of state of Maryland General Obligation and Revenue bonds), the University of Maryland at Baltimore, and extensive state highways (figure 10).[32]

The role of the stadium authority in Baltimore's redevelopment program has now expanded broadly, in part to demonstrate to political leaders a spirit of community engagement. The authority's projects include renovation of some Baltimore city schools, clearing blighted housing throughout the city, and renovating an old downtown theater into a performing arts theater. The authority has also been a force for new schools, campus buildings, and convention centers in suburban locales. Like the UDC, state and city leaders have realized that a robust and competent developer can play an essential role in urban revitalization. Its extensive powers in these social domains can be used to mute political questions about the use of state funds to build and sustain luxury stadiums in a chronically weak city with declining infrastructure. Baltimore's experience raises questions about the latent ability of other stadium authorities in the field of urban improvement. Apparently, they could be a much bigger force.[33]

Massive convention centers, anchors of most American center cities, are usually operated by state-chartered authorities that possess powers of urban redevelopment. According to one of the leading experts on convention center development, Heywood Sanders, "State governments have come to be central players in convention center development and expansion in recent decades." States, encouraged by local elites, stepped in as the price and size of these facilities exceeded the capacity of local government; in addition, state leadership circumvented voter rejection of bond offerings that were becoming more frequent as the price of these facilities escalated (and the local benefits remained minor). Among the many examples Sanders cites as typical are state-led centers in Phoenix, Omaha, Detroit, Tacoma, and Philadelphia. State-sponsored convention centers are ideal for "local business leaders seeking a way to revitalize a downtown core, or local elected officials promoting a major new public project, a means of getting things done" without "any serious debate over local, *city* priorities, ensuring that those interests that want a new or larger convention center succeed."[34]

Two examples amply illustrate a national pattern of state investment in center-city attractions that have significant impacts on their surroundings. The Illinois state legislature in the 1950s created a Metropolitan Fair and Exposition Authority, levied a tax on horse racing, and issued revenue bonds. Business interests and the *Chicago Tribune* used the authority to circumvent determined opponents of a lakefront site. The first McCormick Convention Center opened in 1960 with just 320,000 square feet of space and was a hit. Today's convention center, expanded multiple times, was made possible by strong revenues and a broad mix of taxes over the years (on cigarettes, hotels, restaurants, auto rental, etc.). The multiple building complex now boasts 2.6 million square feet of exhibit space, 600,000 square feet of meeting rooms, and an adjoining hotel. Its economic impact for Chicago is calculated at about $3.5 billion per year.[35]

Another pioneer was the Las Vegas Convention and Visitors Authority.

The authority traces its origins to state legislation in 1955 that authorized a room tax to fund the creation of a convention center (1959). The Las Vegas Convention Center has become a behemoth, with over two million square feet of exhibition space that hosts 21,000 conventions with about six million visitors per year. It is a key force in keeping the Vegas Strip's casinos, restaurants, stores, and bars full of tipsy, affluent, free-spending tourists. At the time of this writing, the authority was moving ahead on an $860 million multiphase expansion and renovation that will create, by 2023, a facility with 3.2 million square feet.[36]

These are two dominant convention centers, but the situation is similar in cities like Atlanta, New Orleans, and Seattle. These state convention center authorities occupy large districts, influence the commercial and residential mix around them, and provide major tourism destinations. States usually secure debt for these facilities and smooth the process of physical expansion through eminent domain and public relations. Experts such as Sanders have criticized the financial commitment that states have made in these facilities in what appears to most like a race to build the biggest and best facilities, even though demand for convention facilities has failed to keep pace with the growing number and size of facilities. The lack of financial transparency of many facilities, the complexity of their business models, boosterish consultant reports, and deep pockets of states have prevented a public accounting and debate about the wisdom of so much expansion.

State Economic Development and the Metropolis

The UDC's and ESDC's pursuit of regional economic development has parallels in various types of state economic development authorities (EDAs). EDAs trace their roots to industrial development and recruitment programs from the early twentieth century in then low-wage, "right to work" agricultural states such as North Carolina, Alabama, and Florida. State leaders in the Sunbelt, aided by federal programs and air-conditioning, scored many successes luring factories and corporations southward. Because even "most new plants in southern and western states" could be "found in suburbs" by 1980, these policies often directly contributed to metropolitan growth. EDAs have today become a national phenomenon, accounting for billions annually in tax incentives, grants, tax increment finance districts, and lightened state regulations. Aggressive venture funds or other versions of "state entrepreneurialism" support business development, identify new export markets, and engage in other high-risk activities formerly the purview of private enterprise. Metropolitan areas, where most Americans live, are the primary beneficiaries.[37]

EDAs, through place marketing, focus on the positive attributes of regions and scrupulously avoid any mention of social, environmental, or economic problems. Enterprise Florida, for instance, is a private/public partnership empowered by the state since the 1990s to recruit business. Its publications tout the state's low taxes, high standard of living, low cost of living, highly trained workforce, extensive higher education system, recreational and cultural facilities, advanced multimodal infrastructure, high-tech infrastructure, robust tourism market, and global expertise and connections. Most of these elements are crucial elements of the state's booming urban regions like Orlando and Miami that host industries such as aviation, life sciences, information technology, clean energy, financial and professional services, and manufacturing. The state's agriculture sector, now being plowed under in the name of urban growth, is a minor element of the total message or emphasis in Florida (population 20.6 million in 2018) or by other EDAs.[38]

Most states hawk similar qualities, or put the best spin on their various assets, to entice businesses to their metropolitan areas. Some have gone as far as denigrating their competition across state lines. EDA cash grant programs considered separately often add up to large sums; for instance, "the Texas Enterprise Fund is the largest of this type of fund, having disbursed almost half a billion dollars since 2006."[39] The value of various tax incentive programs is debated, as they often lead to interstate competition that gives corporations excessive benefits for limited job returns, but they do reflect a sustained state role in urban affairs. EDAs are politically popular at the state level because most voters do not understand how much money is being pledged to these efforts. It helps that EDA benefits may flow to prosperous suburbs, booming downtowns, or poor neighborhoods rather than being targeted solely to high-poverty areas.

These state-enabled economic development efforts sometimes physically shape urban areas in distinct ways. North Carolina's sprawling Research Triangle Park is a widely admired physical planning model for regional economic development. Governor Luther Hodges in the 1950s used a combination of physical infrastructure (roads and developable lots, state highways, and nearby universities) and tax incentives to attract northern companies and federal research facilities. The park started slowly but got a jolt when IBM set up a research facility in 1965. Other companies quickly followed, as did government agencies like the Environmental Protection Agency (EPA). The careful planning of the area, combined with deep state investment in tax breaks, nearby public higher education, and state-funded centers in biotechnology and microelectronics, has resulted in America's largest research park, which now includes 7,000 acres with 250 businesses and 50,000 employees. The park's success has helped generate and sustain a massive process of regional suburbanization.[40]

North Carolina's approach is reflected, if not equaled, in similar research parks across the nation, most of which have a connection to a state-sponsored higher education institution. A 2012 survey of American and Canadian research parks found that they collectively host 379,754 direct jobs with a total employment impact estimated at 941,258. These parks play a crucial role in transferring academic research in areas such as biotech and software to the private sector. One example from among many illustrates the regional impact: "A study of the University of Arizona Science and Technology Park found that the 6,494 jobs in the park supported a total of 14,332 jobs in Pima County, AZ and generated $2.7 billion in economic activity." The current trend is to retrofit low-density research parks for a mixture of uses (restaurants, stores, housing, coworking spaces, etc.) that park managers hope will continue to attract top employers and workers by offering a more urbane "live-work-play" environment.[41]

In coastal cities such as New York, Baltimore, New Orleans, Portland, and Boston, state-enabled port authorities have been powerful forces for valuable economic development program. Among the expanded activities of port authorities are tourism (cruise terminals), airports, industrial and warehouse promotion, shipbuilding, and commercial development. In New York, the powerful Port Authority of New York and New Jersey dominates regional aviation, runs the PATH (Port Authority Trans-Hudson) system, manages the bus terminal, developed and redeveloped the World Trade Center complex, and controls various bridges and tunnels. Port authority administrators in other cities often control the development process on hundreds or thousands of acres of waterfront land formerly used for shipping. In Boston, for instance, Massport controls 10 percent of the city's total land area. Port authorities are usually independent of local leadership, have access to additional sources of capital, and can plan for long-range infrastructure. This independence often raises questions about accountability and suitability of large-scale infrastructure projects to local needs.[42]

Through these diverse means states have played a quiet but powerful role in urban development. Postwar state programs influenced downtown redevelopment even though it sometimes took decades for the vision to be realized. States then became leading forces after the "collapse of urban renewal" in ongoing redevelopment programs, including huge and expensive stadiums and convention centers. In recent decades many of these state efforts, such as research parks, have arguably encouraged sprawl and Sunbelt boom by making suburban areas competitive for high technology and factories. City and state leaders, by developing independent and consistent funding sources, circumvented difficult conversations about who would benefit from the facilities, who should fund them, reasonable returns on investments, and their impact on city centers and neighborhoods. States thus remained crucial players in American urban development.

4

State Capital Office Complexes and Cities

The growing scale and scope of postwar state government services and functions demanded a much more substantial bureaucracy. Between 1958 and 1978, the total number of state employees nationally roughly doubled, rising from 1.4 million[1] to 3 million.[2] By 2012, state governments cumulatively employed a total of 5.3 million mostly full-time workers.[3] The growing ranks of state white-collar workers have expected to labor in offices on par with their peers in the private sector, including modern lighting, air-conditioning, lots of parking, and suburban-level safety—even if their offices are located in otherwise crumbling downtowns adjacent to historic state capitols.

Expanding state universities, hospitals, and prisons absorbed most of these state workers, some of whom were also located in and around state capitals, but expanding, centralized state bureaucracies related to transportation, education, environment, health, etc. had their own distinctive office space needs. Some new state office buildings sprouted in suburban-style office parks, but downtowns of state capitals remained dominant as places of both bureaucratic employment and ceremonial significance. Decades of investments in a center-city physical campus, usually surrounding an impressive capitol building, made it difficult for state leaders nationally to envision a wholesale abandonment of traditional locations.

This dimension of state redevelopment merits a closer look. Planning and urban historians, for instance, have overlooked a collectively large program of urban reconstruction that has had enduring impacts on 50 mostly smaller cities across the nation. Because the states were the force behind offices complexes and mostly built them as planned, they are a variation on traditional urban renewal themes of clearance and failure. Urban reconstruction, often structured around a bold master plan, reached goals thanks to the sustained support and deep pockets of a state government. The collective impact nationally of state office complex redevelopment and renting is huge.

Smaller capital cities like Albany, Sacramento, and Springfield in the postwar years were not resisting urban redevelopment; rather, redevelopment had stalled out or, even worse, bypassed them. With new highways and little center-city market demand, suburbanization eviscerated their commercial vitality. Local elites in state capitals usually jumped happily into state- and federal-funded urban renewal programs and seemed to have faced relatively little initial resistance to their frequently destructive plans. When there was opposition, supporters easily steamrolled the local opposition. From coast to coast, sections of older commercial districts were cleared to make way for new or greatly expanded state office buildings.

Albany was one of many New York State cities that had languished. Albany was "a shabby, dank and crumbling backwater in the early-1960s with about as much pizzazz as a Dutch wooden shoe."[4] State leaders, imposing grandiose downstate tastes on a modest commercial center, had already carved out ceremonial spaces with a scandalously expensive state capitol, a Beaux Arts Education building, and Governor Al Smith's art deco skyscraper that seemed to have escaped Midtown Manhattan. The city surrounding the state offices in postwar years had nevertheless become shabby and "after Nelson came to Albany, he looked out the window of his second-floor office, and he saw a piece of the city of Albany with dilapidated housing . . . and he thought that it should be eliminated and replaced by State Office Buildings."[5] To do so, he would not only have to create new space downtown but would have to restrict the growth of suburban state offices set in motion by his predecessor, Governor Dewey. Many downtown business interests understandably supported such an investment in the center. The city's corrupt, longtime Democratic Mayor Erastus Corning, however, was initially skeptical and even openly hostile. Not only was he going to lose neighborhoods full of dependable voters, but state offices would be untaxable.[6]

The State Commission on the Capital City, led by Rockefeller's lieutenant governor, Malcolm Wilson, predictably recommended a vast urban renewal project for 98.5 acres of central Albany, with a focus on removing the "Gut" neighborhood adjacent to the capitol. The Gut's 1,150 buildings targeted for demolition included many bars and rooming houses occupied by a poor or marginalized urban population (alcoholics, service workers, seniors, etc.) still living in the city center during these years.[7] In the Gut, however, "there was plenty of fine architecture worth preserving, not to mention a couple of churches, a brand new high school . . . saloons, grocery stores and even a police station." Democratic voters that Corning counted on during elections

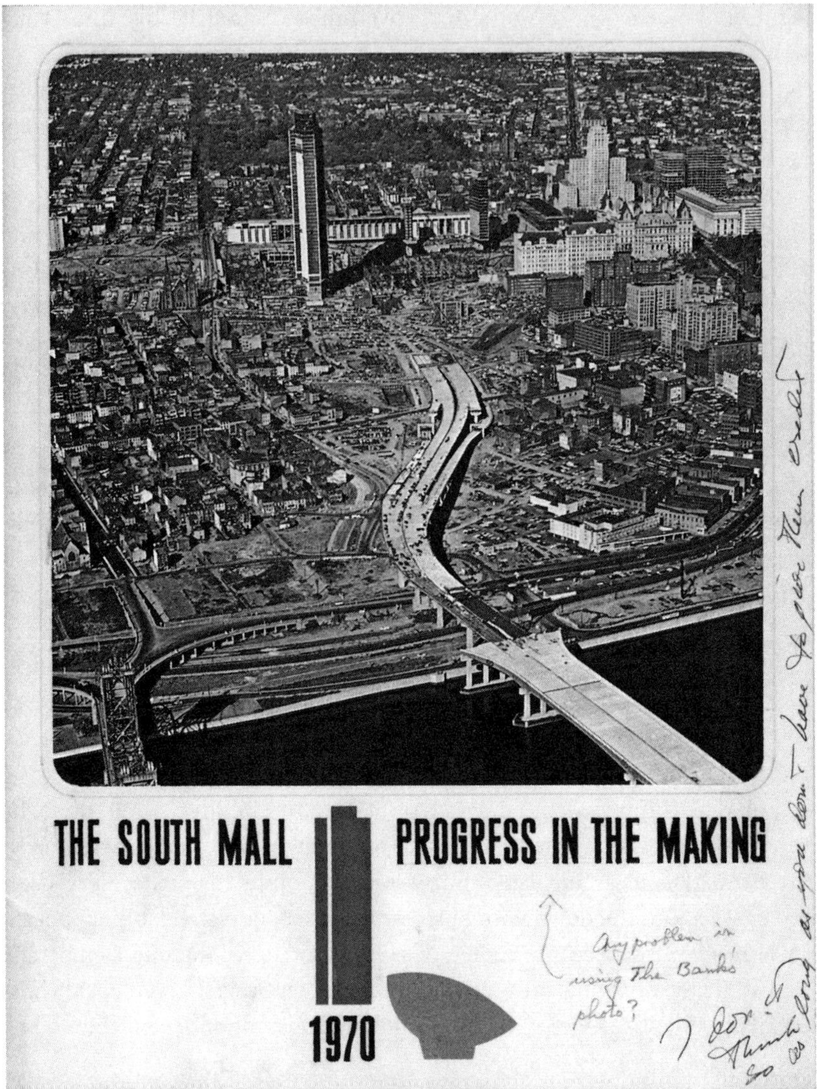

FIGURE 11. The massive reconstruction of downtown Albany in the service of state government. "The South Mall: Progress in the Making," 1970. New York State Archives, courtesy of the Rockefeller Archive Center.

also lived there. Some downtown property owners were fearful of the loss of about 9,000 state workers from offices rented in old buildings mixed into the existing city.[8]

None of these local concerns mattered. By 1962, the state had taken 40 blocks using eminent domain and eventually cleared the site without a valid relocation plan or public housing option for the many poor people displaced. The Temporary Commission had considered many potential schemes, including some more incremental and less disruptive to surrounding neighborhoods, but the one selected on the South Side demanded clearance of the Gut to make way for underground parking and concourses. It helped, in selling the plan, that "the South Mall site was also ideally situated for direct arterial connection to the interstate highway network being spread across the state." A planned highway linking the complex to the riverfront would spirit state government workers in and out of the city at top speed.[9]

The project initially stalled out, however, as the high cost of creating a massive complex made Rockefeller uncomfortable about asking for additional funds from the state legislature. Mayor Corning eventually joined with the governor to keep the project moving and thus avoid the fate of so many delayed urban renewal projects. Corning put together a complex "lease-purchase" agreement that included the transfer of land to city and county, county-issued bonds, county supervision of the construction, and state leasing of the buildings until the state owned them in full (in 2004). The city made up for some of its losses by being reimbursed for lost taxes and gained a free museum, tiny convention center, and lots of downtown parking. The key to such a massive financing scheme was the dependability of the state government needing the space. Eventually, $895 million in Albany County bonds would be sold, which covered only part of an estimated $1.9 billion project. The rest of the cost was begrudgingly financed by the state on an annual basis during the protracted erection of the complex.[10]

The new state compound, which Rockefeller claimed credit for originating in consultation with Harrison, evoked the drama of the Dalai Lama's palace at Lhasa, Tibet. On a flight, the governor recommended to Harrison how it "might be done in a grand style of Brasilia, Versailles, or Chandigarh. He took out his pen and sketched his ideas in black ink." Harrison eventually translated these sketches into the plan.[11] The central pedestrian mall on the top of the massive base had echoes of many previous Wallace Harrison projects. The complex was from the start designed as much for show as function, bringing the drama of Midtown redevelopment upstate. Like many projects of its day, it had a "world's fair" accent that would eventually include vast reflecting pools, fountains, public art, underground shopping and gallery space, lush landscaping, and large plazas for public gatherings.[12] The Albany complex was jammed full of high-rise buildings and offices unnecessary in a mostly low- to medium-rise city with so much available land: "a forty-four-story office tower, four identical twenty-three story agency buildings, a legislative building, a justice building, a headquarters for the motor-vehicles department, a cultural center . . . a meeting center, and a laboratory for the department of health." The platform on which the high-rises sat was a massive 3.8-million-square-foot building (one-quarter by one-eighth of a mile).[13]

The troubles that developed from such a complicated program and design idea were like those encountered in many urban renewal programs of the time. The 40 prime contractors and 70 separate contractors working on the site failed to cooperate for years. Nature was no more cooperative, as the ravine exposed included clay and a stream. Accordingly, "the hole in the ground remained formidable for years. It looked like a deserted Worlds' Fair project when the workday ended, lights erratically blinking in the middle floors of the tower building." A reporter discovered that "the place was chockablock with thievery, no-shows, ridiculous featherbedding, gambling, and a rather spectacular record of arson."[14] An original estimate of $250 million for the project turned out to be entirely wrong, as the price tag rose by hundreds of millions.[15] The large number of state projects in the region—highways, university center, and Albany mall—gave contractors an upper hand negotiating prices for work.[16]

The long-term dividends of such an expensive project were mixed and remain debated. Approximately 10,000 workers, mostly from other downtown sites, were finally relocated to the complex in the 1970s, securing a dominant presence of state government in this expanded section of the downtown business district. But state agencies had a nasty surprise. The "large and elaborate central service cores" in the office towers lining the plazas delivered "an extremely low ratio of usable space compared with the total area of the buildings." The four 23-story agency buildings may have included an impressive 190,000 square feet under each of their roofs, but only 90,000 of that total was usable office space. The state government continued to rent and develop space on its 429-acre suburban-style complex during the 1960s, growing to over 11,000 employees in 20 buildings.[17]

The role of the plaza in reanimating the downtown is equally debatable. The plaza eventually became a tourist destination for hundreds of thousands of visitors,[18] and the Egg performance hall and the New York State Museum are reasonably popular attractions. Studding the lawns and the underground concourse is the fabulous collection of modern art Rockefeller assembled, with state funds, of "New York School" artists. On nice days, "the Empire State Mall is filled with employees and tourists lounging along its reflecting pools, enjoying its eighteen fountains" and public art.[19]

The drawbacks of the planned complex are typical of modern government centers nationally. A large amount of tax-exempt property tied up in the complex hurts city government despite some payments in lieu of taxes.[20] The majority suburban workforce can easily avoid ever leaving the downtown

FIGURE 12. Nelson Rockefeller Empire State Plaza. Photograph courtesy of Jer21999/Wikimedia Commons.

complex. The plaza's elevated plateau is difficult to access from surrounding neighborhoods and often cold and windswept. Many nearby neighborhoods have continued to lose structures and homes because of widespread disinvestment. The plaza transformed urban space but not necessarily the trajectory of the state's capital city.

Rebuilding American Capitals

A similar pattern of state government as office tenant and agent of redevelopment has transformed the economic life and ambiance of center cities across the nation. These efforts have, however, mostly escaped notice, as they are frequently in smaller media markets. Most projects also lack the grandiosity of the Albany plan. Instead, they are designed to match the needs of state agencies and their usually suburban employees for modern office space, vast parking fields, and close connections to new state highways.

Florida's state legislature followed on New York's heels in commissioning an architecturally ambitious capital redevelopment program for Tallahassee. The new complex was part of a 1960s strategy by northern state legislators to head off a move of the state's capital to booming Orlando. In 1969, the state moved ahead with a capitol complex that included a 22-story high-rise executive office building flanked by new legislative chambers. Designed by New York's Edward Durrell Stone—responsible for the Kennedy Center,

FIGURE 13. Florida capitol complex in Tallahassee designed by Edward Durrell Stone. Courtesy of the State Library and Archives of Florida.

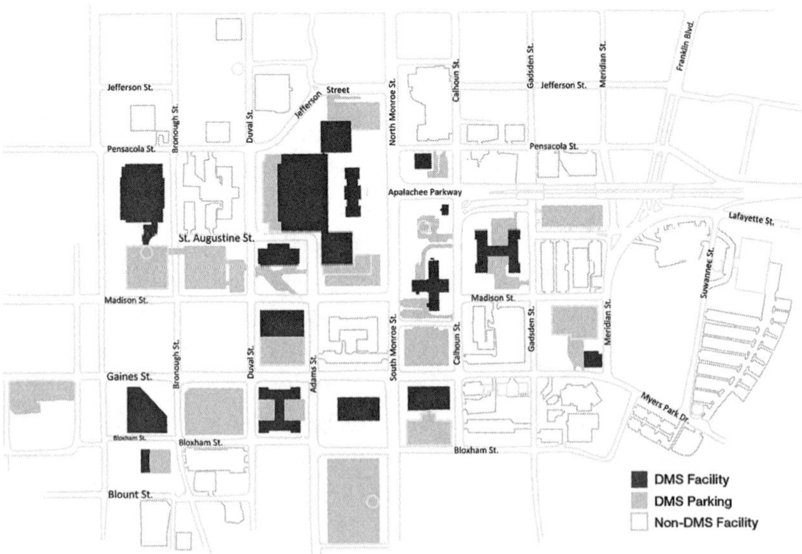

FIGURE 14. Tallahassee reshaped for state bureaucracy, including plentiful space for commuters' cars. Map by Minna Ninova, 2018.

numerous embassies, and New York's SUNY Albany campus—the complex included his modernized neoclassicism integrating whitewashed surfaces, marble, symmetry, and colonnades. The Florida complex has echoes of both Brasilia and Albany's government district. Since the center's creation in the 1970s, additional offices and an enormous amount of parking has been provided to make the offices desirable for state employees.[21]

Sacramento entered an extensive and protracted period of urban redevelopment that rivals Albany's. The aim of focusing state government offices in Sacramento reached back to the 1920s as "scatteration" to San Francisco and elsewhere threatened. New highways and postwar state expansion helped government count for 40 percent of nonfarm Sacramento workers by 1956. City officials were embarrassed, however, by the West End skid row full of "bars, fast food joints, flophouses, employment agencies, and houses of ill-repute" that was home to perhaps 10,000 male transients. A massive clearance program began in 1957, "targeting the area directly in front of the state capital as the first site for rehabilitation." Thousands of residents were displaced from the sites as "demolition proceeded rapidly and before long a new Capitol Mall emerged, providing a sweeping open space between the Tower Bridge and the statehouse." Local newspapers gushed that "where honky-tonks and gas stations once stood, a thoroughly businesslike Capitol Mall sprouted, an appropriate gateway to the Capital." Large, modern office buildings to house state agencies were central to the rise of a sanitized, industrious

FIGURE 15. The impact of state government expansion in Sacramento's downtown is illustrated graphically in this map. Map by Minna Ninova, 2018.

state capital complex. The scale of downtown space developed cumulatively rivals that undertaken in Albany even though it lacks the drama of Albany or Tallahassee.[22]

Even small, urbanized states engaged in large-scale reconstruction. State legislators in Trenton, New Jersey, for instance, cleared neighborhoods to make way for suburban-style state office buildings and parking lots. A tangle of interstates connected the offices to the suburbs while brutally cutting the city off from the waterfront. The damage to the city's fabric is still a legacy of the urban expansion of state offices. In the 1980s, responding to continuing decline, the state of New Jersey created the Capital City Redevelopment Corporation to "ensure that the Capital District is a great place to live, visit, work and conduct business." The corporation claims credit for "facilitating redevelopment," including new hotels, corporate headquarters, and housing renovation. Trenton remains a city in crisis, however, despite sustained state employment and investment.[23]

Some capital reconstruction projects have adopted a contextual approach. The antique core of Annapolis is full of low-key state office complexes that have arguably enhanced the historical flavor of the center city. Some of these new buildings, as in the Annapolis Complex, are designed in a Georgian manner to blend in with the historic city. Others, in the surrounding suburbs, are typical corporate parks. The Annapolis Public Buildings and Grounds today "oversees 26 State-owned buildings, 49 acres of landscaped areas and 24.5 acres of parking lots" that offer workspace for 4,700 state employees and elected officials. The impact on the small city is dramatic and underlines the city's dual role as a capital and famous tourist destination. Thousands of miles away, the New Mexico state government developed a distinctive territorial-style "Roundhouse" state capitol building (1966) that blends in well with the historical and revival styles of surrounding Santa Fe.[24]

Some state office expansion, in cities like Harrisburg, St. Paul, and Austin, took place associated with an existing City Beautiful armature. Many modern office buildings that house state offices, for instance, have sprouted around Texas's neo-baroque capitol and formal grounds. In 1955, the Texas Legislature created a master plan as it began aggressively expanding offices that aimed to create a "grand Congress Mall" for pedestrians, including underground parking, but these public realm goals failed. A 1963 master plan, affirmed in a later report in 1989, stressed the importance of the first plan and the importance of maintaining the impressive views of the state capitol, acquiring additional land, and enhanced public access and open space. The plan, however, was not determinative in setting out the location of office buildings. The result was that the state maintained about 5,000 workers in 22 leased properties in

1.5 million gross square feet of space "scattered" around Austin, mostly right around the capitol.

The Texas Legislature's aim today, as in Albany decades ago, is to consolidate these offices in state-owned buildings paired with thousands of parking spaces. Helping to sell the dramatic expansion in state offices and cars is a renewed push to upgrade the public spaces while still accommodating the state workers and their cars downtown. The appealing *Texas Capitol Complex Master Plan* (2016) by Sasaki and Associates aims to create "grand civic spaces, shaded pedestrian-friendly streets, and connections to the surrounding community," including a "tree-lined promenade . . . that will serve as the northern gateway to the Capital Complex with public green space for tourism, events, and festivals." The plan was still in the early stages at the time of this writing (2018).[25]

These selected examples illustrate the variety and impact of postwar state office building construction on state capitals. The underlying themes unifying the different approaches and scale are the steady growth in state government footprint in these cities and the long-term impact of these offices on city life.

State Office Buildings beyond Albany

States have played a quiet but crucial role in adding workers and new buildings to American center cities that are not capitals. This state investment, usually in the guise of facilities such as department of motor vehicles (DMV) facilities, state offices, courthouses, and prisons, is frequently political in origin. A state agency is a plum award for declining cities looking to firm up an urban redevelopment plan because state offices are steady tenants in an otherwise fickle and competitive market. City-center state offices were controversial, however, when they were part of destructive urban renewal schemes.

Rockefeller generated controversy when he decided to bring "prosperity" to Harlem through the creation of a new state office building on 125th Street.[26] At first there appeared to be a consensus among minority leaders and state officials that a state office project would be good for the neighborhood.[27] State administrator James Gaynor reported that "there is little doubt, even among the black community, that this building, and its related recreational and commercial facilities, will lead to a general upgrading of the surrounding community."[28] If anything, local leaders were dissatisfied that the state plan was too modest. Percy Sutton considered the plans for the state office building a "mere token" compared to planned state offices in the forthcoming World Trade Center in Lower Manhattan.[29]

Rockefeller entrusted the site selection in 1966 to Rev. Wyatt Walker, his aide on urban affairs and a former assistant to Rev. Dr. Martin Luther King.[30] The Rockefeller team would claim that, working with Harlem leaders, they were able to select a site that minimized "abrasive human problems, relocation, economics, etc." typical of redevelopment. A site at 125th Street and Seventh Avenue was chosen quickly, and demolition was complete in 1968. Ifill, Johnson, and Hanchard, an African American architectural firm, designed the complex in the typically brutalist style of the era. The original plan included a 20-story building, a DMV, and a civic and cultural center with three buildings, including multipurpose convention center / auditorium, a 10-story educational building, a little theater for 300, and community plaza. The state legislature had its say, however, and canceled most of the cultural and civic add-ons that had been crucial to gaining broad community support.[31]

Ada Louise Huxtable reported in 1969 that the state office building "has turned into Governor Rockefeller's Vietnam. It is mired in the question of community participation, or the complex matter of who speaks for the real needs and wishes of the Harlem community, or even if anyone can." In 1969 activists occupied the site, making the battle over the state office building an iconic moment in the fight against urban renewal.[32] Radical neighborhood activists sought to derail the plan completely. ARCH, the Architects Renewal Committee of Harlem, young black advocacy planners, during this period offered plans for the whole block, including housing, school, and commerce and opposed any state office building.[33]

The governor found workarounds. During the summer, he transferred the project to a subsidiary of the UDC and pledged five floors of the tower for educational purposes.[34] Some felt that "the young people on the site have indeed won a victory." Rockefeller also promoted black tradesmen and assigned a significant share of the project to black contractors.[35] Rockefeller's Office on Urban Affairs, armed with these olive branches, solicited support from business leaders against a "handful of activists."[36] Those putting their names on the advertisement of support included the head of NAACP New York branch, labor leaders, business leaders, and community leaders.[37] Rockefeller, armed with establishment support on all fronts, announced he was moving ahead with the project on September 22, 1969. The police evicted the protestors, and the program of development began. The complex would not open until 1972. To what extent the complex helped inspire a rebirth of 125th Street is debatable. The relatively small number of state workers and continuing decline in the neighborhood undermined broader investment. Today, the brooding tower and windswept plaza break the flow of shopping on 125th Street without adding any genuine point of interest.

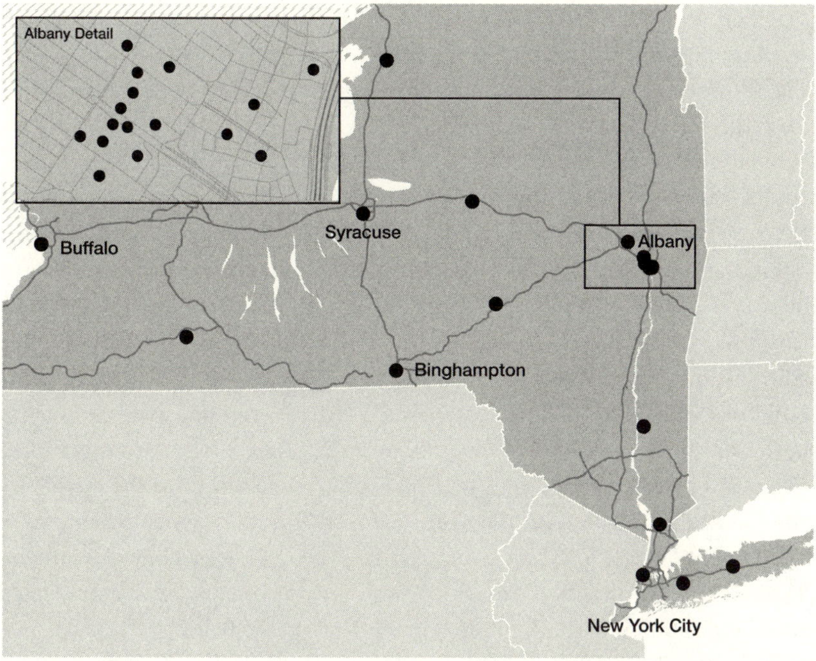

FIGURE 16. New York State offices have an impact in Albany and beyond. Map by Minna Ninova, 2018.

Establishment of state office buildings across the rest of the state, in new and rented space, was welcomed without the bruising fights encountered in either Albany or New York City. The enormous presence of state offices in the Port Authority's World Trade Center provided a steady rental stream in the early days of that complex; even today, the state of New York remains a large tenant in Lower Manhattan. The state bureaucracy also remains an important tenant in struggling urban downtowns across the state. New York State offices are also located in Schenectady, Poughkeepsie, Buffalo, Syracuse, Utica, Oneonta, and Watertown. Complications rising from state office development were not restricted to Albany. A modernist, 18-story state office tower in Binghamton, part of a government plaza urban redevelopment project undertaken at the same time as the Albany and Harlem projects, was poisoned by a toxic fire that made it unusable from 1981 to 1994.

State Office Complexes outside Capitals

Across the United States, state office complexes remain important to regional economies. The offices are to be found in a mix of leased and owned buildings and on both center-city and suburban sites. A few representative examples reflect the broader pattern of urban state office complexes nationally. The importance of state office buildings is geographically broad and extends from the Northeast to the Sunbelt.

Maryland's presence in the Baltimore area is essential to the declining city's remaining health. The state's Baltimore Public Buildings and Grounds Division maintains four buildings with "5400 State employees" and "28 acres of land and parking lots" located mostly in a once controversial modernist urban renewal district that replaced a densely populated minority district adjacent to historic Bolton Hill during the 1950s and 1960s. An additional state administrative unit, the Inner Harbor State Office Complex, includes nine buildings with "1.36 million square feet" of space for 3,000 state workers in both Baltimore and Howard County, including "the Governor's downtown office and 13 state agencies." The expansion of state offices in the city is desired by the powerful local political class to help stabilize the city and takes advantage of large, low-cost commercial spaces in a struggling downtown. The Nancy Grasmick State Education Building, for instance, is in a renovated commercial building (built in 1911) on the west side of Baltimore's downtown in an area targeted for decades as a major redevelopment zone.[38]

Many Sunbelt cities also benefit from significant state office presence. The Texas Facilities Commission leases millions of square feet across the state for various state offices (public safety, attorney general, social services, wildlife, etc.), with significant concentrations in and around the biggest cities.[39]

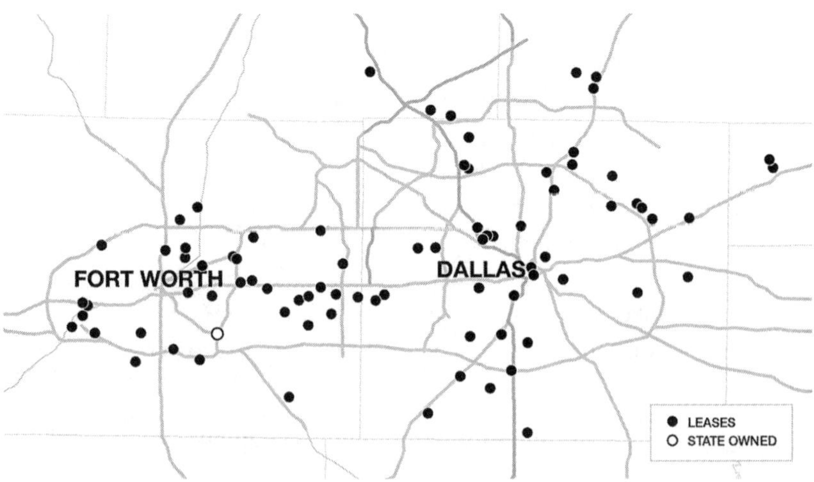

FIGURE 17. Dallas–Fort Worth state office leases indicate the broad impact of state offices in one region. Map by Minna Ninova, 2018.

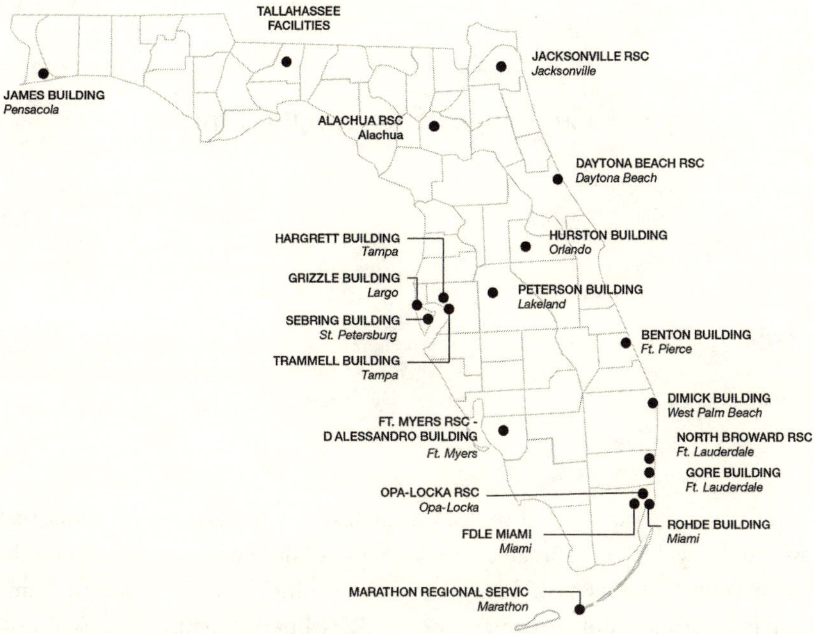

FIGURE 18. Florida maintains many state office buildings in cities across the state. Map by Minna Ninova, 2018.

Other states have commissioned and own the buildings they use as offices. States like California and Florida maintain sizable state-owned office buildings in cities outside their capitals. When added together, the programs in state office development and rentals add up to a large-scale program with metropolitan impact.

5

The Challenge of Regional Planning

State governments seemed to hold a missing key to regional planning that would finally lock up unregulated metropolitan development. Elite and public opinion in the 1960s and 1970s seemed to coincide with a desire to maintain natural and rural areas surrounding cities, but the institutional, political, and economic barriers proved formidable. The Rockefeller administration's efforts in the field of regional planning reflect the challenges for state governments as they looked to address the environmental consequences of sprawl. With a couple of important exceptions, it is more accurate to say that states have been able to plan for sprawl rather than tame it.

New York seemed likely to succeed because the state had served as the nation's urban planning laboratory since the nineteenth century. The Croton and Catskill water systems, the 1898 consolidation of the five boroughs and publicly subsidized high-speed subways (1904–) reflected an emerging regional planning vision. Idealistic New York developers and architects created American-style garden cities at Forest Hills Gardens (1909) and Sunnyside Gardens (1924). The state government prepared visionary plans in the 1920s that envisioned a balance of rural, wild, and urban spaces and created the Port of New York Authority (1921). The privately run Regional Plan Association (1922) researched and published comprehensive, buildable blueprints for a well-regulated metropolis. Robert Moses, who dominated state and city planning from the 1920s to the 1960s, showed a flair for regional planning that involved big projects like parks, roadways, housing, and power facilities.

Even in New York, where planning had demonstrated its value, many critics in the postwar years had come to believe that planning as practiced was not keeping pace with the new scale of the modern metropolis. The merchant builders behind planned communities like Levittown, New York, for instance, created a mix of housing styles and left spaces for schools, shopping, parks, and churches, but "more typical of the postwar years were tracts of a hundred or two hundred houses and a small shopping center," lacking in community facilities, parks, logical street plans, and adequate sewers.[1] New York's and New Jersey's suburbs in the 1950s, because of the aggressive subdivision with

FIGURE 19. Postwar development on Long Island replaced agriculture and compromised environmental quality. State of New York Conservation Department, *Now or Never: A Bold New Program for Outdoor Recreation*, 1960. New York State Archives, courtesy of the Rockefeller Archive Center.

limited planning, added 2.4 million new residents.[2] Once distant Rockland County, when linked to Westchester County by the Tappan Zee Bridge in the 1950s, experienced torrid, unregulated growth: "Today bulldozers rip up the earth to build even more housing developments, shopping centers, schools, and offices where all was quiet and rural a few years past."[3] Upstate suburbs also flowed into the verdant fields around cities like Rochester, Syracuse, Albany, and Buffalo. Between the end of World War II and 1970, "more than two million new homes have been built in New York State, most of them well equipped with modern conveniences."[4]

Most families warmly embraced their homes and lawns, and developers became a crucial progrowth political force in New York. The New York State Builders Association, an affiliate of the National Association of Home Builders, was founded in 1951, with the aim of minimizing regulation, and thus promoting development, through lobbying at the state and national level.[5] But experts worried. Robert Moses, who did so much to create suburbs, was even alarmed. He believed that small-lot subdivisions like Levittown, the result of weak zoning laws, had created "changes in surface and subsurface water, land, trees, watercourses, swales, and drainage" in a "revolutionary," and mostly negative manner. He blamed flooding of parkways on Long Island and uncertain drinking water supplies as "curses of subdivision" that could have been avoided had William Levitt, among others, created larger lots that drained better.[6]

Unregulated growth might even, in the minds of Rockefeller's lieutenants, undo the suburban good life: "The suburbs themselves are straining under problems of rapid expansion. Young families swell the school population. New subdivisions require costly water and sewerage facilities. Leap-frogging development wastes land and causes higher public facility and service costs."[7] A planning expert in 1960 predicted that by 1970 population pressure in Westchester County would "require probably 75 thousand more houses, occupying many square miles of now open land."[8] In the minds of reformers, something should be done to guide and restrain growth.

Making Big Plans

The Rockefeller administration produced a series of regional planning reports that envisioned a transformation of cities and the countryside into much better-organized and environmentally sensitive organisms. The governor also created new organizations to promote planning, such as the Office for Regional Development, the Office of Planning Coordination, the Urban Development Corporation, and the Tri-State Transportation Commission.

The multiplication of plans and agencies like these was a characteristic feature of postwar state government.

The Rockefeller administration's stunning *Change/Challenge/Response* (1964), prepared by the Office for Regional Development, was filled with appealing infographics detailing the rise of the industrial and global economy, the challenge of the contemporary metropolitan system, and a logical plan for compact growth in the state's valleys. The planners envisioned an integrated urban system that would include enhanced regional open spaces, planned new towns to absorb growth, and a modern transportation network. A bleak analysis of the state's future should planning be ignored justified the intervention: "If there is unlimited population growth and a free rein to every pressure to build, New York State could eventually end up a treeless wasteland like much of present-day China." This was a visionary plan, and its recommendations are no less relevant today than they were over half a century ago, but unrealistic given the office's lack of power.[9]

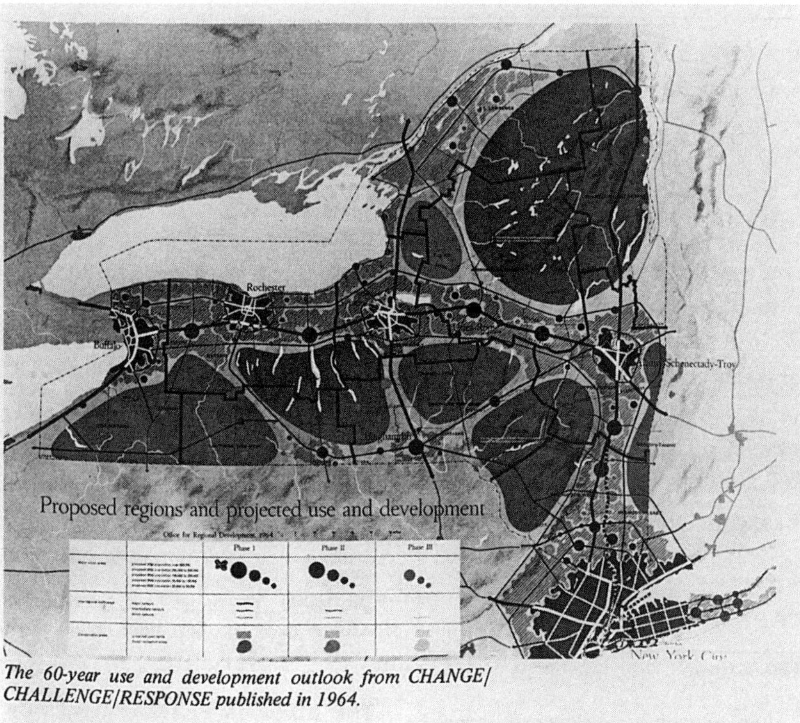

FIGURE 20. What a well-planned state might have looked like. David Brandon, Office of Planning coordinator, "Planning for Development in New York State," 1970. New York State Archives, courtesy of the Rockefeller Archive Center.

Rockefeller knew that planning required more than fanciful visions. The state legislature with Rockefeller's prodding created the Office of Planning Coordination (OPC) to coordinate all state planning, to facilitate state-to-local relationships, to pioneer regional planning, and to develop a comprehensive state plan. The OPC's promotion of regional and county planning boards aimed to encourage sharing of resources and planning across the state's 7,000 governmental units but could claim few practical victories in centralization. The OPC had identified a problem, regional fragmentation, and a solution, consolidation of services at the county level, that remains as relevant today as when it was pursued 40 years ago.[10] The OPC encouraged counties to assume new roles and "many of the functions previously performed at the local level," including sewage treatment, county service districts, and some forms of policing.[11]

The attractively designed New York State Development Plan (1971) by the OPC aimed to control 20 years of future land use "to assure that there will be enough land for people, and at the same time protect large areas vital for farming, recreation, and ecological balance." Urban growth would be restricted "to take advantage of present facilities, such as highways, schools, and utilities," and "multi-use corridors" would funnel growth. The OPC's plans anticipate today's smart growth strategies, but lacked teeth. Consolidation of additional resources and growth controls were bitterly contested by many towns despite high taxes and redundant services in the region's suburbs.[12]

The failure of these grand plans is linked to the deeper political problem of balancing regional ideals with local interests. Exclusivity, and high quality of local services, was a foundational element of the American suburban dream, stretching back at least to the successful resistance of Brookline, Massachusetts, to annexation to the city of Boston in 1873. Suburban elitism led to an end of municipal annexation in the North and thus contributed to the urban crisis of the postwar era. States had granted local governments the power of incorporation or its equivalent; pulling back that grant of local control has proved exceedingly difficult in all but the most extreme cases of municipal bankruptcy. The proposed loss of local control by villages and towns to suburban counties in these 1960s and 1970s plans represented a new assault on suburban rights. Counties were becoming more socially diverse, and it was clear that sharing of services might spread to schools, libraries, parks, and more. Even today in Westchester County, many towns post signs notifying outsiders that a town park is for residents only. Local governments resisted the sharing of services with counties in all but the most expensive or complicated regional services (such as water treatment or mass transit).

The UDC's failure as a regional planning body illustrates in the clearest way the political problems of asserting the state's rights over local government. Rockefeller and the state legislature initially gave Ed Logue and the staff of the Urban Development Corporation (1968–1975) the power to override local zoning and establish regionally based planning. The most ambitious effort was building mixed-income, environmentally sensitive new towns to curb "fragmented development in the van of suburban expansion." Logue and his team scored some success on isolated Roosevelt Island, conceived as a "new town in town" in the middle of the East River, but his suburban new towns upstate failed because of a complex mix of poor market conditions, local resistance (both to planning and low-income housing), and administrative errors. So even though the UDC invested large amounts of money in plans, infrastructure, community facilities, and protected natural features, the towns were a bust. Logue failed to reproduce the nucleated postwar European new towns he and many planners of the day so admired.[13]

The UDC's even more ambitious regional plans for "a statewide project review system; protection of areas of critical state concern; and broad county districting" fell on deaf ears. And when the UDC tried to assert its powers to control development during the battles over subsidized suburban housing, the state legislature, under pressure from suburban residents and politicians, quickly stripped it of that power. The UDC remained a force in urban redevelopment after its reorganization in 1975 but was more narrowly focused on business-friendly redevelopment projects in city centers where the UDC was welcome to flex its muscles.[14]

Another disappointment for many planners was the limited impact of Rockefeller's Tri-State Committee (later Tri-State Commission). Rockefeller launched the organization in 1961 with the governors of New Jersey and Connecticut. Its field of operations technically covered the 11,000-square-mile New York metro area.[15] Among the commission's accomplishments was deploying federal grants in 1961 for "the development of the most comprehensive transportation-land use plan ever designed."[16] The commission recommended rail links to the airports, a new station for the Long Island Rail Road (LIRR) on the East Side of Manhattan, a new Atlantic Avenue LIRR station, and better subways—ideas that were not original but got a good push from the commission's endorsement.[17] The commission became an "official planning agency" of the three states in 1965, in part to meet federal planning requirements. In 1966, the commission proposed a $10 billion ($76.8 billion in 2017 dollars) two-decade improvement plan for subway, rails, and highways. The plan was heavy on highways, potentially adding 1,100 miles in the metropolitan area.[18]

The commission made big plans but in practice failed to deliver a "definitive and comprehensive plan for the future." Its staff mostly cut and pasted projects from other agencies as part of their planning process to meet federal planning requirements.[19] The commission lacked the power to override local planning bodies and thus "deliberately maintained a very low profile" throughout the 1960s and 1970s, occupying itself with "technical analysis of growth patterns, transportation demands, energy needs, and related subjects" rather than revolutionizing regional transportation or challenging entrenched interests.[20] New York City's private Regional Planning Association remained better recognized than most state planning organizations.

Some New York State planners created a land-use planning tool with California's Williamson Act (1965) as inspiration. A report by Rockefeller's New York State Commission on the Preservation of Agricultural Land (1968) called on the state to undertake what today we call "smart growth" policies, including targeted control of state funds for sewer, water, and local roads based upon urban growth patterns. The authors promoted plans to preserve farms through easements, tax exemptions, and cluster development. The state, in response, purchased rural land with voter-approved bonds, but mostly in areas distant from growing cities, where land cost was lower. Cluster development, for instance, remained a local planning prerogative.[21] By 1970 the state had preserved 375,000 acres through open space purchases, but this sounds more impressive as a cumulative figure than as a tool of regional planning in a state with 30 million acres of land.[22] Today, of the 904,702 acres under conservation easements in New York State, fully 777,206 are in the Adirondacks.[23]

The Agricultural Districts Law (1971), the other leg of the agricultural preservation effort, is relatively weak in the face of development pressure. By 2016, for instance, the law in New York applied to 8.8 million acres of land, of which 6.3 million is now in 25,632 farms. The legislation gives farmers some leverage against urbanizing factors such as eminent domain, road expansion, waste treatment facilities, special taxes, and antifarming laws. It is much less generous and restrictive, however, than the Williamson Act, and farmers can easily exit should they wish to sell their land for development. As a result, it is not a very powerful tool for long-term regional land preservation.[24] Land purchases and conservation easements by private groups like Scenic Hudson and the Nature Conservancy have had a broader impact around cities because of the deep pockets of many of their supporters and the long-term protections these easements deliver. The willingness of local, state, and federal governments to allow these land trusts to operate tax-free, despite the high value of the land protected, is an aspect of public policy that is rarely acknowledged. A 2010 estimate counted 9 million acres nationally in various state and local land trusts.[25]

Governor Rockefeller's ambivalence was another crucial source of statewide planning's failure. Not only was he dependent on conservative Republican voters in the suburbs, but like many state leaders of his day and today, Rockefeller understood the attraction of sprawl to his constituents. His team frequently endorsed more radical plans for restricting suburban growth, but the governor remained a proponent of the postwar suburban dream. A screening for the governor of an elitist, antisuburban film by the Urban Development Corporation's Ed Logue featured a "pan across interminable rows of lookalike homes in a suburban tract." Rockefeller scolded Logue: "You'd better be careful, Ed. People live in those houses, and they like 'em."[26]

Rockefeller, like most postwar governors across the nation, sat by quietly as unchecked development ground up more farms and forest. The New York metropolitan region's tentacles crept deeper into the countryside of New Jersey, New York, and Connecticut during his years in office and long after. Nearly all the same problems identified in the suburbs of the postwar era remain concerns today: high-cost local government, redundant infrastructure, horrible traffic, air and groundwater pollution, and loss of habitat.

The American States and Regional Planning

Many states joined New York in the planning game during the postwar era. The federal government was, in general, the primary force behind the rise of state-sponsored or -enabled urban and regional planning. Provisions in the federal Housing Act of 1954 (Section 701), amended in 1959, funneled cash to local government, usually matched by states, for the creation of planning agencies and for small towns to develop comprehensive plans. By 1959, 30 states had designated or were operating planning agencies, although just a few had developed state-level plans.[27] By 1965, there were 29 states with state-level plans under way.[28] By 1971, every state had established a planning agency.[29] A range of federal grants came with a planning requirement in the 1960s, "including federally aided recreation facilities, vocational schools, libraries, hospitals, mental health facilities, sewer and water facilities," and the vast highway programs.[30]

Some state laws in progrowth states tried to counter a debilitating tradition of suburban independence by endorsing rapid, regulated urban growth. Selected state governments by the 1960s had, for instance, "authorized cities to regulate developments within a mile and a half, three miles, or even five miles of their boundaries; others gave municipal planning commissions at least the right to review proposed outlying subdivisions."[31] In 1963, for instance, Texas gave powers of annexation to cities of 300,000 persons or larger to an area reaching five miles beyond city limits. Such an extension of power encouraged the growth of "elastic" Texas cities that have been better able to capture high-value residential, commercial, and industrial growth on the periphery.[32]

Progrowth states like these chose to endorse planning as a critical tool to sustain the suburban "growth machine." The Atlanta region is usually held up as a poster child for sprawl, but according to planning historian Carlton Basmajian, "The present shape of metropolitan Atlanta, lacking limiting topography, is largely a manifestation of a highly developed regulatory framework, with ARC [Atlanta Regional Commission] and the state sitting at the center." He points to extensive postwar cooperative efforts concerning water, regional development, and growth management as evidence of this unheralded engagement. Progressive planners may dislike the outcome, but growing the low-density, car-oriented landscape is the appropriate aim of planning for many politicians, planners, and citizens in Georgia and elsewhere.[33]

Many exceptions to this weak regional planning remain crucial today, and they cumulatively reflect the potential power of states in development. Planning historian Mel Scott highlighted effective metropolitan planning commissions in Indianapolis (1955), Minneapolis–St. Paul (1957), and Chicago (1957) made possible by state laws.[34] Minnesota's Twin Cities Metropolitan Council had "the power to address several of the worst problems caused by urban sprawl including the loss of open space." The council gained planning coordination powers and had transit, subsidized housing, and water treatment as levers to encourage planned growth. The Metropolitan Council remains a powerful force in the region today although it has arguably done little to restrict staggering levels of suburban development.[35]

New Jersey, an urbanized state with severe urban and environmental problems related to growth, also engaged in extensive planning. The New Jersey State Plan (1951), developed "to guide postwar development," influenced the creation of the Garden State Parkway (a landscaped roadway providing easy access of urban populations to the seashore) and the New Jersey Turnpike (linking the region's suburbs and cities to each other and with New York and Philadelphia). The state's Farmland Assessment Act (1964) froze tax assessments to try to protect farms from the rapid pace of development. New Jersey continued to generate new planning laws for preserving the landscapes threatened by urbanization, including the Hackensack Meadowlands Development Commission (1969), the Coastal Area Facility Review Act (1973), the New Jersey Pinelands Protection Act (1979), and the New Jersey Agricultural Retention and Development Act (1981).[36] Laws like these were inspired by fears that "houses, marinas, lagoons, and waterfront restaurants" would be "lining our coast . . . from Sandy Hook to Cape May."[37] These initiatives scored some successes, such as the defense of the Pine Barrens and preservation of many wetlands, but arguably failed to make New Jersey a state where planning, rather than development interests, played a guiding role in shaping urban form on the coast.

A few controversial regional growth programs in northern and western states moved from the planning to the implementation phase. Their success, even with many setbacks along the way, reflected the latent power of state law. Oregon's famous planning initiatives have played a dramatic, visible, and controversial role in metropolitan development. The sprawling suburbs of Portland in the postwar period, which began to scrape up some of the nation's best agricultural land, led to a series of powerful land-use rules. As in many states, including New Jersey and New York, the state legislature offered tax reductions for farms (1961). Senate Bill 10 (1969), championed by Republican governor Tom McCall, required comprehensive zoning by local governments. By all accounts, even with these laws, "local governments largely failed to address exurban sprawl" through planning or any other means. Senate Bill 100 (1973) was, however, transformative. Landscape designer Lawrence Halprin's study *The Willamette Valley* helped galvanize activists, both environmentalists and those representing farming interests. The bill required the development of state planning goals and created powerful new agencies to help local government meet tight deadlines for the development of overdue comprehensive plans. The bill laid the groundwork for regional plans for Portland and the Columbia River area. The ambitious statewide planning goals included preservation of agriculture, forests, air, water, housing, transportation, and more.[38]

The law's most famous provision, Goal 14, required the cities to create urban growth boundaries (UGBs) providing for a planned "conversion of rural land into urban land" based upon conscious thinking, efficiency, market demand, and broader impact. The state empowered local agencies to pursue these goals rather than directly controlling local planning. The Portland region's vote for Metro in 1979, for instance, created a metropolitan government framework in crucial urban service areas. Metro thus became guardian and advocate for the UGB in the Portland area. Oregon's planning framework from the 1970s, including UGBs, has withstood legal challenges and ballot initiatives from property rights groups, suburban flight to nearby Washington State, and suburban towns seeking more land for development. There is a consensus among planning experts as well that "UGBs in Oregon have been shown to be effective tools for focusing population and housing growth within urban areas and for preventing sprawl onto farmland and forestland, as intended by the passage of SB 100 in 1973."[39] Controversy remains over the regional impact of the law, with many property rights groups charging that the rules increase home prices to unaffordable levels and in fact have merely driven many families out of Oregon to less regulated Vancouver, Washington, which has experienced a growth in its population from 46,000 to 173,000 since 1990. Such leakage to neighboring states is perhaps the peril of all state-level land controls.[40]

California's approach to regional planning also reflects the power of state governments to influence local land use. California created early subdivision laws (1893) and general plan laws (1927). The state's pioneering Williamson Act (1965), also known as the Land Conservation Act, now protects 16 out of 30 million state acres, within locally designated agricultural preserve areas, by reducing the tax burden (by 20 to 75 percent) for farmers facing development pressure. Continued support from farmers despite the loss of immediate development rights is linked to the positive economic benefits they gain by participating and the 10-year renewable terms of the contracts they can exit. As many of these lands are valuable for their recreational and scenic beauty (such as in the Napa and Sonoma valleys) or distant from major cities, the public has been supportive.[41]

The massive environmental crisis in the state also resulted in the passage of the California Environmental Quality Act (CEQA) in 1970. Its provisions, which now cover both public and private projects, require careful study of the impact of development on natural, agricultural, and cultural resources. It has thus been used, with varying degrees of success, to fight sprawl. The protections embedded in the Coastal Commissions for areas of significant recreational, scenic, and environmental beauty add additional regulations. Planning experts believe, however, that California's overreliance on "permit" as opposed to "plan" has negative outcomes on a broader scale: "CEQA has given us high-quality development projects, lower residential densities, and site-based environmental impact mitigation, but it has done little to enhance the overall environment" and has "distracted us from the need for large-scale, long-term ecosystem and habitat planning." CEQA has, for instance, failed to stall overdevelopment in the growth corridors of the state such as that running between Los Angeles and San Diego.[42]

The national movement pursuing "smart growth" reflects the continuing pressure in statehouses for regional planning. The concept generated significant excitement in statehouses initially: "From 1991 to 2001, 17 governors issued 19 executive orders on planning and smart growth, and more than 2,000 land use or planning bills were introduced in statehouses across the country, of which approximately 20 percent were enacted into law." The movement is thought, however, to have "peaked" in 2001, "when 27 governors initiated planning and smart growth proposals," as subsequent years saw a rise in anti-planning referendum in many areas.[43]

Governor Parris Glendening (1995–2003) of Maryland was widely admired for his leadership in smart growth. Maryland's citizens pushed back against the loss of the rural landscape, declining cities, and the crash in quality of the Chesapeake Bay caused by suburban growth, agricultural runoff, and inadequate water treatment. The Chesapeake Bay Critical Areas Program (1984) had already created new restrictions on development within 1,000 feet of the shoreline. The governor promoted and accepted PlanMaryland (2011), which leverages state spending on infrastructure, urban redevelopment, and conservation to guide development into already urbanized and frequently underutilized areas. It is too early to analyze the outcome of this state initiative, and its implementation is uneven, but the effort alone indicates the potential of states when it comes to planning.[44]

States have added additional levers on planning due to federal pressure. Legislatures have authorized metropolitan planning organizations (MPOs) required by the federal government for access to transportation funds and other grants. MPOs are empowered, among many roles, to develop regional plans, analyze growth, and create scenarios to conserve land, minimize driving, and maximize transit use. Even though MPOs lack direct power over local government decisions, their control over transportation funds gives them significant leverage. MPOs also often cover vast areas: the one for Los Angeles regulates an area home to 18 million residents in 180 cities. At their best, "MPOs provide an opportunity for local governments and state agencies to coordinate land use planning and regulation, which dictate where people live and at what densities, and transportation planning."[45] In the hands of progressive planners willing to use their leverage over local officials in the service of planning, they can be a force for transit improvements, bike lanes, and transit-oriented development. Some scholars believe, however, that these MPOs have shown a strong bias for expanding road programs.[46]

The Denver Regional Council of Governments (DRCOG), for instance, shifted from serving as a voluntary, highway-centric planning organization of local towns and cities into the state-authorized MPO. DRCOG in the late 1960s and the 1970s, for instance, successfully convinced the state to create what became the Regional Transportation District, including the power to tax regionally and operate mass transit. Denver's widely admired and growing light rail system, which seems to be reducing the number of vehicle miles traveled in the region, is one result. DRCOG has since the 1960s developed most of the ambitious regional transportation, housing, shared facilities, water, and development plans, most of which aim to tame the region's torrid growth. The impact of these initiatives varies greatly. Denver's urban growth boundary is not of comparable impact to that in Portland because it lacks similar control over land-use decisions. Sprawl in Denver by most measures continues despite many excellent plans.[47]

The postwar period revealed the potential of state planning power in the United States. With so many local politicians, citizens, and businesspeople tied up in the land development process—the "urban growth machine"—it has proved difficult, except in a few standout examples, to use the legitimately developed powers of states to tame sprawl. Americans frequently express a desire for regulation, but they have shown a consistent desire in most regions to allow for additional development farther out—perhaps for their children's future homes, a sense of fair play, and to make space for new types of homes. States, as a result, played a more decisive role in center-city redevelopment during the postwar years.[48]

Transportation

6

White-Collar Rail: Mass Transit and Urban Prosperity

The organization man featured on the cover of the *First Annual Report* of the Metropolitan Commuter Transportation Authority (MCTA), the forerunner of New York's MTA, betrays his prosperity in his forward step, mild smile, and neatly pressed suit (figure 21). The report's designer creatively superimposed this commuting hero over an expectant mass of affluent white men and women, a photographic representation of the broader public to be served. The cover can be read as a concise statement of the target audience for state urban policy: those prosperous Americans already enjoying the benefits of a service-based urban economy. The MCTA in 1966 promised more efficient rail service from suburbs to city business centers rather than rebuilding the troubled subway lines that terminated at city boundaries.

That states like New York planned more, and more successfully, for prosperous suburbanites is predictable. States urbanized rapidly, but the new metropolis was more deeply divided along class and racial lines than ever before. The growing majority-white suburbs, with high voter turnout, were ascendant in state politics. Suburbanites demanded and won new services they desired, such as highways, airports, and rail-based commuter lines, and yet they were suspicious and often opposed to funding other transit systems that primarily served center-city residents.

The MCTA planted its seed in the fertile ground of the affluent society. It was not alone. From New York to Atlanta, and from Massachusetts to California, state leaders usually built, sustained, and promoted transit systems just large enough to stabilize patterns where suburban, rush hour commuters still depended upon an existing central business district. Very few states, for instance, maintained robust streetcar lines that had served mostly intracity traffic. Most bus lines, often used by poor, minority city residents, remained

FIGURE 21. Metropolitan Commuter Transportation Authority First Annual Report, 1966. New York State Archives, courtesy of the New York State Library.

of a rudimentary and infrequent type. New York's MTA, for instance, has struggled for decades to sustain its extensive intracity subway and bus systems. Administrators nationally found it difficult, in most cases, to maintain sufficient suburban unity to build transit systems that could compete effectively with highways. Debt financing, high fares, and limited systems usually substituted for deeply subsidized, regionally comprehensive, and widely used mass transit. Even given these the mixed results for transit riders today, the postwar state role in urban mass transit was revolutionary by American standards.

The Transit States

America's private transit systems, upon which the nation's cities had depended for decades, entered a postwar death spiral due to the rise of automobiles, buses, and trucks. Between the end of World War II and 1961, mass transit entirely disappeared from 300 American villages, towns, and cities. In the cities where systems survived, usually with the help of a reluctant public sector, ridership on remaining trains, streetcars, and buses plummeted as fares rose and service quality declined.[1]

Most American downtowns, shaped in the era of rail transit, continued to lose vitality in the postwar years as more space was given over to roads and parking lots. Suburban office parks, subdivisions, and shopping areas became the driving force of urban growth and remain so today. Most Americans, including most political leaders, welcomed and took steps to encourage this decentralization. Cities and suburbs often grew without transit in mind. The middle-class driving public and the politicians who represented them viewed mass transit as a tired, unreliable relic.

America's largest and most concentrated big cities, such as New York, Boston, Philadelphia, Chicago, and San Francisco, faced a more complicated situation. Billions of dollars in downtown real estate values, including a new era of modern office towers, was threatened by the loss of regional mass transit because finding enough parking for commuters without destroying compressed downtowns was almost impossible. Aggressive roadbuilding and parking in and around these business districts failed to resolve the traffic problem of packing workers into older hubs. Not everyone, moreover, could afford cars, and urban neighborhoods in the 1960s and 1970s pushed back on highway expansion. Transportation experts, by highlighting the problem of induced demand, raised doubts about the wisdom of reliance on highways.

American governors and city leaders faced novel pressure from riders and business interests to address the crisis in downtown-focused mass transit. City leaders, who might have been considered natural leaders in saving mass transit, rarely were. They were already grappling with a shrinking tax base, lacked the money or management talent to save bankrupt private transit systems, and usually did not have the legal power to operate regional systems. State government, whose taxing and management powers extended across city lines, thus appeared to many experts and the public as the natural source of leadership, funding, and management of legacy rail systems. Indeed it was.

The 1940s and 1950s ushered in state-sanctioned urban transit authorities, including those in New York (New York City Transit Authority [NYCTA], 1953), Chicago (Chicago Transit Authority, 1945), and Boston (Massachusetts Transportation Authority, 1947).[2] These new transit authorities were hampered, however, by deferred capital needs, limited subsidies, and contentious labor relations. State leadership in mass transit immediately proved more complicated and politically challenging in every state where it took place. The depth of subsidy required, the political dimensions of mustering statewide support for systems with relatively narrow beneficiaries (big-city riders), and the image problems of mass transit bedeviled many elected officials.

The story of New York State's assumption of mass transit during the 1960s vividly illustrates the challenges of state management. New York's regional rail systems downstate were on a stupendous scale, but the problems faced by Governor Rockefeller and his staff in the transit business had many national parallels even in states with much smaller systems. As in other states, meeting needs of commuters and daily subway or bus riders in big cities had to be negotiated to please rural, urban, small town, and suburban interests. New sources of funding for city transit had to be invented or found in New York, just like every state. New York was a transit leader, and its scale alone defied easy solutions, but it was in good company.

Transit and Metropolitan Structure

New York's mass transit crisis of the 1950s and 1960s resulted from a toxic mix of mismanagement and the spatial reorganization of America's largest metropolis. The construction of parkways and limited-access freeways in New York disrupted New York City's existing rail-based, pedestrian pattern of growth. Experts watching the scene unfold, like civic leader and lawyer William Reid, observed that before New Yorkers took to their cars, "absolute dependence upon fixed mass transit dictated a city structure in which practically everybody worked in the downtown business district and lived in nearby residential areas, clustered along transit routes radiating out from the center." By the late 1950s, however, commerce and industry were following "the population migration to the suburbs." New York City lost people during the 1950s at the same time its suburbs swelled with people, homes, stores, factories, and cars. The subways, built for a large working class that once relied almost entirely on rail for commuting and leisure, now struggled to maintain lines with "surplus capacity even during the height of the rush hour" because the city's blue-collar industries declined, relocated, or lost space due to redevelopment across Manhattan and parts of Brooklyn.[3]

Mass transit nevertheless continued to play a crucial role in supporting Manhattan's business districts in the 1960s and 1970s. New York City added more new office space in Midtown and downtown in the postwar era than had ever existed in most other American cities. To sustain these lucrative modern towers and the globalized white-collar employment crucial to the future of the region demanded the maintenance of high-quality mass transit. In congested New York City, after all, automobiles would never serve as a very efficient or environmentally friendly mode of mass commuting from suburbs to Manhattan business districts—and this was true despite one of the most aggressive highway and parkway building programs in the nation. Commuter rail ridership across a vast suburban region had declined sharply from the prewar period but also seemed likely to retain its importance to crucial commuters. Many subway lines also remained popular, and many "suburban" areas in Queens and Staten Island could have benefited from additional service. The suburban commuters, moreover, usually needed a subway connection once they arrived. The challenge was how to preserve a declining transit system and the business districts that profited from it during the urban crisis.[4]

The city of New York compounded the problems by making it impossible since the 1920s for private companies to run a profitable subway system, essentially forcing the companies out of the business of mass transit by refusing to raise the fare above a nickel, even as inflation and other costs skyrocketed. The city government was determined "to 'hold down' the fare" for political reasons so that the system remained cheap for the city's working class. The aim of many subway advocates, after all, was decentralization of the working class from tenement districts.[5] The Great Depression, the nickel fare, suburbanization, and the IND (the city's competitive independent system) killed off the private lines during the 1930s. Mayor La Guardia negotiated municipal ownership and management of all subways in 1940 under the Board of Transportation. Politicization of fares was typical in the United States because of widespread skepticism about the motives of private transit operators, the quality of service, and their monopolistic tendencies.

The city's new public managers, after an artificial boom in ridership during World War II, faced continuing financial problems created by the same low fares and political resistance that had bedeviled the private companies. "Deprivatization" was not the hoped-for panacea.[6] The nickel fare, for instance, had survived for 44 years when public managers finally raised it to a dime in 1948.[7] Ridership shrank 35 percent between 1948 and 1958. The city's loss of industries, the shift to car commuting, additional fare increases, and the suburbs' rapidly growing commercial, industrial, and retail enterprises were all to blame for declining ridership. The enormous challenge of right-sizing vast, expensive, money-losing transit systems to falling public demand was a problem for public transit managers across the nation during these years. Massive service cuts and closing of lines was the typical response in Chicago and most other cities.[8]

The Board of Transportation, and then Governor Dewey's New York City Transit Authority (1953), stubbornly maintained almost the whole subway system, bucking a national trend. The state also began subsidizing and thus preserved most commuter rail service in the 1950s. But the record of management was mixed at best. Standing in the way of improvement was Governor Dewey's requirement that NYCTA, with the aid of some limited subsidies from new real estate taxes, be both self-supporting and debt-free. NYCTA received just half a billion dollars of city capital funds during the 1950s, leaving limited funds for improvements beyond buying a few new subway cars. The unrealism of expecting the NYCTA to pay its way was demonstrated in the long term: by 1971 the NYCTA had lost money in 13 of its 19 operating years.[9]

The results of failing to address the problems fully were evident by the 1950s. By the time Rockefeller arrived on the scene in 1959, most of the subway's rolling stock was old, its stations dirty, and its service unreliable. The system also suffered from revenue losses as sharp city residents swapped out slugs for tokens or just jumped over turnstiles. In the early 1960s, significant losses in subway operations were papered over with the "profits" from the city bus system. These bus surpluses were made possible by the fact that buses, which had replaced streetcars or elevated lines on many routes, ran on roads, not rails, and served some of the remaining middle-class areas in the city. New York City's mass transit was already reliant on "rubber to rail" subsidies.[10]

The commuter rail system run by private rail corporations was initially in even more desperate straits—despite continued demand from upper-income riders. In the late 1950s, plans by the governors of New Jersey and New York to create a Metropolitan Regional Transit District, including plans for public subsidies for failing regional rail systems, passed in New York State only to fail by a thin margin in the face of resistance in the New Jersey suburbs. The failure of this system foreclosed the creation of "an integrated mass transit system for the New York–New Jersey–Connecticut region."[11]

The regional commuter numbers were small, and the problems big, but suburban commuters commanded outsized leverage in Albany. In 1959, there were still 370,000 commuters in the tristate area, many of them "important people both in city and suburbs," with a combined $4 billion in take-home pay. These were many of the managers who had, by the 1960s, made the Manhattan office districts the "front office of the world," and they were the ones who helped maintain "the city's preeminent position in the arts, entertainment, communication" and business fields. One estimate found that their robust salaries created three-quarters of a million jobs in the suburbs because the typical commuter was a "big earner, big spender, and a family man." To hold the city's competitive position in the postindustrial service economy would require maintaining connections to elite suburbs. A rail line could also move 48,000 people per hour, a figure far exceeding the capacity of new interstate lanes.[12]

The Pennsylvania, New York Central, and New Haven Railroads, which collectively provided most of the commuter service in the New York region, had once enjoyed thriving intercity passenger and freight business that had helped cover the high cost of rush hour service (for most hours of the day, cars and staff sat idle or underutilized). By the 1960s, however, there were no more profits to shift around. The faltering private railroads blamed their growing losses on high capital costs and excessive regulation. Railroad executives whined that they paid their way while "merchant marine, airlines, truckers, buses and even the individual motorist benefit from multi-billion-dollar government outlays." It wasn't so long before, of course, that the railroads had dictated generous terms to the government for their benefit, but they failed to recoup their legislative influence in the postwar years.[13] Between 1940 and 1960 national railroad passenger traffic dropped 68 percent, while airline traffic increased 577 percent and intercity automobile traffic increased 268 percent.[14]

Making matters worse for those like Rockefeller seeking a middle path between public and private ownership was the fact that "the public regarded railroad management as a group of robber barons who were not to be trusted and whose sole purpose was accepted to be that of exploiting the users of the railroad facilities."[15] Robert Moses pointed out in 1960 that "the railroads started with enormous grants and subventions; second, that they never retired debt; third, that have been grossly mismanaged; fourth, that they neglected commuters and with few exceptions did nothing to anticipate the competition of truck, bus and passenger auto, air and improved water transportation." Giving money and subsidies to railroads, once a great American tradition, had lost its luster.[16]

The railroad executives were frank about their troubles and impending bankruptcy as a strategy to shed their commuter services. Executives running the Pennsylvania Railroad in the 1950s announced that they were done investing in the Long Island Rail Road. Governor Dewey, in response to the crisis, began the first movement in the direction of public management when in 1954 he created a "railroad development corporation" to operate the LIRR in exchange for certain future concessions from the Pennsylvania Railroad. That organization kept the LIRR in business, raised fares, and made some improvements in service.[17] Dewey, however, turned down Robert Moses's recommendation for a public authority that might have taken a longer view, financed significant improvement, and reorganized service. The LIRR made some temporary enhancements, but service stagnated.[18]

The Interstate Commerce Commission predicted "that railroads would abandon all passenger service within the next decade." This prediction came true in part because federal officials endorsed just such a path. Congress and President Dwight D. Eisenhower in 1958 permitted the railroads, should they choose, to shut down their money-losing systems, just two years after Eisenhower had laid the groundwork for the greatest American road program ever. The private railroads in the New York region, and across the nation, promptly began plans to scale back or shutter their commuter lines.[19]

Reluctant Reformer

The parallel decline of city and suburban mass transit, both public and private, brought Governor Rockefeller and his team much deeper into transit operation and financing than they had ever planned to be. The governor was no great fan of mass transit per se, and he was often suspicious of public enterprise, but he was not going to allow a complete collapse of mass transit, and thus business efficiency and investment, in the nation's largest and richest metropolitan area. All eyes were on New York's bold experiment in state-administered mass transit, even if the state was by no means the first.

In 1959, upon taking office, Rockefeller sharply rejected an interstate transit agency because it would cost "hundreds of millions of dollars" of annual state funds and should only be a "last resort." He made clear that he was "opposed to any large-scale increase in the expenditures of the state" and preferred that the system continue on a "private enterprise basis." Austin Tobin of the Port Authority, who managed profitable bridges and tunnels for cars and trucks, also opposed a "grandiose rail program" that would add money-losing transit operations to the Port Authority and thus damage its high bond rating. Tobin predicted that new highways in New Jersey would "increase the shift from rail to bus in the next decade." The Port Authority had already helped derail an effort in the 1950s by a Metropolitan Rapid Transit Commission to develop overall plans and new sources of funding for regional rail systems. New Jersey voters in 1959 rejected transferring millions in annual surpluses from tolls on the New Jersey Turnpike to mass transit.[20] The advocates of public support for mass transit were in the minority during this time. Nor could they point to any city or state with a significant record of successful, high-quality public management; most transit systems were in steep decline, even where states had created authorities.

In 1959 Rockefeller brought together a small but influential group of business and civic leaders. They recommended additional tax relief for railroads rather than direct management by the government. Rockefeller, understandably pessimistic about a regional solution, acted on their recommendations by creating New York's Railroad Tax Relief Program. He argued that because commuter rail was central to the public well-being, "this degree of public dependence necessarily creates a degree of public responsibility." The tax reductions responded to the fact that New York had the highest taxes on railroads in the country, a legacy of the state's industrial dominance and progressive past.[21] Opponents, mostly Democrats, viewed the tax breaks as a "multi-million give-away to the railroads at the expense of commuters and taxpayers."[22]

Bigger ideas were also floating around the region. Robert Moses in 1960 called once again for a public authority to manage the Long Island Rail Road "to parallel, supplement and be genuinely competitive with the superior road system built and being built."[23] Nassau County Democrats in 1961 endorsed an ambitious plan to increase rapid transit service on Long Island, including a creative if complicated use of subway routes within city limits for LIRR trains.[24] Nassau County political leaders, frustrated with Rockefeller, in 1963 proposed a Long Island Transportation Authority.[25] Rockefeller stuck with more modest plans. In 1960 the state began directly lending millions to the railroad companies. In 1961 the state legislature at Rockefeller's request proffered even more generous tax relief. The management and maintenance of stations were also, in some cases, assumed by city and county governments.[26]

Despite promises from railroads to use the tax breaks and subsidies for improvements, and a high-profile "sprucing up" and repair push by the New York Central after the bill's passage, the effects were uneven. The New York, New Haven and Hartford Railroad declared bankruptcy in 1960 despite tax relief. The remnants of the New Haven railroad still operated with state aid in bankruptcy, but the service on its commuter lines in the West End (southern Connecticut) was awful, with run-down trains and terrible schedule performance.[27] On Long Island, delays at Jamaica Station for engine switching were the result of a system only partially electrified. On nearly all the regional networks, long-distance trains, designed for high speed over long distances, were unwieldy in the stop-and-start commuter routes and had high entries that made loading and unloading people slow.[28] The unions representing the railroad workers believed that the New York Central on the northern routes was deliberately making the passenger experience awful "to discourage commuter travel" and thus get out of the business entirely.[29] Rockefeller's aim of avoiding direct public management of mass transit had been achieved but proved insufficient to the task at hand. By the early 1970s, Rockefeller would admit in retrospect that the initial tax relief strategy "didn't work" to save the commuter lines.[30] As in other states, a more aggressive approach to saving mass transit would be required.

Throughout the 1960s Rockefeller, joined by other state and city officials facing a looming transit bill, lobbied for more federal involvement in mass transit. He believed federal transit funding would help remedy an imbalance in national policy: "Planning that to date has manifested itself in the building of our highways but has been almost totally absent in the consideration of the destiny of the railways and their relationship to the future of our cities and their suburbs."[31] Pressure from states like New York and Illinois created new federal precedents. Limited transit funding in the Housing Act of 1961 and the Urban Mass Transportation Act (1964) offered some direct and minimal support for transit operations, capital improvements, and research. The 1964 act included $375 million ($3 billion in 2017 dollars) in grants for transit improvements but added a rule targeted at New York specifying that no state could receive more than $47 million over the three-year term of the funding.[32] Federal mass grants would improve in the 1960s and 1970s but were never big enough for New York because managers elsewhere were more willing to consolidate and scrap systems to focus on a few lines. Other states were also unwilling to distribute funding by ridership, which would have given New York the lion's share of federal funding.

Rockefeller may have initially dismissed big government takeover of all mass transit in the early 1960s, but he established important precedents for the future MTA.[33] The governor forced the Port Authority of New York to sell bonds for $100 million to cover the cost of new commuter rail cars in a complex lease arrangement with the private railroads.[34] Rockefeller in 1962 also accepted a proposal from Mayor Wagner that the state, for the first time, finance $92 million ($758 million in 2017 dollars) for subway cars in a bid for urban/suburban parity.[35] In 1961 Rockefeller took an even more dramatic step by agreeing to a deal with New Jersey for the Port Authority's assumption of the bankrupt Hudson and Manhattan Railroad (now PATH), which was still carrying over 100,000 daily passengers between New Jersey and New York on a much-dilapidated set of trains and underwater tunnels.[36] Modernizing the H and M system into PATH paid significant dividends to New York property interests, including the Lower Manhattan redevelopment projects championed by David Rockefeller. By 1970, PATH carried 36.8 million passengers annually. These initiatives reflect the national pattern of states using legacy transit subsidies to sustain center-city business districts.[37]

A Deepening Crisis

While Rockefeller's team studied options, and edited around the edges of the transit crisis, the publicized accounting of the costs of sprawl, and air pollution, in the popular media during these years made a solid case for mass transit alternatives. George Saunders, tasked with the glum task of running the faltering Penn Central commuter lines in 1966, criticized federal support for highways: "We are blacktopping ourselves to death in this country. . . . The cloverleaf is becoming our national flower."[38] There were also questions, in New York and elsewhere, about the ability to accommodate cars on highways in urban areas as "increasing resistance to highway locations, rising costs of highway construction and of operating automobiles" was potentially reviving interest "in comfortable and efficient mass transit."[39] New highways had not solved most traffic problems at rush hours, most notably in Long Island, and tailpipe pollution created brown, toxic smog.

Rockefeller's hesitation in taking over mass transit was connected, as it was in many states, to the unsavory issues surrounding mass transit labor relations. The city's subways continued to lose riders during the entire 1960s, while operating costs increased by 100 percent. The total number of transit workers increased from 34,000 to 38,000, but it was collective bargaining agreements that so drove up salaries, wages, and benefits that they accounted for 95 percent of total operating expenditures in 1970, compared with 81 percent in 1960. The Transport Workers Union under the leadership of the legendary labor leader Mike Quill viewed the NYCTA as a typical city bureaucracy, funded out of tax revenues, from which concessions could be endlessly squeezed. Sadly, the NYCTA was still mostly supported out of the fare box. Salaries thus improved, by striking or slowdown if needed, often at the cost of service to passengers. To save money, the public managers reduced the number of subway stations, seldom cleaned cars, and rolled fewer trains through stations. Lindsay was such a weak negotiator in the winter of 1966–1967, during a 12-day strike, that he gave away irresponsibly massive wage and pension concessions.[40]

Management, labor leaders, and politicians shared most of the blame for the crisis, but the public continued to resist reasonable fare increases. The absurdly low fares in the New York City system, for instance, were reflected in thousands of New York City tokens finding their way to buses in Albany, where in 1964 a ride already cost 20 cents, compared to just 15 cents for a more extensive subway trip in New York City.[41] The city transit mess certainly made it difficult to demand significant subsidies from upstate voters and federal officials. The governor, for instance, authorized the 63rd Street subway tunnel project in 1965 to address "the rapid growth and development of the Borough of Queens and Long Island" but expected the city to pay for its construction.[42]

The commuter lines during the 1960s struggled as much as the subways, but for different reasons. The comparatively wealthy white-collar workers riding trains were paying higher fares but could not help but notice the growing difference between their modern air-conditioned offices and the dirty, steaming, freezing, and often late or canceled trains they rode to and from work. The rising cost of commuter tickets and declining service quality encouraged many white-collar workers to seek "alternative employment opportunities to avoid traveling to the city." The suburban office parks and corporate headquarters, aided by the telecommunications revolution, were showing their potential to decentralize both office and industrial employment. Many CEOs needed little urging to move their firms to suburban locales, often snugly tucked away in lush office park campuses close to their tony residences in Connecticut, Westchester, and New Jersey.[43] The city's flourishing service sector, much of it in Midtown, may have counted the greatest number of Fortune 500 headquarters it ever would (over 100) and the world's greatest concentration of bank and insurance assets, but the city's supremacy was under threat if financial and management talent could not get to work in a timely, modern, and comfortable manner.

The state's assumption of both suburban and urban rail systems, a process that started in 1964, resulted from multiple sources. William Ronan's study committee in 1964 included business representatives from leading Long Island employers Sperry Rand and Grumman concerned about the region's economic prospects. They recommended a metropolitan rail authority, purchase of the LIRR, modernization at the price of $200 million with the help of revenue bonds, with an open door on the assumption of other commuter systems. The plan was needed immediately, as the Railroad Development Corporation expired in 1966, which would drop the LIRR back into bankruptcy.[44]

In defending a state takeover against charges of "creeping socialism," Rockefeller responded that "I've been trying to avoid this for six years. The alternative is pretty grim."[45] He could either bail out the LIRR, as he explained to Long Island's business leaders, or "build what turned out to be an additional 24 lanes of highway through Nassau, Queens, and Manhattan to handle the traffic." Rockefeller admitted that to blast these lanes through "tremendously heavily settled population areas was unrealistic and that even if we did put the roads in, when the cars got to New York City, they would all be towed away anyhow. (Laughter) So there was no point in considering this."[46] Rockefeller might have been joking about cars getting towed in Manhattan, but it was unlikely that the city could ever accommodate all the additional cars without a revolution in architecture and planning. New York's powerful traffic commissioner Henry Barnes did what he could during these years to speed up traffic within the city, including turning many of Manhattan's major avenues (such as Fifth, Third, Lexington, and Madison) into one-way streets. He even recommended the addition of 50,000 new parking spaces in or near Manhattan, which would have irreversibly disfigured the city. The City Planning Commission by this time, however, pushed back hard on further conversion of city space to auto space. And it was clear that if Barnes's plans were to be followed, the city's business districts would be less attractive as centers of face-to-face contacts, business lunches, etc. for suburban commuters.[47] Even Barnes's faster north–south avenues had an Achilles' heel, east–west streets: "A motorist behind a 300-horsepower engine takes longer to cross Manhattan Island in midtown than it took a horse and wagon a hundred years ago."[48] Paving over downtowns for cars had failed to save most other American downtowns and promised even less for a city like New York.

Manhattan business leaders, who employed thousands of workers in hundreds of millions of dollars' worth of new office space, lobbied for government leadership for commuter rail. A published statement, signed by 65 business leaders, included the names of top executives from firms such as International Paper, Otis, and Seagram's. These business leaders, demonstrably devoted to free markets, offered their support to publicly subsidized transit despite their feeling that "no responsible business organization desires replacement of private enterprise by government. Only where private enterprise is unable to function is governmental support or subsidization of any kind warranted." They called for government subsidy of commuter rails at all levels yet hedged a little by calling for the state to still rely on "an operating railroad as agent."[49] Their interest was entirely practical. Mass transit was still carrying 90 percent of commuters in the Manhattan central business district at peak time, so even though 67 percent of trips in the region were now by car, the highly centralized business district of greatest importance remained firmly in the rail age.[50]

It was no accident that the state began its deeper involvement in mass transit with suburban commuter rail. To retain and enhance the prosperity of residents in both the city and suburbs, high-profit service industries in New York City business districts, deeply reliant on commuter rail, had to be preserved. William Ronan, for instance, believed that while suburbs would become "growth centers of commerce and industry," Manhattan would retain its "agglomeration of managerial talent, technical talent, legal talent, scientific and recreational talent." Only if a means to save transit could be found, of course.[51] To plan for prosperity in transit meant, in this case, subsidizing the most prosperous commuter first. States duplicated this model across the United States.

Saving Downtown

The legislature, following Ronan and Rockefeller's lead, created the short-lived predecessor of the MTA, the Metropolitan Commuter Transportation Authority (MCTA), in 1965. The new authority counted among its powers—over commuter lines as well as buses, planes, and ferries—the ability to buy or lease commuter lines both in New York and across state lines, issue bonds for modernization, set fares, and charge localities for station maintenance. The city's troubled subways were neither included nor explicitly left out of the law, leaving open the possibility of later integration, but also creating a lingering feeling of insecurity on the part of city leaders.[52] Ronan, as the chair of the MCTA, negotiated a satisfactory deal to buy the entire LIRR system for $65 million ($513 million in 2017 dollars). He also negotiated a complicated scheme to maintain service on the bankrupt New Haven Railroad commuter lines during the 1960s without direct public management.[53]

Visionary flourishes included in early MCTA documents included a rail line, never built, for the center of the Long Island Expressway—symbolically merging the transit needs of both cities and suburbs. Equally novel was an expanded federal role in mass transit funding. Federal funds from the Department of Housing and Urban Development (HUD) started seeping in by fall of 1967 to support the modernization of LIRR, and by the end of 1967, the MCTA claimed $60 million in federal grants either provided or under consideration. The federal portion illustrates the federal government's willingness to subsidize service for affluent commuters and travelers. Many other states had joined New York in this successful battle for federal funding.[54]

Resolving issues at the LIRR, the most extensive commuter rail service, was the primary focus of the MCTA. The administration believed optimistically that a better LIRR under its leadership would "lure additional thousands of drivers from their automobiles" and perhaps "stem the tide of private automobiles clogging Long Island's highways and choking Manhattan's streets and tunnels." The administration also aimed to soothe the tempers of the LIRR's affluent and vocal commuters, of growing importance for Republican power in the state legislature. The LIRR seemed to be a smart starting point for public management because Rockefeller believed that the $65 million in subsidies already received from the state since 1954 had made "a safer, more efficient and better-run railroad" including some new air-conditioned cars, replacement tracks, new locomotives, and more. He was overly optimistic. Just 30 percent of the LIRR's cars were under 30 years old, and the remaining 70 percent were "uncomfortable, unattractive, and, sometimes, undependable."[55]

Ambitious plans Ronan tossed in for good measure included an East Side terminal for the LIRR to save the daily trek to the Midtown East business district for a growing number of LIRR commuters who traveled east by foot or subway from Penn Station. Rockefeller and his team thus decided to endorse the bets placed by real estate developers around Grand Central, such as the Pan Am building, which in one fell swoop added 2.4 million square feet of office space. As a demonstration of good faith on an East Side terminal, Ronan was collaborating with the Transit Authority by 1966 to add tracks for LIRR trains underneath the planned subway tunnel crossing the East River at 63rd Street so that Long Island residents would have a direct ride to the most desirable Midtown office addresses.[56]

Ronan chose to retain most of the LIRR's operating staff to maintain service because of their depth of experience and because federal law (in the Urban Mass Transportation Act of 1964) protected their collective bargaining rights. The retention of the railroad's labor agreements, including retirement rules and benefits, would come to haunt Rockefeller, as the rules hindered improvements and inflation in staff salaries far exceeded revenue. Ronan and his staff in 1966 also ordered 500 electric cars as the first step in aggressive modernization paid for mostly out of a $200 million bond backed by New York State. The LIRR still had a solid base of commuters, 260,000 riders daily, who could look forward to many more air-conditioned cars, quicker start and stop of these self-propelled electric cars, easier entry and exit, and (ideally) speeds up to 100 miles an hour. By early 1967 the MCTA proudly displayed full-sized mockups of the "train of tomorrow" to build excitement about modernization.[57]

The MTA leadership years later explained that the choice of electric, high-performance self-propelled cars was a break in an LIRR policy extending back to 1903, which had required that all new LIRR equipment be compatible with the oldest equipment on the lines. The old policy was practical in the short run, but it also "discouraged technological development." The MTA leadership thought "it necessary to reverse the policy to make a clear break with the past" in part to "make commuting more competitive with the automobile." Unfortunately for the MTA, when the new cars arrived, they forced systemic upgrades, and many of the cars needed many retrofits because they had so many advanced features; only after some embarrassing failures and years of tweaking were they "hailed by rail experts as the most advanced passenger car in North America." The passenger car industry was in decline, to put it mildly, so it is not surprising that there were problems in these early and complicated orders. A city like San Francisco faced similar problems due to the nation's weak rail car building industry.[58]

From MCTA to the MTA

Rockefeller and his team knew that the MCTA in these first years lacked necessary legal and fiscal strength to take over the subways and the remaining private commuter lines. Other states usually managed to paper over losses of smaller-scale systems with special taxes or general revenues, but New York would require a more creative financial approach. The interdependence of commuter/subway systems required a deeper engagement in the everyday transportation network than was typical for many state governments. If all commuters could have just walked from Grand Central and Penn Station to their offices, there is a good chance the state would have ignored the subways, or at least done far less to maintain the system as a whole.

The red ink of subway operations included a $43 million deficit ($330 million in 2017 dollars) in 1966–1967, to say nothing of decades of deferred capital needs. The growing disarray of city transit and pressure from the city for state bailouts kept the pressure on Rockefeller, despite his assertion in 1966 that "the New York City Transit situation was Mayor's Lindsay's problem." Upstate legislators, moreover, viewed the city budget as a "bottomless pit." Most upstate cities maintained small bus systems, and Rochester simply cut its already limited subway service rather than try to save it. The downstate pressure for action on NYCTA, however, was simply too great. A crippling transit strike in 1966, widely publicized service quality decline, demand for city equity with the investments in commuter railroads, and general concerns from wealthy city property owners and retailers could be ignored for only so long.[59]

Suburbanites could also see the wisdom of saving the subways, as many of them descended into subways after their train commutes. State Senator Edward Speno of Nassau County in 1966 called for the MCTA to absorb the NYCTA during the city transit strike because "if the system stops, we all stop.

It is no longer a problem of one city, it is a problem of the State of New York. It is a regional problem." There were very few moments when suburban legislators called for regional solutions, but this was one of them. The self-interest of these commuters generated the concern. The suburban need helps explain why New York's MTA became, and remains today, so deeply engaged in the fraught business of urban intracity transit compared to other state authorities.[60]

City leaders had provided potential roadmaps. The City Planning Commission in 1965 proposed diverting millions of dollars to transit from Moses's Triborough Bridge and Tunnel Authority and, if possible, the Port Authority. Surpluses, they believed, "should be used to improve rail transit systems rather than to finance additional highways into the congested core of the region."[61] Mayor John Lindsay in 1966 adopted the idea to divert excess Triborough Bridge and Tunnel revenues to subways. Lindsay overreached when he sought mayoral control for both the NYCTA and Triborough. He planned to merge powers of five city transit-related agencies and put them under a transit "czar" serving at the pleasure of the mayor.[62] Lindsay's plan fell flat as opponents accused him of plotting a "political power grab." Chase Manhattan, led by David Rockefeller, threatened a lawsuit because of the threat posed by city transit deficits to its $379 million ($2.9 billion in 2017 dollars) invested in Triborough bonds.[63]

Governor Rockefeller and Ronan picked up and adapted the idea in 1967, combining as it did a one-upping of Mayor Lindsay while simultaneously appeasing business leaders, city voters, and suburban commuters. Rockefeller's plan, announced in January of 1967, just after he was sworn in for his third term, proposed the merger of Triborough, NYCTA, Manhattan and Bronx Surface Transit, and Staten Island Transit with the MCTA.[64] The main threat to Rockefeller's plan was Robert Moses. Rockefeller, Ronan, and others claimed that the annual Triborough surplus was about $30 million; after all, in 1966 208 million vehicles paid tolls on Triborough facilities. Moses, for his part, claimed that the capital projects in the works, such as the planned Cross Sound Bridge and the lower deck for the Verrazano, would eat up most of these so-called profits that he estimated, using figures provided by his cherry-picked consultants, at just $5 million a year until 1985.[65] He had an even more powerful threat: "Any effort to place our large, nonexistent, theoretical surplus will have to be met in court by our trustees." Bonds had been sold, after all, on the security of future car tolls, not mass transit.[66]

David Rockefeller now supported the merger proposal, an evolving position that was probably related to his dominant role in Lower Manhattan redevelopment that was so reliant on the subways. He also took a broader view than many bank executives about the health of the city. He and Nelson Rockefeller (and their various lawyers) held a secret meeting on February 9, 1968, in the shadow of Moses's opposition and a lawsuit by Chase. They promised Moses high positions in the new MTA and Governor Rockefeller's continued support for cross-sound bridges. Chase Manhattan continued to be the underwriter for state bonds, while Triborough bondholders received an extra quarter of 1 percent interest and, more crucially, a guarantee of the state's credit for their new MTA bonds. The state's extension of full faith and credit to MTA bonds is rarely given the credit it deserves, but this guarantee has been key to attracting capital to what is otherwise a risky investment.[67]

The MTA opened for business in March of 1968 with "full policy, financing and planning control of all public bus and rapid transit facilities within its metropolitan Commuter Transportation District." It was given responsibility for the city's system as well as transit in Duchess, Nassau, Orange, Putnam, Rockland, and Suffolk Counties. The MTA was and remains an unwieldy organization, described at one point as a "public holding company"; most of its component elements had as many liabilities as assets. Underneath the MTA umbrella was NYCTA (including bus and subway lines),[68] the LIRR, and the New Haven Division, jointly run with the private managers. The MTA also provided public support to commuters on the failing Harlem, Hudson, and Erie Lackawanna Railroads. The MTA sustained service on these lines through the 1970s and eventually created Metro-North (1983) to own and operate commuter service in Westchester County, southern Connecticut, Rockland, and Orange counties.[69]

The MTA Triborough portfolio took longer to yield profits than hoped, as the first cash transfers to transit arrived in 1970, but they proved crucial in the long term. The MTA operated and collected profits from Triborough's seven bridges, two tunnels, two public garages, a parking field, a Manhattan airline terminal building, and the New York Coliseum at Columbus Circle. Triborough managed to double its revenues between 1969 and 1973 by approximately doubling the tolls on its facilities, indicating a much more flexible price structure than mass transit.[70] Triborough funds were, at first, to be used to help the NYCTA alone, but in 1972 the subways began to share the surpluses 50-50 with the commuter railroads despite the much broader problems in the tubes. Such were the perils of city/suburban cooperation for city leaders. Between 1968 and 1974, Triborough contributed $374 million to transit and commuter rail, a not insignificant sum, if one that also paled in comparison to the need of the MTA for either capital or operating funds.[71]

The Triborough merger was a win for mass transit, yet all the rail and subway lines desperately needed capital investments that exceeded what could be provided out of fares, regular state appropriations, city capital contributions, or even Triborough profits. Ronan's team might have blustered about the power and majesty of the new enterprise, and the MTA would eventually be known as the "Wholly Ronan Empire," but in fact, from a financial perspective, the new MTA was, per Ronan, "the biggest collection of losers ever assembled under one roof." Higher than expected operating and capital costs were the typical outcome of state engagement in mass transit across the nation.[72]

To upgrade service in New York would require voter-approved, state-secured debt on par with that which Rockefeller sought for his other programs. Rockefeller's team developed a package of $2.5 billion in bonds that even then many observers believed had much more to please upstate and downstate suburban constituencies than it did New York City residents. To gain legislative approval of an accompanying bond issue, Rockefeller packaged statewide improvements in mass transit (including both subways and commuter rail) with massive highway spending, most of it upstate and some of it of dubious value in the face of growing questions about the environmental and urban price of highways. To keep city voters on board with so much highway spending, he promised to preserve the 20-cent fare (a promise quickly broken). The governor sold the plan hard to the public, reminding the press and legislators, "My great-grandfather was a patent medicine salesman."[73] Labor unions lined up for the bill, as they anticipated the bond projects would be job generators. Voters approved the bond package in 1967.

New York City Transit expected to receive just $600 to $700 million of the $1 billion for mass transit in the $2.5 billion bond package despite moving 4.5 million people each day in 7,000 subway cars on 725 miles of track in 1968.[74] The lopsided funds for city subway projects, in comparison to the tremendous needs of such a large and antiquated system, should not come as much of a surprise. Rockefeller's focus on planning for future prosperity, as much as political realities, accounts for the outcome. If the poor and working class on subways eventually benefited from cleaner cars or better service, all the better, but social equity was not paramount in the era's values at the state or regional level. Many decent subways stations in more impoverished neighborhoods had hemorrhaged ridership compared to their heyday because of unemployment, poverty, and population loss. Arguably, many of the best lines were also in the wrong place by this time, such as Harlem or East New York, where unemployment was stubbornly high. A similar mismatch between resident demand and expensive transit infrastructure also complicated effective management of legacy rail systems in cities like Chicago, Boston, and Philadelphia.

A Transit Plan for the Prosperous

The MTA plans focused on enhancing the health of the center-city business districts by creating an integrated and much improved system of commuter and subway trains. Other states showed an equal bias to central business district efficiency, from Washington, DC, to San Francisco. The biggest of the MTA's new subway projects targeted the city's more prosperous areas, including the farther eastern sections of the Upper East Side (where developers were erecting many middle-class towers) and the middle-class residential districts in booming Queens. Queens was the "wealthiest, whitest, most spacious and fastest growing of New York's four major boroughs," with 40 percent of its residents commuting to Manhattan. The city's pink-collar secretaries, white-collar middle managers, and blue-collar building maintenance staff still lived in areas like Queens—thus enabling large Manhattan employers to maintain their workforces in moderate-cost modern housing.[75] In 1965, the City Planning Commission had already recommended rapid transit improvements to Queens and the Bronx to handle high passenger loads there.[76]

The MTA in 1968 rolled out its ambitious Program for Action for the bond issue. The plan was divided optimistically into a two-phase program that aimed to build on the metropolitan area's remaining middle-class strengths and connections. Among the highlights of Phase One ($1.6 billion) was a four-track tunnel under the East River to reduce crowding on the Queens lines to speed riders to still vibrant, affluent areas such as Forest Hills. A new Second Avenue line would improve service to both the Midtown and Lower Manhattan business districts by the growing number of white-collar workers arriving at Grand Central and residing in new apartment towers on the far East Side of Manhattan. Subway extensions to middle-class neighborhoods in northeastern Queens, new transit for southeastern Queens, and a Nostrand subway extension to Mill Basin were included in the plan although the ridership on these lines from relatively low-density, suburban-style neighborhoods would hardly have compensated for the high costs of development. The growing middle class on Staten Island, just beginning an automobile-centered building boom because of the opening of Moses's Verrazano Bridge (1965), received significant improvements to the Staten Island Rapid Transit Railway, known locally as the "Toonerville Trolley."

In fairness, all city subway riders did score some benefits, regardless of social class. The MTA placed an order for 500 high-speed air-conditioned subway cars. By 1971, the MTA was the biggest buyer of transit equipment in the country, with 2,196 electric cars ordered for all its commuter and subway lines. This large-scale spending helped reinvigorate the transit industry by attracting large, highly skilled companies such as GM, GE, and Westinghouse. State transit arguably saved an industry, most of which was located outside the biggest cities because of cost factors. In this respect, mass transportation generated economic growth.

The suburban emphasis of the Program for Action Phase One is also evident in the significant commitments to upgrading commuter rail, primarily used by affluent riders. To lose the suburban commuter would have been cataclysmic for the city's economic health, as the daily passengers brought much of their disposable income and skills into the city daily. The LIRR used some of its funding to order 350 new cars complete with soundproofing and air-conditioning (aptly christened the "Metropolitan" model), raised more platforms to quicken passenger flow, and pursued electrification to speed travel along its busiest routes. Most ambitious of all, and crucial for the health of the midtown business district, were plans for a new Metropolitan Transportation Center in East Midtown, including an LIRR terminal and high-speed rail to JFK International Airport. The main beneficiaries of this new Midtown station, to be located near 48th Street and Third Avenue, would be property

FIGURE 22. The vision for a Midtown transit hub, while never built, has influenced the MTA since the 1960s. MCTA, *Metropolitan Transportation: A Program for Action*, February 1968. New York State Archives, courtesy of the Rockefeller Archive Center.

owners, large employers, suburban commuters, and affluent business travelers.[77] The project was codesigned with the two-tier subway tunnel at 63rd Street under the East River with space for a new express line (today's F line) on the upper level long sought by Queens politicians and residents. Also, the MTA would build a new people-mover system in Midtown with "high-speed conveyers" that would link terminals, stores, and offices in this bustling district.

The second phase ($1.3 billion) of the 1968 MTA plan included far more visionary flourishes. In these plans, the Second Avenue line extended to Wall Street, with the primary goal of helping major redevelopment projects under way in Lower Manhattan. In 1969, of the 460,000 workers already piling into Lower Manhattan, 80 percent still rode transit because there was absolutely no space for cars and not much more for buses. Nelson Rockefeller's brother David, who created the Downtown Lower Manhattan Association to revive the district, could count "21 buildings now under construction at the cost of $1.3 billion" that "would bring 120,000 more workers into the crowded area south of Canal Street by 1972, an increase of 26 percent." The building he commissioned, the 60-story Chase Manhattan Bank Building (1960) catalyzed redevelopment in the area that would continue for decades.[78] Transit would have to be improved or the district would suffer, as it still does today, from overloaded lines. A Pelham Bay line to Co-op City (a favored housing project of the governor), extensions of the subway in northeast Bronx, and a new route from the LIRR station in Brooklyn to Lower Manhattan reflected the consistent aim of improving service for the city's remaining middle-class and suburban commuters.[79]

The Federal/State/Local Partnership

William Ronan, like his peers in other states, faced significant problems in the legacy core transit business.[80] The first delivery of accumulated Triborough profits, $74 million ($474 million in 2017 dollars), arrived in 1970, but these funds barely made a dent in the mounting operating deficits of the system.[81] The MTA and Rockefeller thus turned to the legislature to approve higher bridge and tunnel tolls and additional direct state aid to transit. Conservative Albany legislators, however, had already lost their enthusiasm for Rockefeller's big projects by this time and only some final arm-twisting in 1971 yielded additional toll increases, loans, and higher fares. The pillars of the MTA were shaky, but they held.[82]

Public transit, like public housing before it, was losing favor not only with many state legislators but also with the state's more conservative upstate and suburban voters. Many did not see why they should have to pay for services that they rarely if ever used. The beginning of the end of the Rockefeller investment in capital was voter rejection (61 to 39 percent) of a $2.5 billion bond package ($15.3 billion in 2017 dollars) in 1971 for road and mass transit improvements.[83] Even rhetorical appeals to the environmental benefits of mass transit and lots of cash for roads in the state could not sway increasingly skeptical voters. During the campaign for the 1971 initiative, Rockefeller muddied the waters by promising voters that capital programs included in "the bond issue would prevent subway and fare increases." Skeptical editorialist Edward Hershey at suburban *Newsday* had supported earlier bonds but voted "no" because he believed government services needed "an approach designed to serve the population instead of the interests of a conglomerate of business, labor and other narrow interests."[84] City officials, such as the borough president of Manhattan, also objected to the governor's unwillingness to guarantee the preservation of the now 30-cent fare.[85]

State voters, even with a softer sales pitch by Rockefeller, rejected a revised version of the bill for $3.5 billion ($19.6 billion in 2017 dollars) in 1973. City politicians objected again to the pairing of mass transit with highway funds ($1.15 billion for highways and $1.35 billion mass transit), and the governor waffled on preserving the 30-cent fare.[86] Some New York City leaders condemned it as "a highway plan in mass transit clothing" because every state dollar devoted to interstates could potentially be matched by nine federal dollars. In retrospect, the rejection of the plan now seems shortsighted, as it undermined the expansion programs for the city's transit system. The rejection of these bonds in 1971 and 1973 directly undercut plans for the Lower East Side subway loop of the Second Avenue line, the Northeast Queens line along the Long Island Expressway, and faster delivery of air-conditioned Interborough Rapid Transit (IRT) lines.[87] Not even gifts like the funding of a dubious modern light rail / subway line in Buffalo (1973) could stiffen upstate support for transit. A smaller transit bond of $250 million ($1.2 billion in 2017 dollars) finally passed in 1974.[88]

The rejection of the bond sales and the continuing financial problems of operating such a large and expensive system set off Ronan's search for "maximum" federal funds. To Ronan, demands for federal funds were the inevitable result of two decades of federal policy favoring cars and trucks that had made "it impossible to operate a nonsubsidized system in competition with subsidized ones."[89] With no state permitted to receive more than 12.5 percent of transit funds, the challenge was to shift the apportioning system and increase the total size of the program.[90]

Ronan used his role as president of the Institute of Rapid Transit and joined forces with the American Transit Association, the League of Cities, and the Fare Conference of Mayors to lobby Congress and President Nixon. Looking back, Ronan could justifiably claim that he had helped federal legislators realize "the importance of urban mass transit to the survival of our cities and suburbs."[91] Ronan admitted in 1973, "We'll take the money from any place, local, state, federal or the United Nations."[92] The *Times* believed that "Dr. Ronan has done more than most public officials to imbue others with that disarmingly simple truth: buses and trains are as much a government responsibility as public parks and fire engines."[93]

By the early 1970s, Ronan prematurely announced a "transit renaissance" spearheaded by the federal government. The Urban Mass Transportation Administration (1968) had helped pay for modernization and new equipment, demonstration projects, technical studies, managerial training, and university grants but not rebuilding or operating transit. Ronan worked as the leader of a coalition "for the enactment of the Urban Mass Transportation Assistance Act of 1970 which authorized substantial federal grants for capital projects."[94] New York State in 1970 sought federal aid in the hundreds of millions, mostly for subways, but this total was considered by local leaders to provide billions less than needed in capital investments.[95] Ronan and his coalition in 1972 next set their sights on efforts "to win Congressional approval of operating assistance to stabilize fares."[96] Accordingly, after much lobbying, in 1973 Congress approved a national mass transit commitment of $11.8 billion ($66.1 billion in 2017 dollars), including both capital and operating subsidies. By the time Ronan stepped down from the MTA in 1974, the federal government had spent close to $650 million for New York City regional capital expenditures for transportation.[97] Rules that accompanied the legislation deliberately set limits on New York, which received about 13 percent of national subsidies despite carrying 31 percent of the nation's riders.[98]

Federal officials remained skeptical that more subsidies, and those for operations that would include labor costs, would necessarily lead to better service. Nixon administration officials, for instance, believed subsidies "mandate low fare and high salaries—if the Federal Government picked up the tab."[99] One Nixon official also believed, with some justification, that mass transit was "a problem in only five large cities" and, in any case, "big-city transit users . . . were for the most part not poor people, but relatively affluent."[100] Federal officials were exaggerating about the social class status of most urban transit riders, but they had correctly identified the underlying bias of state mass transit policies to the prosperous. Federal officials nevertheless finally came through with additional funding, perhaps influenced by the same upscale demographic pressure they decried. The first federal operating grant finally arrived in New York in 1975 and was $87.5 million ($404 million in 2017 dollars).[101] In the fiscal year 1974, however, the MTA operating deficit alone was $411 million ($2.075 billion in 2017 dollars). Federal funds were no panacea.[102]

Turning the Corner on Commuter Rail

The long-term power of suburban commuters in New York and elsewhere is evident in the story of the Long Island Rail Road. The suffering passengers of the LIRR, still America's busiest commuter railroad, had limited patience with Rockefeller and Ronan from the start of the MTA. They had the most extended experience with quasi-state management and were thus least optimistic about the transformative role of government in mass transit. A growing strain of antigovernment Republican ideology in the suburbs like Nassau and Suffolk Counties likely contributed to this skepticism.

The LIRR leadership from the beginning of MTA ownership in 1968 attempted to demonstrate its commitment to service by using the media to feature the advantages of the modern train cars it had ordered. The LIRR unions, more concerned about automation on these cars and their own work rules and wages, dimmed hopes quickly. A work slowdown led, for instance, to the cancellation of service on 738 trains in July of 1968 and a court order in August to resume work.[103] Thirteen thousand respondents to a 1969 survey agreed that service quality had declined since the 1966 MCTA/MTA takeover.[104] The *MTA Annual Report* frankly acknowledged that even in 1969 "much of the year was marked by service problems, labor difficulties and recurrent financial crises."[105] That year, wives staged protests at stations over late husbands. One study blamed the LIRR for "fatigue, conscious anger, anxiety, headaches, palpitations, indigestion, abdominal cramps,—and even sexual problems," in 200 commuters surveyed by a doctor at the Nassau County Mental Health Board.[106]

Rockefeller tried to shift the blame to broader trends: "This problem is a national problem. And if you lived in Westchester and were trying to commute on the New Haven, which is still in private hands, or even on the Penn Central, which is one of the finest railroads in the country, you would recognize the fact that there are basic, deeply disturbing problems in our commuter railroads."[107] The governor, sensing a softening in his ordinarily firm suburban Republican support in Nassau and Suffolk Counties, stepped in and made the situation even worse. In August 1969 he foolishly promised that the LIRR in just two months would "be the finest" commuter rail service in the country. He made these promises, after being flown in by helicopter to a meeting on Long Island, based on the expected delivery of new cars, longer trains, fewer cancellations, better labor relations, and the sad fact that there were so few other functioning commuter railroads in the United States.[108]

The progress in the next two months was both visible and uneven. Fewer of the new train cars than hoped arrived, and many had teething problems; trains continued to be canceled and stall out.[109] The railroad lacked the minimum number of functioning trains needed for standard daily service. The governor urged patience, no doubt regretting his hasty promise: "They say it is darkest before the dawn. And I think we are in that moment—just before the sun comes up over the horizon on this service." As the deadline loomed, he still promised the "finest commuter service anywhere in this country or anywhere in the world." He defended Ronan, now in the crosshairs of angry commuters, as "one of the ablest men in our state" and blamed delays on a system suffering from "50 years of neglect" and poor labor relations. The LIRR's maintenance facility, for instance, was not producing at a sufficient level to keep service at a consistent level despite the LIRR spending 80 percent of its total budget on salaries and benefits.[110]

As the October deadline neared, Rockefeller's advisors wrote to him that they thought it best "for you to stay off the trains. All you need is an entourage of 75 newspapermen delaying a commuter train half an hour—or pictures of you sitting in a stalled car halfway between Babylon and Jamaica."[111] His advisors were worried he might ride on a Monday morning when trains were more likely to stall. Instead, they advised him to ride on a Tuesday and for just a few stops in Suffolk County to Nassau County's Garden City. He did just that.[112] The best that he and his team could report to the public by the two-month deadline was that "the LIRR has improved much of its service during the last two months" in part by reducing "by half . . . [the] number of cars out of service."[113] A few years later even Rockefeller admitted the LIRR was not the finest: "I wouldn't say we exactly achieved that, but—close enough."[114] The *Times* mocked his promise in a telling description of the Babylon line: "Yesterday, after the line became the finest in the country, the 7:42 out of Babylon was dusty and littered and noisy and had some cracked windows and a few doors that did not close." It was also 11 minutes late.[115] An impressive 40 percent of Manhattan-bound commuters avoided the LIRR by 1970. They faced the horrible traffic rather than ride such a fine railroad.[116]

Commuters were vocal, as were their representatives, but their loud voices in 1969 and 1970 obscured real progress. As the new cars finally arrived, and adjustments were made to them and systems to make them compatible, LIRR service probably could have been considered one of the finest in the nation. By 1970 the MTA had already refurbished 295 cars, completed the installation of high-level platforms system wide, and installed more reliable power.[117] By 1971, moreover, the LIRR had put its 620th Metropolitan rail car in service, thus allowing the railroad to junk all its pre–World War II passenger cars. The LIRR added 150 additional Metropolitans to its order in 1971, to be delivered in 1972, and predicted an all Metropolitan fleet by 1972 on its electrified lines. Indeed, by 1973 the LIRR was offering all Metropolitan service on its electrified, and busiest, lines.[118] Fares were higher, and ridership had slipped further, but service quality was up. For most but not all riders "the new air-conditioned M-1 Metropolitans have provided a measure of comfort unknown on the lines a few years ago." They were paying more for the pleasure of riding, however, having grudgingly accepted 18 fare increases since 1947.[119]

The LIRR had made significant progress but was still running deficits, primarily because of outsized labor costs. Continuing labor issues and deficits undermined the accomplishment in the eyes of the public; the railroad hit a $50 million operating deficit in 1972 ($297 million in 2017 dollars). The railroad's workers demanded a 36 percent wage and benefit increase for non-operating staff and went on strike in 1972, further damaging the railroad in the eyes of the public and permanently losing many riders.[120] The line's regular commuters resorted to cars, buses, and subways to get in and out of the city and sided with the LIRR.[121]

Despite the many setbacks, a 1974 *Times* LIRR rider survey provided third-party confirmation of a qualitative shift in service. According to the survey, "Most of its 221,000 daily riders now seem agreed that the improvement . . . has been worthy of a salute in double highball in the bar car." A rejiggered schedule for faster service was now "providing 49 new trains, faster running times, fewer stops generally and fewer bothersome changes at Jamaica." The survey also found "widespread approval of the railroad's new look and new attitude in tackling problems." Its running fleet of 596 electric trains were "now all equipped with the handsome new 85-foot air-conditioned Metropolitan cars, which now total 775." The 145 diesel runs also had air-conditioned cars. Trains system wide were much more likely to run on time, on smoother rails, and at higher speeds.[122] The Westchester and Connecticut commuter lines, serving both tony inland Westchester suburbs like Scarsdale and the river towns on the Hudson, turned around more slowly under MTA control than many riders might have hoped, but by the mid-1970s riders also enjoyed new cars, station upgrades, and better on-time service.

Some of these improvements in regional commuter service proved fleeting, and by the late 1970s commuters felt that service had again slipped, but the same joy, however brief, was never shared by subway riders (many of whom were also suburban commuters catching connections in the city). The financial, physical, and management structure of the commuter lines proved far better suited to MTA management and resources than the far larger, politically hamstrung, labor-intensive, fraying, and complicated subway system.

Failing the Subway

New York's subways were a "meat and potato" intracity network that absorbed lots of funds but offered mostly headaches and little payoff for state or city politicians. Riders understood full well that the scale of investment required to make a first-class system—to rival highways or commuter rail—was not on the menu in Albany. The MTA Board was full of "affluent people who rarely use the dirty, unreliable, overcrowded, cold, dangerous New York City Subways." City residents also objected, time and again, to proposed fare increases, even though slowly rising fares were not by any reasonable standard keeping pace with operating costs. The city, in a familiar refrain heard to this day, was already paying "over $100 million a year to subway costs while suburban counties contribute token sums to commuter railroads."[123] The broader truth is that the MTA system, a result of a regional compromise with upstate voters with no interest in mass transit at all, better addressed the financial and operational needs of the smaller commuter service that mostly served rush hour needs. The four million daily subway riders thus waited on filthy platforms and had to stand or sit in dirty, frequently delayed subway cars.[124]

The complex labor rules of the city inhibited service improvement. When the MTA took over the subways, it had to accept Lindsay's labor contract, which had given workers generous pension benefits after just 20 years. Approximately 4,000 employees jumped at retirement in 1968, roughly four times the average retirement levels. Retirement numbers leveled off in subsequent years, but the MTA now had mounting pension costs and the added burden of training thousands of additional workers. To improve service, the NYCTA added thousands of additional employees during this period.[125] Between 1965 and 1970, wages at the NYCTA also increased 70 percent. Such a large portion of subsidies diverted into worker salaries and benefits was a political and public affairs liability. For every 35 cents the subways collected for a ride, it was spending 52 cents to provide the service. One of the few bright spots was the use of the Transit Authority employment rolls as a stepping stone for minority social mobility. In 1971, 75 percent of transit workers were African Americans or Puerto Ricans who, because of the Transport Workers Union's skill in gaining wage and benefit increases now earned decent salaries and excellent benefits.[126] A few years later, however, one business group would criticize the MTA for raising salaries of Transport Workers Union employees faster than those of workers in the private sector.[127]

Within a decade of their launching, the air had gone out of subway expansion plans. In a modern era of labor unions, complicated urban politics, and inflation, subway lines turned out to be far more expensive to build than in the early twentieth century, when cheap immigrant labor had been key to rapid, cost-effective subway construction. Suburban commuter rail riders, by contrast, had benefited from the fact that the capital program for their systems addressed the efficiency of service and did not require eminent domain, tunneling, or major construction work. Every subway expansion in the city, by contrast, demanded complex political and physical engineering. Even basic renovation of subway stations required extensive tile work and renovation of steel supporting structures astride block-long platforms.

The termination of the East Side Els, on Second Avenue (1942) and Third Avenue (1955), had been carried out with promises of new subways to replace hulking, loud steel structures that had played a key role in East Side transportation. The Upper East Side was left with just the Lexington line and vague promises. Developers switched out tenements for enormous market-rate high-rises in the district even without additions to the overloaded Lexington subway line. When the MTA called for and then began work on the Second Avenue subway in 1968, the line's route and priority became a point of contention. Populist politicians viewed the new line as a "rich man's express" that linked upper-income areas on the Upper East Side with Midtown and, eventually, Lower Manhattan business districts.[128] The Board of Estimate, for instance, thought the Lower East Side deserved more attention in the Second Avenue plans, forcing Ronan to make promises for more stops and a less direct route to the financial district downtown. Governor Rockefeller and Mayor Lindsay broke ground for the Second Avenue line in 1972, and some construction got rolling in sections, but multiple "no" votes on the state transportation bond program posed an existential threat to subway expansion. By 1974 the line's completion had been put off until 1986 because "costs have spiraled greatly." Debates about ideal routes now appeared to be a waste of time.[129]

The MTA still claimed in 1972 to have three subway lines under construction and eight in the design process. These expansions, it promised, would create new lines to Brooklyn, the Bronx, and Queens, "where extensive development has taken place during the last twenty-five years." Cancellations for nearly all additions, some of which were of dubious value in the first place, rolled in during the 1970s as the costs and complexity of construction increased and the city's and state's finances declined.[130] Delays, for instance, plagued the Manhattan-to-Queens subway tunnel and line addition. The NYCTA only lowered the first section of the new 63rd Street tunnel into the East River in 1971. Administrators optimistically aimed to commence service between Roosevelt Island and Queens by 1978—a link that would not open until 1989.[131]

The continuing mediocrity of the subways added to Rockefeller's political vulnerability in the state and nationally. The "crumbling service and rising fares" in New York City were widely publicized during this time in the region's national newspapers, television shows, and magazines.[132] A system "plagued by breakdowns, delayed trains, begrimed stations, bands of hyperkinetic youths roving the cars after school, robberies, and molestations" was not only embarrassing but continued to threaten the city's economic vitality.[133] Riders were finally paying more for a ride, but it was hard to see the justice in supporting a system that was still dirty, loud, and modestly updated, at best. Fares steadily increased during this period, from 20 cents in 1966 to 30 cents in 1970, 35 cents in 1972, and 50 cents in 1975. Commuter rail riders were also paying much higher fares, but they were more affluent to begin with, and they got much better service for their extra dollars.[134]

The problems of the subway system, or other intraurban transit systems nationally, were not as simple an antiurban animus among upstate politicians and their suburban neighbors. The enormous gap between what the subway and commuter rail each required for decent service was considerable. The MTA was, in just a few years, able to electrify much of the LIRR and switch out most of the old cars for modern, air-conditioned ones. In 1968, by way of contrast, just 300 of 800 air-conditioned subway cars ordered by NYCTA were in service, so new cars made up a tiny part of the 7,000-car system. By 1972, just 1,100 new subway cars were in service and another 745 on order. The newest on order boasted air-conditioning, a smoother ride, higher speed, more soundproofing, and updated interiors. The chances of riding on one of these excellent cars, however, were slim.[135] The MTA finally scrapped all the antique cars from 1925 that had stayed in service far beyond their expiration date, but they were forced to keep in service 1,690 subway cars dating from 1930 to 1940. Stepping into subway cars like these was unpleasant time travel for riders.[136]

A system built in stages by different entities also bedeviled renovation plans. The IRT system's small tunnels made the introduction of air-conditioning so difficult that the modernized cars purchased for the line by the NYCTA before the MTA takeover had lacked air-conditioning even though the cold air was technically possible and much desired by riders. An earlier generation of passengers would have been content with just modern cars, but in an age when air-conditioning was becoming typical in homes, offices, and even apartment housing, riding in hot trains sizzled many riders. To replace so many cars in a short time, moreover, took a great deal of money and time. By the end of 1975, for instance, just 44 percent of the 3,781 cars on the Brooklyn Manhattan Transit and Independent lines boasted air conditioning.[137] The NYCTA finally started adding air-conditioning to old IRT trains in 1973, but just 5 percent of the IRT's cars were air-conditioned by 1978, as reengineering them proved difficult.[138]

The new air-conditioned subway cars, when they did arrive, were a mixed blessing. In 1976 managers reported that air-conditioned cars broke down at a rate far higher than older ones because of "sophisticated equipment" for controls.[139] The agency, in any case, did not plan to have the system fully air-conditioned until 1980. During the 1970s, by contrast, suburban commuters were already enjoying air-conditioning systems as an expected, if unreliable, amenity. What this meant in practice was that during the first decade of the MTA most subway riders continued to ride old, hot, cold, screeching, and substandard cars most of the time.[140] Even in 1982, only 82 percent of subway cars were air-conditioned and often imperfectly. In much of the world, and for most of human history, people coped without air-conditioning. But in a prosperous postwar society, where cars and buildings cooled with a touch of a button, the failure to add this amenity on a full basis was another strike against the system for those with alternative options.[141]

The contrast between subway and commuter rail stations was equally sharp. The MTA could offer LIRR and Westchester commuters new platforms and many station upgrades because, in part, commuter stations are composed mostly of semi-covered platforms and small waiting rooms. Subway stations were far more complicated to build, maintain, expand, and renovate. Subway riders enjoyed just one new station in this era, at 57th Street and Avenue of Americas, which opened in 1968. It was the first new station to open since 1928 and had a nominal effect on quality of life for most system riders. It was nevertheless a welcome upgrade for the investors and professionals in the modern office towers above, including the Rockefeller family.[142] In 1972, just three stations, all in Manhattan in business districts, were even being remodeled: the Bowling Green, 49th Street, and 50th Street stations, all of which addressed service quality for Manhattan business districts. Most stations continued to be unsavory at best.[143]

Declining conditions on the subways in the 1970s are reflected in spending for station "amenities" unnecessary on suburban railroads. The MTA announced in 1971 the installation of 100 bulletproof subway attendant booths in high crime areas to protect staff. The necessity of spending to protect staff reflects the fact that the city's crime wave had made the tunnels more dangerous.[144] In 1974, for instance, police nabbed a Bronx gang of teenagers who were believed to have robbed 60 subway booths, grossing $1,000 per day for two months.[145]

The MTA also had to pay for cleaning stations and scrubbing cars from a lean budget in the 1970s as vandalism lent the system a visual profile of disorder. Kids and adults "bombed" cars and stations with cheap spray paint and permanent markers. One transit official remembered catching "a 14-year-old girl marking up the brand-new R-44 cars at 1 AM." The MTA devoted about half a million dollars per year in the early 1970s to removing graffiti. The number of transit officers increased significantly, but they usually issued youthful offenders cards rather than seeking criminal prosecution.[146] In 1972, for instance, the MTA police referred 40,130 juveniles under 16 to the youth aid department of the New York Police Department.[147] This soft touch, poorly secured train storage yards, and cleaning backlogs helped sustain a golden age of graffiti art but also undermined any sense of progress for many mainstream riders.

Local politicians, including Democratic rival Arthur Goldberg, pounded the governor and Ronan over the declining conditions. Goldberg sought to differentiate himself in 1970 from Rockefeller by calling for a permanent state subsidy for subway operating expenses because "only a subsidy can end the Rockefeller policy of mass transit management by crisis." Goldberg promised that if elected governor he would fire Ronan.[148] Then city comptroller Abraham Beame demanded in 1970 that the MTA cede control of the subways.[149] The city's elected leaders and much of the population believed that they were "being shortchanged to the benefit of the suburbs."[150] It was remarkable, however, that upstate voters tolerated as much subway subsidy as they did. William F. Buckley, reflecting broad sentiment, dismissed the state writing a blank check for subways: "There is simply no obvious reason why Cayuga County apple pickers need to be taxed in order to subsidize the 5,000,000 New Yorkers who regularly ride the subways."[151]

Most transit professionals considered subway service to be better than it was at its lowest points, but NYCTA continued to lose customers. Between 1962 and 1973 the system was losing riders even faster than the city was shedding jobs. The Times Square station slipped from 40 million passengers in 1962 to 27.7 million in 1973.[152] In 1974, ridership slipped to its lowest level since 1918, 1.098 billion.[153] This service decline, to the frustration of remaining riders, was overseen by a surprisingly affluent working class. The average salary of city transit workers by 1974 had risen to $15,125 ($76,389 in 2017 dollars), and the number of these workers had also increased substantially from

1965 to 1974, growing from 33,826 workers and 1,146 transit police officers to 38,066 workers and 5,101 transit police. The perils of public management are reflected in this growing cost of personnel.[154] Most workers were dedicated and managed to keep the old system in motion, but multiple studies by outside sources "found gross examples of overtime abuses, absenteeism, loafing and poor productivity and supervision" costing New York City Transit millions a year.[155]

The MTA deficit by 1975 was up to $470 million ($2.175 billion in 2017 dollars) for just subways and buses.[156] Triborough profits and federal operating subsidies could not even patch such a large hole. Between 1968 and 1978, for instance, Triborough provided $831 million for transit.[157] When the city's finances collapsed in the mid-1970s, it revealed a crucial flaw in the MTA financial structure. The city traditionally contributed to the transit police and provided hidden subsidies to pay for rides of the elderly and children. The city also gave $100 million minimum per year to the subway system's capital needs per the arrangement to share in the Triborough surpluses. From 1967 to 1974 New York City had quietly provided $750 million to fund capital improvements, mainly for subways. A broke city threatened the flow of subsidies.[158] When Mayor Beame asked the MTA to cut its budget in 1974, the ax fell hard on MTA planning and operations. Beame's six-year capital plan omitted the Second Avenue program, and most other expansion plans, leaving just the 63rd Street express line and the Jamaica Avenue/Southeast Queens extensions—all of which were delayed and over budget.[159] New MTA chair David Yunich grudgingly agreed that the MTA needed to be "realistic" and ended work on everything but the Queens line extension.[160]

A city commissioner in 1976 believed that the state of the subways still threatened the city's economic health: "The businessmen who formerly used the Lexington Avenue express between the downtown and midtown business districts . . . are seen less and less now on that line because of the uncontrolled proliferation of addicts, winos, beggars and other unfortunates." The vandalism and graffiti had become moving symbols "of the chaotic mismanagement under which our subways are run."[161] The agency sidelined hundreds of cars because it lacked the money to run them, while remaining trains in service were packed. Trains broke down too frequently, derailments spooked customers, and track and car fires disrupted service frequently.[162]

The Long-Term Payoff of State Investment

The late 1970s and early 1980s were dark days for city transit, but the system did not collapse, because the state remained engaged. As in other states, legacy mass transit proved its value during the gas crisis of the 1970s as systems experienced significant if temporary ridership increases. Most cities, including the city of New York, experienced such deep financial problems that only state sponsorship prevented the evaporation of entire transit networks. We can praise states like New York for sustaining the systems while still criticizing them for their limited commitments.

By the 1980s it had become clear to political and business leaders in New York that the interrelationship of commuter rail with subways meant that *both* would have to be upgraded to maintain central business district efficiency. Much has been made about the quality-of-life issues for city residents addressed in the 1980s subway turnaround, such as crime reduction, but the moving factor was still the reliance of the Manhattan business districts on both subways and commuter rail. It is unlikely that state leaders would have allowed so much debt to be issued in the name of city residents alone.

During the 1980s and 1990s the powers of MTA as a regionally operating state authority, rather than a municipal or private manager, finally paid off with massive bond sales and the healthy mix of direct subsidies for rail. The fare box in 1985, for instance, still provided only 43.9 percent of operating funds, so the rest came from the federal operating subsidy of 2.6 percent, Triborough Bridge and Tunnel Authority (TBTA) tolls of 9.4 percent, and local subsidies of 11.5 percent. A robust set of additional state-enabled regional taxes (mortgage transfer, commuter taxes, etc.) of 14.7 percent were crucial in subsidizing operations of the rail system. The addition of these taxes was the result of hard-fought battles by the downstate region's state legislators and business interests.[163]

The state most crucially in the 1980s allowed for bond sales for major capital improvement, secured by the state's credit, despite the sketchy state of MTA finances. Without this financing of capital improvements, it is likely that the subway system would have failed to offer anything remotely close to world-class service expected in a reemergent global financial capital. Experts estimated in 1982 that the loss of commuter rail alone in the New York City region would have added at least 150,000 automobile commuters to jammed roads; the subway's functional collapse, which was once entirely possible, would have left 1.4 million daily workers commuting on buses, cars, bikes, or shoe leather.[164]

Developer Richard Ravitch, who became chairman of the MTA, deserves much of the credit for the capital program of the 1980s. Ravitch faced down politicians who viewed fare increases "as an invitation to political suicide," demanded an end to "deferred maintenance practices," suffered stoically through a damaging strike, confronted state and federal officials, and got a firm number on the MTA's needed revenues for the next decade ($14 billion) to reverse "an unsustainable downward course" in the subways. Ravitch convinced politicians in Albany to permit the sale of revenue bonds, "serviced by MTA revenues, including fares," thus laying the groundwork for billions in bond sales for capital upgrades. By selling bonds, backed by future revenues, the state broke through the dysfunctional upstate/downstate conflict that sunk the voter-approved bond programs. Ravitch had to give bond investors promises of priority of payment and a pledge to never seek bankruptcy to calm their nerves in the face of low bond ratings. The MTA without the state, after all, was a bad bet.[165]

State leaders supplemented bond offerings with fare increases, regional transit taxes, federal grants, state grants, city grants, and TBTA revenue bonds. The MTA between 1982 and 1991 thus secured an impressive total of $16.122 billion in capital funds. The scale of this spending was crucial, particularly for the subways, because even adjusting for inflation, these funds were much greater than those available during the Rockefeller period. The NYCTA received $12 billion, the LIRR $2 billion, and Metro-North $1.6 billion in the period. The willingness of states to underwrite bond offering for transit capital spending has been crucial to building and sustaining regional mass transit.[166] City/suburban compromises were made to close the political deals. The capital plan spending for MTA from 1981 to 1996 divided on a politically derived formula of 77 percent for the city and 23 percent outside: "Because most of the assembly majority has been from the city, and the state senate majority's base has been strongly suburban, this insures regional balance between commuter and subway rider interests and between the suburbs and the city."[167] Today, the MTA claims to have spent $102 billion during the past three decades on capital funding for improvements and restoration.[168]

Riders felt the difference in both commuter and subway lines. During the 1980s, suburban commuters scored new trains for one-third of the fleet, an enhanced program of car maintenance, a new train yard (for the LIRR), and additional electrification (the upper Harlem lines). Penn Station, or what was left of it, was renovated, and Grand Central was spectacularly overhauled. Federal funds helped fund new cars and additional improvements.[169] The MTA in 1983, through the creation of Metro-North, took over direct management of northern commuter routes from Conrail, which had managed them since 1976 for the MTA.[170] Both Metro-North and the LIRR continued to suffer under public management from high personnel costs, occasional labor problems, and fast-rising costs that made it prohibitive for anyone but the middle class to use the system regularly. Yet commuter lines reborn during the Rockefeller era, once given new financial and managerial tools during the

1980s and 1990s, became functioning lines with better on-time performance, safe platforms, modern cars, and more attractive central stations.

The transformation of the subway was even more dramatic than commuter rail during this period. Managers of the subway showed renewed vigor and now had the funds to back up their ambitions. NYCTA president David Gunn in the early 1980s, taking a page from the private sector, created 1,200 new managerial position exempt from civil service and union rules. With this new leadership, he began closely managing repair shops, reorganized many departments, and invested heavily in transit police. He prioritized cleaning graffiti from cars and transit policing that in a few years achieved a nearly graffiti-free car system. The cleaner cars and stations helped draw many more riders to the system. By the end of 1988, the NYCTA had overhauled 60 percent of the subway cars, restored most of the system's 1,400 miles of track, and ordered over 1,000 new cars. In 1988 "construction activity on the subway reached its highest level since completion of the system nearly half a century before."[171] The MTA also renovated many subway stations, often adding attractive public artworks, and could finally announce that it had installed air-conditioning in all subway cars.The result of new investments by the late 1980s was an acknowledgment that "service has dramatically improved at the MTA" because "of extensive capital investments." The central Manhattan business districts could still be efficiently served by rail; in 1988, 83 per-

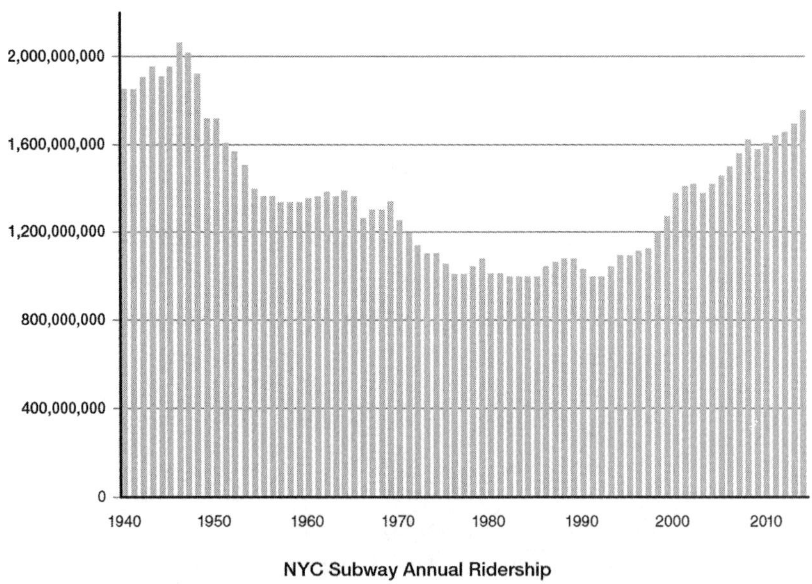

FIGURE 23. The MTA, and a recovering economy, stopped the ongoing collapse in ridership. Chart by Minna Ninova, 2018, from data by Charles Komanoff, 2015.

cent of workers arrived by rail for jobs in a still-expanding service sector.[172] The commuter rail system enhanced the city's central land values and that of many high-priced suburban towns en route. Developers since the 1980s have added tens of millions of additional square feet to Manhattan and Brooklyn commercial rental markets while adding very little additional parking. These additions of thousands of workers, and billions more in tax revenues, would be impossible without rail.

The reemerging problems of today's MTA have their roots in the same stresses and strains that were on full display in the 1960s. Priority has been placed on big-ticket items given to suburban commuters such as East Side Access ($11 billion at minimum), restarted in about 2006 after falling victim to the 1970s financial crisis, to bring Long Island Rail Road passengers directly to Grand Central. Penn Station, which is overwhelmed by a daily flood of LIRR, New Jersey Transit, and Amtrak passengers, is also benefiting from a state-designed expansion program under the post office next door. Wealthy East Side residents and developers have also benefited from the first phase of the Second Avenue project ($4.45 billion) that as of this writing extends only from 72nd Street to 96th Street. Investment in the subway's hundreds of other miles of lines, hundreds of dreary stations, and ancient control systems has not kept pace with demand. The city's bus service is in steep decline due to poor service and competition from private ride-sharing and shuttle-bus service. Personnel costs absorb most of the MTA's enormous annual budgets. Service reached such a low point that Governor Andrew Cuomo was forced to focus on the system's problems in 2017–2018.[173]

What reporters and Governor Cuomo discovered, and the riding public already knew, would be all too familiar to Rockefeller and Ronan. State, federal, and city government since the 1990s have forced the MTA to subsist on a mix of debt, legacy funding sources such as TBTA tolls, miserly federal grants, and rising fares rather than robust state funds or regional taxes. It is still hard to convince upstate legislators, and even many representatives from downstate suburbs, that transit is a financial priority for them—especially given what they hear about the comparatively booming downstate economy and inflated MTA labor and construction contracts. Debt and fare box revenues solve the political problem of maintaining the state's hand in mass transit but have a fatal flaw. The accumulated $34 billion in MTA debt for capital projects now consumes approximately one-fifth of annual revenues just for debt service. Bond holders and contractors get rich, and fares rise, without buying much better service.[174]

Governor Cuomo, because of Rockefeller's decision to assume management, is nevertheless forced to confront the needs of all transit riders. At the time of this writing, the governor had succeeded in funding a Subway Action Plan with a mix of state subsidies, city funds (only agreed to by Mayor Bill de Blasio under duress), and fees on taxis and Uber service below 96th Street. Congestion charges on vehicles entering Manhattan that might have yielded sustained funds were resisted, however, by outer-borough car commuters, their state legislators, and the mayor, illustrating the persistence of fraught transit politics stretching back decades.

New York State saved America's most extensive system of mass transit, but service quality has fluctuated widely, depending upon variables such as regional politics, management, and the economic context. New York State's mixed record on transit is widely shared.

American States and Mass Transit

The *Book of the States*, comprehensively documenting state activity in the postwar period, only added a Mass Transit section in its 1966–1967 edition, mostly related to new federal programs. Chapters on highways and aviation long preceded those sections on mass transit, indicating the state interest in these modern, adequately funded, and more universally popular forms of transportation.[175] Despite their late arrival, the entry of state governments in transit proved just as crucial to transit survival in other cities as in New York.

States in the postwar period, mostly for the first time in American history, provided direct subsidies to municipal transit.[176] Pennsylvania's government, for instance, pumped enough funds into some of its legacy urban mass transit systems to keep them alive and to study additional options.[177] Generating these funds sometimes required new revenues, including "a cigarette tax in MA, higher gas and electric rates in New Orleans, LA, a half-penny sales tax in CO, a special property tax in Toledo . . . payroll tax in Portland." States frequently provided tax relief or rebates to transit operators to keep them in business.[178] Cleveland's Regional Transportation Authority in the 1970s was underwritten by a 1 percent regional (Cuyahoga County) sales tax. The Illinois General Assembly in 1979 created a regional sales tax to help fund Chicago's Regional Transit Authority. California in 1979 was spending $350 million ($1.2 billion in 2017 dollars) to aid transit development, twice the level of federal support to the state. Many states directly operated and funded transit systems in smaller towns and cities.[179]

The total squeezed from state legislatures was always low compared to the enormous expense of financing, building, operating, and maintaining mass transit. The federal government, which had demonstrated vision and generosity on highways, became the natural target of transit activists. Antihighway politicians and activists were eager to divert some of the surfeit of highway money into mass transit as part of a strategy of reducing the scale of urban interstates. An early result was the Urban Mass Transportation Act of 1964. The program was modest at first but, as described above, eventually became more robust.[180] Among the winners in federal capital funding for urban mass transit from 1965 to 1977 were New York ($1.48 billion), Pennsylvania ($410 million), Illinois ($749 million), and Sunbelt darlings California ($784 million), Georgia ($698 million), and Texas ($89 million).[181] These substantial totals can be traced, in part, to a change in 1973 that allowed states to transfer funds from the Highway Trust Fund to mass transit.[182] The transfer provision by 1999 had generated "$6.8 billion in funding for more than 50 transit projects, most notably in Washington, DC ($2.1 billion), Boston ($1.5 billion), Chicago ($882 million), New York City ($884 million), and Philadelphia ($354 million)."[183]

New or expanded transit systems, however, were rarely large enough or of sufficient quality to alter regional transportation patterns. Because the typical transit funding ratio in the late 1970s (about 20 percent state, 60 percent federal, and 20 percent local) was less generous than that for federally aided roads (90 percent federal), and construction costs were coming in much higher than expected for transit development, many politicians grew skeptical of transit's return on investment. Only Washington, DC, developed a new, regional, high-quality subway system, an achievement made possible by enormous and sustained federal subsidies unavailable nationally. The quest for mass transit economy in most metropolitan areas had led to a boom since the 1980s in light rail systems with a strong suburban bias. Analysts believe, however, that light rail, which carries a relatively small percentage of most regional riders, contributed in many cities to diversion of funds from more heavily patronized inner-city buses.

The federal government continues to favor roads over rails and buses. The Intermodal Surface Transit Efficiency Act (1991), championed by Senator Patrick Moynihan (D-NY), aimed to make transit development an important factor in reducing air pollution, but the limited funds available and various project delays, have again led to limited results.[184] Today, the federal government provides about $12 billion per year to mass transit subsidies (funded from a portion of the gas tax) for all American rural areas, small towns, and big cities combined. This is approximately one-quarter of what the federal government spends on capital needs for interstates. I have not found a similar cumulative figure for all state spending on mass transit, but it is undoubtedly a fraction of the $100 billion annually spent by local and state government on highways.[185]

Frustrated urban voters have, in recent years, approved separate taxes on themselves for transit improvement. Some of these local tax initiatives have yielded transit improvements, as in cities like Seattle and Los Angeles, but they also reflect the failure of the state/federal partnership to deliver high-quality mass transit to the transit authorities they authorized decades ago. States such as Texas, Florida, and California have shown a predictable interest recently in expensive, intercity rail lines that are likely to benefit affluent intercity travelers rather than daily city transit riders.

A National Pattern of Transit

Every region has a slightly different history of transit, but the patterns of development of state-run mass transit are more similar than different. There are many parallels in the following short vignettes to the struggles that emerged in transit-rich New York.

New York's regional partner, New Jersey, while unwilling to join in a regional mass transit agency, did eventually step up to preserve commuter rail. As in New York, to get state voters to approve transit, government officials had to buy off drivers. New Jersey voters in 1968, for instance, approved $640 million of a $2 billion planned, decade-long expansion program. Of that $640 million, however, only one-third found its way to transit, while two-thirds went to roads already underwritten by local, state, and federal sources. New Jersey also failed to upgrade or reorganize mass transit at the same scale as New York. New Jersey Transit finally rose in 1979 from the shells of dying private rail companies. This delay in launching a state system echoes today in terms of service quality problems, including time-consuming transfers, limited tunnel space between Manhattan and New Jersey, and a crowded terminal at Penn Station. The costs to update these systems have mounted ever higher, and state voters remain reluctant to fund transit improvements for a system most never or rarely use.[186]

Coalitions of suburban and urban activists and academics around Boston, as in other cities, put up fierce and active resistance to more highways during the 1960s. Governor Sargent canceled a planned inner-belt highway, admitting that "the old highway planning game is over." The state created the Massachusetts Bay Transportation Authority (MBTA) in 1964 (replacing the Metropolitan Transit Authority, 1947) as a regional authority for 78 towns. On paper, at least, it appeared to be a "perfect model of a single authority, transcending all jurisdictional lines, with the power to tax the people of the serviced communities to make up any deficit." The MBTA eventually upgraded subways (with some lines modernized and expanded) and commuter rail, mostly with the help of federal capital grants.[187] The system quality was uneven because of antiquated policies that favored the suburban/downtown routes, high employee salaries, patronage, deficits, and union rules. Still, New York City residents looked in envy at the "statewide tax funds devoted to transit improvement" mostly in and around the state's biggest metropolitan area.[188]

California's legendary traffic and smog, urbanized structure (most of the state's population lived in urban places), and fast-rising population made it a likely candidate for mass transit development. Highway interests had won thousands of miles of freeway in the postwar period, and the auto lifestyle became synonymous with the California Dream. During the 1960s, however, residents in San Francisco, Beverly Hills, Laguna Beach, and Santa Barbara often resisted additional highways. The Planning Conservation League, created in 1966, included 87 groups fighting for housing, mass transit, scenic roads, billboard controls, and emission control.[189]

In Northern California, transit moved ahead with state support, and the emphasis on the prosperous parallels that in New York and other states. Bay Area Rapid Transit (BART) traces its origins to studies by cooperating governments in the 1950s. The multicounty consortium received an official blessing from the state in 1957. BART could sell voter-approved bonds, tax property, issue revenue bonds, and tax the region for operating subsidies. BART promoters aimed, among many goals, to link the East Bay with San Francisco, preserve central city values by aiding suburban/downtown commuting, link poor people to suburban factories, and better integrate university campuses in the metropolis. The construction of the 75-mile system, which began in 1964, was delayed, however, by multiple issues, including the loss of two counties as participants, spiraling costs, an increasingly skeptical state legislature, a legal challenge, and more. Construction even halted between 1967 and 1969 because of insufficient funds.

As in New York, technical innovation added delays. The designers aimed to avoid the high labor costs of legacy systems by relying on automatic controls, but the high-tech, fast, lightweight, air-conditioned cars rolled out slowly because of engineering problems. Total costs soared so much that the original aim of primarily relying on bridge tolls and fares had to be supplemented by a regional sales tax.[190] When the first BART section opened in 1972, there were only 30 cars in operation because of manufacturing delays, "strikes, lawsuits, inflation and a string of fiscal and technical crises."[191] By the late 1970s about $1.6 billion had been spent on the system, with an average cost of $22 million per mile. Federal funds counted for $768 million of the total.[192]

If the BART system had achieved its goals of diverting traffic or otherwise reaffirming center-city land values, it would not serve as a key example in Peter Hall's famous study, *Great Planning Disasters.* The system was carrying roughly half of the predicted passengers in the mid-1970s and required a permanent sales tax subsidy to pay its bills. Hall points out that the subsidies drawn for the system were arguably regressive because "the poor are paying; the rich are riding. . . . BART was designed from the start to connect white-collar suburban commuters with downtown San Francisco and Oakland." Even in 1982 "the effect on traffic is so slight as to be undetectable," as just 2.5 percent of all trips and 5 percent of peak trips were on BART. Hall believed that "the system could have worked, in fact, only if Californians had abandoned Californian living patterns and had taken up European ones." The system was underutilized because the major goals were "preservation of urban centers, the generation of higher property values, prevention of sprawl, better employment conditions and access to social, cultural and recreational facilities," rather than transit efficiency and point-to-point times. BART looks better today, carrying 400,000 daily riders and undergoing extensive modernization, but it still serves a relatively small section of the sprawling Bay region.[193]

The comparative success of California's northern neighbor in mass transit, Oregon, has been widely noted in planning circles. Portland's Tri-Met system (1969), run by a state-controlled transit agency, today provides quality service to three urban counties. Tri-Met, over decades of regional management, transformed failing private bus systems into a national model that today has 77 routes and 683 buses. Tri-Met's now famous light rail service, the roots of which can be tracked to a 1970s transfer of highway funding to transit, has grown from a single line in 1986 to almost 60 miles (2018) that span both city center and many suburbs. This transformation succeeded with a mix of fare box revenues, federal funds, state funds, and a regional payroll tax. The state's essential role is sometimes left out of this story, but it is worth emphasizing that Portland would not be the poster child of American mass transit without state legislative action. The city of Portland, for instance, entirely lacked the funds or authority to develop a regional system of equivalent quality.[194]

Maryland's state-run Maryland Transit Administration, serving the Baltimore region, has a mixed record of development that reflects the complexity of creating new transit systems in automobile-oriented cities. Its challenges and accomplishments are typical for medium-sized, car-oriented American urban areas. The Maryland DOT, through sponsorship of today's Maryland Transit Administration (established 1970), took on "the sole responsibility for providing public transport (bus and rail) in the Baltimore metropolitan" area. Baltimore's declining downtown business center was unable to benefit from an original plan (1971) for a 71-mile regional subway system because only a small section was ever built. The limited, expensive, mostly federally funded section that finally opened in 1983 primarily ran through neighborhoods suffering from disinvestment. These benefits for minority riders should be applauded, but the unimpressive ridership in a very expensive system makes it difficult to justify heavy rail systems like this. The Maryland Transit Administration subsequently added just a few extensions to the subway system but primarily invested in lower-cost options such as a separate low-capacity north–south light rail line and Maryland Area Regional Commuter rail between Washington and Baltimore. Maryland Transit Administration systems thus remain weak competitors with the automobile both within the city and into the suburbs.[195]

Similar mixed outcomes are illustrated further south. The Georgia state legislature laid the groundwork in 1965 for a metropolitan-scale system when it authorized the development of the Metropolitan Atlanta Rapid Transit Authority (MARTA) rail system. The project, initiated in 1971, quickly lost three of five participating counties, leading to a more conservative program of just 48 miles of track. The fast-growing rural/suburban counties refused to join the system because of cost to taxpayers, lifestyle differences, and fear of city (i.e., minority) people and potential crime. The state government, in the years since its creation, has also refused to provide dependable subsidies to the authority. Robert Ashe, MARTA's current board chairman, boasts a 95 percent on-time rate for a system that takes "nearly 400,000 passengers to work, school and other destinations every day" on 350 rail cars and 103 bus routes. Yet the Atlanta region now sprawls over 18 counties, and the millions of drivers there logged 143,994,000 daily vehicle miles traveled in 2012, or 28 miles traveled per day, per capita. MARTA coverage compares unfavorably with the massive highway programs that by 2012 included 6,201 miles of regional interstate/freeway, principal and minor arterials, and collector roads. Atlanta's horrible traffic and air pollution have, however, so damaged the region's national reputation that plans are finally under way to focus growth around MARTA stations, add counties to the system, and expand rail and bus lines.[196]

These valiant efforts on the parts of states, the federal government, and many local governments were not sufficient to create rail or bus systems that can compete with cars. Most rail or bus commuters in the United States moved more slowly, in worse conditions than their peers in private vehicles. The number of American public transit riders on an annual basis dropped from 23 billion to 6.8 billion between 1950 and 1974, despite national population growth, because "the public clearly prefers the automobile at the expense of such public modes as buses, subways, surface rail, and trolleys." State management was insufficient to turn the tide; instead, states prevented the total evaporation of the sector.[197] A slight uptick during the gas crunch during the 1970s (eight billion riders in 1979) turned out to be temporary.[198] Ridership on expensive new rail lines since the 1970s has been offset by the exodus of passengers from frustrating, lackluster bus systems. Ridership levels on mass transit nationally remain about where they had dropped to by the mid-1970s after the massive postwar collapse of mass transit: under one transit trip per person per week.[199]

It is simplistic, however, to blame state officials and transit managers because many factors influencing ridership are beyond their control. Even the much-admired bus and light rails run by the Minneapolis–St. Paul region's Metro Transit (1967) has trouble competing with the excellent roads and decentralized lifestyle in this sprawling midwestern metropolis. The transit system has grown during the past few decades with the help of state, local, and federal operating and capital subsidies. Management has a good reputation. Researchers in a 2010 study found, however, that driving still accounted for 84 percent of all trips in the region and that there were even more walking trips (6 percent) than transit (3 percent). The figures for daily commuters

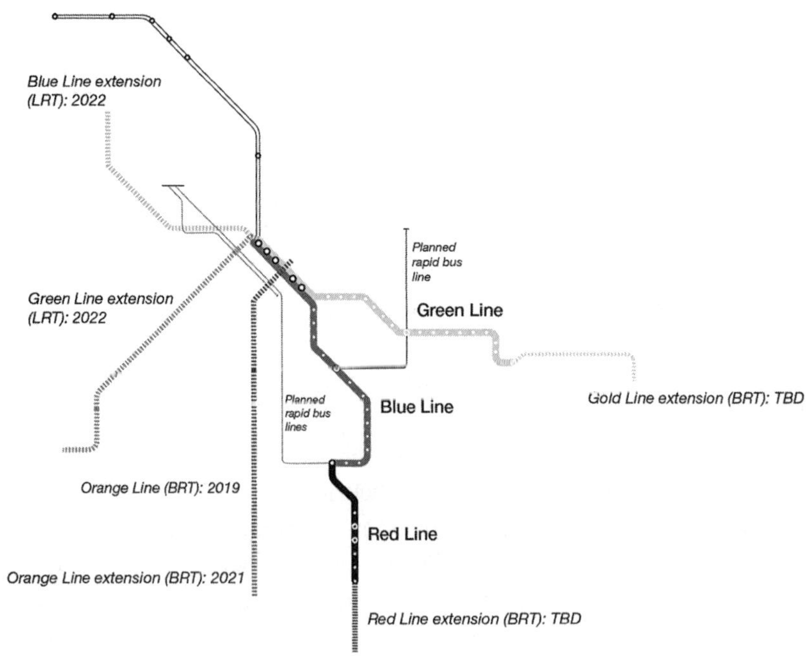

FIGURE 24. Minneapolis Light Rail system with existing and planned additions. Map by Minna Ninova, 2018.

were just as grim: 90 percent in cars and 6 percent on transit. Metro Transit has gained commuting riders since this study (11 percent of commuters in 2016), and transit is expanding, but system ridership remains small compared to automobiles, which remain faster, relatively affordable, more comprehensive, and reliable.[200]

The usual terms by which states entered transit, to maintain vestigial service or enhance downtown business values, undermined the long-term sustainability and expansion of expensive regional systems. State governments had the latent power but lacked the unified political will to create and sustain regional transportation systems that would be competitive in quality or time with the much more deeply subsidized road network. Americans may complain about poor transit service, especially when they can no longer drive for reasons of age or health, but not enough of them depend upon it to make a crucial difference in public policy. We get what we pay for, and most Americans do not pay much to support rail or bus lines. In retrospect, it is impressive to consider how much states have accomplished, and the creativity of many efforts, given the weak political support and small number of transit riders nationally.

7

State Government and the Metropolitan Highway Network

The cautious approach of states in the urban transit business contrasts sharply with their enthusiastic leadership in highway development and maintenance. Many state officials may have recoiled at the high price and political complexity of building and maintaining mass transit systems, often leading to partial or lackluster service, but the same is not true of state highway networks. States engaged in long-term planning, pushed roads through delicate natural and urban locales, funneled and fought for massive subsidies of every imaginable type, and accepted high casualty rates that would be front page news if they happened daily in mass transit.

The high-profile subsidies of the federal government associated with the Interstate Highway Act (1956), and the dominating physical presence of these roads, have often obscured the major planning role and significantly deeper and longer-term subsidies provided by states to highways. State highway departments, for instance, planned the routes of today's federal interstate system in partnership with federal and local officials. States also remain the primary sponsors and managers of designated US highways, despite some federal aid. Many of these state highways formerly served rural areas but now have mostly urban functions for commuting, shopping, and inter/intracity travel across metropolitan areas.

By the 1960s, the combined scale of state and federal highway programs had achieved the fondest hopes of many original advocates. The benefits to growth and circulation to most of the American public were real, and they loved driving almost better than anything else, but the costs of building and maintaining highways were much higher than predicted. Unlike criticism of "gold-plated" mass transit systems, the broad middle-class constituency for roads quietly swallowed significant increases in the gas and related taxes at the state and federal levels, and use of general revenues when needed, to pay for expensive road projects.

State roadbuilding and planning has continued despite significant local resistance to urban interstate construction on the grounds of environmental and social impact. Roads that were successfully plowed through neighborhoods far outnumbered the few highways eventually stopped because of citizen activism (the freeway revolt) or funds diverted to mass transit. Highway expansion programs are still under way in Sunbelt regions like Arizona, Texas, and Florida despite serious environmental impacts. The central role played by states in shaping patterns of metropolitan growth through the planning, construction, and maintenance of highway networks merits greater analysis.

States and the New Metropolis

The impact of the automobile on the shape of American cities was evident by the 1920s and 1930s. The rising generation of suburbanites, unlike their predecessors in railroad or streetcar suburbs, mostly drove and only occasionally rode a trolley, train, or bus. They were delighted to trade in tokens and coins for the comfort and privacy of car commuting: "The population of the central cities of 140 metropolitan areas increased by only two and a half million in the decade from 1930 to 1940, while in the same period the urbanized area outside the central cities gained almost three million."[1]

State leaders accepted early the responsibilities that came with the rise of the infrastructure required for an automobile society, at least outside of major cities. As early as 1917 every American state operated a road department of some type. Oregon led the way when it initiated a gas tax in 1918. Gas taxes and similar user fees provided a protected, steady funding stream that would be crucial for building state and federal roads to the present. States such as New York, Pennsylvania, California, and Connecticut pioneered limited-access parkways and toll roads during the 1920s and 1930s (some with federal help). Direct fees and tolls, and an emerging arrangement of one-to-one federal-state funding (dating first to 1916) did not come close, however, to paying for the emerging state road network. Historian Owen Gutfreund discovered that "between 1921 and 1932 American governments spent $21 billion on streets and highways and collected only $5 billion from motor vehicle users." He concludes that "auto subsidy" from general revenues and municipal bond sales became an accepted practice for state and local government despite the high price tag.[2]

The contrast between the provision of both general revenues for roads and dedicated revenue streams (such as gas taxes) contrasted sharply with

FIGURE 25. American Association of State Highway Officials, United States System of Highways, 1926.

the absence of public transit funding in this era. Roads, cars, and trucks were widely viewed as a populist and progressive movement in this era, freeing up citizens and cities from the domination of horses and mass transportation monopolies. Americans, of course, also loved the comparative freedom (routes and hours), the speed, and the privacy of auto travel. Cars and gas to fuel them were cheap. The federal work programs of the New Deal added new subsidies and favored road projects, which complemented state and local revenues.

The postwar years cemented the reliance on roads. War rationing temporarily restricted motoring and gave many mass transit systems their final hurrah, but a flood of American drivers took to the roads when the fighting stopped: "October of 1946 produced the highest volume of traffic for that month ever recorded for the United States as a whole."[3] Americans were ready to pick up the pace of decentralization, but the country's urban roads were not ready for them. Thomas MacDonald, commissioner of public roads and a legendary force for the federal/state road partnership, reported that "the worst traffic congestion is in the cities" because cars were bogged down "on main city arteries . . . designed for horse-drawn traffic." He already predicted that "construction of expressways at large cost offers the only hope of ultimate solution of large city traffic problems." MacDonald was a diehard highway man, but the facts reflected the dreadful reality in most cities. The nation's city streets counted for 9 percent of all roads but 50 percent of all national traffic.[4]

States in this period funded most highway building with a rural bias, but urban highways received recognition and a small boost with the creation of a new Federal-Aid Highway Act program in 1944. States like Ohio, Kentucky, and Michigan initiated planning for expressway systems during the war years.[5] The first phase of the planned interstate system was a balanced state/federal partnership where states provided a 50 percent match to federal funds. The act provided $500 million for three years and specifically targeted $125 million of the total for urban areas. This sum was far less than needed in cities, and even less was appropriated than called for in the act, but it represented a fundamental shift in the relationship of local, state, and federal governments. Now state governments, with federal urging, would be taking a more critical role in urban traffic. The growth of many of today's state highways can be traced to the federal aid program (often known as the ABC roads).[6]

The balance of road building, even counting these new federal funds, during the first half of the 1950s remained with the states. The network proved adequate to sustain the shift to cars and trucks, although the flood of cars overwhelmed downtowns and many neighborhood surface streets. Surging demand created even more pressure for more roads and accelerated industrial, residential, and commercial decentralization. The process accelerated as rail companies dumped many of the commuter and freight systems. By the early 1950s, 90 percent of the nation's passenger miles were driven on highways, and most of the nation's produce moved in trucks from city to city and countryside to city: "Highways are now as vital to every phase of national activity as railways, or mining, or industry. The economy as we know it cannot function without the automobile and the truck."[7] In this period, almost all highways, even ones with some initial federal aid, were constructed and managed by state highway departments.

States were aggressive in this period as underwriters of the new automobile-based economy at a time when they still provided almost nothing for rail subsidies. State governments funded highways at $2.9 billion in 1952 versus $562 million provided by the federal government. California in 1953, for instance, had launched a $3.4 billion plan ($31.7 billion in 2017 dollars) for 12,000 miles, and Pennsylvania had 12,000 miles of highways under way at a price tag of $1.5 billion ($14 billion in 2017 dollars). States drew heavily on gasoline taxes and registration fees, federal aid programs, and in most cases, general revenues. States like Maine, New Jersey, New York, Ohio, and Pennsylvania also charged tolls on many new turnpikes because "high-speed, limited access highways" were turning out to be "extremely costly."[8]

A radical change in the scale of federal subsidies, the result of active lobbying by the automobile/trucking industries and state highway officials for "free" highways, was enshrined in the Federal-Aid Highway Act, or National Interstate and Defense Highway Act (1956). The act "tremendously increased the amounts available, accelerated the whole program to meet the traffic expected in 1975, and raised the standards of design." A plan for an interstate highway system had emerged in the 1940s, a combined state and federal effort, but only limited sections of designated interstates were built because of high costs and a lack of sufficient federal or state financing. The 90/10 federal/state split in the 1956 act represented the long-awaited federal catalyst. Cities did not get as much as they wanted, but the act was far more aggressive on urban interstate development than anything that came before. Under the 1956 act, which called for an estimated 40,000-mile system, "the interstate highway system was to link most of the state capitals and 90 percent of the cities with populations 50,000 or more and was to include 6700 miles of four–eight lane, limited-access routes through urban areas." Many rural interstates were also arguably on their way to becoming suburban highways because land developed so quickly around extensions and exits. Within a few years of their construction, many sections of rural interstates became effectively suburban

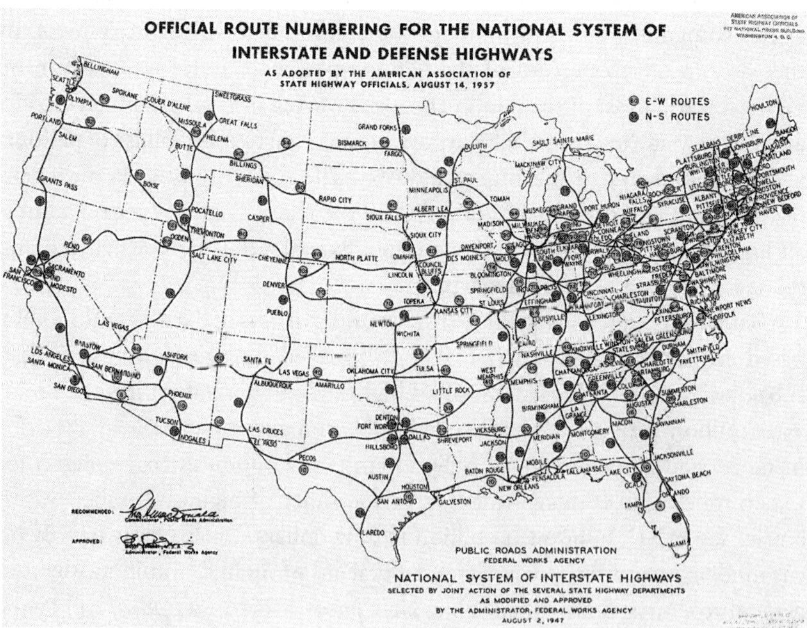

FIGURE 26. The text reflects the federal/state partnership in the selection of routes in what became the federal interstate system. American Association of State Highway Officials, 1957.

in function and audience. Federal officials in fact added additional miles to the interstate system in 1968, mostly for expansion of suburban beltway systems that pushed out the edge of urbanized regions.[9]

Federal interstate funds proved necessary, but it would be incorrect to ignore the crucial and dominant role still played by states in the highway business during this period. According to highway history authorities Mark Rose and Raymond Mohl, "In 1956 . . . Congress and President Eisenhower reaffirmed the long-standing principle that the locus of authority in highway programming rested unambiguously in the hands of state highway officials," who cared about traffic flow and not much else.[10] Not only were state highway departments making critical decisions about interstate location and design, but they were spending more than the federal government to create a comprehensive network of roads that could serve to expand metropolitan areas. In 1962, during one of the greatest eras of federal interstate development, of the approximately $12 billion ($98.9 billion in 2017 dollars) combined in funds spent nationally for highways, the *states* were the largest single source, providing $6.5 billion ($53.5 billion in 2017 dollars), versus $3.3 billion in federal ($27.2 billion in 2017 dollars) and $2.4 billion ($19.7 billion in 2017 dollars) in local funds. The price of roads stressed many states to the limit, but they persevered. America would still have become a highway nation even without the Interstate Highway Act of 1956.[11]

State Highways and the Urban/Suburban Network

New York was a highway pioneer, but in most respects its experience with highway development was typical. We see in New York the pioneering of urban parkways and toll roads, the influential role of state highways in urban development, the massive scale of the state's commitment to roads versus mass transit, and the consequences of such a large-scale state commitment to the fortunes of cities and suburbs.

Robert Moses was a leader in the national movement for high-speed roads, yet he mostly built state highways and parkways—laying the groundwork for lasting intervention of state government in regional road networks in and around the state's big cities. His works came to include many landscaped, limited-access parkways, magnificent highway suspension bridges, and high-speed tunnels. In the New York metropolitan area, Moses controlled parkways, the federal interstate highway program, and the Triborough Bridge and Tunnel Authority.

The notion that Moses single-handedly drove highways through urban neighborhoods is a myth encouraged by the vivid storytelling in Robert

Caro's *The Powerbroker* (1974). Powerful organizations had in fact supported high-speed roads since the 1920s, including the Port Authority, the Regional Plan Association, and the City Planning Commission. Moses, as postwar construction coordinator, joined with the Port Authority to forge a powerful "highway coalition" that pushed local, state, and federal officials for more funding.[12] Most of New York's city political leaders until the 1960s encouraged limited-access highways within city limits as tools for linking booming suburbs and downtown, reducing local traffic, and creating new social boundaries in a time of white flight. Most suburbanites, including those living in subdivisions within the corporate limits of the city of New York, welcomed the creation of a complex road network that would allow them to live in green subdivisions so close to America's largest business center.[13]

Robert Moses also had many allies in Albany. Governor Dewey's construction of the New York State Thruway, the first section of which opened in 1954, had been funded almost entirely by bonds sold based upon future toll revenues. During the first half of the 1960s, Governor Rockefeller, like his contemporaries across the nation, pursued transport policies that prioritized planning and construction of high-speed expressways. Rockefeller drove fancy cars or was chauffeured or flew above it all his entire life despite having residences in transit-friendly districts of New York City and Westchester County. His family's fortunes, through Standard Oil and its descendant corporations such as Exxon, were multiplied by the rise of the internal combustion engine. He even allowed a sizable four-lane highway to be constructed through his family's rural property in Westchester County both to divert traffic around the central section of the estate and, perhaps more crucially, as part of a projected expressway on the east side of the Hudson.

Boasting multiple times of a "record highway program" in the early years of the Rockefeller administration, the state's Department of Public Works spent approximately $1 billion per year in 1959 and 1960 for new highways using a mix of state and federal money. The New York State sections of the national system of interstate and defense highways was 90 percent federally funded, so the state had a financial incentive to think even bigger about roads. Interstates such as the Northway and North–South Expressway opened "new areas, particularly upstate" and linked New York with the industrial areas of Canada.[14] From 1959 to 1964, the state awarded contracts for 6,994 miles of highways, or an average of 1,199 new highway miles per year.[15] In 1965, the state even eliminated a 50 percent funding requirement by local government for arterial highway land acquisition, thus accelerating highway development sought by city leaders.[16]

A great many of these new highways, by design, were urban. From 1959 to

1963, the state claimed to have launched the "greatest arterial highway construction program—122 projects in 28 cities." In New York's northern suburbs the list of new or expanded state roads included major investments in the Taconic and Heckscher Parkways and the vital Cross Westchester highway to tie together many north–south routes. Robert Moses in New York City built out sections of the Clearview and the Cross Bronx, among many center-city highway projects.[17] Moses tied together these various systems through the creation of dramatic suspension bridges. By the mid-1960s, the "highway coalition could look on results with satisfaction: the Verrazano-Narrows Bridge (1965) . . . the Throgs Neck Bridge (1961) . . . [and] second deck on the George Washington Bridge." Staten Island experienced a suburban development boom once it was connected to Brooklyn and New Jersey by new highways and bridges.[18]

Long Island had gotten a fast start in suburban growth before the Second World War with the launching of Moses's Grand Central / Northern State and Belt / Southern State parkways. Moses in the 1950s and 1960s pushed the Long Island Expressway, with federal funds and Rockefeller's support, through Nassau County and into the more distant agricultural lands of Suffolk County. State and federal contributions to roads in the New York City-Nassau-Suffolk area totaled $781 million between 1957 and 1963.[19] One estimate counted roughly $200 million ($1.5 billion in 2017 dollars) in highway expansion still under way in 1966 on Long Island alone, thus bringing into the suburban orbit lands farther east in Suffolk County.[20] Assembly Speaker Joseph Carlino called the Long Island Expressway "the Island's main economic artery through which will flow the very life-blood of commerce."[21]

Today, New York State remains a key player on Long Island in the many parkways, the Long Island Expressway, and a network of state highways. The DOT pays 1,000 people in the Region 10 Long Island area to maintain and supervise 5,300 state highway lane miles and 546 bridges located there. These serve as crucial elements of the road network for the 2.8 million people in Nassau and Suffolk Counties in 95 incorporated villages, 13 towns, and 2 cities. Just maintaining this state system of roads is an enormous expense. Roughly 1,800 lane miles and 156 bridges have been rebuilt or replaced since 1995. The representative map from the district reflects the crucial role of the state in this suburban district. The maintenance of these roads represents another hidden state subsidy for the suburban lifestyle, as there is not as robust a network of similar state highways within city limits.[22] A similar pattern of state investment in suburban Westchester County created a powerful combination of federal interstates, state parkways, and state/US highways.

The state took an equally aggressive role in rebuilding upstate cities. The

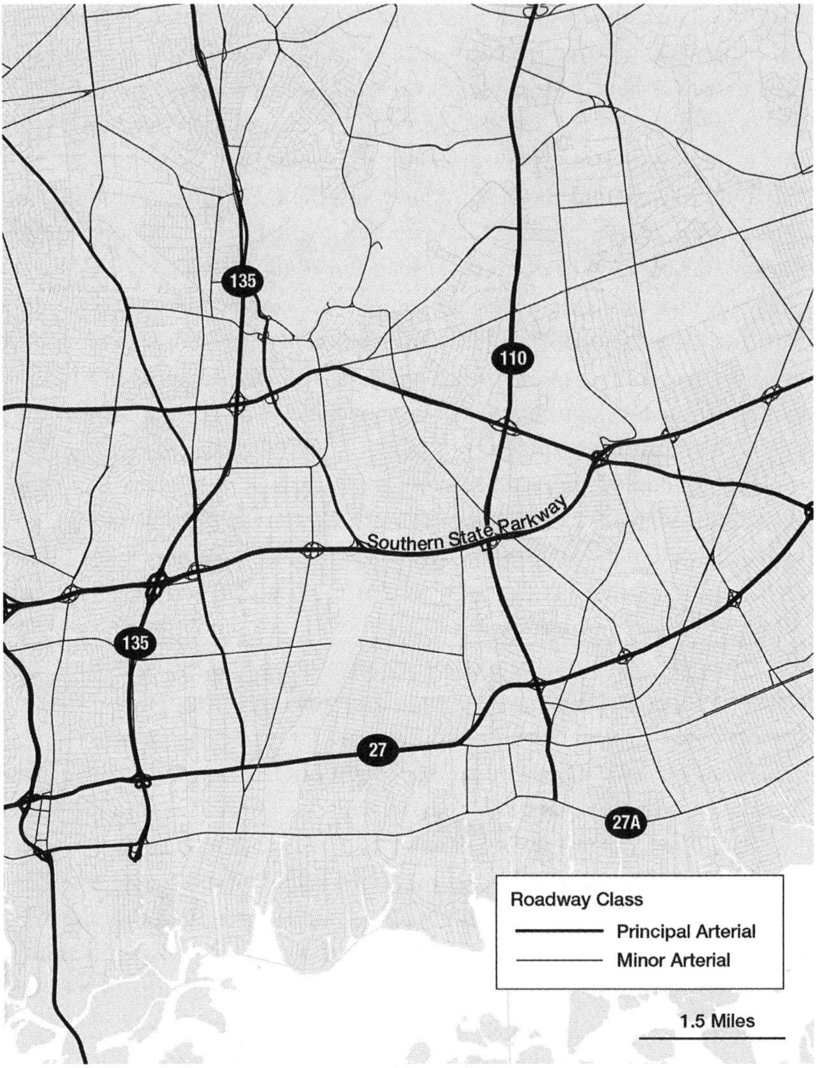

FIGURE 27. Long Island's state highway network, as in most states, is crucial to suburban functionality. The principal arteries on the map, running both east–west and north–south, are primarily state-supported roads. Map by Minna Ninova, 2018.

highway network ended up overbuilt in cities like Albany, Syracuse, Rochester, and Buffalo because of the dramatic loss of industry and population that eventually gripped most of these center cities during the postwar years. Syracuse's story is typical of upstate cities (and most medium-size cities across the Northeast). During the 1940s the state Department of Public Works prepared detailed plans for limited-access expressways running north–south and east–

west through Syracuse. The state also advanced funds in the late 1940s to turn selected Syracuse streets into "arterials" that would feed into the expressway system. During the 1950s, state and local officials used highway development programs to clear minority neighborhoods as part of urban renewal. City officials were eager to get their share of federal highway construction activity. Rockefeller pumped record amounts of money into the Syracuse project: "By the mid-1960s, the center of Syracuse was the site of high-speed divided overhead interstate highways running north-south and east-west." Ethnic neighborhoods along the route were trashed, and the city continued to lose people and businesses. Many who had formerly supported the roads had become skeptical. Most of the roads were too far advanced to stop and large areas of the downtown were given over for parking. The downtowns of Schenectady, Albany, Rochester, and Buffalo were similarly reshaped thanks to highways and the combined impact of federal/state urban renewal. Many of these cleared areas, unfortunately, remained low-value surface parking for decades.[23]

Backlash

New Yorkers took to the roads in record numbers, and the access afforded by roadways created a higher standard of living for an emergent middle class, but the enthusiasm for road building had its limits. Rockefeller, in aggressively pursuing roads, ignored an expert report in 1960 that warned: "The grim traffic situation in our cities will not be alleviated by building more and larger highways since these only encourage a greater number of motorists to drive downtown."[24] Highways intended to enhance downtown/suburban links also contributed to a hollowing out of the core by destroying the quality of neighborhoods and bringing new land within reach of developers. Roadway expansion began to stall out as wealthy and articulate urban and suburban residents turned against new bridges or roads that might speed cars on a regional basis. Lawsuits and raucous public meetings were a political liability for both Moses and Rockefeller. Many roads were already so advanced that stopping them was unlikely, but resistance can be read today in the missing pieces in the regional road network. Similar dead ends or incomplete systems can be found in cities across the nation.

Road builders like Moses and Rockefeller created the baseline highway network but in the longer term failed to maintain the necessary scale of highway construction or expansion to keep pace with the skyrocketing pace of car ownership. Both men fought battles over road and bridge expansions in Manhattan, Staten Island, Brooklyn, Queens, Fire Island, Long Island, and Westchester County. The result was a growing list of canceled or delayed

One of the most important Interchanges on the Niagara Section, Oak-Elm Streets, gives a heavy volume of traffic easy access to the heart of downtown Buffalo.

FIGURE 28. Highway construction in upstate cities like Buffalo smoothed the flow of suburban commuters in and out of downtown but came at a high cost to many old neighborhoods. New York State Thruway, 12th Annual Report, 1971. New York State Archives, courtesy of the Rockefeller Archive Center.

roads. Rockefeller chastised Long Island residents in 1969 because "you want roads. But when those roads are going to go through your community, you don't want them. And I can make more friends today by canceling roads, the construction of roads, than I can by building them."[25]

Neighborhood pushback, in time, damaged the operation of the urban interstate network by pulling out key links such as the Clearview Expressway extension to JFK International Airport, the Lower Manhattan Expressway, the Mid-Manhattan Expressway, the Bushwick Expressway, and the Cross-Brooklyn Expressway. Some losses were more serious than others. Crowding of taxis, cars, and trucks on the Van Wyck Expressway to JFK International Airport, which might have been relieved by the completion of the Clearview, made that airport less efficient and attractive to passengers and freight traffic for decades compared to Newark and its national peers. Even the completion of these routes would not, of course, have necessarily solved the traffic problem, because of induced demand, but the lack of connections made the aim of a seamless flow of trucks and cars across and around the city impossible except at off hours. Cars and trucks that managed to get to the city often headed onto already crowded city surface streets, undermining one of the primary goals of interstates in the first place. Many neighborhoods, even today, are plagued by slow-moving truck traffic on crosstown or otherwise non-local routes.

In the suburbs, roads also ran up against a growing environmental movement made even more potent by the deep pockets of those impacted by road projects. Cars were the lifeblood of suburban communities, but roads also had the potential to rob homeowners of their hard-won tranquility. Rockefeller, for instance, did nothing to stop Interstate 87 blasting through scenic Chestnut Ridge in Westchester County, taking with it the serenity of beautiful estates in the horsey towns of Bedford and North Castle.

Suburban activists scored some crucial victories. They secured federal designation to stop Rockefeller's and Robert Moses's highway plans for isolated Fire Island that likely would have brought more dense development. The result was the Fire Island National Seashore Act of 1964, a landmark bill that brought federal control over local development and zoning. On the north and south shores of Long Island, environmentalists spent years to win federal protection for natural areas to stop a large cross-sound bridge also favored by Moses and Rockefeller.[26] In his backyard, Rockefeller encouraged a proposal for a Hudson waterfront expressway from Tarrytown to Beacon that was only killed in 1971, and then after a few highway sections had already cut off Peekskill and Croton on Harmon from their waterfronts further north.[27]

The number and timing of cancellations like these were not sufficient to save most of the areas designated for highways in the postwar period; nor did they prevent the creation of auto-dependent suburban towns and villages and the lifestyle that went with it.

Shaping City Regions

Aggressive state highway building in other states easily matched that in New York. A 1972 National Transportation Report discovered that driving dominated all modes of travel by 10 to 1. In the nation's sprawling urban areas, 98 percent (94 auto, 4 percent bus) of travel was on roads. Even in most big cities with surviving mass transit, rail and bus carried a low percentage of daily commuters.[28]

The sprawling profile of most American cities created a dramatic role for state governments in America's Sunbelt, for instance. In areas of high growth, state highway divisions that formerly focused upon rural roads upgraded both interstates and state highways to meet increasing traffic demands in and

MAJOR PROJECTS UNDERWAY:

- US 290: reconstruction and widening from I-610 to FM 2920 - $2.4 billion
  - Anticipated completion: 2018
- SH 288 toll lanes in Harris County: construct 4 toll lanes from US 59 to Harris/Brazoria County line. Comprehensive Development Agreement for $815 million.
  - Construction began October 2016
  - Anticipated completion: Late 2018
- I-45 South: widening from Nyack to FM 2351 - $77 million
  - Anticipated completion: Summer 2017
- I-45 South: widening from El Dorado to Medical Center Drive - $93 million
  - Anticipated completion: Fall 2018
- US 59/I-69S: widening from FM 762 to Spur 10 - $135 million
  - Anticipated completion: 2018

PLANNED MAJOR PROJECTS:

- US 59/I-610 West Loop Interchamge reconstruction*: estimated cost $287 million
  - Anticipated letting: Summer 2017 with completion targeted for Spring 2021
- I-45 South*: Nasa Road 1 to FM 518; estimated project cost $132 million
  - Anticipated letting: Spring 2017 with completion targeted for Summer 2022
- I-10 West*: FM 359 to Brazos River; estimated project cost $242 million
  - Anticipated letting: Summer 2017 with completion targeted for Spring 2021
- SH 99/Grand Parkway Segments H and I: design-build contract to construct 6.5 miles of new toll lanes; estimated cost $1.1 billion
  - Conditional award and start of construction anticipated in FY 2017
- SH 249 in Montgomery County and Grimes County: estimated cost $400 million
  - Conditional award and start of construction anticipated in FY 2017
- I-45 North: from downtown to Beltway 8
  - Currently in environmental impact statement phase; anticipating clearance in FY 2018

FIGURE 29. Houston (2016), like most American urban regions, benefits from an extensive state highway program. Image adapted by Minna Ninova from information provided by the Texas Department of Transportation, 2018.

around cities. They were eager to accommodate suburban growth by widening roadways on the periphery, including the addition of beltways. Even a massive displacement crisis due to road construction only stopped a few highways. Approximately 37,000 people, disproportionately low-income and minority, were displaced annually in the 1960s by urban segments of the interstate system. In response to massive resistance to highways in the 1960s, the federal government finally allowed a modest diversion of highway funds to mass transit, paid for regional transportation planning (usually toothless except when it encouraged growth), offered some more money for relocation, attacked clutter along highways, canceled a few urban interstates, and made other window-dressing efforts. Highways mostly grew where they had been planned, and most remain in place to this day. Our cities would look very different had there been more than just a couple of roadways canceled on the waterfronts of cities such as Portland, Baltimore, New Orleans, and San Francisco.[29]

Owen Gutfreund's portrait of Denver in *20th Century Sprawl* illustrates how a city shifted rapidly from streetcars to auto dependence. Mayors and governors, under pressure from a growing automobile lobby, began paving and widening roads, added traffic lights, and redesigned circulation to the benefit of cars and trucks in the first half of the twentieth century. Denver leaders accepted their responsibility for roads even though they were not receiving a fair share of state highway funds compared to rural areas. The era of interstates and federal funds hastened the trend. New interstates, including an additional beltway loop added in the late 1960s, prioritized suburban locations, new office parks, subdivisions, shopping centers, and defense plants at the expense of the city's downtown. State officials further encouraged decentralization by allowing developers to borrow vast sums to develop infrastructure in remote sites. By contrast, city and state officials did everything they could to hasten the demise, and nothing to save, the streetcar companies. The state's regional transit system (1969) was funded at a shallow level and thus served a tiny portion of the metropolitan area's riders. Denver has an aggressive program of light rail under way today, but it will have trouble diverting large numbers of passengers, as the region's form is already entirely built around the highway network—and it continues to sprawl outward.[30]

These patterns were repeated nationally. States remain deeply engaged in road building as an adjunct to urban development. Around both Houston and Dallas, for instance, the Texas DOT has a large footprint that has enabled the region to grow at record pace. The Dallas region in 2016 amassed $1.6 billion in construction and maintenance costs for 10,624 lane miles (and

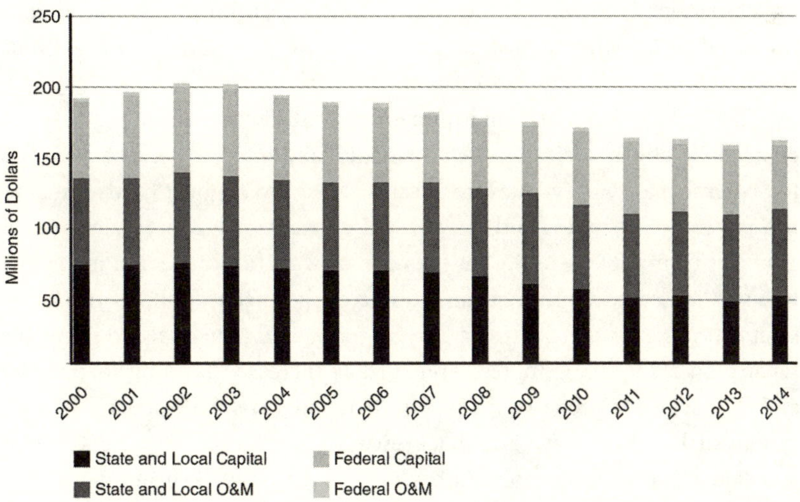

FIGURE 30. States and local government are still the main sources of funding for America's highways. Infrastructure Report Card, adapted by Minna Ninova, 2018.

over 6,000 bridges) in a mix of interstates and state highways. The DOT was engaged in major extension and widening programs of the interstates, US highways, and state highways to accommodate growing suburban and urban traffic. Another 10,567 lane miles around Houston absorbed an additional $1.6 billion in maintenance and construction funds for a similar mix of interstates, US highways, and state highways. The expansion of US highways and state highways, including new interchanges, is an essential element in supporting the interstates and opening new areas for development.

The Favorite Son

The costs of the highway building campaigns exceeded initial estimates. By the mid-1960s, it was already clear that the interstate system would consume billions more than projected. The cost of land acquisition was higher than expected; rising engineering and construction costs were also blamed. The result was not cancellation or diminishment of programs as it often was for mass transit projects. Instead, the federal and state administrations made up the difference and provided more money for relocation.[31] America built not just 40,000 but 42,500 miles of interstates, including a larger than anticipated number of metropolitan beltways with nominal "interstate" functions.

State and local government continued to carry the burden of maintaining road networks. The federal government covered 90 percent of the costs of building interstates but often failed to cover the associated increases that came from maintaining the network. By 1971–1972, state and local governments nationally were covering $12.3 billion ($75.6 billion in 2017 dollars) in capital costs, while the federal government was spending just $2.6 billion ($15.9 billion in 2017 dollars) for interstate development.[32]

The 1970s inflationary environment proved disastrous for highway cost controls. Highway maintenance costs nationally rose 328 percent from 1967 to September 1979. Revenues from various taxes to support roads remained flat as people drove less and bought fuel-efficient cars. Most states boosted gas taxes from 1968 to 1978, "yet the revenue was still considered inadequate to cover increased highway costs." Some of the first sections of the federal interstate system were nearing a 20-year mark, and many needed significant repairs. In response, Congress dramatically increased funding for highway and interstate maintenance in 1978.[33] A national state and federal highway system sucked money at a rate that even advocates found sobering. Congress and state leaders found more money even as the price of sustaining such an enormous system came into focus.[34]

Today, state and local governments remain the key source of funds for

FIGURE 31. SUNY Binghamton reflects the national preference for large, peripheral campuses linked to interstate highway networks. Aerial by State University Construction Fund, 1972. Courtesy of the New York State Archives.

highways. Capital spending in 2014 was split between federal ($43.5 billion) and state and local ($48.3 billion) governments, but state and local funding of highways for operation and maintenance was $70 billion, compared to just $2.7 billion by the federal government. The states and federal government often use general revenues to supplement various fees and taxes paid by drivers. Toll highways are coming back into fashion to meet escalating demand. The failure to raise the federal gas tax since 1993 is often blamed for this imbalance. The American Society of Civil Engineers (ASCE) says the nation's existing highways alone have a $420 billion repair backlog. ASCE envisions another $167 billion for expansion to handle the additional traffic: "More than two out of every five miles of America's urban interstates are congested and traffic delays cost the country $160 billion in wasted time and fuel in 2014. One out of every five miles of highway pavement is in poor condition."[35]

A few progressive planners doubt that highway expansion can ever resolve traffic problems, as drivers inevitably crowd new roads, but the question on the minds of the public, civil engineers, and most politicians remains how to fix, expand, and improve the highway network, not a search for alternative modes of travel. Since 1980 Americans have been driving more, not less: "The number of miles Americans drive has grown three times faster than population, and almost twice as fast as vehicle registrations."[36] Those who dream of a Europeanized America should control their excitement. Electric, hybrid, and self-driving cars are likely to increase miles driven, along with distances between work and home. Politicians in both cities and suburbs understand that road maintenance, and in some regions, constant expansion, is a key element of the American creed.

Higher Education

8

The Metropolitan State University System

A short drive in any metropolitan area of the United States can take a college student to a sprawling parking lot serving a state-subsidized higher education campus. The unprecedented rise in the scale of these systems is a direct result of concerted state initiative. The federal government's crucial role in expanding access to higher education through the GI Bill, federal student loan programs, and defense-related research is already famous. Overlooked, or at least deemphasized, in the story has been the parallel role state governments played in building America's high-quality, metropolitan-scale, democratic public higher education system.

State governments after World War II provided the largest share of capital and operating costs for America's public higher education systems, set up financing vehicles to build new campuses at record speed, determined the location and number of campuses, selected the architectural and planning concepts, and set the rules on student demographics, degrees, research focus, faculty roles, diversity, and more. The differences in quality, quantity, and accessibility of higher education across the nation reflect the importance of state decision making. Variations aside, generations of Americans have become accustomed to public-supported state colleges as dependable, convenient, low-cost fixtures of their surroundings.

These campuses and affiliated medical centers are as ubiquitous in the suburbs and some cities as fast food chains, shopping malls, and interstate highways. The growing size and number of campuses eventually gave them crucial roles in regional economic development, ambiance, health care, and culture. To build, maintain, and expand so many campuses engaged the talents of politicians, administrators, professors, architects, lawyers, and many others. State systems now produce the bulk of America's trained workforce in both cities and suburbs. Political leaders of both parties have largely endorsed state university expansion as an unmitigated good, a rare area of agreement in government policy. Erase state-sponsored universities from the American metropolis, both in center cities and suburbs, and they would be very different indeed.

Expanding public higher education systems was a widely shared state goal in the postwar era. In the 1945–1946 school year, state governments sponsored just 624 higher education institutions nationally, but that number rose quickly during the postwar years.[1] Massive increases in operating and capital spending made expansion possible. Between 1959–1960 and 1969–1970, states increased spending on higher education by 337 percent. The result of the shift was a greater dominance of the public sector in higher education. The ratio of public to private college students enrolled nationally changed from four to three in 1960 to five to two in 1968.[2]

The federal government was a crucial partner in this extraordinary growth. By 1963–1964, Federal funds counted for 22 percent of operating costs at universities, and universities swallowed up three-quarters of federal research funds.[3] Universities nationally enjoyed approximately $3 billion ($23 billion in 2017 dollars) in federal research aid by 1966 from agencies such as the National Science Foundation, Department of Defense, National Aeronautics and Space Administration (NASA), and Atomic Energy Commission (AEC).[4] The Higher Education Facilities Act of 1963 helped build the big new campuses with "a combination of federal matching grants and loans for the construction of facilities for undergraduate instruction in science, mathematics and foreign languages." The federal government even kicked in funds for buildings related to graduate research.[5] Federal loans and grants to students provided another steady operating subsidy to the state university systems as tuition rose. By 1979, federal Office of Education student aid grants "reached 3.9 billion, more than four times the 1972 level. This total does not include the $4 billion in support of student loans."[6] The federal/state higher education partnership proved remarkably durable, popular, and productive throughout the postwar era, but the stories of federal largess have overshadowed the cumulatively more substantial commitment of American states to higher education.

The Rockefeller administration's redesign and expansion of the State University of New York system in the 1960s exemplifies the expansionist mood in state-supported public education across the United States. The scale of the SUNY system had few rivals, but in other dimensions it was more similar to than different from other state university initiatives. As at SUNY, promoters of higher education expansion in other states started with bold plans, created innovative financing schemes, built modern campuses, and favored metropolitan areas over rural collegiate traditions in their plans. As at SUNY, administrators elsewhere faced long-term challenges maintaining political support, balancing demand with budget realism, and answering calls for diversity and equity. Most states, including New York, also had to wait longer than anticipated to meet promised technology transfer goals. In the long run, as in New York, states that invested deeply reaped major long-term economic gains, metropolitan anchors, and a better-educated population.[7]

SUNY and Urban Interests

SUNY is not widely viewed as an urban-oriented system because most of its campuses are in the suburbs or small towns upstate, but the system would never have amounted to much without New York City. The city's ethnic and religious minorities, outraged by discriminatory practices in New York's dominant private education system, identified a new state university as a priority in the 1930s. They faced off, however, against conservative private colleges and universities that belonged to the Association of Colleges and Universities of the State of New York. Private colleges and universities at the time generated most of the state's college graduates, absorbed many public subsidies, dominated statewide policy through the Board of Regents, and openly maintained quota systems to limit ethnic students. The state government only supported small "normal" schools (for teacher training), agricultural training schools, and agriculture and forestry research/training in partnership with Cornell and Syracuse.[8]

The Second World War temporarily muted debates over higher education, but as the GIs came home, urban civil rights leaders returned to the field of battle. They attacked the private schools' ethnic quota systems successfully by "building on the rhetoric of the recent conflict between democracy and fascist racism." Discrimination against Jewish and African American students in the private colleges was dubbed "Hitlerite" and contrary to the dominant postwar ideology of ethnic assimilation and social mobility. Governor Dewey had deferred to the private colleges and upstate interests, but Jewish activists and others forced his hand in exchange for their political support.[9]

Governor Dewey established the Temporary Commission on the Need for a State University in 1946 to debate, and many thought delay, the difficult political decisions about the future of higher education. The commissioners were politically divided, Dewey noncommittal on many points, and so much back-channel pressure came from both sides that progress was slow. The leaders of many private schools believed that opening the gates to Jews would lead to a flood of Semites on their campuses. Father Robert Gannon, president of Fordham University, who served on the committee, aimed to "prevent the creation of this absurdly expensive Jewish university," referring to plans for SUNY.[10]

Because most private colleges failed to expand on a permanent basis to accommodate growing numbers of veteran students, a comparatively narrow fight over civil rights turned into a broader debate about access to quality higher education of any kind. The commission's staff demonstrated that in 1946 the combined public/private systems were already 64 percent overfilled and many veterans lacked access to affordable education in the state. Many of the best students headed out of state. The combined private/public system in New York as it existed would fail to meet the future demand of roughly twice the number of students seeking higher education expected by 1960.[11]

New York was a laggard in this arena of state activity. State-subsidized systems in California, Michigan, and Wisconsin expanded more impressively for returning veterans. By embracing growth, they also took full advantage of $14.5 billion for the GI Bill in the first decade of the program—an economic boost for these states. New York had expanded some temporary technical institutes following the war, and private schools had stretched a little, but the state lacked the number or scale of public or private institutions to handle significant expansion.[12]

The Truman administration's *Higher Education for American Democracy* report, calling for a major expansion in federally supported higher education and endorsing community colleges, is believed to have finally pushed Dewey (and state leaders nationally) off the fence. Truman was Dewey's political rival, and although the federal program proposed in the report remained hypothetical, it gave Truman an edge. Dewey and the legislature now pushed past continuing resistance from the private schools to create SUNY in 1948, including a SUNY Board of Trustees, integration of the "normal" (teacher education) schools into SUNY, expansion of medical education, and responsibility for the expansion of county-based community colleges.[13]

Governor Dewey's creation of the SUNY system in 1948, the result of horse-trading among different interest groups, bore the marks of compromise. The new SUNY did not fundamentally change the relationship of state-sponsored higher education to leading private schools or urban areas. During the 1950s, SUNY still supervised an uneven and uncoordinated set of teaching and agricultural colleges, mostly in small towns upstate. SUNY's leaders made crucial forays, however, into the domain of private institutions. They created Harpur College in 1950 (which started as an extension of Syracuse University in 1946) in Binghamton as the state's only public liberal arts institution; opened medical and dental training centers (private medical colleges converted to public control, upstate in Syracuse and downstate in Brooklyn); and planned the nucleus of a new university on Long Island in science, engineering, and education at the Planting Fields estate (later moved to Stony Brook) to meet growing suburban demand.

The total budget of SUNY, despite growing responsibility, rose very slowly between 1949 and 1959, rising from $29 million ($303 million in 2017 dollars) to $44 million ($376 million in 2017 dollars). Anemic growth of the total student body from 26,000 to 39,000 in these years reflected the insufficient support and damaging compromises with the private schools.[14] Private colleges even pushed back on a consultant report in 1957 recommending a central campus to enhance SUNY's research profile, as it was clear that New York was not keeping pace with the development of research flagships in other states. SUNY president William Carlson, who supported the flagship idea, was fired that year.[15]

The SUNY trustees created pressure during the 1950s for the expansion of state-supported liberal arts by investing in the state's community college system. States in the West and Midwest, like California and Illinois, created model community college systems; SUNY did what it could under its budgetary and political constraints. Administrators converted temporary postwar institutes of applied arts into permanent community colleges at urban sites such as Binghamton, Buffalo, New York City, Utica, and White Plains and in many rural counties, bringing the number to 18 by 1960. Local or county governments operated the community colleges, with the state government generously contributing one-third of the operating and half of the capital costs to build whole new campuses. The community colleges, with minor admission requirements, addressed the need for some advanced education, including vocational options, for high school graduates who were less prepared, poorer, or less motivated to attend traditional colleges with higher standards.

The community college system was an acknowledgment that strong hands and backs were insufficient in a society of greater technological sophistication. Cheap cars, vast parking lots, and new highways made suburban community colleges hum with life as students tacked back and forth from home to work to school. Community colleges rose in every county of New York State, regardless of population, but the largest of the community colleges, such as Nassau Community College and the Borough of Manhattan Community College, grew rapidly in and around the state's largest cities. The community colleges were ideal for families who could not afford to pay for their new homes, cars, and consumer goods as well as tuition and dorm charges. They were also suitable for students who, for one reason or another, were not prepared for a typical four-year education. Adult women and other nontraditional students with time and money to advance their careers poured in as well.

The Intellectual Capital for Capitalism

The growth of New York's community college system exposed the gap in state-funded upper-level higher education as these students added credits and associate degrees to their achievements.[16] The number of K–12 students in New York State increased from 2,465,000 in 1950 to 3,503,000 in 1960, with 80,000 more students per year expected in the school system during the 1960s. Just educating these students in the K–12 system would prove a challenge, demanding as many as 12,000 additional teachers per year, taxing the capacity of the state's public and private teacher colleges. The state government deeply subsidized high-quality K–12 education across the state, including generous grants for new school buildings demanded in fast-growing suburbs. Quality instruction created pressure for improved access for higher education.[17]

More of these metropolitan students were also likely to attend college to compete for good jobs in a service-oriented, professional society. In 1950, for instance, 40.8 percent of 18-to-21-year-olds attended some college, but by 1960 that number had jumped to 55 percent. More students, and more in college, meant larger colleges.[18] The growing number of women attending college in this period played an essential role in this change. New York was still exporting tens of thousands of talented students to public and private colleges across the country—a potentially dangerous sign for the region's future should this pattern continue.[19]

A reinvented SUNY during the Rockefeller years now rested on two major foundations: deploying universities as key elements of statewide economic development and meeting baby boomer demand in modern metropolitan areas, mostly in fast-growing suburbs. Concerns about discrimination against urban minorities may have dominated the debates in 1948, providing the impetus for SUNY's creation, but social equity was just one of many reasons, and not the most important one, for SUNY's massive expansion during the Rockefeller years. Jews and other European ethnic minorities were quickly becoming "white" and suburban, thanks in no small measure to Dewey-era higher-education antidiscrimination legislation signed in 1948. The pressure in the late 1950s and early 1960s was part of a general liberal preference for activist government assuming a broader role in daily life (akin to the new role of government in urban services like mass transit and housing) rather than an ethnic strategy of social mobility.

Rockefeller and his administration gazed longingly on the prime contracts for military research lavished on the University of California system that helped build laboratories and whole campuses, the state's international reputation, and broader economic development made possible by skilled labor, technology transfer, and statewide university employment. Governor Edmund "Pat" Brown built on the strategic planning of his predecessor Governor Earl Warren to expand the scale and quality of the system. Clark Kerr, as the new president of the system in 1957, became the force behind the admired *Master Plan for Higher Education in California: 1960–1975*. The master plan, as adopted in 1960, sustained open admissions for the growing number of state high school graduates to the community college system while retaining selectivity in a fast-growing four-year state college and university systems. Most large California campuses sprouted in urban or suburban locations (Berkeley, Los Angeles, Santa Barbara, Irvine, Long Beach, Riverside, Davis, San Diego, etc.), a striking change from the pastoral campuses of the Northeast and much of the rest of the nation. California's three-tiered system of community colleges, state colleges, and universities was America's best, but even the large "flagship" schools in many states (such as in Madison, Wisconsin, and Ann Arbor, Michigan) cast New York's lackluster system in a harsh light.

New York's delay can be explained in the unprecedented national shift to a high-technology service economy. New York State's older factories remained at full tilt after World War II, creating a false sense of security. The state in fact possessed "an industrial plant older and more outmoded than the burgeoning new industrial areas of the land could boast." California's booming cities, for instance, tested New York's supremacy by competing in new industries demanding more scientific and management talent. California in the early 1960s had captured 21 percent of the nation's electronics production, 23 percent of the nation's defense contracts, 25 percent of NASA contracts, and the primary operations of three of the top five defense contractors. These Cold War contracts employed and developed a highly trained workforce, successful civilian applications, and related university and private research and development labs. Rockefeller and his team never mentioned the Stanford Industrial Park, as it was still small, but a growing dimension of California's higher education reputation was derived from technology transfer as pioneered in the aerospace industry and at privately run Stanford University. Texas also benefited from military spending and contracting that, combined with its booming oil business, spurred massive urban growth, including a rapidly expanding system of public higher education. North Carolina's Research Triangle was snowballing with a heady blend of fast-growing universities, government contracts, and private investments. The affluent urban society for these reasons was heading to these and other Sunbelt states.[20]

Cutting-edge private research labs at General Electric, IBM, Corning Glass, General Telephone, Eastman Kodak, and Sperry Rand were a source of complacency in New York; so too were the federally sponsored Brookhaven National Laboratory on Long Island and the research programs at Cornell, Syracuse, Columbia, and New York University Medical. So "although New York's knowledge industry has not been able to match that of California in its ability to capture prime military contract, the state has done reasonably well compared to the rest of the country." In 1964, for instance, New York managed to secure 10 percent of the nation's prime military contracts, 9 percent of the research and development contracts by the Department of Defense to education, and 6 percent of the nation's space contracts. These proportions aligned with the state's 9.4 percent share of the national population. New York's companies were also at the forefront of research in computers and profitable industries that would streamline office work in the postwar era. It was IBM's Eliot Noyes, after all, who designed the IBM Selectric typewriter (1961) that revolutionized office productivity and dominated office landscapes for decades. New York's Xerox corporation introduced the Xerox 914 (1960), the first production copy machine. Such advanced thinking, however, could not be taken for granted as the country's resources tilted to the sunny, air-conditioned West and South. IBM, for instance, built a modern plant in Austin, Texas, to produce and refine its Selectric line. Modern businesses would remain upstate only if the surrounding environment contained a superior level of well-trained managers, engineers, and scientists. The state was now expected to provide the intellectual capital for capitalism.[21]

Governor Rockefeller drew the connections between research and economic development many times: "If we in New York are fully to share in the fruits of new industry drawing upon scientific and technical advance and to remain in the forefront of modern industrial development, we must develop even more fully the intellectual resources in our State," he said. Federally funded Cold War–related scientific research opened the opportunity for the "practical application" of the "results of research for the defense of the Nation and for the advancement of the living standards of the Nation's families." The administration understood, however, that the benefits of the new research-driven economy would be distributed unequally because "it is around these centers of basic research that modern industry and science, with their reliance upon scientific and technical learning cluster." States without the most competitive universities and research programs in and around cities, what Margaret O'Mara aptly calls Cities of Knowledge, would likely slip into decline. The high cost of building and staffing new campuses was thus outweighed by the enhanced economic competitiveness of the state because leading schools would attract "the industry and business activity that means jobs and well-being to all citizens of the community."[22]

The state's modern industries also demanded a generation of workers with more advanced skills that corporations could not or did not want to develop for reasons of cost or complexity.[23] Ronan believed that with the "constantly increasing sophistication and technological innovation in industry, business, and commerce, a high school diploma . . . was grossly inadequate for young people of the 1960s."[24] An expanded and targeted SUNY, by contrast, could finally meet "the needs for technically trained manpower as well as for the professions" particularly "for teachers and engineers, and for scientists and technicians to man the growing number of research laboratories in the State."[25] The Rockefeller planners believed that the liberal arts, including the hard sciences, would be crucial to managing a more complicated society: "Increasingly, business and industrial enterprises, and employers in service agencies are demanding of their potential employees a thorough grounding in liberal studies." At the undergraduate level in the SUNY system, liberal arts and sciences students made up just 1,700 out of 75,000 students in 1960. The liberal arts and sciences, therefore, became the crucial aspect of new colleges in the SUNY system. Engineering and preprofessional training received emphasis as well.[26]

The New System

The watershed for SUNY was Rockefeller's commissioning of the Heald Report (1960). This concise plan laid out a broad, attractive outline for future expansion that was instantly useful to Rockefeller and his team. The report came with excellent credentials, as two of its three members were New Yorkers at the forefront of educational reform: Henry Heald of the Ford Foundation and John Gardner of the Carnegie Corporation. The importance of this report was the willingness to stake out a new ambition for the public system. Heald believed that only a reversal in the relative share of public/private education (then 60 percent private, 40 percent public), at a much larger scale, would accommodate future demand. To achieve public leadership the state would have to invest at a rate comparable to its peers. New York, at the time, was ranked eighth in per capita higher education spending, behind states such as California, Michigan, Indiana, Minnesota, and Texas and just above North Carolina. Structurally the SUNY system was also rigid, with "less administrative and management freedom of operation than almost any other publicly supported institution or group of institutions in the United States."[27] The Heald Report recommended that the Board of Regents step back and let the SUNY trustees and chancellor run the system, release SUNY from most civil service requirements, and grant more freedom of construction and design to SUNY.

Heald was sensitive to urban patterns, recommending that 60 percent of the total state-sponsored community college seats be in the New York metro areas, including Nassau, Suffolk, Westchester, and Rockland Counties; another 20–25 percent of the capacity was to be located near Albany, Buffalo, Rochester, and Syracuse. Transfer from these mostly metropolitan-based community colleges to new liberal arts or research colleges, some in more distant locales, would be seamless. While sensitive to the needs of the private schools, including a new system of student aid, they proposed that the regents convert all the state colleges of education (many in small towns like Cortland and Geneseo) into liberal arts colleges. At the graduate level, they envisioned two research-oriented university campuses and expanded medical education. Responding to suburban growth on Long Island, they called for Stony Brook to become a research-oriented institution. Another university upstate, to spread the wealth to other metros, would be destined to be counted among the "finest in the nation."[28]

Rockefeller endorsed the Heald Report in multiple speeches and lobbied the state legislature in 1960–1961. The ethnic tensions that had defined the acrimonious debates of the 1940s had dissipated once private schools opened their doors to high-achieving Jewish students. The private institutions at the time enjoyed strong demand, large federal research grants, and solid tuitions,[29] and any concerns were allayed with generous state-sponsored tuition assistance programs to private schools.[30] The governor and the SUNY trustees in 1961 moved on the Heald recommendations, including a master plan process, conversion of "normal" schools to the liberal arts, creating four university centers (combining undergraduate and graduate training), the unification and upgrading of City College to become the City University of New York, and the creation of the State University Construction Fund. The Muir report in 1963 fleshed out the Heald recommendations on health care that provided critical medical services (in the guise of teaching hospitals) in mostly urban and suburban areas. SUNY was finally to become a metropolitan-scale higher education system. [31]

Heald and the commission promoted expansion but advised a strategic approach. The report warned that "if the State University were to continue to follow historically accepted space utilization practices during the next ten or fifteen years, appropriations for new buildings to meet the enrollment demand would have to be greater than the grand total provided for college buildings by the Legislature during the past century." The authors called such physical expansion "unreasonable." They discovered, for instance, that existing SUNY lab and lecture space was underutilized much of the time. They proposed that the colleges consider new schedules on a daily and yearly basis, shorter and combined degree programs, and prior learning for credit—elements that were pursued at SUNY but not with the same enthusiasm as campus expansion. A 1961 plan by Rockefeller, for instance, to convert the state university campuses to year-round use fell flat. Later attempts to fully utilize physical resources at alternative times also sputtered out in the face of dominant patterns of vacation and summer jobs. By failing to rethink utilization, the state's leaders committed to a large construction and planning program.[32]

A Decentralized, Metropolitan System

State officials, including Rockefeller, resisted the widespread "view that educational excellence should be limited to a few 'flagship' institutions, to the detriment of tens of thousands of students attending the non-flagship institutions."[33] The administration pursued an alternative route: specializations in areas such as the arts, research, teacher training, liberal arts, and technology defined campuses. The four university centers (Albany, Buffalo, Stony Brook, and Binghamton) developed research specialties, often in overlapping areas, rather than a single campus dominating in all areas as was typical in a flagship system.

This decentralized strategy meant that many more urban areas stood to benefit from hosting substantial higher education institutions, with major political dividends: "The Geography of the systems—CUNY in the city, SUNY on Long Island and upstate, and the privates throughout the state—gives politicians a vested interest in the well-being of public higher education, since a campus in one's district brings opportunities for constituents and economic development for communities surrounding the state and city systems." Even in the post-Rockefeller 1970s era of austerity and neoliberal retrenchment, the state legislature pushed back hard on plans to privatize, shrink, and potentially close many campuses that were often crucial to a region's financial fortunes. Not a single SUNY campus has closed despite multiple economic crises, cutbacks in many graduate programs, and weaker demand at many upstate campuses.[34]

The new SUNY system was decentralized, but it served cities mostly, and the biggest ones more than others. The trustees addressed the needs of the service economy in the New York City region, including both the city and its suburbs. The trustees believed that by 1970 New York City alone would provide one-third of the four-year students of the SUNY system. The four metropolitan counties surrounding the city would produce another 50,000 students. The trustees concluded that "when reported expansion plans are related to this geographic breakdown it becomes immediately apparent that the most serious concentrated problem in 1970 will exist in the four metropolitan counties." [35] New York's suburbs won new community colleges, undergraduate colleges, and universities. CUNY gained university status and the funds to aid expansion of the number and quality of city colleges (described in the next chapter) to help meet the projected demand.

Long Island, one of the state's fastest-growing suburbs, had almost no public higher education in place and only a few small private colleges to meet the educational needs of a large generation of middle-class children. Long Island became the most massive single target for expansion, ultimately including Stony Brook (25,000 students, 2017 enrollment numbers), Old Westbury (4,000 students in 2017), Farmington (9,000 students in 2017), Nassau Community College (23,000 students in 2017), and Suffolk Community College (26,000 students in 2017). Nassau Community College opened with just 219 full-time and 415 part-time students in 1960 in a "hodgepodge of buildings" at the former Mitchel Air field yet aimed to have 16,000 students by 1970.[36]

Westchester County, another booming suburb, benefited from a lavishly provisioned four-year SUNY liberal arts and college and conservatory at Purchase as well as an expanded community college. Just up the thruway from New York City in New Paltz, another multipurpose college popular with downstate students rose. Rockland Community College grew to meet the demands of residents pouring from the new subdivisions made possible by the Tappan Zee Bridge. The SUNY promise in 1964 of open access to its community college campuses helped drive up the number of students. Areas around New York City seemed to have an insatiable demand, however, for higher education. Even in 1971, the *Times* reported that "Nassau and Suffolk Community colleges do not have the facilities to admit all applicants for their full-time day programs," whereas many community colleges upstate remained roomier.[37]

Upstate cities and suburbs did well during this expansive era. Syracuse benefited from a major expansion of the Upstate Hospital Center and School of Forestry adjacent to Syracuse University. SUNY four-year programs at Fredonia, Alfred, Geneseo, and Cortland were within easy drives from Buffalo, Syracuse, and Rochester. The trustees prioritized transforming older campuses at Albany (public) and Buffalo (private), in densely populated and highly industrialized regions, into "university centers" with branches of these campuses in both city and suburban locations. Buffalo benefited not only from continuing support of Buffalo State, mostly engaged in teacher training, but more crucially the transformation of the private, ailing 10,000-student University of Buffalo, with established professional schools, into the largest upstate SUNY campus. The president of the University of Buffalo, Clifford Furnas, with help from the state senate majority leader, successfully convinced the Rockefeller administration to absorb the private school and to build a new campus. An undeveloped site at suburban Amherst would be the main campus, while the older Main Street campus would focus on the health sciences and design.[38] The city of Binghamton benefited directly from the transformation of Harpur College into SUNY-Binghamton. The new campus, designated a university center in 1965, rose in Vestal on the suburban fringe: the school became a top-ranked comprehensive university in a region in steep decline.[39]

The colleges of education, many in small cities around the state, became multipurpose liberal arts colleges that provided equally critical economic benefits. As their student populations grew and the steady flow of state aid put up new buildings and staff, the new or expanded SUNY campuses boosted local economies in small upstate cities such as Oneonta, Cortland, Plattsburgh, Genesseo, and Canton. College students became significant percentages of town populations, patronized local stores, and added, over time, to the educational quality of the workforce. New or expanded community colleges made similar contributions.[40] The movement of students had the added benefit of shifting dollars north from the New York City metropolitan area upstate: "Thousands of Long Island students flock each year to Oswego, Oneonta, New Paltz, Cortland, and Fredonia." The flow of money and students northward from the New York City regions to upstate institutions and towns remains crucial today.[41]

The decentralized, undergraduate-oriented plans had many benefits, but it immediately compromised the goal of using the university as a catalyst for top research programs and spinoffs. State leaders, including Rockefeller, failed to understand the depth of commitment required to build and staff top-rank universities or the difficulty of turning older state institutions, with a legacy of teaching faculty, into research universities. *Newsday* in 1962, for instance, proposed that Stony Brook university center become the system's flagship research campus, developing "prestige and impact" rather than "scattering and duplicating facilities" across the state. Their suggestions were predictably ignored in Albany.[42]

A 1964 report by higher education experts commissioned by the state legislature already found worrisome signs of "slippage" attributed to the "range, quality, and extent of graduate education and the university research carried on at its two large public universities," referring to the SUNY and CUNY systems. They found that "research activities . . . have had meager budgets, the faculty has had heavy teaching loads," and the system lacked the high salaries demanded by the top researchers. They claimed that elsewhere state governments were funding "85 percent of the scientific, engineering, medical, and agricultural research now being conducted in universities across the country." States provide the "seed money . . . the original facilities, the talented faculty members, the leadership, and the initiative." New York had created the State University Research Foundation and some research chairs, but the experts demanded that the legislature support research centers in the master plans, develop "peaks of excellence" at each university, imitate the Research Triangle strategy of offering matching funds from federal or private sources, and even make direct grants for researchers. It would take decades in New York, however, for state leaders to embrace this engaged strategy.[43]

The research program faltered, but SUNY campuses benefited from the fact that Rockefeller, like most governors of the time, retained his faith in higher education. By 1973 SUNY included 14 colleges of liberal arts and sciences, 3 specialized colleges, four university centers, 6 agricultural colleges, 5 statutory colleges, and 38 community colleges.[44] Annual spending for higher education rose from $88 million in 1959 ($752 million in 2017 dollars) to $972 million in 1973 ($5.45 billion in 2017 dollars).[45] By 1973–1974, SUNY counted for almost 20 percent of the state's growing budget.[46] Between 1958 and 1972, SUNY grew from 43,000 full-time students to 169,000 even as the quality of entering students system-wide increased. Community colleges increased their numbers from 31,000 to 196,000 students, many of them part time.[47] SUNY graduated what was called the world's largest graduating class in 1973, 52,000 students, including 20,000 bachelors', 27,000 associates', 4,000 masters', and 1,200 doctorate degrees.[48] These record numbers in the late 1960s tipped the balance in New York State from a private to a public majority and fed the labor market with educated graduates. The fact that "every state resident could commute to nearby colleges as a result of this expansion," helps explain this new productivity.[49] Between 1959 and 1970, the number of SUNY degree programs grew from several hundred to about 2,000 and the faculty from 5,000 to 15,000.[50]

Dr. Samuel Gould, recruited from the University of California at Santa Barbara, was appointed chancellor in 1964 and has been given much credit for steady leadership and good rapport with Rockefeller.[51] SUNY had been initially overwhelmed by the rapid expansion plans and was "plagued with massive internal red tape, [and] lack of leadership in its top echelons." Gould, with Rockefeller's support, avoided civil service requirements to hire top professionals, added administrators, and sped up purchasing.[52] Gould was proud in 1970 that despite unprecedented growth, the design of the system had avoided "inhuman bunching and depersonalization" characteristic of very large campuses: "only five institutions out of 67 with more than 5,000 full-time students and one (the University of Buffalo) with more than 10,000." He was equally proud of experimental campuses at Purchase, Old Westbury, and urban career prep programs that contrasted with "higher education as the isolation, rigidity and snobbery of college and university learning."[53]

An Engine for Growth

To serve all these students on so many new and expanded campuses required an unprecedented building program, one that ranked as one of the most expensive public infrastructure projects in the United States to that date. To pay for the construction of such an extensive, decentralized system in just a decade also required a level of funding that could not be realistically addressed either by annual state appropriations or voter-approved bonds. Initially, in 1961, Rockefeller had proposed to fund the construction program through voter-guaranteed bonds of $500 million ($4.163 billion in 2017 dollars) to be funneled through the State Dormitory Authority. Even then he and his staff realized that these generous funds were insufficient to build the number, quality, and scale of campuses envisioned. The State Dormitory Authority would remain an essential partner in developing the new colleges, as were similar dormitory authorities elsewhere, but a more radical approach was required.[54]

Rockefeller received permission from the state legislature in 1962 to direct the Housing Finance Agency to funnel $700 million ($5.77 billion in 2017 dollars) in moral obligation bond sales, pledged with future tuition (introduced at SUNY in 1963) and fees, into a new State University Construction Fund (SUCF). The fund would plan, design, and construct the new campuses in partnership with SUNY officials and leading architects.[55] The state legislature, which had previously resisted significant funding for university buildings, accepted the spending, as the legislators believed that the costs of these buildings, including debt service, would be covered out of tuition and fees. States developed similar financing vehicles, utilizing revenue bonds, during these years to fund campus and dormitory growth. The HFA bond funding, as in other states, was complemented by federal funds for facilities such as Graduate and Health Science Center grants.[56]

The financing strategy worked, and quickly, to supercharge campus expansion. By 1966, the HFA had financed 126 buildings at 26 campuses. When added to the State Dormitory Authority funds, the results were often extraordinary.[57] The State University Construction Fund sprinted from design (commissioning significant conceptual and technical work from private architectural and engineering firms) with the help of 200 of its staff, including 130 architects, engineers, lawyers, and other professionals. Because of the scale of the system and the complexity of campus requirements, the fund was an early adopter of a computer system to control and organize the construction process.[58] By the late 1960s, one analysis noted, "All over New York State students move into new dormitories that are ready for them, eat in new dining halls, attend class in new lecture hall centers or classroom and lab buildings, study or do research in special new libraries, practice the creative arts in new fine arts centers which include studios, theaters, and concert halls, and get to know each other in new student activity buildings."[59]

The total development program, if added together, would have been enough to build a large American city. Between 1962 and 1995, SUCF counted 3,000 different building projects, giving rise to a system of 2,522 buildings with 73 million square feet of interior space—making its combined square footage portfolio a rival to almost any American downtown. By 1995 the SUCF oversaw an infrastructure program of 110 miles of sanitary sewers, 81,000 parking spaces, 460 athletic fields, and massive boiler, electric, and air-conditioning systems on a total of 34 campuses. The SUCF remains the force today for campus renovation, new master plans, and additions to the SUNY system, pumping in hundreds of millions system-wide annually. SUNY campuses present well today, with many modern structures, due to this consistent support.[60]

The SUCF built across the state but deliberately skirted the upstate architects, civil engineers, and administrators in the conservative Department of Public Works that had previously overseen, and value-engineered, the buildings on SUNY campuses. The dynamic fund administrator, Dr. Anthony Adinolfi, and architect George Dudley (a Rockefeller confidant, architect, and SUCF trustee) rejected a "one size fits all" approach. According to Dudley, "We had to try to find a plan and a design structure, some organized scheme, which would make each campus a being unto itself, with its own personality and its own strength."[61] The governor's promise that "only the fund, one overall architect, and one general contractor had any real say over the cost, design, and construction of a college campus" meant a rare opportunity to design ensembles rather than just individual buildings.[62]

For the architects engaged by SUCF, the fund's projects were both lucrative contracts and an opportunity to demonstrate the positive role modern design could play in postwar life. With deep pockets, zoning exemptions, and large sites, the designers made grand, bold, collective statements. Many new state campus master plans across the country shared in this tradition of architectural experimentation, including the University of Illinois at Chicago, University of California, Irvine; University of California, Santa Cruz; and University of Massachusetts, Dartmouth. Community colleges often included innovative megastructures built around interior atria and quadrangles, reminiscent of the era's shopping malls, which facilitated a community vibe for commuter students.[63]

SUCF's ability to operate outside the state lines, hiring based on talent and taste, created concerns for those on the margins of the most fashionable design circles. Rockefeller "had a very deep concern for harnessing the creativity and sensitivity of the private sector"[64] and "made it clear he wanted the best architects in the country to design SUNY buildings."[65] With so many leading firms in New York City, and Rockefeller's infatuation with big-name practitioners, the negative consequences for small, regional firms were quickly apparent. Buffalo's architecture community, for instance, objected to the "tendency of the state to take important work from them and divert it to New York and Chicago firms" for early campus planning at Buffalo. They called for the governor to create a national architectural competition for the Buffalo campus instead of making local firms "minor adjuncts to out of town firms." The governor and SUCF leadership, however, were not convinced.[66]

Trustee George Dudley defended the selection process in 1963, claiming that the SUCF had interviewed 200 firms before making final hiring decisions. From these the trustees chose a small number of "motivated" firms to serve as "campus planning architects," a powerful role that included designing master plans (in coordination with academic and other leaders), creating the "first key buildings," and selecting additional designers as the campuses expanded. The campus planners, in sum, established a "design vocabulary . . . to achieve and insure a visual continuity and harmony of all elements." Dudley tried to finesse the dominance of Manhattan firms: "Our spread in the sense of Upstate vs. New York City firms was a good reflection of the actual geographic distribution of our architectural resources." In other words, SUCF was justly tapping the rich vein of architectural talent in Manhattan rather than deliberately ignoring architects statewide.[67]

New York City's architectural community would dominate the commissions for the SUCF, including a mix of famous, fashionable, and emerging architects and firms: Edward Durrell Stone; Edward Larrabee Barnes; I. M. Pei, Ulrich Franzen; Jon Johansen; Alexander Kouzmanoff; Philip Johnson; and Davis Brody and Associates. Chicago-based Skidmore, Owings, and Merrill (SOM); Perkins and Will (with a branch in White Plains); and the legendary Harry Weese were also big-city-based firms the Fund and Rockefeller preferred.

Governor Rockefeller by 1971 would claim that thanks to such talent, the SUCF had demonstrated that public buildings "need not result in stereotypes, mediocrity, and dullness."[68] Advanced design thinking from ambitious architects would hopefully contribute to a more cosmopolitan atmosphere in the suburbs and upstate. *Architectural Record* in a lavish endorsement in 1971 claimed that SUNY "students are consciously and unconsciously learning about architecture and becoming aware of what a better environment can be."[69] Ultramodern structures on the campus, in a small and conservative upstate town like Canton or Fredonia, decentralized cultural production so that the benefits of modernism spread outside the big cities: "It is to the credit of SUCF that it puts leading architects to work on modest budgets to create—far off the beaten track—esthetic and functional amenities solely for the users—students, faculty, and people from the town and outlying region."[70] The results of architectural innovation, in the long term, were more complicated.

The Campus as Planned Community

The SUCF settled into a planning formula that reflects broader patterns of postwar modernist planning and university expansion. Older "normal"/education SUNY campuses converted to liberal arts schools followed a process of campus expansion and accretion. At Geneseo, for instance, the planners hired by SUCF worked with town leaders to avoid a "brutal invasion of the structure of the town" and instead sought to use the campus to "revivify its own Main Street with common arcades bringing town and gown together, designation of common parking areas, the rear yards cleaned up, and some streets closed."[71] The older New Paltz campus was redesigned "to take best advantage of site," including views of nearby mountains.[72] New SUCF-sponsored buildings on these converted campuses filled out or added new quadrangles, plazas, and pedestrian spines. Architects made a genuine effort to carry themes from old to new buildings through the application of a modern academic styling that integrated reinforced steel and concrete columns, exposed-concrete floor plates, brick walls, horizontal roofs, and plate glass windows in a rhythm and scale that often complemented the older academic buildings.

Many of these campuses, like those at Cortland, New Paltz, or Geneseo, were close enough to existing main streets to provide a walkable environment despite the provision of additional parking lots on campus. As these

FIGURE 32. The new SUNY Albany, rising on the edge of an aging city, was linked by highways to the region. Aerial by State University Construction Fund, 1972. Courtesy of the New York State Archives.

campuses grew, the student populations helped maintain retail vitality in old towns even as everyday shopping stores, such as supermarkets, moved to suburban strip malls. Many students eventually moved off campus, providing a key stimulus to small town rental markets that were suffering economic decline. A symbiotic, if sometimes tense, atmosphere developed between "town and gown" despite the countercultural habits and bigger-city demographic profile, of the students and faculty. Residents in New Paltz, one of the hubs of the upstate counterculture, "found themselves outnumbered by the sudden influx of students, cars and the trappings of youth culture." New Paltz, a town of just 6,000 people, was being flooded by 8,000 students and their hippie hangers-on. Locals cited rising crime and traffic as an outcome of college growth. Most residents of small SUNY towns admitted, however, that "students mean money, and you got to admit they provide a lot of people with a living."[73]

The same symbiosis never developed at the suburban "mega" campuses of the Rockefeller era, including Albany, Buffalo, Binghamton, Purchase, and Stony Brook. The aerials of most large SUNY campus sites from the period of growth reveal new greenfield sites close to the expanding highway network and new suburban subdivisions rather than in crowded downtowns or even small towns. Cheap land on the urban periphery (Buffalo-Amherst and Albany rose on former golf courses and Stony Brook on a donated estate) was more attractive for large-scale campus planning. Displacement was minimal, the target suburban market for many campuses lived nearby, and the extensive modernist physical program was hidden from public scrutiny within hundreds of acres of forests and fields.

The determination to build such large campuses for the modern age, most of them heavy with daily commuters (including students, faculty, and staff), usually led to buildings set within forested greenbelts that separated them from surrounding neighborhoods. Understated entrances led drivers to looping ring roads that brought commuting students to huge parking areas around centralized, pedestrian cores and plazas. The spatial logic of the era's shopping malls inflected these spaces. Landmark towers or otherwise eye-catching buildings studded the hearts of campuses. Clusters of dorms, usually in the woods or fields nearby, were separated from the teaching and student life areas, in modernist fashion.[74]

As at most postwar state universities, the car was king at SUNY. The designers provided extensive parking lots for students, staff, and teachers, many of whom lived in the region or commuted to the campus from off-campus private or family housing. Acres of bland parking lots thus defined the edges of many campuses. By 1970, for instance, there were 7,500 registered cars on the Stony Brook campus. Stony Brook, while designed as a residential campus, operated as a quasi–commuter college because of the ease of driving from home (or off-campus housing) to school on the island's parkways and the Long Island Expressway. Campuses within a metropolitan orbit, such as Buffalo and Albany, had a similar character. Expensive dorm complexes system-wide were underutilized in the early 1970s, for a variety of reasons (counterculture, dorm charges, unattractive facilities), but the ease with which mobile students could live elsewhere, and usually for less, was a factor.

The SUNY campus design program remained comprehensive but shifted somewhat during the 1960s. SUCF initially sought out established modern architectural firms such as Skidmore, Owings, and Merrill and Edward Durrell Stone, who delivered modern campuses with a recognizable neoclassical flair (rows of columns, symmetrical arrangements, and quadrangles) that either enhanced existing campuses or, as at Albany, offered a modernist interpretation of collegiate traditionalism. As time progressed, and "as master plans became more clearly outlined," the administrators found opportunities for more building projects that could be farmed out to "younger and smaller firms."[75]

What began with a monumental, neoclassical approach at Albany by Stone shifted to a function-oriented brutalist approach still noticeable today at Purchase, Old Westbury, Stony Brook, and Buffalo-Amherst. The SUCF made much of its program-oriented policies after the mid-1960s—working with faculty and staff to create modestly priced structures that responded directly to the needs of academic departments, for "new and creative teaching methods."[76] They boasted of winning architectural awards for designs that may have ignored traditional collegiate design expectations but delivered great spaces for rehearsal and teaching: "The fund has exercised great care to the end that buildings accommodate the university's academic programs, not vice versa." They highlighted the creation of "new types of facilities" such as instructional resource centers and instructional communications buildings for multimedia presentations. Innovative structures became typical elements of state university campuses, for better and worse.[77]

Many of these campuses seem cold today because so many of these structures prioritized internal academic functions such as darkened theaters, lecture halls, and carefully lighted galleries. Windows, and a sense of transparency that might brighten and lighten public spaces, was a victim of the scheme. One of the administrators in the SUCF program claimed that "user satisfaction" by students and faculty was "very positive,"[78] but they overlooked the accumulated impact of their strategy. Visitors and students by the 1970s encountered at Stony Brook, for instance, "a stark group of completed and half-finished buildings described variously as 'neo-penal colony.'"[79] The

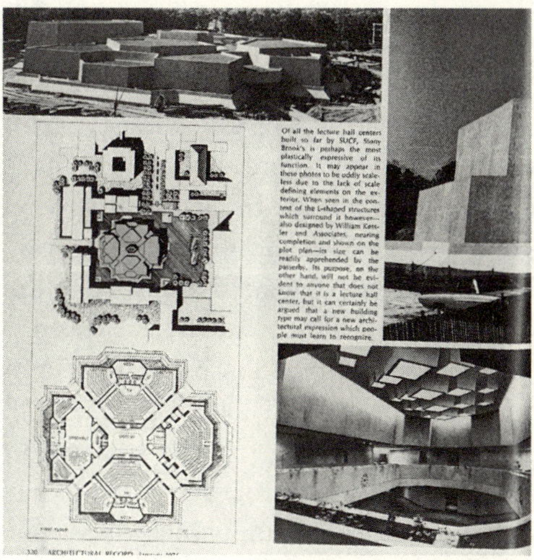

Of all the lecture hall centers built so far by SUCF, Stony Brook's is perhaps the most plastically expressive of its function. It may appear in these photos to be oddly scaleless due to the lack of scale defining elements on the exterior. When seen in the context of the L-shaped structures which surround it however—also designed by William Kessler and Associates, nearing completion and shown on the plot plan—its size can be readily apprehended by the passerby. Its purpose, on the other hand, will not be evident to anyone that does not know that it is a lecture hall center, but it can certainly be argued that a new building type may call for a new architectural expression which people must learn to recognize.

FIGURE 33. *Architectural Forum* celebrated the adoption of modernist design in new campuses like Stony Brook in New York and elsewhere. *Architectural Forum*, January 1971.

same was true at Fredonia, Buffalo, and many other new campuses. The architectural fashions of the day favoring sculptural brutalism in concrete or brick, often shaped into large interrelated megastructures, frequently created unfamiliar landscapes, confusing pedestrian and automobile circulation systems, and gloomy interiors. The contrast between the dense "urban" ensembles and megastructures and their pastoral surroundings was an intentional break both with the traditionalist suburban context in which most rose and the American campus planning tradition. SUNY has substantially altered/updated many modernist/brutalist buildings on its campuses, raising questions about the wisdom of investing deeply in avant-garde architecture during the 1960s and 1970s.

The planning model of large inwardly turned, auto-oriented campuses became even more attenuated when applied to campuses with specific urbanistic pursuits. Rockefeller promoted the SUNY Purchase campus in Westchester County, for instance, as a bold experiment combining the liberal arts and high-quality performing arts training. A highly praised megastructure and world-class studios occupied the center of a vast estate by the early 1970s. Purchase in fact received recognition for the quality of its dance, fine arts, and performing arts programs, but the vision would probably have worked better if it had not been isolated in the middle of a wealthy Westchester community. Campuses like Buffalo, Alfred, Old Westbury, Purchase, and Stony Brook today have new master plans, lovely new buildings, landscaping, fountains, and signage, and many excellent programs, but they remain isolated in ways that frequently undercut their identity and mission.

Pressure for Social Equity

At the very same time the state was investing in its system of mostly suburban and small town campuses, new pressure came from urban activists for a fair share of the benefits of a highly educated society. SUNY, like many state systems, was highly segregated. Its elitism during the civil rights movement stood out given the rhetoric of integration promoted by campus administrators, faculty, and students. SUNY leaders thus pioneered programs to bring social diversity to otherwise isolated suburban or small town campuses.

Stony Brook, for instance, was socially and geographically distant from its nearby metropolis. In 1967, just 20 out of 4,447 students on the Stony Brook campus were minority, the lowest proportion of minority students of any campus on the island. Nassau Community college was not much better, with just 198 of 4,547 students. Both schools were in fact worse than the University of Mississippi, which by 1967 hosted 101 black students out of 7,921 undergrads. President Toll of Stony Brook admitted, "We are not satisfied with the proportion of Negroes among our students and faculty"[80] and aimed to bolster the numbers on his campus. The SUNY Master Plan of 1968 was also "designed to help the poor obtain improved education, employment, better housing, and self-respect."[81]

Rockefeller introduced a series of initiatives to make SUNY more accessible to urban minority students. In 1970, for instance, the governor's Full Opportunity Program admitted 6,300 students to four and two-year campuses using a less rigorous admissions standard.[82] The Educational Opportunity Program (EOP) scholarship and academic support system introduced in 1966, pioneered by outspoken African American civil rights leaders Percy E. Sutton (Manhattan) and Arthur Eve (Buffalo), was a direct response to SUNY's lopsided white profile. EOP developed, and maintains today, a strong track record supporting minority students within the SUNY system. SUNY also planned centers at Syracuse, Mount Vernon, Wyandanch, and other minority-accessible sites to "prepare students for college through a variety of remedial courses."[83] Indeed, SUNY's track record on minority access improved significantly over time because of programs like these (as well as downstate's role as a global immigration hub). As of 2017, SUNY was 58 percent white.[84]

SUNY faculty and staff demographics also failed to reflect the urban diversity of the state, raising doubts about the role that such a fast-growing system might play in addressing the educational and occupational needs of upwardly mobile minorities. SUNY, as one of the largest regional employers of college graduates in every one of the state's metro areas, failed to hire many minority college graduates. In 1972, of 660 faculty members at Stony Brook, just 13 were black.[85] In 1971, of the 4,204 tenured faculty members in the SUNY system, only 36 were black and 6 were Puerto Rican. The system wasn't changing fast enough to meet changing social expectations. Black faculty members counted for just 283 out of 9,492 full-time faculty that year.[86]

While the lack of minority faculty was blamed on the lack of productivity of minority PhD's nationwide, the same excuse could not be used to paper over the lack of minority staff members, many hired with more modest academic qualifications. Of 3,056 professional administrative staff in the SUNY system, just 257 were black and 14 were Puerto Rican. That so many of the campuses were in lily-white suburbs and small towns upstate was likely a determining factor. The state government was creating many steady service jobs for whites primarily while simultaneously fighting private-sector housing and employment bias. The New York State Advisory Committee of the United States Commission on Civil Rights accused SUNY of "grossly discriminatory" practices in 1971.[87] In 1976, African American faculty still comprised just 3.1 percent of the total faculty system-wide. The advisory committee was not pleased by the slow progress.[88]

Even in 2013, underrepresented minorities were just 12.4 percent of the total faculty and staff of SUNY statewide, and African Americans separately comprised just 7.5 percent of the total. Changes in the ethnic identity of staff and faculty are proceeding far more slowly than changes in student demographics.[89] SUNY is just one of many high-quality government programs that white, suburban, or small town middle-class families benefit from despite remaining skeptical of government social programs for city-based minority families. Questions about access to state universities by minority students, along with equity in hiring at state campuses, remains a concern across the nation, even for many universities located in center-city locations.

Rethinking Campus Life in an Urban Age

A standout leader in urbanizing SUNY was Chancellor Ernest Boyer, who disparaged the modern campus as "a ghetto for the young."[90] He emphasized overcoming the physical and social isolation of many campuses that he believed housed a pampered and entitled middle-class youth culture. Boyer's interest in engaged campuses was shared by many state university leaders concerned about urban affairs.[91] The Stony Brook Urban and Policy Sciences Center, for instance, helped rethink sanitation in New York City and regional air traffic control. The Farmingdale campus offered two-week courses for welfare mothers seeking a better life.[92]

The controversial "poor people's college" at Old Westbury continued to receive Boyer's support despite a rocky start. Founded in 1967 "to serve the historically bypassed" black and Puerto Rican population, it responded to social unrest in cities and campuses nationally despite its location in polo country on Long Island's North Shore.[93] Peace Corps veteran and the college's first president Harris Wofford's intention "to establish temporary working parties and even permanent centers in the heart of the slums" encouraged a countercultural, urban activist spirit in the early years as the college took form.[94] Old Westbury's first academic village was aggressively urban, expressing the campus's "social justice theme" pursued by the academic leadership. The nearby multistory Central Core academic megastructure featured a grand, urban-style multilevel conservatory with multiple areas for socializing amid the horse pastures and forests.[95] The founding image of Old Westbury continued to shape the school's faculty and student body. By 1979, 52 percent of the student body was still minority, as was 55 percent of the faculty.[96] Even today, Old Westbury stands out as the SUNY campus with the highest percentage of underrepresented minority students among the 13 comprehensive colleges in the SUNY system (53.3 percent, in 2014).[97]

Boyer's most radical plan, the Empire State College, almost entirely dispensed with stand-alone campuses. The "open university" concept was not Boyer's invention; rather, it was part of a global movement that aimed to deliver higher education to nontraditional students.[98] It was novel, however, for Boyer to apply this approach to SUNY, considering the massive investments already made in physical campuses. Students of Empire State gained credit for their experiences and could take classes at a campus of their choosing or through tapes, TV, fieldwork, and even travel. The program quickly attracted hundreds of students, many of them older with some professional experience. Boyer argued that "the academic seriousness would improve when the props have been removed—the buildings, the units, the calendar," thus leaving "the crucial questions of content and quality" to faculty and students.[99] The five learning centers of Empire State College were created in Rochester, Saratoga, Albany, New York City, and Long Island to reach commuters and underserved minority students.[100]

One of the biggest tests of the ability to urbanize the SUNY mission, while continuing to pursue megacampuses, took place in Buffalo in the late 1960s and early 1970s. The outcome of the experiment reflects the difficulty faced by those seeking to create a more balanced urban/suburban system both in New York and nationally.

The site planning in the 1960s at Buffalo had a rocky launch because of a conflict over the best use of state resources. Downtown boosters and civil rights activists wanted to know why the new campus could not be built downtown where there was plenty of available land due to deindustrialization and corporate flight. Civil rights leaders, students, and liberals "believed a university close to the ghetto could satisfy the legitimate demands of a disadvantaged population for the aid up the social ladder a higher education could give." A state review, however, of the downtown concept concluded that the site was too far from the existing Main Street campus and would be more expensive to develop. But one suspects that just as important was the opportunity to plan grandly from the ground up for a vast suburban site.[101] The SUCF's Adinolfi later revealed that suburban Amherst was planned to be large enough to handle "the educational load of Western New York."[102] The suburban Amherst plan thus moved ahead but would continue to be caught up in interethnic competition in areas such as construction hiring.

SUNY leaders justified abandoning downtown in part because the Urban Development Corporation planned to create a campus-oriented, urbanistic

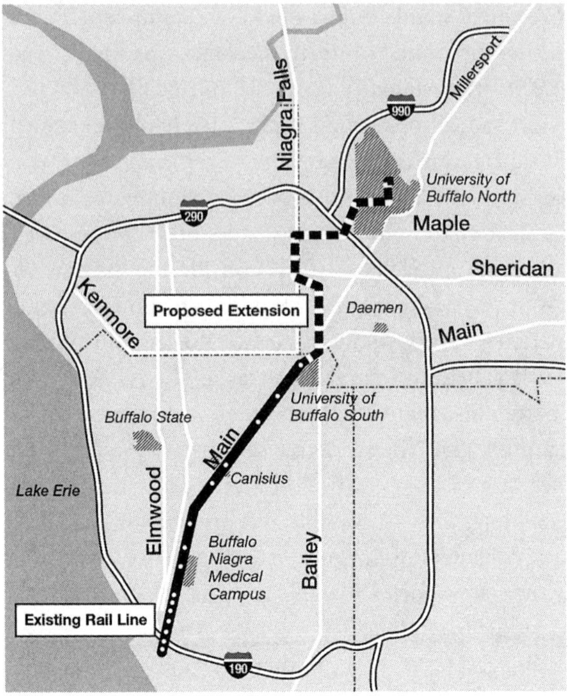

FIGURE 34. Numerous state university investments anchor Buffalo's limited mass transit and slowly recovering downtown. Map by Minna Ninova, 2018.

new town in Amherst, known as Audubon. British planner Richard Llewelyn-Davies, the designer of the Milton Keynes new town in Great Britain, provided the blueprint. The new town on 2,400 acres would provide shelter for 200,000 people within 10 to 15 years, thus providing a lively, mixed-income setting for a large faculty, staff, and student body—and would contrast with campus isolation at other large SUNY campuses.[103] The UDC promised, through this planning process, to "protect Amherst from falling prey to the undesirable urban sprawl and strip development" of typical suburbs. Architectural Forum predicted that "'it will be a city in the country—a dense concentration of housing and services' surrounded by natural areas."[104]

Suburban leaders did not feel that they needed rescuing from their suburban paradise and sued to stop the plan, delaying it long enough that it fell victim to the 1970s recession. Audubon ended up with some parks, a few hundred homes, and industrial parks but failed to become an urbanistic enclave. The campus surroundings thus developed into a more typical car-focused suburban mixture of garden apartment complexes, single-family homes, recreational lands, hotels, and shopping plazas. The campus's many brutalist buildings stood out isolated and exposed in the cold Buffalo winters.

Too Big to Work? Medium-Term Problems

The SUNY master plans, like those of nearly all state systems during this time, assumed an explosive, sustained rate of growth in both enrollment and state support for the university's mission. By 1970, however, "hard demographic data made it very clear that the enrollment projections underlying the plans for further huge construction of public higher education facilities were grossly exaggerated." The weight of everything planned, and so many different campuses, raised questions about the large-scale, decentralized model.[105]

SUNY endured a series of punishing budget cuts and tuition increases (1972, 1976, 1979).[106] The state legislature, facing a state and city budget crisis in the 1970s, demanded that SUNY provide more revenue to help pay off dormitory and construction bonds.[107] As early as 1972, *Times* architecture critic Ada Louise Huxtable acknowledged that the SUCF may have had "so strong a program, in fact, that there are now serious doubts about overbuilding causing tuition rises and questions as to whether the plant has become more important than the availability of the educational product."[108] Chancellor Ernest Boyer (1970–1977) admitted that the campus planning process might have been less than systematic: "I mean, ten years ago we just took everybody's wish list, and added them up and got a master plan."[109] Boyer defended the slowdown in construction and campus creation by pointing to the fact that "we already have 72 separate campuses with 72 libraries, student unions, administration buildings; and we've had to ask ourselves: Where does it end?"[110] Decentralization, administrators now realized, brought both costs and benefits.

SUCF found itself defending its ambitious building program by reminding an auditor that "the goals set for the State University of New York are not the goals for a minimum type of state university. The excellence of the academic program is a prime objective. . . . The space standards therefore are based upon what is considered good, sound, academic practice among the better public universities in the country."[111] Many politicians had already forgotten that the realization of such grand campuses aligned closely with Rockefeller's aim to transform SUNY into the top American public state system in just a few years: the massive scale of the system was intentional.

The late arrival of the SUNY system, despite the Rockefeller speed up, turned out to be a significant disadvantage in technology transfer. According to higher education expert Roger Geiger, the Rockefeller planners did not adequately foresee the changing national research picture in the 1960s:

> During the great post-Sputnik expansion of the university research system, established universities were far better suited to take advantage of federal largesse. By the late 1960s, as the SUNY centers were gearing up, the federal research economy was beginning to spiral downward. The peak year for federal support for academic research was 1968, followed by eight years of stagnation. Other federal programs for graduate students and developing science departments were reduced far more. Moreover, when university research began to recover in the late 1970s, the growth areas were no longer in the arts and sciences—the darlings of the 1960s and the focus of SUNY graduate departments.

SUNY campuses fared poorly in applied research, and faculty seemed to be reluctant or unable to adapt. For example, SUNY rankings for industry-sponsored research remained low.[112]

Stony Brook leaders in the 1960s, for instance, had "looked specifically at UC San Diego, where an explicit commitment to build a leading university had included years of planning. It had been built from the top down—eminent professors and strong graduate divisions first, followed by fairly small undergraduate programs." Stony Brook administrators had to fight hard to maintain this vision with state leaders because of changing priorities.[113] The first sale of HFA bonds after the financial crisis, which provided $137 million for SUNY Stony Brook hospital, reflects the enduring vision.[114] Many other SUNY graduate programs and campus research initiatives faltered in the 1970s; few achieved national or international recognition and many received insufficient funding. Administrators terminated many liberal arts graduate programs as cost-cutting measures over the decades. The lack of state support for the graduate mission reflected the fraying vision of SUNY as the vanguard of a new economy.[115]

Boyer's successor, Chancellor Clifton Wharton, toured the system in 1978 and found common concerns about "student performance, about unfinished plans of the expansion years of the 1960s, about competition from private institutions, and about facilities that are quickly becoming obsolete." The colleges were in survival mode.[116] In the late 1970s, SUNY leaders admitted to a significant backlog in quality and amount of "movable equipment" such as classroom furniture, scientific equipment, and computers: "I suppose we were so busy opening new facilities in the 1960s and 1970s that replacing equipment was just not given priority consideration." The rapid construction of so many facilities, moreover, bunched together replacement needs as "the life expectancy for each facility's original equipment began running out at the same time, creating the huge backlog."[117] Limited funds for modernization inevitably damaged the reputation of the system and its research capabilities, even with campuses full of relatively new buildings. Increases that did arrive were absorbed quickly into financial aid and personnel costs rather than program growth.[118]

Transforming the public sector into both an educational and economic force proved far more difficult than the waving of a Rockefeller wand. The entrepreneurial state, it turned out, required more risk and less reward than planned. When Governor Mario Cuomo took credit in the 1990s for creating Centers for Advanced Technology, the ones he praised most highly, outside the contract research system at Cornell, were private schools like Rochester, Syracuse, and Rensselaer Polytechnic Institute. The governor admitted that "it disappoints me our state's high-tech reputation is not better known beyond our border," which he blamed on the fact that "leading high-tech companies are not crowded together in a single region with a convenient label, like 'Silicon Valley' or 'Route 128' or the 'Research Triangle.'"[119] The alternative explanation was that SUNY had underperformed due to the combination of extraordinarily ambitious plans with inconsistent funding. The state may have had the "second largest concentration of doctoral computer scientists, life scientists, and engineers—and the largest concentration of Ph.D. chemists and mathematicians" in the nation, but they were not clustered effectively in research clusters at most SUNY schools. Private institutions like Columbia and Cornell still stood "among the best in the world," while SUNY colleges were "best buys" for undergraduates.[120]

Long-Term Urban Dividends

Governors since the 1980s, responding to upstate decline in industry and population and the SUNY system's underperformance compared to peers in places like California and Texas, have pushed for SUNY to decentralize, specialize, fund-raise, and develop campus identity programs. Governor Mario Cuomo, for instance, claimed to have invested billions in SUNY during his terms in office. State leaders in general now expected the system to be more performance driven and industry focused: "Higher education was a service industry, an all-important engine in the process of economic growth."[121] Additional state funds for research and associated development have backed up the renewed vision.

The state's long-term investments today yield major dividends. SUNY's 64 campuses had 431,855 students in fall 2017, including both full- and part-time students, of which over 90 percent are from the state. The goal of keeping more of New York's talent in state universities, set in the 1960s, has been realized. There were 2,999,549 total SUNY alumni in 2014, with 2,432,942 living in New York State.[122] A 2011 report by the Rockefeller Institute and the University of Buffalo Regional Institute quantified both the broad and local economic impact of the SUNY system. As hoped, the system (graduating 78,000 students per year) produces large numbers of workers in fields that require more advanced training such as health care, education, business, and engineering. As a contributor to the state's urban service economy, the SUNY system is itself crucial to maintaining prosperity in nearly every region of the state. SUNY directly employed 83,800 employees and had a $19.8 billion economic impact in 2008–2009. The system supported 173,000 full-time jobs statewide, most of them clustered in and around the major metropolitan areas. SUNY is a good bargain for taxpayers today, as the state provides just $3.9 billion in direct funding to the system out of $10 billion in revenues (most of which come from tuition). The degree to which SUNY is an economic force in Western New York, reeling from massive deindustrialization, is striking, including a $3.7 billion impact and 32,000 jobs. SUNY employees, alumni, and staff combined comprise 24 percent of the Western New York population.[123]

SUNY campuses are, as was hoped decades ago, anchor institutions in many cities large and small, with crucial importance to maintaining the vitality of upstate cities: "The campuses themselves are full of energy, as classrooms and quads bustle with activity and debate, buildings and landmarks are constructed or revitalized." The off-campus spending of students, estimated at $2.3 billion total, or about $5,000 per student per year, would be sorely missed in upstate cities that have shed so many jobs: "Businesses catering to SUNY students, faculty, staff and visitors—from cultural centers to coffee shops—are drawn to the area, creating a critical mass of jobs, services and amenities for the population." The 2011 Rockefeller Institute / University of Buffalo report found that many college towns "are more pedestrian friendly than are surrounding areas, with diverse amenities within walking distance of where people live, including coffee shops, grocery stores, and theaters." Cultural and volunteer activities "filter" into the community. The report found that "SUNY institutions are landmarks in the cities, towns, and villages of New York State," reflecting the aim of using these campuses to help steer urban growth. The students flowing in have helped to change their surroundings: "Compared with their surrounding county, SUNY hosts communities are younger, more diverse and more highly educated." In the Mohawk Valley, however, three-quarters of graduates leave because of the limited economic opportunities there and the less diverse surroundings. This brain drain undermines some but not all of the arguments for higher education decentralization.[124]

Rockefeller's plan that SUNY would help make New York a national leader in advanced technology is, after more than half a century of investment, just beginning to reach scale. The long wait for technology transfer and spin-offs at SUNY is typical in American higher education, despite the many promises made for this sector.[125] Beginning in the 1980s system administrators looked to the Research Triangle approach of using university resources and/or state resources, the "state as entrepreneur," to encourage university/corporate partnerships and research.[126] Applied research and professional programs such as business, rather than the liberal arts, received new priority.[127] As of 2014, SUNY's combined campuses were 31st among the top 100 universities for patents. The state maintains programs worth hundreds of millions of dollars to help incubate new research enterprises on a competitive basis only within SUNY and CUNY. The major growth in technology-related fields, as expected, is around the research centers in Buffalo, Albany, Stony Brook, and various contract and medical colleges. Research center campuses alone generated roughly half of the $1.3 billion in SUNY research revenues (2008–2009).[128] The race is on to use the research campuses to save the state: "Much of SUNY's research is conducted with the end-view of transforming New York's (particularly upstate New York's) status as a Rust Belt state through advanced technology."[129]

Upstate cities and towns have benefited from the work of an entrepreneurial physics professor originally from SUNY-Albany, Dr. Alain Kaloyeros, "the 'Johnny Appleseed' of nanotechnology." He became the force behind SUNY Polytechnic Institute, including both an educational and a research facility, that generated billions in private/public investment and houses hundreds of thousands of square feet of modern university/industry research space on the edge of Albany. The NanoTech Complex expanded from just 72 positions in 2001 to an estimated 2,600 scientists in 2011. The state acted as the project's venture capitalist, creating a foundation that provided superior facilities for the corporate research labs. This is deeply subsidized capitalism. Between 2000 and 2009 the state's investment of $876 million was multiplied by the private sector's $5.5 billion investment. The state's reliance on Dr. Kaloyeros, and the shallow regional roots of the initiative, was revealed after his indictment in 2018 on corruption charges related to lucrative contracts associated with Governor Andrew Cuomo's "Buffalo Billion" program. The NanoTech Complex as of this writing (2018) was still successful, but also losing partners and positions due to Dr. Kalyeros's legal troubles. Investing in public/private partnerships comes with risks for state governments.[130]

By all accounts, suburban Long Island is still the region with the most profound SUNY presence. There are still five SUNY campuses, and three of them are among the five largest. The suburban region accommodates 85,000 SUNY students. Compared to the 1960s this is a much more diverse population, as one in three students are now minority at the SUNY campuses there. A remarkable 325,000 alumni live on the island, and of those 85 percent went to a SUNY on the island, reflecting an insular higher education culture that has developed, and which may have its perils. The island derived $3.9 billion in economic benefits from the SUNY outposts, including jobs for 16,000 faculty and staff. Stony Brook remains the SUNY campus with the dominant state-supported academic research enterprise outside New York City, in part created by the major and early investment in faculty and facilities (the hospital, most notably) made decades ago. Stony Brook's leaders see its research program as helping the island transition from defense spending to a "diversified high-tech economy," and the campus supports over 100 specialized research facilities and multiple business incubators. Regional political leaders, however, would like Stony Brook to play an even larger role in regional economic development, on a par with schools such as Stanford, UC–San Diego, or Wisconsin.[131]

The American States and Higher Education Systems

Similar patterns of state government investment in postwar higher education took place across the nation. States invested in multitiered systems, built most large new campuses on greenfield sites favoring white suburban or small towns, renovated and expanded older campuses in cities and small towns, invested in public/private research programs with potential spin-offs, tapped federal aid, and eventually shifted to a tuition-, grant-, and endowment-based model of funding. States that made the most substantial investments now reap the greatest rewards in research, technology, and educated workforces.

Designers of a rising generation of community colleges and state colleges across the nation used automobiles as "a principle factor in postwar campus planning," leading to a typical "linear arrangement of buildings along a road and parking lots, and a 'ring road' type of plan, in which vehicles were kept mainly on the outside of a central campus area." Most of the new campuses, from the University of South Florida to the University of California, Irvine, responded to suburban lifestyles and expectations by making enormous provisions for parking and highway access. Most of the new campuses also shared in the preference for pedestrianized centers or atria that would create a shared public space despite the heavy emphasis on regional mobility.[132]

California remained the pioneer and leader in higher education after World War II, and it created a system with metropolitan impact across the state. Its three tiers—community colleges, state colleges, and universities—offered degree programs to 1.2 million students by the early 1970s. Suburban students found they could drive to nearby community college campuses for as much or little education as they wanted. State universities offered the next step up to four-year education. The University of California system remained the most prestigious, and campuses grew quickly. The explosive growth and high quality of the university system played key roles in the state's urban development, clustering primarily in and around the Los Angeles, San Diego, and San Francisco metropolitan areas. The leaders of the system invested in expansions of older, urban-based campuses (see next chapter for more details) as well as large-scale new campuses on the fringe.

The University of California, Los Angeles's (UCLA's) established West Los Angeles campus was complemented by new and exciting megacampuses at Santa Barbara and Northridge. South of Los Angeles, the Irvine campus, designed in a futuristic style by architect William Pereira, was the nucleus of a carefully planned suburban new town during the 1960s. Within a short drive of Irvine were additional campuses at Fullerton, Riverside, San Bernardino, Pomona, Cerritos, Long Beach, and Dominguez Hills to accommodate suburban growth regionally. Just down the interstate the suburban University of California, San Diego, campus in La Jolla became known for science and oceanography, as well as other advanced research, helping to diversify the economy of a city known mostly for recreation and navy ports. In the north, Berkeley remained the crown jewel of the system, with continued strength in technology-related research, and the campus gave its town an international reputation as the heart of the antiwar movement and counterculture. New megacampuses in the system, including Santa Cruz and Davis, constructed on large peripheral parcels of land near existing urban centers, provided options for the growing percentage of students pursuing higher education.[133]

Governor Ronald Reagan and the state legislature, and many conservative state residents, took out their unhappiness with the counterculture by cutting California's higher education budget in the late 1960s and 1970s, leading to tuition charges, weaker salaries, some program cancellation, and other fiscal strains common to universities during this period. Questions emerged about the wisdom of commissioning defense-related research in such politically charged atmospheres. The system, like New York's, also appeared to be overbuilt in the 1970s. But the California system's established reputation and popularity, many federally funded grants and labs, out-of-state students, the state's growing population, and loyal alumni and faculty allowed the system to endure and ultimately prosper.[134]

The rise and expansion of public higher education systems in California, New York, and other states put the laggards on notice. New Jersey, for instance, finally embraced higher education improvement in the late 1960s. In 1968, the state was still exporting 98,710 students to out-of-state universities. Rutgers, its branch campuses, new medical schools, and a range of new or expanded public institutions were serving 85,000 students by 1975. In time, these state institutions, and other state-sponsored institutions such as New Jersey Institute of Technology, would become essential to the economic life of the state's cities, including Newark, Camden, and New Brunswick.[135] Governor Rhodes in Ohio convinced voters to support a $665 million bond issue to support expansion from 5 to 12 state universities, a medical school, and new branch campuses. As in New Jersey, campuses in cities such as Cleveland, Cincinnati, Akron, and Toledo have become crucial to sustaining and renewing many center-city neighborhoods.[136]

The investment in higher education extended deep into the Sunbelt, reaching Texas, Florida, and Georgia. Florida, not formerly known for ambitious state education, planned to build community colleges within driving distance of all the state's students.[137] Between 1957 and 1962, the percentage of Florida freshman attending junior college campuses zoomed from 20 to 50 percent. Experts also recognized North Carolina for an aggressive program of community college and state university expansion. Texas higher education underwent a massive expansion during the administration of Governor John Connally (1963–1969), including many new branch campuses in both center-city and suburban sites across the state.[138] Arizona State University, now one of America's largest universities, grew rapidly in the postwar era thanks to sustained financial support by Phoenix business interests seeking to establish a major engineering and high-technology training and research center.[139]

The public support for state university systems, and rising tuitions, largely insulated them from the worst possible cuts possible during the 1970s. National state expenditures for public higher education institutions was over $31 billion ($127 billion in 2017 dollars) by 1977–1978, with state taxes covering about $19 billion ($78 billion in 2017 dollars) of that total. State support for higher education, even during a punishing recession, increased over 200 percent from 1969 to 1979. The rising costs resulted from inflation and the growing number of public institutions (1,478), with 8.8 million students in 1979. The total number of campuses was roughly equal to the total number of private institutions (1,685), but public system enrollments (due to so many more large campuses) dwarfed the 2.5 million students served in the private sector. State leaders, however, tended to rely much more on tuition than they had in the 1960s, a trend that has continued and now seems to be accelerating or permanent. In 2013, after dramatic cuts in state support, 11 states spent a higher percentage of their annual general fund on corrections than higher education, including Michigan, Oregon, Pennsylvania, Colorado, and Massachusetts. These funding totals, however, usually leave off important subsidies universities continue to receive in areas such as low-interest bonds and tax-free status.[140]

Flagship Urbanism

A specialized city region has developed since World War II because of sustained state and federal investment in higher education. SUNY leaders may have resisted the flagship development process, but the urban dividends for systems elsewhere that have concentrated resources in one or two locations are often significant. Today, many flagship cities have changed from modest "town and gown" college towns into small cities with highly educated residents, extensive cultural activity, high-value homes, low unemployment, and strong economic growth. The patterns of urban flagship transformation are national in scope and include a remarkable range of fast-growing small cities such as Madison, Ann Arbor, Athens, Charlottesville, Tempe, Austin, Gainesville, and College Station.

State governments, even with cuts in direct support, continue to underwrite debt that allows flagship universities to build and renovate cheaply; authorize confiscatory out-of-state tuition rates; and shield these institutions from major local tax bills despite their outsize economic dominance, use of local municipal services, and profit-making enterprises. Because these dividends of state investment are unequally distributed statewide, the differences in urban health between flagship towns and other cities are often stark. Booming college towns in the otherwise suffering Rust Belt or other economically depressed areas appears to have had political ramifications. State legislatures are now forcing the flagships to subsist primarily on tuition, contingent labor, fund-raising, and various federal or other grants. The recent sizable cuts to the University of Missouri, Columbia, indicate that state legislatures can do real harm to both town and gown. The perception of state universities as rich, liberal institutions may also hurt the case for the typical teaching and community colleges in systems that still educate most students.

The University of Wisconsin–Madison, for instance, has grown during the postwar period from a large, land-grant educational institution in a small town into a massive, multibillion dollar urban-based multiversity. Its vitality has directly contributed to the surrounding region's prosperity, making the city's economy distinct from Wisconsin's Rust Belt pattern of industrial disinvestment and center-city decline. Wisconsin's 21,000 faculty members and staff and 43,000 students collectively spend approximately $5 billion per year, mostly in and around Madison. The university boasts over 300 Madison-related startups providing 25,000 jobs, many of which grew from research in university labs or affiliated incubator/research parks. The university spends over $1 billion annually on research in modern facilities on both the campus and surrounding areas.[141]

The university's physical footprint in the city has expanded, including new student housing, research facilities, technology research parks, and student services. The market demand related to student and faculty housing has maintained rental housing in the city's downtown districts despite aging frame houses and growing suburbs. The downtown commercial corridor, along State Street, thrives only because of the campus connection. The lack of social and racial diversity on the Madison campus has, however, been a concern for decades to many activists and administrators. In the spring of 2018, for instance, the administration reported only 1,210 African American and 2,025 Hispanic students on a campus of 41,520 total students. Given the growing importance of the high-skill, research-based economy, the lack of minority residents at flagship campuses like Madison deprives many minority college graduates access to the brightest careers in many regional economies.[142]

Madison's success has not gone unnoticed in the state legislature, just a few blocks from campus, which now provides just 15 percent of the university's revenue. Federal grants and tuition now provide the lion's share of university support. University administrators are understandably frustrated about declining state support, which in the late 1970s accounted for over 40 percent of revenue, and predict various doomsday scenarios, but it is also possible to see this retreat as a success story for state investment. After decades of state support, a $3 billion university enterprise appears to be mostly self-supporting. The perceived value of the degree nationally now allows the college to charge high out-of-state rates that keep in-state tuition more affordable (16,583 of 41,520 are full-time nonresident students). Thousands of foreign graduate students study and support top-ranked research labs. Alumni give at an annual rate that almost matches state support. Declining state funding, rooted in envy and anger about activists in Madison from more conservative regions of the state, has so far had a minor impact on the area's success.[143]

Many southern flagship cities are also booming. North Carolina continues to attract new business and migrants because of the Research Triangle Park and three major universities, the leading pair of which are state sponsored. North Carolina State has a $3.3 billion impact in Wake County, accounting for approximately 6 percent of the county's gross regional product. North Carolina State–related startups add a $1.1 billion impact on the Triangle Park region alone. Its massive campuses (2,090 acres total) dominate the city of Raleigh and include both a traditional older campus and a vast new research-related campus that mimics the Triangle Park.[144] Just down the interstate in Chapel Hill, not only do the University of North Carolina (UNC) campus (729 acres) and the affiliated hospital physically dominate their setting, but UNC contributes $7 billion to the state's economy, most of which sloshes around vibrant Chapel Hill and the Triangle Park region. Approximately 150 startups with 8,000 local employees can be tracked to UNC research. The combined force of these two large research institutions with privately-run Duke and the state-sponsored Triangle Park has sustained a vibrant, decentralized, suburban-style region for decades. These schools have also successfully weathered declining state support with a mix of tuition, grants, entrepreneurialism, and donations.[145]

Public colleges and universities, of a bewildering range of types, are now vital to the health of nearly all American metropolitan areas. They serve as more than just educational centers: they are frequently large and stable regional employers, health care providers, technology hubs and incubators, cultural centers, athletic facilities, sources of state pride, and more. An observer transported from the 1940s to today's massive state-sponsored higher education landscape could scarcely have imagined the change. Most Americans may not view university expansion as a form of state government urban policy, but the record speaks otherwise.

9
Unheralded Anchors: Center-City State Universities

Most large American cities have become dependent on the economic, social, and physical impact of at least one center-city state university. The decline of downtown as the premier space of American business and commerce made space for large-scale higher education. Universities cleared old buildings, built on derelict parking lots, and adapted old commercial, factory, and warehouse spaces. Many states have now invested deeply in campuses that have become indispensable center-city anchor institutions from Baltimore to San Francisco. The range of institutions is impressive, including community colleges, state and city universities, professional schools, teaching hospitals, and specialized learning centers.

The attraction of higher education to city officials is linked to the resilience of higher education as an enterprise. Campuses have continued to grow even as many center-city neighborhoods and downtown business centers around them suffered from disinvestment and crime. Universities arguably surpass most state and city economic development programs in generating sustained investment and spillover effects. Universities renovate and add buildings on a district-wide scale; attract prosperous students, faculty, and staff; generate steady revenue from tuition, patents, grants, gifts, and medical services; and operate on a long-term basis despite the ups and downs in the national and local economy. Imagining the center cities of Cleveland, Baltimore, Birmingham, Detroit, and Denver without these campuses gives a sense of their importance.

For most of American history, city-based public higher education was small or poorly organized compared to private institutions. The entrance of state government into urban public higher education, as a result, was usually welcomed by nearly all city leaders and residents. New York State's investments were complicated by the prior existence and independence of a city-sponsored university system in New York City, but the long-term outcome of that state investment has parallels across the nation in urban higher education. The crucial role played by the state government in building CUNY into a high-quality system, one much better than a city government alone could fund, is typical nationally. The debate in New York about the relationship of publicly subsidized institutions to minority neighborhoods is also often at the heart of town/gown debates in other major cities, although these fights often simmer under the surface elsewhere.

Becoming a State-Sponsored University

New York City government has sponsored higher education since before the Civil War, first with City College (1847), then Hunter (1870), Brooklyn (1930), and Queens (1937) Colleges. The system enjoyed an enviable reputation in the postwar years, compared to its state-run peers, for high-quality programs and students. The excellence had less to do with the quality of its faculty or its facilities, which was uneven, and much more to do with an accident of social geography. Thousands of high-achieving Jewish students attended the city system's senior colleges in the first half of the twentieth century, including many graduates who became Nobel laureates, city politicians, and successful businesspeople.[1]

The highest-achieving students attended for free, helping to maintain the competitive and elite flavor of the system's senior colleges such as City and Queens Colleges. In 1957, for instance, 36,000 students, from the top 25 percent of city schools, enjoyed tuition-free education, while 24,000 students paid $300 a year to attend part or full time in the four senior colleges. A community college system, partly funded by the state government and partly by tuition, grew to include campuses in Staten Island, the Bronx, and Queens after World War II. Even those who paid something in these two systems paid very little; those who attended for free were understandably proud of both their accomplishments and thriftiness.[2] The state government already played a quiet but crucial role in this excellence by providing partial funding for both community colleges and teacher education within the city system, providing approximately 45 percent of the system's operating costs.[3]

During the 1950s, the city colleges retained their excellent reputation even as many of the city's other public systems (transit, hospitals, sanitation, etc.) declined. In 1960, the Board of Higher Education, which administered the system, created an ambitious plan to upgrade to a city university, to be developed from four senior colleges and three community colleges. The transformation to a city university, in the context of SUNY's ambitious expansion plan, would mean "two great co-equal university centers." The board demanded greater financial parity between state and city institutions, while it rejected deeper state oversight and tuition charges recommended by the Heald Report (and which might have been expected in exchange for deeper subsidies).[4] In 1961, Governor Rockefeller dutifully approved the transformation of the city colleges into the City University of New York. Becoming a university allowed CUNY to develop doctoral programs and potentially achieve national recognition. Provision for advanced training added to the city's attractiveness in a knowledge-driven service economy on the rise. Graduate students would also be charged tuition if they came from outside the city, contributing to more robust budgets; in 1962, the state began to provide funds to graduate education.

CUNY leaders, students, faculty, and staff welcomed the state government's change of its status and new funding, but city leaders and alumni were determined to retain their administrative independence from SUNY. CUNY champions viewed SUNY as permanently second rate. Students, faculty, and administrators also continued to resist broader tuition charges. Free tuition had become an article of faith for some city residents, as politicized as the uneconomic subway fare—and with arguably similar results on service quality. For some defenders of the status quo, free tuition guaranteed the attractiveness of the city system to top (then mostly white) students, many from the prosperous semisuburban outer boroughs, who might otherwise go elsewhere. City College, for instance, "maintained its traditional academic standards . . . up through the late-1960s" despite a growing range of options for top city students, including SUNY, other senior colleges, and private schools. No tuition and just a few low fees were a major draw for commuters despite neighborhood disinvestment.[5] The shifting urban conditions citywide, however, raised questions about these policies. The senior colleges were still "overwhelmingly Jewish," but now many of their families were "more prosperous, even middle class, at the time that admissions requirements to qualify for the scarce seats in the municipal colleges were becoming ever more stringent." In 1967, CUNY was still 82 percent white, 10 percent black, and 3 percent Puerto Rican.[6]

CUNY boosters, ignoring calls for social equity, suspected that Rockefeller and the SUNY trustees sought control to enhance SUNY's reputation as it was "still fair to say that none of the undergraduate units of the state system can be compared in quality with the best of the city colleges." City leaders were, however, ignoring the impact of the state's massive new investments. The old guard was also tone deaf about ways in which state funds could address social justice issues at CUNY. The state's scholarship program would have had an outsize effect on access for lower-income New Yorkers.[7] Rockefeller continued during the mid-1960s to pressure the city to end free tuition. He now drew on growing support from minority leaders and students who believed that a modest tuition charge for middle-class students would cross-subsidize generous scholarships for poor students in the CUNY system. The lines in the fight over urban higher education reflected a dimension of the fracturing Jewish/minority civil rights coalition.[8]

A longtime CUNY administrator acknowledged a risk of this strategy of delay: "CUNY missed the golden age of the sixties when college construction was booming everywhere, and campuses were being overbuilt."[9] The city even pushed back on the governor's proposals for new SUNY programs within the city limits in 1966. Experimental two-year technical colleges, for instance, would have accepted students without a high school diploma in Harlem and Bedford-Stuyvesant. Rockefeller highlighted the urban need even if city officials denied it: "It is apparent that many young persons past high school age living in the culturally disadvantaged areas of New York State's great cities are not getting the kind of higher education they need to compete." At another point, Rockefeller hastily suggested adding five new SUNY colleges to the city to meet local demand for four-year degrees.[10]

A new CUNY chancellor recruited from California, Albert Bowker, sensed the changing social climate and introduced a plan for open admission in 1966 (with the goal of full implementation by 1975). In the meantime, demand would be met with more community colleges and additional senior colleges.[11] In 1966, Rockefeller and the Board of Education finally compromised on 50-50 matching for operating funds for CUNY, initiated the City University Construction Fund with $583 million ($4.48 billion in 2017 dollars), added state representation to the governing board and launched the Search for Education, Elevation and Knowledge (SEEK) Program. SEEK responded to pressure for broader access by offering less selective admission to senior colleges paired with extensive academic or remedial help. The construction fund aimed to make space for 39,000 additional students by 1972. The City College campus in Harlem, for instance, bursting at the seams, could finally add a new science building, student commons, and more. City leaders scored this state aid while maintaining most of the system's independence and mostly free undergraduate tuition.[12]

The compromise had unlocked state aid but still did not satisfy many city residents locked out from CUNY. The senior colleges in the late 1960s were not losing their white students as fast as many city neighborhoods were losing their white residents; the CUNY system now looked like an anachronism, or worse. The perils of failing to address this racial divide could be seen just over the river in Newark, New Jersey. An elite, state-sponsored medical school for white students was an aggravating factor in riots there in 1967. Rising on the site of a cleared minority neighborhood, with all the displacement that entailed, the medical school promised very little to the city's minority majority in exchange for so much disruption. More education, in this case, was not an unqualified urban benefit.[13]

The inequity was evident in New York as well. CUNY may have guaranteed entry of associate degree recipients from the community colleges to senior colleges, but the community colleges were relatively small and selective compared to their SUNY counterparts. The city's minority students and families could send their children to SUNY if they had high enough scores or the funds to support their independent living, but this choice often landed minority students in seas of white students on isolated suburban or upstate campuses. Dorm life upstate, even with the financial aid that covered SUNY's tuition for poor students, cost much more than commuting to a free college on the subway. Most of the city kids accepted at SUNY (about 8 percent of the total enrollments) entered with relatively high scores, indicating that it probably was not a first choice, or very accessible, for poorer, minority students.[14]

Accelerating Open Admissions

Activists across the city's many campuses pushed hard on CUNY leaders in the late 1960s. SEEK had placed only 1,100 minority students at senior colleges by 1968. Brooklyn College was still 96 percent white in 1968, and City College was 91 percent white.[15] These high white populations contrasted sharply with the 40 percent African American and Puerto Rican enrollment in the city's high schools. Student activists highlighted this mismatch in 1969 by hanging a sign at City College reading "Harlem University."[16] The maintenance of an elite, mostly white citadel at City College in Harlem seemed particularly insensitive in an era of urban crisis.

Had CUNY leaders accepted state plans and funds earlier, they might have been able to manage the adjustment better, but now they merely caved. Bowker justified moving up the open admission target to 1970, without the planning or facilities to handle the historic change, because the "admissions criteria at the city's public colleges were systematically excluding those whose need for entry into higher education was most pressing." Open admissions was a transparent attempt to make up for decades of ignoring the changing social composition of the city.[17]

Under CUNY open admissions, the system guaranteed admission to a senior college for the top half of graduating classes in the city, looking past the radically different quality of city schools and family background in poor neighborhoods versus middle-class neighborhoods. The remaining lower half of high school graduates would be placed in hastily expanded community colleges. Total part- and full-time students in the CUNY system increased from 172,000 to 259,000 between 1969 and 1973. Minority and Hispanic enrollment rose from 18.8 to 35.6 percent in the same period. Citywide, CUNY was spending $30 million annually in the early 1970s on remedial tutoring for large numbers of accepted students, many of whom could not read or write at a college or, in some cases, even high school level. College graduation rates plummeted from their formerly high levels. The system was losing its status among better students, often viewed as a "last resort" below either SUNY or private alternatives. SUNY applications from the city soared.[18] Some of this uptick in SUNY demand was driven by "general unease on the part of the middle class, regarding the future of the City University."[19]

Legendary socialist Michael Harrington, reflecting the sentiment of some leftist CUNY faculty, believed that graduating even small numbers of many students admitted through open admissions was an "incomplete success" because, in his view, addressing the needs of these students was both more difficult and crucial for a better society than serving the more privileged. Older alumni, by contrast, believed open admissions destroyed the system's quality and reputation.[20] The chaos of open admissions became additional evidence of the city leadership's chronic mismanagement. The fact that similar debates were not so public in other cities should not lead one to think that similar tensions were not just below the surface. In Newark, Detroit, Cleveland, and Chicago it was clear to many minority residents that states used urban land and conveniences to support comparatively elite state universities that drew students from a broad region rather than addressing local issues of equity.

Rockefeller, watching the chaos from a distance, proposed in 1972 that SUNY absorb the City University to help meet the challenge of open admissions and restore some fiscal balance. Former mayor Robert Wagner and those on a study commission he led still believed that a merger—despite the clear benefits to quality—would lead to the greater evil of broader tuition charges. The commission boldly proposed, instead, that the free tuition policy be preserved, CUNY retain its independence, and the state increase its support to 75 percent of CUNY operating costs. Wagner's commission was skeptical, for instance, that tuition would lead to more state funding and believed that city residents were already contributing disproportionately to SUNY through the state's tax system (a familiar refrain today in New York City). Understandably, the state rejected this proposal, which gave it no more control over CUNY while asking for far more money. Many state legislators remained skeptical about the labor arrangements at CUNY, which they believed would simply vacuum up additional subsidies. This rejection left CUNY highly reliant on the weakening city government.[21]

By sticking to the free tuition model, CUNY administrators made it challenging to fund desperately needed expansion and provided limited opportunity for scholarships financed by higher-income students. One estimate determined that CUNY was forgoing $40 million in revenue when combined with potential state aid.[22] The CUNY operating budget increased from $325 million in 1969 ($2.2 billion in 2017 dollars) to $565 million in 1974 ($2.85 billion in 2017 dollars), a worrying trend for a city on the edge of municipal bankruptcy, even with a 50-50 split with the state government.[23] A task force in 1969 had already stressed that CUNY had a "lack of physical space to absorb the increased students."[24] A one-third increase in daytime student populations from 1970 to 1973, reaching 133,999 students, was a challenge. The space allocated per student at CUNY was roughly half that at SUNY and one-third of typical private colleges. The senior colleges began building and renting millions of square feet of new space, at a cost of approximately $1.5 billion, when the city's budget was already stretched.[25]

The resistance to state interference for almost a decade and a half, in the context of such a massive increase in students, made CUNY's looming financial crisis far worse than it would have been otherwise. The state in 1975 spent $3,300 per student ($15,272 in 2017 dollars) at SUNY senior colleges versus just $1,300 ($6,016 in 2017 dollars) for each CUNY student.[26] When Mayor Beame slashed city aid to higher education as part of citywide belt-tightening during the municipal financial crisis, state officials initially refused to bail out a system they did not control. The Board of Higher Education thus began significant cuts in late 1975, raised admission standards to slash enrollment, and furloughed many staff and faculty.[27] The state offered to cover 75 percent of the operating costs, up from 50 percent, if CUNY simply added tuition charges. State officials pointed out that 75 percent of students would not pay anything even with charges because of the scholarship programs in place for poorer students.[28]

The city finally surrendered. The governor gained the right to appoint a majority of the board members, and the system officially ended free tuition in 1976 to access state funds. The damage had been done to the reputation of the system and the city. Cuts to faculty and staff still had to be made in the context of the state's financial crisis.[29] By 1980, the total number of CUNY students dropped by 62,000. Many crucial research and facility improvements were put on hold. Even the hoped-for benefits to minority students were threatened by the delays, with an embarrassing 50 percent reduction in black and Latino first-year students in the CUNY entering class in 1980.[30]

A Secret Romance: CUNY and the State Government

State aid, as in other American cities, proved transformative in New York City for the quality and scale of urban higher education from the 1970s to the present. When the state's budget crisis subsided in the 1980s, the cash spigot sputtered back on. In the decades that followed, CUNY would reassert selectivity in its senior colleges, maintain low tuition, sustain new campuses with minority focus (such as Medgar Evers and York Colleges), and mount a major faculty research program. Steady state support has similar effects on downtown state colleges across the nation, from Wayne State in Detroit to Georgia Tech in Atlanta.

The senior colleges have enviable regional reputations today and are highly competitive. The campuses are expanding and modern and remain anchors of their respective neighborhoods, including Harlem (City College of New York) and the flatlands of Brooklyn (Brooklyn College). The current system has 270,000 degree-seeking students and an $8 billion economic impact; 60 percent of students attend tuition-free (and more will soon because of newly created Excelsior scholarships from the state), 85 percent stay in New York City (adding educated citizens to the labor market), and merely maintaining the campuses requires hundreds of millions in annual construction spending. The senior colleges justly celebrate their success in securing upward mobility for its students and are today 75 percent minority.[31]

Not all these changes are the result of state or city investments. As in the early twentieth century, the system's reputation benefits from highly competitive immigrant children, now more often from Asia, South America, and Africa than Europe. Nor has the return of competitive entry at CUNY senior colleges been warmly welcomed by all activists. The remigration of higher-income, higher-achieving students into the senior colleges and the concentration of poorer students in the community college system mirror somewhat the situation during the Rockefeller years. Community college students benefit from fewer resources, and the graduation rates are very low compared to the senior colleges. Low community college graduation rates have in recent years led to experiments like Guttman Community College, which provides a smaller, more supportive environment.

The depth of state subsidy to CUNY will probably surprise most New Yorkers. CUNY now includes 7 community colleges, 13 senior colleges, and 4 professional/graduate schools. In 2017, Albany provided $1.2 billion in

FIGURE 35. The City University of New York system is in fact a state-subsidized education system. Map by Minna Ninova, 2018.

direct aid to CUNY senior colleges, which represented 60 percent of their funding, a figure higher than the 40 percent SUNY schools get from direct state funds. The state also guarantees the bonds of the City University Construction Fund, makes available building programs through the State Dormitory Authority, and provides hundreds of millions more in financial aid and debt service payments. The city, by contrast, provided a paltry $30 million for the senior colleges in 2016. The state also underwrites New York's impressive network of community colleges, most of which have expanded during the past four decades.[32]

If direct funding were the determining factor in "ownership" of the system, CUNY should probably be renamed in honor of the state. In fact, in other states, it would probably be a state-associated system by name. CUNY faculty and administration remain dissatisfied with Albany's declining support in recent years; the state hasn't matched funding to growing student numbers, but without long-term state support CUNY would not have anywhere near the academic quality, benefit, salary levels, and low price that it does today. A city-supported institution like the University of the District of Columbia has fewer resources. It is no accident that most urban higher education institutions are state run.

New York State's direct role, through SUNY, in urban higher education statewide has also grown significantly since the Rockefeller years. SUNY administrators are adding facilities at urban sites because of their availability, appropriateness for specific programs (public policy or medicine), and attractiveness to many students. The rapidly growing Buffalo Niagara Medical Campus, a nine-million-square-foot colossus on the edge of downtown, now includes facilities for treatment, research, business development, and more. The state government is the lead investor in changing an ordinary urban hospital complex into an ambitious technology incubator. The University at Buffalo's impressive New York State Center of Excellence in Bioinformatics and Life Sciences, for instance, is deeply subsidized by the state to generate technology transfer and cooperation. The goal is to create a "hub of life sciences expertise" upstate that, among other projects, can use supercomputing as part of bioinformatics focusing on cancer, pathogens, and more. The University at Buffalo administration's decision to relocate the Jacobs School of Medicine and Biomedical Sciences to the downtown campus, from the older Main Street professional campus setting, cements the state's presence downtown. SUNY suburban and small town campuses continue to add most of the new academic and residential buildings system wide, but a notable trend is the new investments in center-city locations, such as these buildings in Buffalo and a new engineering school in center-city Albany.[33]

American Center-City State Universities

Cities in most states are closely aligned with state university interests. Declining cities are eager for investment, many older public and private universities viewed state government patrons as saviors, and many students and faculty enjoy living downtown. The campuses promise additions of new educational options for city residents; the potential for new services that might be expensive to fund otherwise (private security, health care, social work); and physical redevelopment of whole districts without much city help. Most of these benefits have been delivered.

Many urban districts, frequently old warehouse or other commercial areas, have been cleared, either rapidly or incrementally, as part of these urban higher education programs. Large institutional buildings often create fortresslike environs, with elevated walkways and private lobbies, commons, and offices, that can be secured by university police forces. Many state universities have recently become lead developers for new commercial centers, cafés, tech incubators, apartment buildings, and other schemes to upgrade surrounding neighborhoods. Questions remain, however, about minority enrollment at the most elite and competitive of these institutions within majority-minority cities. Gentrification associated with these campuses is also often valued more by city leaders and business interests than long-time neighbors experiencing pressure on rents.

A number of these institutions resulted from state takeovers of formerly private urban universities that faltered during the postwar era because of changing demographics and limited fund-raising ability. Cleveland State University (CSU), for instance, traces its roots to a state takeover in the 1960s of Fenn College, a career-oriented private institution. The opening of the Cleveland State era in 1965 was a direct result of Ohio governor Rhodes's campaign promise of a "state university within a thirty-mile radius of every citizen." The governor also insisted that the university remain and expand in the downtown. The 1966 master plan called for a 100-acre academic core for 20,000 students and 7,500 parking spaces. The plan's advantages included "easy and quick access from the Innerbelt" highway and "availability of nearby land to be acquired through urban renewal." Indeed, CSU purchased and cleared large numbers of older buildings. The campus launched with a typical elevated brutalist megastructure that walled off the mostly white student commuters from the city outside.[34] Only one phase of the megastructure rose, and it was not beloved.

Administrators have transformed CSU since the 1990s into a "city facing" campus that begins at the gates of the revived Playhouse Square district of downtown. Urban redevelopment now means civic engagement on multiple levels. The Euclid Avenue spine of the campus, now threaded by the popular Silver Line Bus Rapid Transit system, includes glass-fronted academic buildings, collegiate shopping and living options in adapted old and new buildings, and extensive landscaping. CSU administrators have also developed scholarship and similar outreach efforts to make the campus more reflective of the majority-minority city in which it resides—a typical complaint of neighbors surrounding state universities. Cleveland State is today 61.4 percent white in a city that is 53 percent African American. African American students make up only 16.9 percent of the Cleveland State student population.[35]

Professional campuses, filled with older, career-focused students working and studying long hours, are natural urban anchors. The University of Maryland at Baltimore (UMAB) campus, for instance, has grown from modest beginnings into a large (58 buildings on 60 acres) medical-related complex on Baltimore's once decayed Westside downtown commercial district. The

FIGURE 36 AND 37. Cleveland State University Master Plan (1966), partially realized, typical of "fortress" urban state universities at the time, replaced an older commercial district. Courtesy of Cleveland State University Facilities.

medical, law, and dental schools trace their roots to the early nineteenth century; later additions brought schools of nursing, pharmacy, and social work. The 1,200 faculty today secure half a billion dollars in annual grants in areas such as cancer and genomics. The adjoining hospital complex of the University of Maryland Medical System, always in some phase of renovation and expansion, provides care and serves as a teaching hospital to city residents and others. Its shock trauma center is nationally famous for pioneering medivac helicopters and EMS training in the early 1970s thanks to the support of Governor Marvin Mandel. The UMAB campus planning office created distinctive architectural palates, new public spaces, extensive landscaping, and expanded parking facilities. The thousands of medical and associated students have created demand for renovated lofts and apartments in surrounding neighborhoods.[36]

The adjoining UMAB BioPark (2003), planned to eventually include 1.8 million square feet of space of labs and classrooms on 10 acres, is under way through a nonprofit subcorporation. It reflects the urban spillover effects sought by many urban private and public universities. The BioPark is rising on the west side of Martin Luther King Jr. Boulevard, in a poor neighborhood that was the former site of a tower-block public housing project redeveloped under the US Department of Housing and Urban Development's Hope VI plan. The leadership acquired vacant land with the help of the city, secured additional police protection, and attracted commercial tenants. The BioPark already includes half a million square feet of space, many startups and spinoffs, and a massive parking ramp, key for its affluent employee base who likely have concerns about working in one of Baltimore's violent Westside neighborhoods. The effort includes community outreach programs in areas such as science, technology, engineering, and math education, an acknowledgment of the tensions that simmer between elite, whiter, urban state universities and their surroundings. UMAB's African American student population, for instance, is only 18 percent in a city that is 62 percent African American. This level of integration is, however, significantly better than the situation decades ago, when Maryland's professional schools banned enrollment of any minority students.[37]

Center-city campuses and affiliated medical centers are also crucial elements of healthier Sunbelt and western city regions. UCLA, in West Los Angeles, employs approximately 47,000 people, who receive a total of $3.2 billion in compensation. The economic impact is vast, with an estimated 94,000 positions supported in direct/indirect/induced fields. Nearly 40,000 students form a core of renters and consumers. UCLA's economic employment impact exceeds 61 of 87 industry sectors in Southern California.[38] The University of California, San Francisco (UCSF) Medical Center and health-related graduate schools have similar power. UCSF remains today a major anchor institution, with 24,000 employees and an $8.9 billion economic impact in the Bay area.[39] Other standouts that deeply impact urban conditions in the West include the University of New Mexico campus in Albuquerque, the University of Arizona in Tucson, the University of Denver, Portland State University, and the University of Washington, Seattle. Southern cities have quietly benefited from professional campuses, including the Georgia Tech campus in Atlanta ($2.87 billion annual economic impact) and the vast medical center / research campus of the University of Alabama at Birmingham ($7.5 billion annual economic impact).[40]

State universities in center cities have sustained the urban redevelopment goals of the postwar era. Their growing influence reflects what can be done for urban districts when states maintain funding and focus for decades. These urban universities exist at a remove from their still-struggling neighbors and contribute less than private businesses in taxes to support local government, but realistically these cities would be even worse off without them. Cities would lose some of their largest employers, thousands of renters and consumers, crucial medical services, sustained infrastructure development, and extra security in and around the campuses. In this dimension of postwar policy, states have played a vital role in center-city stabilization.

Metropolitan Housing

10

Housing Finance Agencies Rethink Subsidized Housing

State government deserves more attention for its role in postwar housing policy. National agencies such as the Federal Housing Administration and the Department of Housing and Urban Development, and federal programs such as public housing and Section 8, have dominated headlines and scholarship for decades. Not only did states serve as crucial partners with federal and local agencies in programs like these, but the direct influence and investment of states in housing has grown significantly since the 1960s. State housing agencies have become deeply engaged in regulating and subsidizing America's contemporary affordable housing production system. The fact that states are not recognized for this role, outside specialist circles, merits correction.

States, responsive to progressive city leadership, entered private housing regulation decades before the federal government. In the nineteenth and early twentieth centuries, in response to horrible tenement conditions highlighted by visionaries like Jacob Riis, "legislatures in the major cities and in states across the country adopted building regulations to suppress the tenement and ensure that the poor would have access to air and light."[1] State-enabled zoning law addressed public interest in protecting residential neighborhoods from unwanted uses and density. Many state governments in the 1930s created pioneering public housing authorities with novel powers such as eminent domain and long-term housing ownership and management.[2]

A common thread of state housing policy, despite federal promotion of government-owned public housing, was the enduring and prescient emphasis on public/private partnerships. By 1949, for instance, many states had taken a cue from New York's success attracting large insurance companies like Metropolitan Life to middle-class housing. Twenty-three state legislatures by 1949 had created legislation to encourage insurance company investments "in the direct financing, building, and management of large-scale, moderate rental housing."[3] California's successful veteran housing program, with the state buying the houses and selling them to veterans who might not have qualified otherwise, successfully moved about 176,000 privately developed homes to new owners between 1921 and 1960. Oregon took a similar tack in a program that from 1945 to 1961 provided $250 million in loans for 33,000 veterans to buy homes. Puerto Rico, Arkansas, and Hawaii were given credit for early leadership on condominium authorization in the 1960s, "a new form of homeownership expected to aid the middle-income family."[4]

New York State was early to the field and built the biggest projects, but far more important than timing or scale was the state's many experimental housing programs that have shaped the contemporary affordable housing industry. New York placed pioneering emphasis on private/public housing partnerships, mixed-income projects, tenant "demand side" subsidies (vouchers), subsidies for renovation, and more. New York's experience illustrates the ups and downs, impact on cities and suburbs, and unintended consequences of these pioneering housing programs.

New York State's Pioneering Efforts

In response to famously substandard housing conditions in New York City, the state legislature had progressively developed the nation's most aggressive series of tenement house laws. The aim was to regulate and thus sustain a massive, privately run, low-cost urban housing market. The New York State Tenement House Act of 1901 was a watershed nationally for establishing minimum modern standards. The law created a boom in privately developed, higher-quality "New Law" apartment buildings in New York City neighborhoods, often around new stops on the emerging subway system.

New York was also one of the first American states to subsidize private, moderate-cost housing. Governor Al Smith's State Housing Act (1926) attracted leftist labor unions in New York City, and a few desperate private developers during the Great Depression, who were willing to accept the limited profit requirements embedded in the law. The state's Redevelopment Company Law (1942), championed by Robert Moses, brought forth a revolutionary, if limited, generation of huge middle-income housing projects such as Parkchester and Stuyvesant Town developed by insurance companies seeking stable, long-term urban investments.

In the postwar years, the combined federal and city programs were, at first, more aggressive in middle-income housing than the state's existing laws. Moses's Slum Clearance Committee (1948) blended city, private, and federal Title I funds to replace tenements with middle-class enclaves that would deliver more property tax and thousands of solid citizens. By 1957, the program counted for a total of $881 million in city, federal, and private investments to build 38,000 new apartments in comprehensively planned "tower in the park" complexes. Yet the challenge of clearing 27,000 existing units on targeted sites (and other buildings), relocating tenants elsewhere, and developing the new housing projects ran into many snags during the 1950s. Delays in the program, empty lots and rotting buildings, and the social cost of relocation were political liabilities so severe that they undermined Moses's tight hold on urban renewal. Title I in other cities, while smaller in scale, ran into similar problems.[5]

The state's powerful role in low-income public housing revealed different liabilities. State-sponsored public housing for poorer city residents was not unique in America, but it was singularly large in New York thanks to Moses's need for site relocation. By 1958, New York State's many housing authorities had cleared 42,000 "substandard" housing units and produced 99 new housing projects offering 61,030 units. Most state-sponsored public housing apartments sprouted in New York City (in 43 projects), but the greatest number of projects (56) were in other cities or towns statewide. The New York City Housing Authority's (NYCHA's) many large projects with over 1,000 units each accounted for this lopsided statistic. The federal government sponsored tens of thousands of additional public housing apartments after the passage of the Housing Acts of 1949 and 1954. The state and federal projects collectively displaced tens of thousands of additional site residents without rehousing many of them in new redbrick minimal towers or garden apartments.[6]

These public housing communities rose very quickly, but the achievement in New York City and upstate raised many questions. Housing advocates in the 1950s realized that most public housing projects "were individually too big and almost unmanageable" because the tenants were poorer than planned, rent collection was weak, and many families had complicated social problems. Cities with public housing usually lost about as many units as they gained and effectively signed away decades of future tax revenues from the cleared sites. New York State housing administrators in the 1950s and 1960s experimented with the privatization of selected public projects and better-quality garden apartments to try to save the program, but most state voters and legislators had so soured on the concept that the state program ran out of funds by the early 1960s. A similar revolt against public housing gripped other states, although in most other states the federal government had been the primary sponsor.[7]

The frustration on multiple housing fronts during the 1950s and 1960s contributed to the creation of Mitchell-Lama (1955): an umbrella term that refers to New York's pioneering program of state-subsidized lower- to middle-income housing. With bipartisan support in Albany, including crucial leadership of Robert Moses and future New York City mayor Robert Wagner, Governor Averell Harriman's administration and the state legislature initiated the Limited Profit Housing Company Law (1955), or Mitchell-Lama. Unlike most public housing, and reflecting the income groups targeted, the program was designed to be "entirely self-liquidating." The law targeted "low-income families whose needs could not be met by the 'unaided operation of private enterprise,'" a deliberately vague social definition that would "encompass a 'middle income' group." With an upper rental limit for entry at six times the annual rent plus utilities, and possibilities for rent surcharges for existing tenants should their income increase, the state intended these projects to encourage social mobility and mixture. The program openly encouraged the use of "undeveloped" sites "to eliminate the need for relocation of site tenants," a clear response to growing public unhappiness over urban renewal and public housing policies in New York City. The state's Division of Housing and Community Renewal (DHCR) negotiated directly with private sponsors and local governments rather than relying upon local public housing authorities or redevelopment authorities that had become so controversial.[8]

The state's voters approved $50 million in state loan funds to back the program and in 1958 approved another $100 million ($861 million in 2018 dollars). Local governments could also issue bonds and make loans. New York City, for which the program had been created in the first place, issued $100 million in loans by 1959. Developers applied to participate in a program that offered low-risk loans (covering 90 percent of project costs) at a rate of 3 percent interest and partial local tax exemption, enticements that somewhat compensated for a 6 percent cap on profits. By the late 1950s, colleges and hospitals joined the program to create housing for faculty and medical personnel, investments that provided another potential boost to urban economies and urban neighborhood social mixture. The Mitchell-Lama program, however, underperformed in much the same way earlier state programs had.[9] The state legislature in 1957, to spur private-sector interest, reduced the time period that owners were required to remain in the program from 50 to 35 years. By 1959, however, there were still just eight projects for 2,079 families completed or in construction.[10]

Inventing the State Housing Finance Agency Model

By the late 1950s, New York's politicians and housing leaders believed that subsidized working/middle-class housing desperately needed additional stimulus. The route selected by the Rockefeller administration, wise to the growing sentiment opposed to public housing, was to double down on private-sector participation.[11] Rockefeller's Task Force on Middle-Income Housing (1959), led by Otto Nelson of the Metropolitan Life Corporation, called for better intergovernmental cooperation, more generous tax abatement, integration of the program in urban renewal projects, and creation of new sponsor committees to overcome development complexities. The most controversial proposal was to sweeten the pot for developers. They believed that the limits of profit before taxes provided "little encouragement of private enterprise." Few developers had the patience to wait 35 years for full private ownership. Developers, the task force thought, should be given the "opportunity for transferring the new housing to full private ownership after a period of 15 years."[12]

Shortening the mandatory regulated term to twenty years, as agreed to by the governor and state legislature in 1959, finally attracted many more developers to the program. These easier terms would result in quicker profits, more high-quality urban housing, and a quicker boost for faltering municipal tax revenues when housing developments timed out of the subsidy and tax abatement programs. Rapid conversion to market rates also encouraged developers to build housing for middle-class standards because the units could be sold or rented at higher rates in the future. Conversion to market rents on a shorter term was not an accident or compromise; instead, it was a program goal that aligned with the Rockefeller administration's emphasis on planning for the upwardly mobile or already prosperous. The planned reversion to market rents to entice developers anticipated today's LIHTC affordable housing projects, but planned market conversion would also create problems for later politicians entrusted with "preserving" units in a program designed, at heart, to harness developer greed and boost city tax revenues. Those 20 years passed all too quickly for many tenants and activists.[13]

Rockefeller's team leveraged these more generous terms with an innovative and influential financing program. The state's many public authorities had demonstrated for decades that the private sector could be a robust source of private funding for public works if a clear revenue source could be promised to secure those bonds. Middle-income housing would now follow in the footsteps of the Port of New York Authority, TBTA, and NYCHA, responsible for "construction of housing, airports, highways, and many other facilities without which our urban, airborne, automotive society could not function."[14] Rockefeller's administration during the 1960s conjured up two new state organizations—the New York State Housing Finance Agency (1960) and the Urban Development Corporation (1968)—public benefit corporations with the ability to sell "moral obligation" tax-exempt bonds to investors that would be repaid and/or secured out of project revenues (rents, fees, etc.) and federal grants.

Selling these riskier bonds, according to administrator James Gaynor, was not the first choice. Gaynor had first tried in 1959 to convince the private sector to make a substantial commitment out of civic spirit but after a year of cajoling found that the altruistic approach was a "bomb. It won't fly, because these people are stewards of somebody else's money. . . . Housing is a very risky business." Gaynor had worked at NYCHA in the 1950s where he was impressed with "a program of housing without cash subsidy. We used no subsidies, but used the credit of the City of New York."[15] NYCHA sold bonds to finance self-liquidating public housing projects, for what was known as the "no cash subsidy" program. This independent program eventually gave rise to over 30,000 semi-middle-income NYCHA units in New York City—an impressive level of productivity for a nonfederal-funded housing program and one that had no equal in the United States at the time.

Gaynor, who reported support for the idea from Wall Street lawyer John Mitchell, convinced Rockefeller of the soundness of this procedure for a new state housing program. The key to the HFA's self-liquidating projects were the "moral obligation" bonds, which were sold without an accompanying and absolute state promise to backstop the bonds in case of default. Voter-approved bond debt, in contrast, had first call on the state's tax revenues (the full faith and credit of New York State), making them very secure, and therefore sellable at lower interest rates to investors. The HFA's moral obligation bonds had to be sold at higher interest rates because they were backed up by project revenues, and the HFA's reserve fund in the worst case, so the risk exposure for investors in case of default was higher.[16]

Gaynor and his colleagues doubted that Rockefeller entirely grasped the financial dimension of the program; instead, they thought that he "believed they were just a whole pack of user fees. . . . paid by a municipality or a college student or it came out of a rental fee."[17] Maybe he understood better than they realized. His secretary, Al Marshall, admitted years later that "unlike a lot of liberals, he wasn't turned off by somebody making a buck off a socially worthwhile program, like banks and bond buyers getting in on his housing projects. He was enough of a capitalist to wonder how good the motivation was if somebody couldn't make money on it." The HFA had the ability, through the incentives it could offer, to "take a project that private enterprise won't touch, and then make it commercially appealing."[18] Indeed, investors cared less about the social mission than the profits to be made in holding such high-interest debt. Companies involved in the quietly negotiated and private bond sales included Lehman Brothers, Smith, Barney, and W. H. Morton. The selling of tax-exempt bonds at high interest rates may have helped mute criticism from the elite concerning the growing scale, scope, and cost of New York state government during the Rockefeller years.

The moral obligation approach also worked in practice to build support among state legislators for the generous authorizations granted to the HFA. The state legislature could comfort itself that it was only morally obligated to backstop debts, not legally required to do so. The legislature's first authorization for HFA housing was for up to $500 million in bonds (ca. $4 billion in 2017 dollars) to be sold for limited profit housing at 4 percent interest for investors. This sum represented a figure many times the amount approved by voters for Mitchell-Lama up to that time and much more than could be expected directly from the legislature. By 1961, the administration already counted 11,415 apartments in 15 new projects and 6 others scheduled to go into construction that year. New York City was also able to finance thousands of additional apartments under the new program.[19]

An innovation of equal importance possessed by the HFA was short-term construction financing, or the "bond anticipation" program, which delivered loans to the many housing sponsors, often nonprofits, needing immediate construction financing.[20] The short-term program was designed to speed up the plodding process of urban redevelopment, which was as much on trial as slum clearance. Empty lots, or rotting buildings used for developers milked for profits in redevelopment zones, were an embarrassment to politicians. The bond anticipation program would by the 1970s sell and redeem billions in short-term notes for HFA projects. Indeed, projects moved much more quickly from proposal to completion thanks to the short-term financing.

The governor, once armed with the permission of the state legislature, gave Gaynor a relatively free hand in implementing these methods of self-liquidating projects and moral obligation bond offerings in overlapping positions leading the New York State Housing Finance Agency, the DHCR, the SUCF, and the Health and Mental Hygiene Fund. The HFA arranged the financing while these various agencies arranged the development details, including plans for revenues that would cover debt service and operations. Some skeptics raised early questions about the financing method. In 1964, an audit already criticized both the high interest rates and the noncompetitive sale of the bonds that contributed to these costs. Additional interest costs were in fact passed along to tenants and managers of the projects financed by them. The auditors wanted the public sale of bonds and potentially lower interest; after all, the bonds had "a very high level of investor acceptance due to the substantial security behind the bonds, including what the financial community characterized as a 'moral' pledge of state credit." The HFA, however, continued selling through "a syndicate of 200 major investment banking firms" rather than selling publicly. The interest totals incurred by the university, housing, and mental health projects raise questions about the price paid for circumventing voter approval. The interest paid for the long-term bond program by 1982 would total $9.6 billion in today's dollars.[21]

Mitchell-Lama projects rose primarily in New York City (comprising approximately 90 percent of all HFA-financed projects) thanks to the combined impact of state and city programs; only a few projects rose in cities such as Yonkers, Buffalo, and Rochester.[22] New York City was the clear winner: "Over 400 Mitchell-Lama rental properties with 165,000 units were funded from 1955 to 1978 in New York State. Of those, 271 properties, containing 139,400 units, were developed in New York City, including 174 rental properties with 69,800 units and 97 cooperative properties with 69,800 units." The program addressed middle-class housing on an unprecedented scale.[23]

New Urban Communities for the Middle Class

One of the opening notes of the Rockefeller administration on housing was a bold initiative to build large middle-income projects using air rights in New York City. Concourse Village, a 5,206-unit, middle-class cooperative in the Mitchell-Lama program planned for a platform over train yards in the Bronx, was cited admiringly in state housing materials for the "first use of air rights to create new sites for middle-income housing." The multiple slab tower blocks, surrounding acres of play space on the new platform, seemed to float in the middle of the track yards and were hailed as a "first in a rapidly developing trend toward utilizing air rights to create sites that will provide housing for middle-income families within the urban areas."[24]

James Gaynor led Rockefeller's Study Committee for Urban Middle-Income Housing (1961), which proposed that the city and state, using air rights, could add a million middle-class residents in just 10 years (250,000 apartments) without any significant displacement. This would have been a major and creative revision in the bulldozer urban redevelopment approach up to that time. The committee included close Rockefeller associates William Ronan, George Dudley (director of the state Office of Regional Development and a trusted architect and partner with Rockefeller since 1940 on projects including prefabricated housing in Puerto Rico and elsewhere), and Rocke-

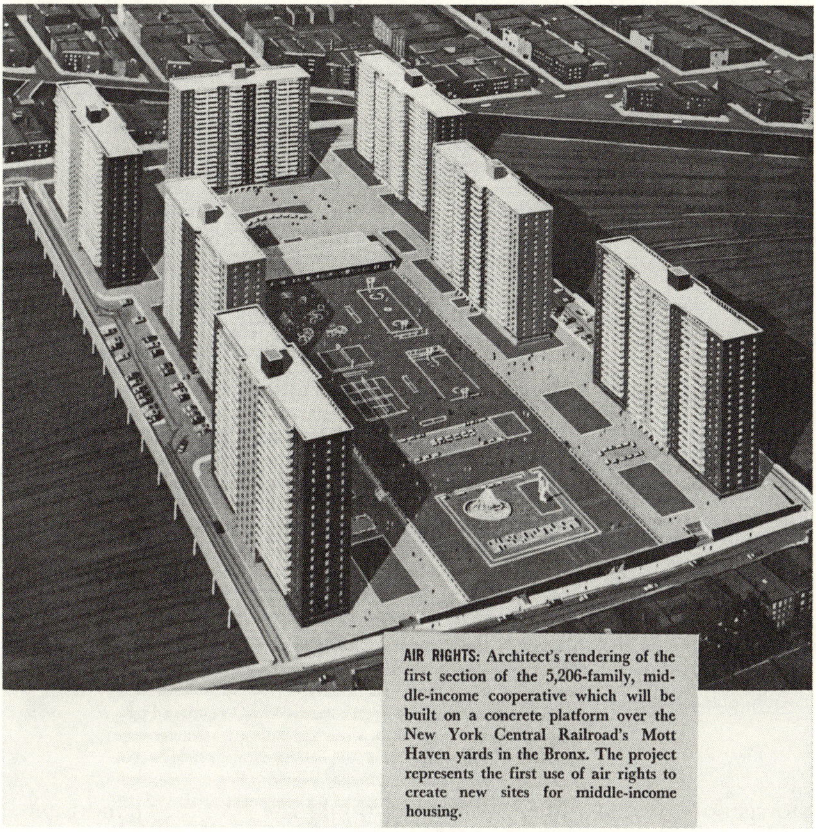

FIGURE 38. Concourse Village, rising on a platform above rail yards in the Bronx, inspired bold plans for new housing above infrastructure. New York State Division of Housing and Community Renewal Annual Report, 1960–1961. New York State Archives, courtesy of the Rockefeller Archive Center.

feller's friend modernist architect Wallace Harrison, the force behind the cooperative teams that built the United Nations, Lincoln Center, and various world fairs.

The visionary brochure for the proposal, reflecting the brightly colored modernist vision of Harrison, envisioned a citywide program with new housing over city infrastructure such as highways, piers, rapid transit storage tracks, parking fields, tunnel entrance plazas, and new schools. The project for a housing project over the IRT storage yard in northern Manhattan would have hidden the tracks under housing, parking decks, new play areas, shopping, and other buildings. The apartment buildings would not only add units but would help stabilize the "predominately middle-income walkups and elevator apartments" in nearby Inwood. Another project would recover 26 acres in east New York for urban living space by covering the IRT subway

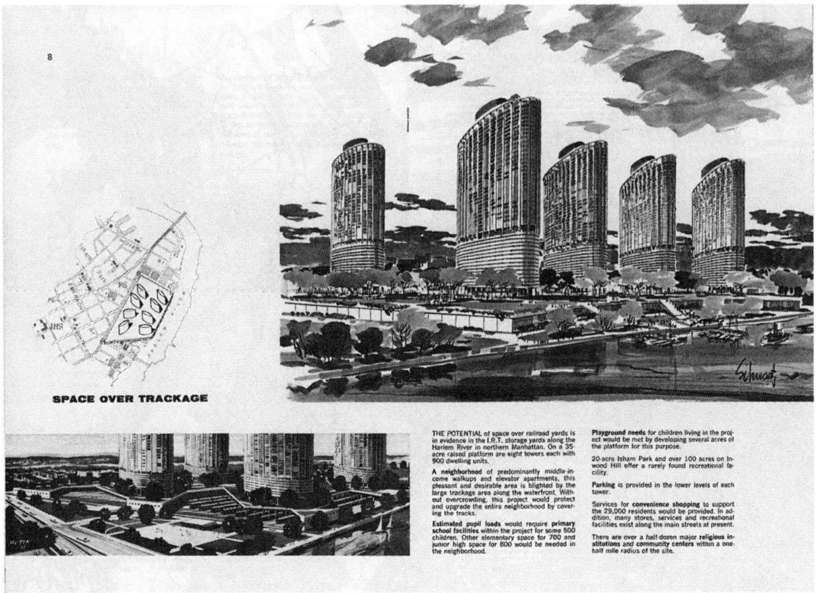

FIGURE 39. Vast middle-class communities to rise above the city's infrastructure. Study Committee for Urban Middle-Income Housing, "Space for Urban Living: A Plan of Action to Provide Urban Homes for Middle-Income Families Utilizing Air Rights Over Public Facilities," 1961. New York State Archives, courtesy of the Rockefeller Archive Center.

storage lots. Vast apartment complexes would rise over the Grand Central Parkway in Queens. Two 30-story towers over FDR Drive would begin to diversify East Harlem's tenements and public housing by adding units for "middle-income families, many having close ties with the neighborhood, thus giving balance to the neighborhood." This statement was a veiled reference to the need for middle-class minority housing of a high standard in a segregated city; a successful program like this could evidently help maintain the lines of the emerging second ghetto. The report projected $75 million in additional taxes yearly to the city even with major tax breaks for developers. After 30 years, and the expiration of state oversight, those taxes might well jump to $150 million per year.[25]

This well-intentioned initiative to add middle-class residents, hide many highways, and prevent the need to "tear down any existing structures" was greeted with howls of displeasure from city leaders.[26] Newbold Morris, New York's commissioner of parks and a Moses admirer, defended urban parkways as "true parks just as Central Park or any other. They have important recreational value of a different kind . . . their miles of seldom interrupted greenery, the feeling of 'rus in urbe' which has appealed alike to the motorists and to the dwellers in the adjacent communities." He claimed that for the middle class "the City's parkway system in its present beauty and convenience is an important element in making urban life not only bearable but attractive for them."[27]

The state might have moved ahead more aggressively despite the criticism, but the higher costs of building platforms and complex foundations threatened in most cases to "jeopardize the economic feasibility of such projects for middle-income families."[28] The concept of creating large middle-class, master-planned communities on sites not requiring displacement remained a lodestone for agencies such as the HFA, the UDC, and the Battery Park City Authority. The concept has been reinvigorated today with large-scale projects like Hudson Yards, Atlantic Terminal, and a visionary plan for Sunnyside Yards.[29]

Mitchell-Lama Islands

New York had the funds and the power to pull off large-scale projects that would provide refuges from declining urban neighborhoods, while leaders in other states and cities, lacking equivalent political support for subsidized housing, rarely ever built on such a scale. By the 1970s, however, many state leaders had learned cautionary lessons from New York's overly ambitious and supposedly sure bets on Mitchell-Lama projects as they developed their own, and quite different, housing finance programs.

The Mitchell-Lama program initially delivered high-quality middle-income communities with few notable social problems. Across the board, in the state program, the sponsors produced brick towers set back in lawns that offered respectable lobbies, relatively spacious and bright apartment layouts, lots of parking, and private balconies. The exterior design was intentionally secondary: "acceptable as far as appearance, acceptable as far as design, and acceptable as far as costs are concerned" rather than endowed with architectural flourishes that would cost residents (more concerned about "interiors") and taxpayers more.[30] A Mitchell-Lama rental apartment in New York City was a real prize, averaging 1,500 square feet.[31]

The Mitchell-Lama projects frequently looked like public housing to outsiders, except perhaps for the balconies, but looks were deceiving. Mitchell-Lama rentals and cooperatives gave private management more leeway in management policies, screening, and design than public housing. The program, compared to public housing, had wider permitted income levels and permitted surcharges for improving family economic circumstances. Sponsors often token-integrated their projects rather than promoting true racial integration as was pursued in public housing.[32]

The strategy of using Mitchell-Lama projects like these to stabilize declining or racially changing neighborhoods is still evident in parts of Manhattan, Brooklyn, and the Bronx. Many rose in stable middle-income areas, but figure 40 reflects the degree of risk leaders took in the placement of new projects in or near to areas of lower-income residents. A great many floated precariously in mostly poor neighborhoods. State housing leaders in the 1960s almost immediately recognized, however, the difficulty of maintaining socially and ethnically mixed Mitchell-Lama projects in neighborhoods changing faster racially and socially than anyone could have predicted. State leaders decided that they would have to offer more "security," broadly defined. One

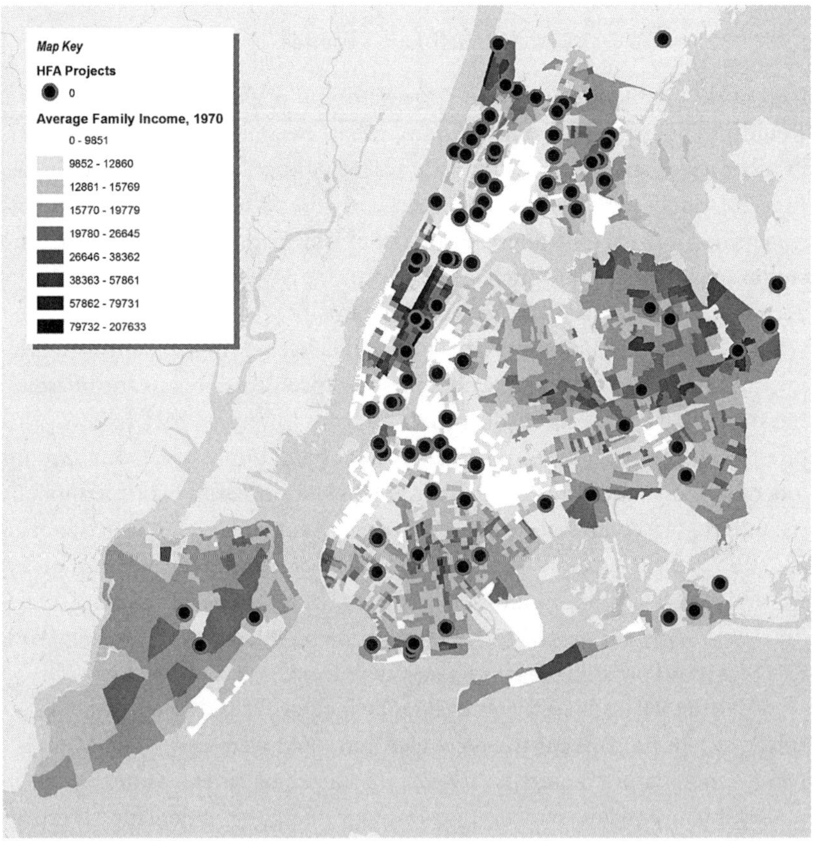

FIGURE 40. Mitchell-Lama invested in both prosperous and poor neighborhoods as part of a strategy for neighborhood stabilization. Map by Minna Ninova, 2018.

small project or two in a poor neighborhood, they found, faced obstacles as a strategy of social integration because "building on a small scale and marginal or deteriorated areas means the children will have to go to school in potentially dangerous situations, and mothers will have to walk to troubled areas to do the family marketing." Large-scale planned communities, by contrast, extended that security to the public realm because they "can contain their own schools, shopping and recreation areas and even their own security forces to augment the protection provided by the city."[33]

Some of the most eager institutional participants in Mitchell-Lama turned out to be nonprofits. Various socialistic unions, under the umbrella of the United Housing Federation, already dominated Mitchell-Lama housing, but a greater diversity of nonprofits joined in with state encouragement. By 1970, the nonprofit program included 16 projects, 6,627 apartments, and an investment of over $200 million. Many of these nonprofit towers provided housing for senior citizens with some measure of on-site support. Some of these units were located adjacent to urban hospitals in New York City and other cities, providing quality housing for professionals working within the growing urban medical system. Roosevelt Hospital's 465-unit staff housing project in Manhattan's Hell's Kitchen, for instance, aided neighborhood redevelopment along middle-class lines.[34] The state eventually halved equity requirements, which were too high for many nonprofits, and offered 95 percent and, later (1970), even 100 percent loans. The strategy of using nonprofits to lead housing development, despite many managerial and financial problems, became an essential element of New York and state HFA programs elsewhere and remains so to this day.[35]

The Enclave Strategy

A program of "new town"–scale projects became the central feature of the major projects in the state Mitchell-Lama program. Robert Moses and allied insurance companies had pioneered large-scale planned communities within the city limits at Parkchester and Stuyvesant Town during the 1940s. These communities were large enough to employ security forces, support shopping centers, and create landscaped environments distinct from the surrounding neighborhoods. They were also racially exclusive for years, much to the satisfaction of their white resident base. The "success" of the strategy was reflected in their continuing high occupancy rates in the 1960s despite surrounding urban abandonment in areas like the Lower East Side and the Bronx.

The HFA/DHCR, in partnership with Moses and the United Housing Foundation (UHF), built a new generation of urban new towns, now racially integrated by law, on a scale to rival those once created by the postwar insurance company giants. The HFA financed commitments to individual projects that alone would have consumed the proceeds from multiple voter-approved bond issues. The initial Co-op City loan, for instance, of approximately $250 million (ca. $1.9 billion in 2017 dollars) was a record for a mortgage (and eventually swallowed at least $350 million), large enough to create a community for 50,000 working and middle-class people within the boundaries of New York City. Rochdale Village (1960, 5,860 units), Co-op City (1965, 15,000 units), Starrett City (1976, 5,888 units), and another nine large projects such as Trump Village III and IV (2,820 units total) dominated the portfolio, although there were many smaller projects as well. By 1970 the DHCR, with the help of HFA financing, had approved mortgage loans of $1.189 billion ($7.63 billion in 2017 dollars) for 63,314 apartments statewide. Most of these launched after Rockefeller's term started in 1959 (93 of 106 projects).[36]

Abraham Kazan and other labor leaders participating in the United Housing Foundation he led pursued limited-profit cooperative ownership, cooperative enterprises, racial integration, community centers, and community-owned power plants. Modernist community planning, the famous "towers in the park," is on display at these complexes. The various projects boasted cookie-cutter brick tower blocks by architect Herman Jessor with relatively spacious apartments, lots of windows, formal modern layouts, and balconies. Inhabitants of these buildings were also "owners" of cooperative apartments rather than just temporary renters, a strategy influenced not only by Kazan's socialist leanings but a vision of anchoring the middle-class in self-regulating communities within the city.

The vast Co-op City (1965, 15,000 units) in the northeast Bronx mixed 35 24- and 33-story buildings, and eight parking garages to offer living space for approximately 50,000 people and their cars. The towers covered only 15 percent of the 300-acre site, as the vertical parking ramps reduced the need for large lots. The landscaped grounds featured extensive community facilities and neighborhood shopping centers. Most attractive to the tens of thousands new residents fleeing declining neighborhoods across the city were low-cost cooperative apartments featuring two-bedroom units of 1,200 square feet, central air-conditioning, parquet floors, sunlit dining areas, and layouts that emphasized family privacy by separating circulation from living spaces. The residents of Co-op City could, if they wished, eat, shop, learn, socialize, and exercise within the planned district. The community lacked a direct transit connection, which had some advantages in the minds of many residents turned off by the growing crime in the subways, but buses provided relatively quick access to nearby transit and downtown. Co-op City's direct connection to the region's highway network and ample space for cars was rare within city limits, opening many more opportunities for work and leisure.

The sponsors understood that these housing projects had become exercises in community planning: "Each project has increasingly provided more and more of the infrastructure and supportive services needed to adequately service the residents." The aim of such large projects was not only to reduce costs through mass construction but also to make "available the elements that make what could be a cold housing project into a total viable community."[37] Architectural and planning critics mostly panned these UHF complexes, which failed to respond to the turn against the "tower in the park" typology, but these negative reviews did not dim the public enthusiasm. Indeed, Co-op City and Rochdale Village offered a standard of living far beyond that available in many neighborhoods in the city. These communities attracted and retained the middle class, which might otherwise have abandoned the city entirely. The emerging minority middle class found these communities particularly appealing, as they were filled with moderate-cost, high-quality apartments that offered opportunities for ownership and pioneered racially integrated (sometimes temporarily, as it turned out) living in a sharply divided city.

Program administrator Charles Urstadt in the early 1970s remained "convinced that new housing can best be built only on a large scale, that is, in developments with at least 5000 units."[38] He dismissed NYCHA's smaller "scatter site" and "vest pocket" public housing developments as "not the stuff of which New York City's housing solutions are made" because of "the production of the smaller units takes more staff time, more dollars per unit and more aggravation." He challenged critics of the design to talk to residents directly because the "sales record at Co-op City indicates in loud, clearly understood terms the satisfaction of those for whom the housing is intended."[39]

Mixing Middle-Income Projects

In response to a lack of ethnic and income diversity in many Mitchell-Lama projects, the Rockefeller administration during the 1960s embarked on two major programs that it believed answered many of the concerns activists had both about the comparative exclusivity of the middle-income programs and developing concentrations of poverty in public housing. This overlooked but revolutionary program in New York State helped point the way to later federal rent supplement programs.

The Housing Finance Agency in 1962 began to provide 10-year low-interest loans for down payments required in cooperative buildings. The Home Owners Purchase Endorsement (HOPE) Program developed so that lower-income families could benefit from middle-class environments and address the shortage of minority buyers in mostly white cooperatives. By 1969, the program had provided over $6 million in loans to 23 housing companies for purchases by 3,581 mostly minority families. This investment represented a significant sum. More minority families probably gained access to large-scale cooperatives like Co-op City and Rochdale Village because of civil rights laws and white flight than through affirmative loan programs of this type. The use of homeownership as a tool of social integration was nevertheless pioneering.[40]

Rockefeller in 1964–1965, after some initial setbacks, was also successful initiating a "program of rent subsidies to low-income families" funded directly out of state appropriations.[41] The aim was to create "a limited number of apartments in middle-income developments . . . rented to low-income families who, apart from their income, are considered desirable tenants."[42] Known as the Capital Grant Low Rent Assistance (CGLRA) Program, up to 20 percent of families paid one-fifth of their income (or rent equivalent in newest state public housing), whichever was greater, and the state made up the difference of the rental costs. The state legislature later allowed higher percentages of families in a building to sign up to help struggling developers of Mitchell-Lama middle-income rental buildings facing declining market demand.[43]

DHCR administrator Charles Urstadt, in a 1972 *New York Times* editorial, favorably compared the state rental assistance programs to more overt attempts by the city to scatter public housing units in otherwise middle-income neighborhoods. The state, by way of contrast, preferred the "scattered apartment" approach as embodied in the capital grant low-rent assistance program because the program had by this time discreetly mixed in 2,300 low-income families in 55 different projects. The "children of these lower income families are able to grow up in a middle-income environment. They are not stigmatized because they live in low-income buildings, and they need not play in segregated playgrounds surrounded by, but not in contact with, their more affluent neighbors."[44]

Urstadt understandably glossed over some critical program issues reported internally.[45] The small number of families in the CGLRA Program that had transitioned to full rents by the 1970s were, for instance, becoming a severe financial problem. Only 5 percent of families in the program from 1969 to 1971 had been "able to assume full rental charges and terminate their rent assistance which suggests that few who enter the . . . program are economically able to move out of it." The state would be potentially required to provide hundreds of millions in additional subsidies. A ladder to social mobility was quickly becoming a semipermanent benefit.[46]

Urstadt's trumpeting of a large, successful state housing program in 1972 on the editorial pages of the *New York Times* does not seem accidental and may have been timed both to burnish Rockefeller's national reputation and influence federal officials then overhauling federal housing policy. The CGLRA Program was part of a general trend in the United States away from direct public ownership and management of low-income projects. During the 1960s, the Kennedy and Johnson administrations had also started to experiment with rent supplements for lower-income residents in private housing. Yet federal officials, facing an even more polarized political situation, failed to overcome combined opposition from public housing defenders on the left and anti-integrationists on the right. Rent supplements remained small at the federal level until the 1970s.

President Nixon's surprisingly strong support in 1973 for what became Section 8, motivated in part by his Watergate troubles and his moratorium on traditional public housing, proved crucial in making "demand"-side support, of the type Urstadt highlighted in New York, the dominant form of subsidized housing in the United States. Section 8 (which came in many different flavors, impacting new construction, substantial rehabilitation, and existing housing) was a public/private partnership that proved popular with the public, politicians, tenants, developers, and landlords. The federal government, unlike the states, had the deep pockets to make Section 8 a semipermanent benefit for millions of families. Section 8, for instance, remains an essential backstop for many privately managed affordable housing projects constructed with the help of LIHTCs because these complexes otherwise lack an annual operating subsidy that would make them affordable to lower-income tenants.[47]

Mitchell-Lama under Pressure

The scale, innovation, and speed of the Mitchell-Lama program and its associated income-mixture programs were breathtaking, but the rhetorical equivalence between housing projects and other public programs (such as airports that collected steady and increasing revenues) collapsed by the late 1960s. Production sputtered despite continued demand and political support from those who hoped to escape the city's deteriorating private housing stock. The Mitchell-Lama program in the late 1960s became more challenging as developers faced higher than expected construction cost, limited urban sites, complex local approvals, and limited profits. Rockefeller acknowledged that the Mitchell-Lama program had also bogged down due to "dozens of bureaucratic steps promoters of middle-income housing had to go through," including land assembly, local zoning, code changes, and tenant relocation. Developers often had "to tie up their venture capital anywhere from five to eight years and pay taxes on it."[48]

Co-op City was a standout problem project for decades despite its long-term success. The community had multiple problems on the construction front, bruising fights over neighborhood school districts, interethnic tension, and a prolonged rent strike in the face of rising maintenance charges due to "unrealistically" low initial carrying charges. The state characterized residents in 1974 as "highly organized and extremely militant."[49] White families, many of whom were initially enthusiastic, eventually abandoned the complex in the 1970s and 1980s and were replaced by an aspiring middle-class minority population. Co-op City remained a desirable place to live, isolated as it was from the chaos of the South Bronx, but it was more segregated and had to be more deeply subsidized than the UHF or HFA had envisioned.

Co-op City had many partners in trouble. Rochdale Village in the late 1960s suffered through a divisive fight over school integration, was damaged by the continuing decline of surrounding neighborhoods, and ended up losing its integrated character even faster than Co-op City. UHF's large Twin Pines (now Starrett City) community in East New York had to be completed by another developer after the UHF collapsed in 1972. Twin Pines had been promoted by city leaders "to keep middle-class families of all races in the city." The new developer converted it from cooperative to subsidized rental status—thus undercutting some of the key justifications for the big projects such as rooting the middle class in the city. Many large-scale state-sponsored projects never left the planning stages; others, like Battery Park City, were delayed so long that they changed beyond recognition. The 12,000 units targeted for the Sherman Creek area in northern Manhattan as a "totally balanced residential community," and ambitious new town plans for Floyd Bennett Field and Staten Island never advanced. Reality finally set in that the program was overextended.[50]

The inflationary environment of the era threw another wrench in the rent/income structure. The Mitchell-Lama housing cooperative companies and private owners found that "the cost of maintaining the state assisted cooperatives—and to build them—have risen so much that the rents are no longer sufficient to operate the developments and meet the mortgage." Residents of these complexes on the lower income side, including many senior citizens on fixed incomes, believed that the state, nonprofit developers, and even private developers had promised to maintain these places as moderate-cost islands no matter the financial drag, and they often resisted maintenance/rent increases. Nor did the hope that cooperative ownership would lead to owner residents willingly shouldering higher maintenance costs always pan out in practice.[51]

Higher-income Mitchell-Lama tenants were a different but equally worrisome challenge. The high rents in a few buildings allowed families (some with incomes up to $25,000/year) to gain access by the late 1960s. While only one-quarter of applicants from 1965 to 1969 were above $10,000/year family income, any high-income residents were a political liability considering the deep subsidies. What was worse is that higher-income residents often refused to pay surcharges required by state law. They resisted certifying their income annually, and managers were often reluctant to press the point for fear, perhaps, of losing them. In 1970, for instance, 20 projects in New York City failed to collect any surcharges at all. The buildings full of seniors and hospital staffs could be expected to collect few surcharges, but the same could not be said of Warbasse Houses, Concourse Village, and Rochdale Village—all of which had plenty of middle-class families and zero surcharge collection.[52]

Auditors pointed out that high-rent income residents not paying surcharges might consider their resistance a victimless crime, but they denied local government a legitimate source of income, as the state sent the surcharges to local governments to make up for property tax rebates. Not a single family had been removed from its apartment under Mitchell-Lama by 1972 for having excess income (greater than 25 percent than when admitted).[53] A letter from a Co-Op City resident in 1973 reflects the twisted logic of many upper-income families, warning that "unless the surcharge formula is changed, Co-Op City will lose its middle-income families, both black and white." By this reasoning, the state was expected to forgo contract and law, and millions in revenue that serviced debt, for the benefit of maintaining a few thousand middle-class families in New York City. State programs since this period have been much more careful to collect higher rents from higher-income residents both in New York and other states.[54]

This toxic combination of variables, created by a social mixture strategy with complicated and unexpected outcomes, created a grave situation. Developer Daniel Rose, who was deeply involved in the program, reported, "It is no secret that 90 out of New York's 125 subsidized middle-income projects are in arrears or default."[55] The HFA's program, and the moral obligation bond concept, now seemed risky rather than visionary. The HFA was forced to offer very high-interest rates (9–10 percent) on its bonds to entice investors, which boosted the operating cost of the projects it sponsored. The constructive "program that was supposed to have cost nothing was turning out to cost an enormous amount."[56]

By the early 1970s, the HFA was leery of underwriting any additional projects at all as the deteriorating "market situation" was creating a toxic situation of rent increases because of "spiraling" operating costs and taxes. Co-op City exposed major liabilities for the HFA.[57] In 1973, the state legislature clipped the HFA's wings and, hoping to reassure bond buyers, transferred $3 billion ($16.8 billion in 2017 dollars) of the HFA's borrowing authority to a new Medical Care Facilities Finance Agency and $400 million to the Battery Park City Authority. These new agencies would be able to finance projects that more reliably serviced the debt issued by the state.[58]

The Rockefeller administration had underestimated the political and social complexity of housing management and finance. The program, shaped in the era of the affluent society and rising incomes, did not calculate factors such as the deepening urban crisis, stagnation and aging of New York State's population, inflation, higher than expected construction and energy costs, design flaws, and the politicization of rental/carrying charges. There was, for instance, little or no compelling evidence at the time that the program "alleviates neighborhood deterioration or halts outmigration of families from the cities." In sum, many of the assumptions used for estimating future operating costs, and the idealistic hopes of stabilizing neighborhoods, were wrong or debatable.[59]

The HFA problems reached an existential crisis during the financial meltdown of New York City in 1975 when the HFA was cut out of the bond market. The HFA only righted its financial ship through a series of complex bailouts aided by New York State, including new state reserve funds, successful negotiations with Co-op City residents, state purchase of HFA offerings, second mortgages, use of county funds for hospital projects, selected foreclosures of housing projects, and conversion of high-interest short-term debt to long-term debt. Most of the cooperative and rental buildings limped along and, in many cases, deferred basic maintenance.

The continuing danger of politicizing rent became apparent in 1977 when the state legislature turned back a plan by Richard Ravitch to allow market rents immediately in vacated Mitchell-Lama apartments. According to Ravitch, by rejecting the plan, the government extended financial problems in these developments for many more years.[60] In 1980 the HFA offered another subsidy program to work out problems in Mitchell-Lama projects with construction defects, including Co-op City.[61] Many buildings in the troubled urban rental housing program had to be backstopped with Section 8 vouchers.[62]

In 2011, while tens of thousands of Mitchell-Lama units owners had privatized their operations, as Rockefeller and his team had planned, city and state leaders have devoted significant funding during the preceding few decades to "preserving" about 65,000 cooperative apartments and 33,000 rental apartments at below market prices and rents in New York City. The political pressure for preservation comes from the many senior or lower-income families that view Mitchell-Lama as a permanent subsidized housing program rather than a contractual, private/public partnership with multiple program goals. Such was the peril of using subsidized middle-income housing to stabilize neighborhoods in a city like New York.[63]

Pioneering Mixed-Income Housing

In the late 1960s, as the HFA faced declining interest from developers and mounting financial problems, Rockefeller created the Urban Development Corporation to supercharge subsidized housing development. The agency was fueled in the housing field by a new set of federal subsidies that, responding to state pressure and the problems of public housing, encouraged social mixture. The housing activities of the UDC helped pioneer, along with other state HFAs, today's federal/state/local/private mixed-income housing partnerships. The UDC also tested the limits of the emerging strategy to use subsidized housing to stabilize rather than replace declining neighborhoods.

Residents and leaders of New York's largest city continued to push for state action on housing despite the growing issues associated with subsidized housing. The challenge of quality housing in New York City became more severe in the late 1960s due to slum clearance and the declining conditions of older units. Of the city's 2.7 million housing units in 1970, 60 percent were more than 40 years old, and 500,000 were considered substandard. About 100,000 apartments had been lost to abandonment by 1970, and another half million were on their way to vacancy. Upstate cities suffered from similar, sometimes even more dramatic urban disinvestment.[64]

The UDC overcame investor skepticism for many sites and tenant mixes by becoming the lead developer of a project, only turning the buildings over to private interests relatively late in the development process or even after construction ended. Public risk and private profit was thus built into the model.[65] The UDC combined this engaged development process with the moral obligation financing system and a new federal subsidy program, Section 236. The

1968 Housing Act, according to Ed Logue, "finally brought the United States up to the level of commitment found in most of the advanced countries of Western Europe." Section 236 of the act offered 40-year contracts that dramatically reduced interest costs on loans, making it "a whopping subsidy. It cuts monthly payments almost in half."[66]

The Section 236 program was popular in New York and other states because it addressed the mainstream values of state leaders that emphasized public/private partnerships and social mobility: "While the 235–36 program generally has not been able to reach families with the lowest incomes, as public housing has, it nonetheless has been more popular on the whole than public housing because the occupants typically are employed and pay full property taxes, and the projects have tended to avoid massive concentrations of the poor in huge, isolated high-rise complexes." Sponsors had some flexibility to subsidize lower-income tenants if they wished, but serving the neediest was not a program priority.[67] Deliberate social mixture occurred in some HFA projects after the development process, but the Urban Development Corporation pursued income blending as a starting point. The UDC thus "built for a mix of moderate or middle-income families (70 percent), low-income (20 percent) and low-income elderly persons (10 percent)."[68] Logue adopted an intentionally broad definition of low-income that "allowed leeway to the point of providing housing where the private market was incapable of meeting the demand."[69] The flexible income structure, it was hoped, encouraged an "up and stay" strategy: "Families who improve their income are not forced to seek out another apartment—a problem often faced by families in public housing." Instead of eviction, "income improvement is encouraged in UDC developments, benefitting the community, the tenant, and the development itself."[70]

These were not to be federal and state government poorhouses but dynamic neighborhood apartment buildings that would contribute solid citizens and community cohesion even within declining neighborhoods. Sensitive to the growing clamor over slum clearance, UDC minimized slum clearance and offered existing residents, veterans, and those displaced by construction priority in the new UDC projects. The emphasis on income mixture at UDC was typical for state agencies using these federal programs during these years.

A New Machine for Building

Logue set up the development pipeline in 1969 and by 1972 had 30,759 units completed or under way in 44 different locales, a building program with a total value of $1 billion. Section 236, in addition to the funds generated by moral obligation funds, would be a key financing element for 28,350 of those units.[71] UDC lived up to its commitment to urban housing: by 1972, 86 percent of UDC-sponsored housing was in cities, 74 percent in the Big Six cities, and about half in New York City alone.[72]

The UDC mixed-income approach aligned with the thinking of influential planners, politicians, and urbanists of the day. In New York City, for instance, leaders were still more concerned about the loss of the middle class than adding more low-income units to NYCHA's already enormous public housing system. Mayor Lindsay eventually invited the UDC to work in eight renewal areas in 1969, including Welfare Island and ongoing projects in Harlem, East Harlem, the Bronx, and elsewhere. The UDC promised to act as a builder of housing and brought significant funds to the table rather than usurping the city's planning functions. Logue counted 11,000 apartments under way in the eight areas. The UDC picked up several smaller city projects in the pipeline, such as Twin Parks.[73]

UDC built very quickly, as its proponents had hoped, because its powers "contributed significantly to expedite negotiations for the design and location of housing developments," making it possible, in some cases to turn design concepts into apartments in just 18 months. Logue invested heavily in industrialized building methods that yielded mixed long-term outcomes due to technical problems typical of experimentation. The construction process itself became a tool of social mobility. The affirmative action program for minority construction workers, led by Kenneth Clark, by 1972 scored an impressive rate of 21.9 percent minority workers, a figure higher than the minority population statewide (18.9 percent), and a stark contrast to the white-dominated construction trade at the time.[74]

The UDC made a point of developing excellent apartment layouts, even duplex apartments, with lots of light. The Twin Parks complex featured a plan where "new buildings have been fitted between old ones or on small vacant lots so as to reduce large-scale clearance in the neighborhood."[75] While UDC supporters believed that the agency had "managed to break the traditional image of publicly assisted housing as a row of standardized redbrick towers" with experimental projects imagined by designers such as Paul Rudolph, Richard Meier, and Davis Brody and Associates, others were less convinced.[76] The alternative modern vision pursued at the urban projects was different in the context of rarefied architectural debate but still far from the American standard. In fairness to the UDC, however, there were many projects in the suburbs and in cities "designed to achieve compatibility with their surroundings . . . to avoid the stigma associated with publicly-assisted housing." The UDC developed, for instance, a robust collection of garden-style apartments throughout the state.[77]

The Crisis of Mixed-Income Stabilization

Below the surface, however, the UDC program was showing signs of strain. Requirements that residents pay 25 percent of their income tended to make UDC projects less attractive to the higher-income families with more affordable private market options. Many higher-income residents, on the other hand, were turned off by the location of so many UDC projects in poor, minority areas like the South Bronx and the center of Coney Island. Recruitment of white families failed and seemed unfair when so many minority families were applying for these good units.[78]

The financial mechanism failed at different levels. By 1972, "the independent accountant declined to render an affirmative opinion on UDC's financial statements" because of declining federal support and the small number of completed projects.[79] The price of the Schaumburg Towers project approached $65,000 a unit, as much as a nice house in the suburbs. Projects like these appeared to some as "a designer's dream, a foolish fraud upon the taxpayer and the citizenry, including the poor."[80] The UDC bundled its various projects into a general obligation / general purpose bond offering that included both "good and bad" loans. This misleading packaging and the inability to spin off individual low-performing projects contributed to the UDC's problems in the 1970s.[81]

Nixon's national moratorium on housing subsidies on January 8, 1973, struck "at the heart of UDC's ability in the future to create housing" because the UDC depended on programs like Section 236.[82] The UDC halted construction on many projects or tried to reorient them to higher-income families.[83] Rockefeller's successor, Governor Carey, considered the UDC another dangerous reminder of his predecessor's penchant for big thinking. High vacancy rates in housing developments in Niagara Falls and Buffalo, construction defects in others, and general disarray left the UDC politically exposed.[84] The UDC was in such a sorry state in 1975 that it required a mix of state and private loans to cover its immediate loan needs.[85] The governor was ready to approve financial aid to the UDC,[86] but the state legislature was skeptical.

Governor Carey enlisted Richard Ravitch to right the ship. Behind the scenes, Ravitch negotiated hard with the state, federal officials, and the financial community to cobble together the $690 million ($3.1 billion in 2018 dollars) in cash he believed was needed to build out and stabilize the UDC operation. He was determined, in fact, to build out as many projects in the pipeline as possible, as "if the projects were finished, they could produce enough revenues to cover the cost of servicing the debt that would need to be incurred to complete them." Failure to finish would also embroil the state in a legal morass that would end up in the courts, destroy contractors, and produce no housing.[87]

Ravitch's key innovation was to leverage future Section 236 federal funds to borrow $500 million through a new entity, the Project Finance Agency (PFA), that would be separate enough from the UDC to restore banker confidence in the bonds issued.[88] Legislators, on the edge of a UDC bankruptcy, eventually agreed that they could not let the state default despite the state having only given its moral obligation to the debt.[89] Big banks, in the person of David Rockefeller, sensed that the state would not default and, worried about the impact of a default on their bond holdings, finally came through with millions to allow the UDC to finish its projects.[90] Seeing the private investors step up convinced the state legislature to approve its share of the bailout.[91] Ravitch used the state bailout and PFA to build out the $1.5 billion in projects under way.[92] A new construction group was found to complete 11,000 of the 33,000 housing units in process. Half of the UDC staff was fired and future housing projects canceled.[93]

The financial danger of mixed-income, moderately subsidized projects continued to haunt the people living in and managing UDC projects during the 1970s and 1980s. With weak rent returns, the state had been forced to use creative accounting methods to refinance the portfolio in 1975, such as counting temporary state aid on the books of many projects to make them appear "viable." Tenant "resistance against rent increases" in the late 1970s, unfortunately, remained widespread, continuing to wreck the financial model. Federal subsidies under Section 236 were only ever projected to cover 65 percent of debt service, leaving rent payments to cover the remainder of the operating and capital costs. The rent crisis caused serious damage. Approximately 70 of 113 projects in the late 1970s had rents too low to cover operating and debt service costs, often leading to deferred maintenance, changing management, and general dissatisfaction. A rent increase at the Broadway East project in the small upstate city of Kingston, for instance, "drew immediate strong protests, from the tenants." They started moving out en masse into a city with a large stock of inexpensive and underoccupied private housing.[94]

The noble goal of building mixed-income buildings to increase urban social diversity in troubled areas contributed to this misfiring. In 1977, the UDC portfolio still suffered from a 7 percent vacancy rate in its apartments. The Twin Parks developments, for instance, were stricken by Bronx neighborhood decline, rising crime, and high utility charges. The Twin Parks NE recorded a 10 percent vacancy rate in 1978. It was not alone. Coney Island projects, also in a district with significant social issues, were highlighted for high vacancy rates. In 1978, 64 of 113 UDC residential projects were recorded as having vacancy rates 5 percent or higher. The social situation was in part to blame: "Most of the projects built by UDC are located on sites in the inner cities and were, in many cases, part of an urban renewal program. Although the new housing has upgraded the areas, it did not completely eliminate the endemic problems." Additional security guards required "to attract tenants" was another factor driving up costs.[95]

The accomplishments and succeeding troubles of the HFA and the UDC were known nationally. Among the many cautionary lessons embedded in the story for housing experts was the risk of state overreliance on federal programs lacking ironclad agreements; the crucial importance of filling mixed-income projects with a sufficient number of market-rate tenants; the challenges of building and tenanting new housing in urban areas of declining market power; the danger of mixing high-style architectural design into a subsidized housing program; and the necessity of taking great care in the selection of private managers. Many of these hard lessons are reflected in the different approach of today's affordable housing enterprise.

New York State Helps Reinvent Affordable Housing (Again)

The administration of Mario Cuomo (1983–1994), responding to a continuing housing shortage, strongly reentered the affordable housing field in the 1980s and 1990s as the downstate regional economy recovered. Although the federal government had slashed support, Governor Cuomo took a page from Rockefeller and invented new financing vehicles that relied on state-secured debt, private partners, nonprofits, and mixed-income tenancies, including homeownership.

The successful national affordable housing movement of the 1980s and 1990s, which continues today, was shaped in part by the creative response of housing advocates in New York and other states to the troubles of private disinvestment and crisis in older subsidy programs. New York's housing leaders retained the public/private approach, but there was an even more significant role for community-based partners, the city government, and private developers. Slum clearance was out, as were big projects, replaced by new strategies to stabilize older apartment buildings and add new buildings in surrounding vacant lots. The architects dutifully switched out grand statements for incremental, contextual, neotraditional, mixed-use dwellings.[96]

The HFA by 1994 had issued $587 million in new bonds to help create 8,450 units of affordable housing. The Homeless Housing Assistance Program (1983), responding to a highly visible and growing street and shelter population in New York City, provided capital grants for 5,232 units of permanent, transitional, and emergency housing. The Affordable Housing Corporation (1985) Cuomo created had by 1993 spent $265 million on purchase, rehabilitation, and improvement of 22,000 homes. Cuomo designated $326 million in tax revenues for affordable housing through the Infrastructure Trust Fund (1988). The state of New York Mortgage Agency provided $3 billion in loans for 49,000 buyers, including those in the world-famous Nehemiah program of moderate-income homeownership in East New York and the Bronx. The Battery Park City Authority, by this time generating robust revenues from commercial and mostly luxury development, in 1986 transferred millions in its commercial revenues to affordable housing across the city. Programs like these helped moderate-income families rent quality apartments and buy thousands of small homes within New York City that collectively helped stabilize suffering neighborhoods. Governor Cuomo claimed credit for 280,000 units created or renovated between 1983 and 1992. This state program played a critical role in Mayor Ed Koch's successful and more famous program of affordable housing development and preservation. [97]

State agencies like the HFA and DHCR since the 1980s have proved their value in helping to arrange the complex financial packages of state, local, and federal subsidies required to build assisted housing. Governor Andrew Cuomo, building on the family housing tradition, has promised to commit $20 billion to build or preserve 120,000 units over five years statewide. State dollars, for instance, have been key to sustaining older Mitchell-Lama buildings at below-market prices or rents. Albany remains a major contributor to publicized affordable housing efforts in New York City by Mayor Bill de Blasio: "From January 2014 through December 2017, 20,598 apartments—or almost one fourth of the 87,557 affordable housing units created or preserved by the de Blasio administration so far—had some form of state involvement, according to HPD."[98] It is worth acknowledging, however, that state-aided new construction and preservation aid has been offset, in part, by the state government's weakening of rent protections in New York City at the behest of landlords since the 1970s (and which Governor Rockefeller also promoted). Deregulation is nevertheless consistent with postwar state housing policies that favored urban investment by private investors.[99]

New York State's broad participation in working/middle-class housing and public/private partnerships since the 1960s established national precedents in financing, partnerships, and design. Rockefeller and subsequent

New York administrations, by sticking with programs even when they ran into trouble, demonstrated the long-term positive role a state government could play in center-city housing conditions. Programs in new construction, renovation, supportive housing, and tenant subsidies remain dominant today not only in New York but in many other states.

The Rise of the HFAs

The states, with New York as a leader, dramatically reentered the subsidized housing field in the 1960s and 1970s. Some state officials had "become convinced that neither the federal government nor city governments, acting without state legal and financial assistance, can adequately achieve the commonly accepted goal of a 'decent home and suitable living environment for every American family.'" Among the new tools they utilized for reengineering urban housing markets was "the establishment of housing finance agencies, development corporations, statewide housing authorities, industrialized housing certification programs, central relocation agencies, zoning appeals procedures, and state offices of community affairs."[100]

The successes and failures of this era helped shape our contemporary cities. The result of state interventions, usually packaged as complex state/federal/local/private partnerships, is collectively impressive. Today, hundreds of thousands of renters and owners across the nation have federal and state government agencies to thank for their comfortable, subsidized apartments, supportive housing (for the formerly homeless, veterans, etc.), and even many single-family homes. An impressively wide range of tenant families has been housed in a diversity of settings, at least compared to traditional public housing. The cumulative scale of the state investment in housing is counted in the many billions of dollars, even though the visual impact on urban landscapes is deliberately low profile.

New York's Housing Finance Agency, and its cousin, the UDC, proved to be enduring financing models for state-level affordable housing despite the problems they faced. The revenue bond approach, which circumvented rural/suburban opposition to subsidized housing in so many state legislatures, was just too good to ignore. By 1973, 29 states had joined New York in sponsoring similar agencies.[101] Like New York's HFA and UDC, they enjoyed "relative autonomy and flexibility, with the authority, in some cases, to act on their own initiative as land developers, limited-profit housing sponsors, and low-rent housing agencies." Many played a key role in reviewing or acquiring sites, architectural contracts, and tenant mix. Like the HFA, they could "sell revenue bonds, make loans, and provide technical and consultative services."

With their bonds exempt from federal taxes, they attracted investors at lower interest rates, the proceeds of which could be loaned at lower rates to developers for the creation of more modestly priced rentals.[102]

State HFAs relied initially upon the Section 236 program, which offered "administrative flexibility contained in the 'annual arrangement' to adjust rents and provide a greater economic mix in their projects, as well as to provide certain types of social amenities, such as recreation and community centers and, in a very few cases, swimming pools." Greater social mixture meant for many leftist activists a different kind of failure, as "state agencies do not reach the very lowest income families, particularly in rural areas and in urban centers of our central cities." Program administrators seemed too conservative to many activists because of their connection to the bond markets. By 1974, HFAs were given credit for creating 250,000 units, indicating that the programs in other states were often substantial. This level of productivity was impressive, given that in 1974 only half of the existing HFAs were fully operational and many were still hiring staff. The Speaker of the Michigan House of Representatives praised HFAs for being able to "locate housing and community facilities where job availability, housing demand, and other factors create a need for low and moderate-income housing." In other words, they could be in more than the poorest urban neighborhoods. State HFAs avoided both the dramatic architectural statements of the UDC and the bland towers in the park of the New York HFA. They also appear to have avoided the massive and unwieldy enclaves of the New York approach. Still, various state HFAs shared in some of the same 1970s troubles felt in New York. "Severe problems" developing in the HFA programs, Section 236 most notably, as well as those in traditional public housing, were blamed for the 1973 federal moratorium. The Nixon administration aimed to back off subsidy of new housing and replace these expensive programs' cash assistance with "demand"-based strategies such as Section 8.[103]

HFAs proved their value by surviving and then adapting to the new federal housing landscape. By 1980 HFAs could be found in 37 states and Puerto Rico. They continued to use revenue bond programs and now sometimes combined them with federal Section 8 subsidies: "State housing financing agencies are financing approximately one third of Section 8 new construction/substantial rehabilitation units each year, or about 50,000 units." A rate of production that high indicates the potential of so many state agencies.[104] HFAs were in fact given credit for the strong showing of the Section 8 program, which counted 927,000 units in the program by 1980.[105]

The cumulative HFA funds applied to housing nationally is impressive. The $192 billion in tax-exempt mortgage revenue bonds issued by 2004 and

$55 billion in multifamily bonds have generated roughly 2.4 million in home loans and 687,000 apartments.[106] The states rely on the federal government to underwrite their efforts, including annual authorizations of tax-exempt mortgage revenue bonds, LIHTCs, community block grants, and HOME Investment Partnerships Program. Credit for these complex partnerships also needs to be shared with community development corporations, LIHTC syndicators such as the Enterprise Foundation, and various city and state leaders.[107]

Active HFAs can achieve substantial production levels through these combined public/private partnerships. Florida's Housing Finance Corporation in 2016 took credit, in one year alone, for helping 12,400 families buy or save for a home, and the agency played a role in the creation or rehabilitation of 9,200 affordable units.[108] The affordable housing sector in the state pales, however, in comparison to both the need for low-cost housing and the productivity of the private sector: "Florida added 839,527 rental units between 2000 and 2014, but only 115,740 were affordable to renters with incomes below 60 percent of AMI."[109]

State housing trust funds, originating in the same creative era as HFAs, provide additional support in 40 states. Drawing from multiple sources, including general revenues, they offer "matching funds for federal programs, down payment assistance, predevelopment funds, technical assistance and project-based rental assistance." Some of these funds are large, as in Florida ($166 million in 2005), while others are modest.[110]

Some housing experts today, as they did decades ago, criticize states for not prioritizing the housing needs of America's poorest citizens. State-sponsored multifamily programs, according to housing experts Alex Schwartz and Elizabeth Mueller, "provide far less subsidy per unit than public housing, vouchers, and other deep-subsidy programs, and seldom assist extremely low-income households unless they also hold vouchers."[111] Persistent American attitudes about the deserving versus the nondeserving poor probably play some role in this outcome, but today's state administrators and developers face constraints similar to those of the Rockefeller era. States would struggle to provide sufficient annual operating funds for low-income projects they sponsored; as it is, they already rely on a variety of federal-sponsored programs and vouchers. Participating developers, as a result, are required to generate sufficient rents to cover the costs of operations and future capital needs. Developers thus target a broad range of tenant income levels, a low percentage of whom are very poor (compared to public housing) to maintain project solvency and higher standards of management.

State housing agencies helped pioneer today's dominant paradigm of mixed-income, mixed-location, and public/private affordable housing. The contemporary system is open to criticism that its definition of "affordable" is frequently so broad that the housing needs of the poorest have sometimes become secondary. Yet today's tighter financial structure appears to be more politically and economically sustainable than deeply subsidized programs like public housing. The modern approach grew incrementally out of diverse efforts by states to find a workable alternative to market and public housing options that did not work well for many families. There were many bumps on the road, but programs persisted thanks to talented private-sector partners, dedicated city and state leaders, and many supportive managers, activists, and residents.

11

The Sad Tale of Decentralized Subsidized Housing

Racial and economic divisions grew sharper and more dangerous in the postwar years, contributing to frustration and social unrest in American cities. Activists in the civil rights movement of the time viewed discriminatory housing practices—contributing to differences in education, occupation, and quality of life—as crucial sources of anger. During the 1940s, for instance, the NAACP mounted aggressive challenges to race-based restrictive property covenants, culminating in the *Shelly v. Kraemer* (1948) decision declaring such covenants unenforceable by the government. Activists in the 1950s also confronted William Levitt, and most of the white residents of his new communities, who openly endorsed segregation as a desirable community attribute.[1]

These high-profile postwar challenges changed policies and influenced public opinion, but they also tended to increase the determination of most suburban towns and developers to resist "social engineering" through other means. Among the tried and true tactics was unspoken pressure on realtors, elitist zoning with minimum and large lot sizes, limits on multifamily housing, environmental or tax burden objections, and painfully slow approvals. These techniques discouraged even some of the most idealistic and patient developers of multifamily subsidized housing.

By the 1960s, activists realized that while they may have won key battles on the suburban frontier, they had lost the war for equal access. Two strategies emerged: building subsidized housing in suburbs and fair housing laws. Liberal governors in states like New York, Massachusetts, New Jersey, and California were innovators in these fraught social integration enterprises. At first, it seemed they might successfully use the power of state government to cut through suburban resistance. The reality was more complicated and politically costly than they could ever have imagined.

Northern Suburban Elitists

The suburbs of New York reflected the growing segregationist pattern in the North. Suffolk County's African American population increased from 32,000 to 52,000 (1950–1960), but the fastest growth took place in just a few towns, indicating that the growth of minority residents was uneven. Growing segregation by town was also typical in Nassau and Westchester Counties. For those in the mainstream of the civil rights movement, in the NAACP or Urban League, and many liberal government officials, housing discrimination threatened to create new suburban ghettos that would inhibit the social mobility of minority families.[2] Manhattan Borough president Percy Sutton asked the question on many people's mind in the 1960s and 1970s: "Where do black people and Puerto Rican people turn if they want to change their lives and not be forever restricted to the ghetto?"[3]

UDC in the late 1960s became the hammer in Rockefeller's biggest attempt to change metropolitan housing patterns. Logue justified taking on the suburbs directly because "housing shortages are no respecters of boundaries." He took the notion of the UDC as a state entity seriously, so "the execution of its statutory obligations must be, at the very least, regional or metropolitan." Ed Logue's desire to see affordably priced housing in middle-class and wealthy suburbs, and certainly beyond the political boundaries of cities, was widely shared by those vitally interested in minority social mobility. Logue aimed to build moderate-cost, mixed-income communities rather than minority communities, but these complexes were widely viewed by both supporters and opponents as potential minority footholds in affluent white suburbs.[4] In the suburbs, after all, "exclusionary zoning practices were shown clearly to have resulted in de facto segregation. Most blacks were unable to afford the prices of single-family houses and were unable to move out of core city areas."[5]

Logue had scored some legal and political victories upstate that he incorrectly believed augured well for a move into the New York City suburbs. The UDC in Rochester aimed for "free flow of housing opportunities in and out of the City." To that end, Logue planned subsidized, mixed-income projects in a few Rochester neighborhoods. He attributed his success in Rochester not only to a favorable court ruling—the state supreme court upheld UDC's right to override local zoning—but also to strong support from Rochester business leaders such as the chairman of the board of the Xerox Corporation. By 1972, a Rochester-UDC subsidiary had built 3,042 units in the city of Rochester and an impressive 3,008 units in 12 different Rochester suburbs. That the UDC created mixed-income complexes that were designed to blend into the suburban setting likely helped. A development in Penfield, New York, included 350 townhouses with patios, balconies, open space, and gardens. The percentage of minority residents in these apartment complexes is not clear from the record, however.[6]

The troubles mounted when Logue decided to bring his suburban income integration strategy to Westchester County, one of the wealthiest and most segregated counties in the nation. In Westchester, his staff had found that "despite their offer to build low-density, garden style, landscaped units in the suburbs, the only acceptance it gets is in suburban cities that already have a low-income population."[7] Logue and Rockefeller overlooked, or seemed to dismiss, the growing management problems Mayor Lindsay faced with his "scatter site" public housing program in New York City. White middle-class residents in the city's outer boroughs mounted a vicious and successful public attack on NYCHA's plans for smaller projects in neighborhoods such as Forest Hills. The language of resistance to so-called liberal social engineering, including stoking fears of overcrowded schools and portraying minorities and the poor as de facto bad neighbors, played well in the press. Mario Cuomo, then a lawyer, eventually worked out a compromise in Forest Hills but not before subsidized housing turned into a political liability for Mayor Lindsay, NYCHA, and liberal housing promoters more generally. Some even believe that the nationally famous Forest Hills debacle contributed to Nixon's national moratorium on subsidized housing in 1973. Rockefeller and Logue, armed with the powers of the state, apparently believed that they could be successful where Lindsay and others had failed.[8]

Since the early twentieth century, Westchester's elitist leaders had openly used the power of zoning and decentralized local control to resist extensive apartment building development outside the county's few small cities, such as Yonkers, Peekskill, and White Plains. The lack of apartment options contributed to a deserved reputation for racial discrimination in the county's many towns and villages. The Regional Plan Association scolded the county in 1971: "Westchester is adding to the Statue of Liberty message: 'Give me . . . your poor: but only during the day to man the factories, clean the houses and maintain the hospitals."[9]

Persistent elitism mattered because New York's suburbs in the postwar years were changing rapidly from sleepy bedroom communities, closely tied to the city center, into the most vibrant shopping and commercial centers in their respective regions. Employment increased by half a million jobs in the New York / New Jersey suburbs between 1950 and 1970.[10] General Foods executives moved their national headquarters from Manhattan to a custom-designed White Plains campus in 1954—an early and ominous sign of changing corporate preferences.[11] IBM's Thomas Watson Jr. built a major research center and a new corporate headquarters in suburban Westchester County in the early 1960s; PepsiCo decamped for a luxurious complex in Westchester in 1970. Stamford welcomed corporate headquarters of Continental Oil, General Electric, Xerox, Shell, and other companies that desired to be "close enough to New York to reap its big-city benefits and far enough away to escape its big-city problems."[12] The migration of so many jobs to the suburbs raised the stakes for integration. Many experts feared the growing "mismatch" between the distant homes of minority workers and hard-to-reach suburban locations.

Progressive opinion in the metropolitan area was firmly behind Logue's building subsidized housing in Westchester County to encourage minority access to the better jobs, housing, and schools concentrated there. The fast rate of black suburbanization made the question of suburban integration crucial to many liberals in the 1960s and 1970s. A planned and orderly integration process might forestall further ghettoization, racial conflict, and white flight characteristic of older urban centers. New York's suburbs started with a small minority base in 1950, but the trend was clear: between 1950 and 1960 Nassau County's minority population grew about 137 percent, or 24,000 persons, and Westchester County's grew by about 61 percent, or 23,000 persons. Elmer Carter, a civil rights leader, attributed this rapid growth to African Americans having made "great strides toward normal mobility."[13]

African American families that managed to escape the ghetto often ended up in aging industrial suburban towns like Yonkers or segregated black middle-class enclaves in Mount Vernon that did not always boast the newest schools, most affluent residents, or best services. New racial ghettos formed as whites again dispersed.[14] The UDC had in fact focused its efforts up to that point in the "urban areas" of Westchester. The 2,400 units of mixed-income housing UDC planned for towns like Yonkers, Ossining, New Rochelle, and Peekskill underlined a continuing and deepening segregation by zip code. The more affluent Westchester areas had shown little interest in UDC-subsidized projects and remained overwhelmingly white. Realtors and developers fearlessly discriminated in many different types of housing, both rental and privately owned.

Economic and racial segregation was, in the context of the civil rights movement, soft-sold in wealthy towns through manipulation of the zoning process to favor large lots, ostensibly to protect open space and a rural landscape. The Regional Plan Association, in association with the UDC, saw through the strategy and identified vacant land parcels within 30 miles of Manhattan that could accommodate 1.3 million people if zoning were revised in elitist enclaves. Radical planners Paul Davidoff and Neil Gold joined the battle in 1969 by founding the Suburban Action Institute in the suburban city of White Plains to sue the suburbs over restrictive zoning. They discovered that 68 percent of land in Westchester County had been zoned for lots of at least 1 acre each and that 80 percent of the black population lived in towns counting for just 9 percent of the county's land. A legal strategy, given this clear pattern of segregation, seemed possible.[15]

City officials and some business leaders could also be convinced that excessive reliance on zoning would hurt future economic prospects. Planners forecast a need for 92,000 new housing units by 1980 to keep pace with the booming commercial and service industry in the county and New York City. Subsidized housing advocates also pointed to the 17,500 substandard houses in the county, even in many otherwise affluent towns, as another justification for dispersing affordable housing.[16]

A Strategic Error or a No-Win Situation?

The Westchester Development Corporation, a subsidiary of the UDC created in 1970 with the full cooperation of the Westchester County executive (a long-time Rockefeller insider), announced six demonstration projects in suburban towns. Logue made clear that while he might steamroll opposition by relying on the agency's delegated powers, he preferred consensus. By 1972, however, only projects in Yonkers had gotten off the ground. Opponents stymied his middle-of-the-road attempts to build faculty housing at Manhattanville College in tony Purchase. He even struggled to build staff and student housing for New York Medical College in Valhalla on an isolated parcel. Logue's generous offer that towns could choose the income mix failed to entice greater participation.

Logue announced a more aggressive plan in 1972 that would potentially override local zoning to build 900 units across nine Westchester towns. Logue presented his Nine Towns plan to Rockefeller, who told him to "go ahead." The governor even offered 20 acres of the Rockefeller property in Westchester for low-income housing (his family members ultimately vetoed the donation).[17] Sy Schulman, former Westchester County planning commissioner and paid consultant to the UDC in Westchester, arranged meetings with town supervisors to move the program forward.[18] The UDC subsidiary took options on nine rural sites and hired architects for feasibility studies. Towns had zoned most of the places for single-family homes with minimum lot sizes of up to four acres, so Logue asked for a rezoning but was prepared for an override if needed. As a peace offering, he offered priority to local residents in these mixed-income communities, which may have backfired among those uncomfortable with any low-income residents in their areas.[19]

The plan generated a bitter and aggressive response. Rather than making opposition an embarrassing situation for leaders in a single town, Logue awoke a sleeping giant. "The people of Westchester will not tolerate having big brother dictate ill-conceived and costly projects for their communities, projects on which they have no real voice and no approval and no funds to take care of services," railed Democratic Representative Ogden Reid, who led the charge against low- and moderate-income apartments in Westchester County. An organization calling itself United Towns for Home Rule emerged as a countywide group to fight the UDC.[20] The UDC did not help its case by choosing many sites that were "remote" and poorly served by services needed by a low-income or elderly population.[21] Opponents of the projects, wary of being tagged as racists or snobs, claimed with some justice that the apartments would be "out of place in rural communities, will impose tax burdens on the towns and will impinge on local controls over developments." Some leaders, however, were blunt: "If we want New York City to move into Newcastle, we'll tell you."[22]

A survey of Westchester County residents revealed greater than majority support for low- and moderate-income apartments in principle but also lopsided support for local development rather than UDC (which raised the question of who would undertake such an effort). Opinion divided further when it came to race, the underlying issue despite all the talk of density and ambiance. Respondents who believed that Westchester had already gone too far to help "black residents" also opposed the UDC; predictably, racial progressives who believed that not nearly enough had been done for minorities strongly supported Logue's efforts.[23] Logue tried to move ahead despite opposition. He used the UDC's power to override zoning ordinances in Bedford, Cortland, Greenberg, Harrison, Lewisboro, Newcastle, North Castle, Somers, and Yorktown.[24]

Rockefeller had been supportive publicly of Logue but finally intervened, under the gun from many Westchester politicians, as the rhetoric grew heated and politically dangerous. He established a "cooling-off period" allowing a delay in the plans for the nine towns in the fall of 1972. The towns were told to come up with their plans by January 1973 or the UDC would move ahead without their permission. A standstill in the fall and winter of 1972 generated some positive steps. Some Westchester towns under pressure hired consultants to provide alternative plans. By January 1973, four towns had submitted alternative plans, two towns said they would accept UDC proposals, and three towns remained opposed to conciliation. The threat of UDC override had worked to move the needle on income integration, illustrating that in New York a state agency with the right powers and goals could make a difference.

Behind the scenes, however, Logue's opponents had the final say. Had the state legislature left the UDC unanswered, they would have been opening the door to subsidized housing in the suburbs across the state. Now, for instance, trouble was brewing in Long Island over a multifamily complex UDC and community leaders had planned for Wyandanch. Affluent towns there were just as reluctant to provide a fair share of subsidized housing within their borders. In June of 1973 Governor Rockefeller, under continuing pressure from Westchester County, agreed with the legislature to take away the UDC's power to override local zoning in towns and villages.[25] Legislators from Westchester County led the charge on stripping the UDC of its power. The legislators who still supported the agency wanted it to refocus on its primary mission: urban development.[26] The revised law strategically cut UDC's powers only in towns and villages, not cities, an obvious sop to suburban opponents. The state legislature packaged it with an expansion of the agency's bond capacity, now desperately needed considering a 1973 federal moratorium on new public housing. The UDC thus "retreated from Westchester County after encountering a fusillade of opposition from residents who complained of diminished property values, the threatened export of city crime to their streets and the erosion of their suburban lifestyle." Davidoff shuttered his Suburban Action Institute because of determined resistance to low-income projects in Connecticut and Westchester.[27]

New York's high-profile failure contributed to national debates about housing, helping both to undermine support among suburbanites for subsidized housing of any kind and to discourage many advocates from seeking similar programs in their states unless they were willing to go to court. One need look no further than Westchester today to see the scope of the problem. Even a new brand of affordable housing decades later could not overcome the political resistance to subsidized housing entirely. In 2017, many affluent Westchester towns successfully maintain their opposition to federal requirements for even the most benign forms of affordable or "workforce" housing. Almost 50 years after Logue failed, the elitist, leafy towns are still winning. No strategy seems to be strong enough. Today, as in the past, getting subsidized housing built in the suburbs—in New York or elsewhere—is a hard sell.

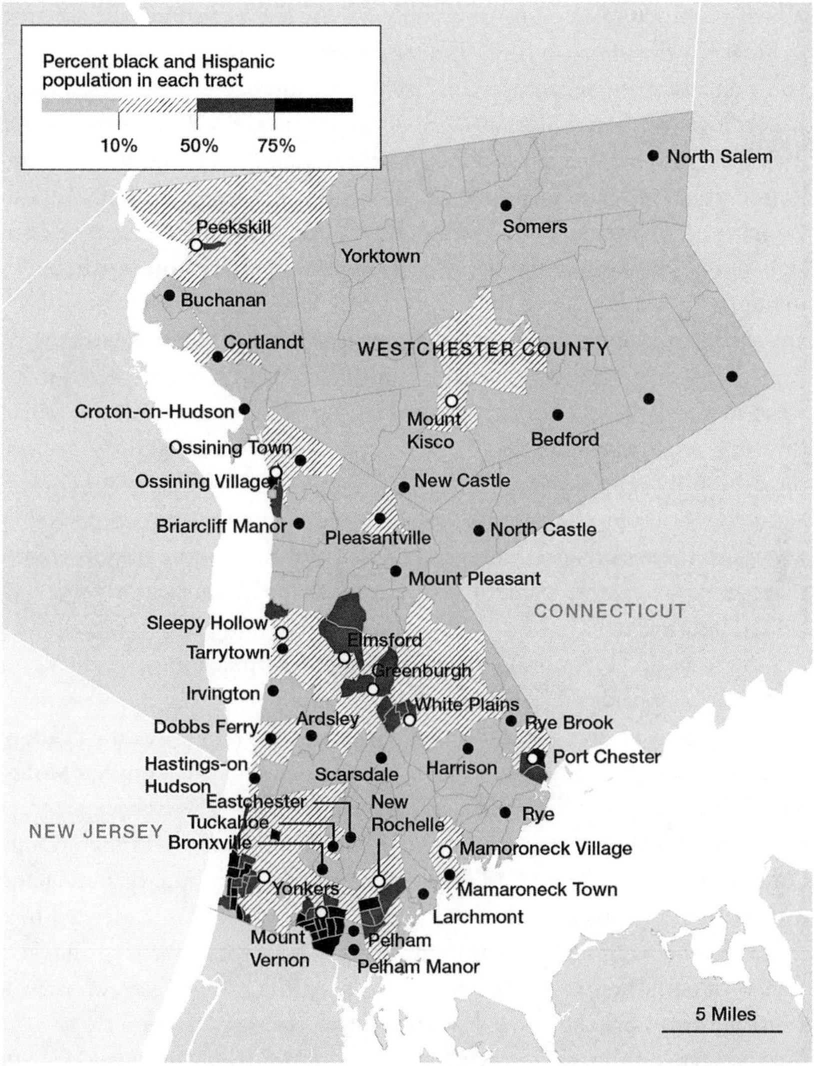

FIGURE 41. Westchester communities that Obama-era HUD believed needed additional subsidized housing are indicated with the solid circle. Logue targeted many of these same towns in the early 1970s. Map by Minna Ninova, 2018.

Decentralizing Subsidized Housing

The dangerous politics of decentralizing subsidized housing in New York has many parallels in other states. The net effect was not merely a rejection of these types of fair share programs but an organized resistance of suburbanites to subsidized housing of most types. The wide publicity given these efforts, and their generally dismal results, has discouraged broader imitation.

Massachusetts created an "anti-snob" zoning law, passed in 1969, designed to break down suburban resistance to low-income housing, and a $515 million bond issue to encourage construction of low-income housing units.[28] According to urban historian Peter Siskind, however, "Putting this novel legislation into practice proved more difficult than the law's authors—a collection of liberal state legislators—had hoped." The state's Housing Appeals Committee, a product of the law, stood firm against many local zoning decision, but it "did little or nothing to remove other practical hurdles to building in the suburbs such as stalling tactics by localities, environmental laws, and the institutional weakness of so many low-income housing developers." Even a well-organized and -financed housing effort in suburban Newton fell apart in the early 1970s when "significant public outcry created a familiar, tortuous process: lengthy hearings, tactical compromises, and determined opposition by critical town officials." The Massachusetts Housing Finance Agency, as a result, was only able to build one-third of the 25,000 units it financed in the suburbs, and these were mostly for the elderly. Siskind reports that even in 1989, there were still 95 towns in Massachusetts without any subsidized housing at all.[29]

The 1970s and 1980s brought an expansion in formal, long-term plans for inclusion of subsidized housing in the suburbs. One of the more dramatic state programs to encourage income and racial integration was the result of legal challenges by housing activists to zoning decisions in suburban Mount Laurel, New Jersey, that they believed were designed to thwart the construction of affordable housing. New Jersey Republican governor William Cahill (1970–1974), their ally, was an outspoken critic of exclusionary zoning and a proponent of subsidized housing in the suburbs. He was succeeded by a Democratic governor, Brendan Byrne (1974–1982), who shared his integrationist values. Their combined actions to open the suburbs were, however, consistently thwarted by town leaders and state legislators.

The State Supreme Court of New Jersey in *Southern Burlington County N.A.A.C.P. v. Mount Laurel Township* (*Mount Laurel I*, 1975) took the activists' and governors' side and required affordable housing plans by local governments that had used zoning to lock out lower-income minority residents. Governor Byrne's support for meeting the Mount Laurel guidelines, including a statewide tax for affordable housing, was nevertheless rejected by voters—making progress difficult because of declining federal support for housing in this era. So determined were opponents that for years they sought a constitutional amendment that would push the courts out of zoning issues. The election of Governor Thomas Kean (1982–1990), a Republican, brought an end to an aggressive executive order by his predecessor; Kean was openly noncompliant with the court rulings.

Because of local and state resistance, the courts and housing advocates pressed the issue again in 1983, resulting in a set of decisions known as *Mount Laurel II*. These affirmed the earlier decision, gave developers more power to build affordable housing in the face of local opposition, and once again demanded stronger state action. Governor Kean in 1984 decried the rulings as "undesirable intrusion on the home rule principle" and even "communistic." The governor and legislature's much-delayed and compromised response to court pressure, the New Jersey Fair Housing Act (1986), modestly funded affordable housing, allocated moderate-cost housing on a fair share basis, created a weak state agency, and provided opportunities for localities to fund housing outside their borders. Most towns refused to comply with even these modest requirements, and the state encouraged "regional contribution agreements," allowing towns to pay for affordable housing somewhere else so that they could remain elitist.[30]

The results of so much legal and legislative wrangling in New Jersey have been mixed, with a total of 80,000 units statewide attributed to the Fair Housing Act between 1985 and 2016, mostly in mixed-income, privately developed and managed complexes. The state supreme court has recently stepped back into the fray by confronting the many holdout towns that remain. The towns are now to develop, finally, updated "fair share" local plans statewide. Considering their successful resistance for decades, there are reasons for pessimism.[31]

California has one of the most robust planning programs on the books related to fair share housing. California, through its state-authorized regional councils of government (COGs) began to plan for a statewide forecast of affordable housing based on the Housing Element Law (1980). The 37 COGs assign portions of the housing needs (hundreds of thousands total, including low and moderate cost) every few years to cities and counties (482 municipalities in California). Local plans, evaluated through factors such as zoning capacity for high-density housing, must reflect these goals. These requirements, until recently, have been limited in impact by the absence of generous local, state, or federal funding programs to build the subsidized housing called for in plans. Many towns also throw up various roadblocks in the zoning and building approval process for high-density housing.

Due to a current housing emergency in California, impacting a broad range of income levels, major changes are now under way as the state legislature and governor debate new laws to overrule local zoning to expedite the approval of multifamily housing. Many of the predictable opponents of higher-density housing in suburbs have surfaced, but even many affordable housing advocates fear that additional housing density may lead to more low-income displacement in the absence of robust subsidy or rent regulation programs.[32] Other states have pursued similar programs to expedite multifamily housing development with similar mixed results. Florida's State Housing Initiatives Partnership program, for instance, provides modest funds to local governments that develop partnerships to create affordable housing and reduce regulatory barriers to low-income housing development.

The resistance to affordable housing in suburbs, more successful in most respects than any of the countermeasures described above, makes even less sense today than it did decades ago. Affordable housing projects under the state/federal LIHTC program, for instance, are better spread across metropolitan areas than public housing projects of an earlier era. The new projects include a range of medium-rise buildings, garden apartments, single-family homes, or attached housing. They are attractively designed, often neotraditional in style, and landscaped so that they blend in well with their surround-

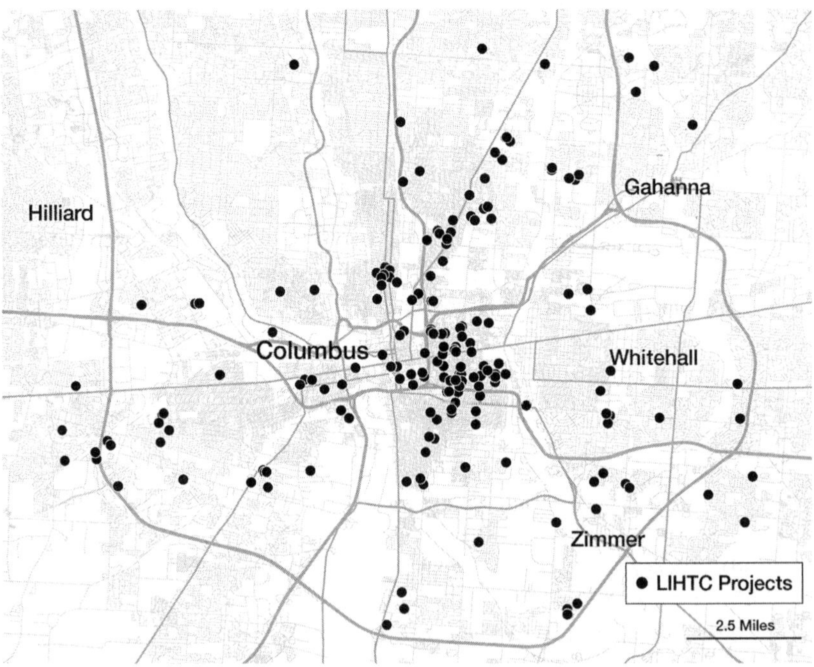

FIGURE 42. Columbus, Ohio, LIHTC projects illustrate a mix of center-city and suburban sites that compares well with older center-city public housing but are more concentrated than many advocates would like. Map by Minna Ninova, 2018.

ings. The range of income levels is much wider than public housing and usually includes middle-income families. Home ownership is often encouraged. Yet better design and mixed-income communities have still not been enough to overcome suburban resistance.

The growing concentration of today's affordable housing apartments in mostly city neighborhoods, or poorer suburbs, due to elitist zoning has led to a new generation of lawsuits and pressure on the federal government to aggressively enforce the goals of "affirmatively furthering fair housing" in the Housing Act of 1968. Studies finding better outcomes for families living in subsidized housing outside traditional ghettos bolstered the arguments for decentralization, although even nonexperts had understood for decades the advantages for most lower-income children and families living in higher-income neighborhoods. The result of this new era of liberal housing activism was an initial burst of enthusiasm nationally during the Obama administration and then a conservative backlash. The Trump administration predictably viewed the HUD effort as "social engineering" and shelved the program to please elite suburbs, including Westchester County.[33]

Neither the state nor federal programs were of the requisite size or strength to change broader trends. State legislators, sensitive to their suburban constituents, decided to play it safe. Politicians successfully played upon fears of "social engineering." The plan for using subsidized housing to integrate suburbs bore little fruit, especially compared to the massive political capital expended in New York and other states.

12

States and the Limits of Fair Housing Laws

Building subsidized housing in suburbs was one path to social and ethnic integration but also appeared to be the most expensive, politically vexing, and time consuming among the different methods. States thus served as pioneering sites of fair housing laws in the United States. These laws promised, by prying open the private housing market, a fair shot for minority families at neighborhoods in cities and suburbs with better quality housing, new schools, and lower crime. By appealing to the nation's promise of equal protection and the momentum of the civil rights movement, advocates were initially hopeful of meaningful changes in New York and other states. Many activists believed that state fair housing laws, properly designed and forcefully implemented, might address residential segregation in cities and suburbs on a scale that would systematically improve minority social mobility.

Passage of fair housing laws in northern and western states in the 1950s and 1960s, however, often shielded darker truths. White violence and token integration frequently substituted for true integration. Realtors, property owners, and developers found plenty of low-key ways to discriminate. Whites often fled city neighborhoods and suburbs in droves rather share lobbies, hallways, laundry rooms, and schools with minority families. Racist politicians fought for and often won changes in state fair housing laws that rendered enforcement agencies weak or ineffective. States were innovative and in most respects preceded the federal government in this crucial field of civil rights, but state governments also proved to be imperfect weapons against social discrimination.

Integrating Subsidized Housing

New York had a comparatively long, if imperfect, tradition of fair housing law that used the justification of state investment for policing residential racial integration. New York State's pioneering 1938 fair housing law, for instance, banned discrimination by race in publicly assisted state-sponsored public housing. Officials might turn a blind eye to private housing segregation, but to actively promote segregation in housing it subsidized looked awful. The law had the intended effect of forcing NYCHA and other state housing authorities to abandon or at least tweak segregationist policies that led to all-white or all-black projects.

The broader movement for postwar civil rights inevitably addressed segregated housing in New York. In 1945, in the context of sustaining wartime antidiscrimination progress, Governor Dewey and the state legislature created the nation's first antidiscrimination laws for the workplace, to be enforced through the New York State Commission against Discrimination (SCAD).[1] SCAD did not at first have any power over integration in the state's growing subsidized private housing system, which led to extreme and open segregation of key middle-class housing projects like Stuyvesant Town. This oversight forced civil rights activists to undertake years of public litigation and protest against racially conservative owners.

The state government finally barred discrimination in all public and publicly assisted housing in 1955, giving SCAD supervision of 2 percent of the state's housing. In 1956, the Harriman administration and state legislature extended SCAD's oversight again, this time to housing where state money or guarantees were used in private housing.[2] SCAD proudly reported that by 1959 all state-assisted private developments, 70 projects in total with 40,000 units, were integrated. Such an announcement should be read, however, in the context of a state with millions of housing units (two million in New York City alone). Many of these integrated projects, moreover, would today be considered "token" integrated. Some Mitchell-Lama complexes intentionally dragged their feet on integration, particularly in areas that remained whiter, thus making them a target for activist lawyers. Even in the early 1970s, for instance, activists successfully sued Fred and Donald Trump for their discriminatory renting practices at the middle-income subsidized Trump Village in Brooklyn.[3]

Resegregation by minority families was, unfortunately, a frequent byproduct of the successful application of these state fair housing laws in subsidized housing both public and private. The white flight from New York City's public housing in the 1950s, despite many white families in need, was so swift that the entire system became minority majority by the late 1950s. Administrators in the Mitchell-Lama program also acknowledged the "vast increase in the number of Negro families applying for middle-income projects [was] creating [an] integration problem" in the early 1960s. Whites had plenty of segregated options in the private market and exercised that option freely. State administrators marketed to white families to maintain some balance, but in so doing faced "the problem of how to achieve a racially-integrated tenantry without violating the laws against discrimination."[4]

White families remained in Title I and city Mitchell-Lama projects in a few highly desirable Manhattan and Brooklyn neighborhoods, but most state Mitchell-Lama projects quickly added minority families in the 1960s and 1970s.[5] Complexes like Rochdale Village and Co-op City offered thousands of new high-quality apartments for middle-class minority families with few options outside the city limits. The resegregation, and loss of integrated living in these communities, was a disappointment to many sponsors and residents on both sides of the color line, but the laws they had created tied their hands. Sustaining integration proved difficult because to promote white residence penalized minority families in greater need of new high-quality housing. It was clear, moreover, that if the much larger private market remained discriminatory, integration in subsidized housing would be difficult to sustain and, in any case, would impact only a small number of families.[6]

Integrating Private Housing

The housing discrimination problems of publicly subsidized housing looked tame in comparison to those in the vast private market in New York and other states. Racially progressive leaders in states, however, could pass the laws they wanted rather than having to wait on a national consensus required for congressional action. New York, New Jersey, Massachusetts, Oregon, and Washington entered the fair housing field earliest, but the rules they created were relatively weak and, as in New York, narrow. By 1959, in the context of the growing civil rights movement, five states had banned discrimination in renting or selling in the private housing market: California, Colorado, Connecticut, Massachusetts, and Oregon.[7]

New York reflects a national pattern of seemingly aggressive action in northern and western states. Housing expert and lawyer Charles Abrams, who led SCAD from 1955 to 1959, sought "patterns of open occupancy within a market area" to help "professionally trained and technically skilled Negroes, recruited by vital industries . . . in upstate communities to find suitable housing accommodations for themselves and their families." Without a state law covering fair housing in the private market, he had limited success.[8] Private racial discrimination was widely accepted by sellers, realtors, bankers, and neighbors in New York as a legitimate way of "defending" neighborhoods, attitudes reflected in an otherwise pathbreaking law of the time. The city of New York, with the passage of the Fair Housing Practice Law (Sharkey-Brown-Isaacs Law, 1958), blazed the path on desegregating private housing. Yet the city government exempted owner-occupied two-family buildings and apartment houses with fewer than 10 units—an acknowledgment of deep-seated animosity to fair housing rules by northern whites.[9]

Rockefeller, in partnership with the legislature, made fair housing law a priority. The governor took a broader view of harm brought by discrimination. For him, and many civil rights leaders, housing discrimination represented a roadblock to prosperity for upwardly mobile minority families because "equal opportunity in housing is vital to equal opportunity in education." With massive state investment in roads, higher education, and K–12 school facilities, a case could be made that minority families deserved a fair share of the good life. The state legislature joined Rockefeller to create "broadened jurisdiction" in private housing through the Metcalf-Baker Law (1961). The law barred discrimination in 2.5 million housing units, housing about 10 million of the state's 17 million citizens, mostly in New York City or other big-city apartment houses. The new law also banned 27,500 real estate offices and 39,000 realtors from the use of discriminatory advertising and outlawed "blockbusting in the State of New York."[10]

To demonstrate the broader justification for the integrationist effort, Rockefeller renamed SCAD the New York State Commission on Human Rights.[11] An early and widely publicized case settled under the new powers, in late 1961, opened an apartment in suburban Great Neck to a successful black family.[12] Another case in 1962 allowed the family of a minority business owner to rent an apartment in Rye, New York, a tony suburb.[13] The commission's powers bolstered "secret shopping" in Nassau County by activists in the Congress of Racial Equality who focused on racist builders and brokers who discriminated against black families by demanding higher down payments, lying about the sale status of a home, or denying the availability of mortgages.[14] The emphasis in all these efforts was helping upwardly mobile minority families find space in affluent suburbs where they could enjoy better schools, safer neighborhoods, and high standard housing.

Rockefeller, like his counterparts in the city in 1958, had compromised to get Metcalf-Baker passed. The racist views of millions of small owners had been accommodated in the name of passage. Metcalf-Baker, by focusing on apartment houses, covered just 15 percent of housing outside New York City (and much of that 15 percent was in other big-city centers). The law, by leaving out single-family units, two-family units, and rentals in owner-occupied three-family units, de facto accepted discrimination in a vast portion of the state's housing, particularly the best new single-family housing rising in the suburbs. Rockefeller, making law during the high point of the civil rights struggle and looking to burnish his national credentials in his constant run for the presidency, sought and won revisions in the law in 1963 to cover discrimination in *all* private housing. The state government also gave the commission the power to request enforcement in the state supreme court.[15] The 1963 law extended coverage to 95 percent of the state's housing. This law was justifiably celebrated by the administration as a landmark national achievement.[16]

Bark versus Bite

An enforcement system developed both to gain support from civil rights leaders and mollify powerful opponents in the real estate community inevitably disappointed. The commission, even after the 1963 revision, seemed more therapeutic and educational than punitive. The commission in typical cases provided a 60-day procedure to conciliate the grievance, only after which the commission would determine if there was sufficient evidence for a public hearing. Reputation was the coin of the realty profession, so the state optimistically reckoned that an open airing of bad behavior would be undesirable to some realtors. The hearing would be the opportunity for the commission to determine the penalty, including an order to rent or sell to the aggrieved party, a misdemeanor charge (and up to one year in prison), or up to $500 in damages (with some leeway for compensatory or settlement payments). The decision could, however, be appealed to the state's court of appeals.[17]

By 1963 civil rights leaders were already unhappy about the weak penalties and the fact that the commission could not instigate investigations.[18] The commission in 1965 was thus empowered to create a special investigations unit. By all accounts, however, it lacked the staff to make much progress in complex cases against well-heeled defendants.[19] The various paid commissioners serving on the commission, spread across the state, were believed to operate as "feudal baronies" and resisted central control that might have rationalized enforcement.[20] By 1965, civil rights leaders were doubtful that the state was "vigorously" enforcing laws, as not a single real estate license had been revoked since the passing of the laws. They cited notorious cases of realtors with multiple violations still practicing their trade in Yonkers. Nor had the state imprisoned any realtor or seller. The commission mostly sent warning letters and posted signs in windows of offending agents highlighting the antidiscrimination laws. The fact that the Real Estate Board of New York praised the commission for "an admirable job" was telling. What had appeared as a major victory in practice looked much less impressive.[21]

The NAACP in 1967 wanted the state to take a more "militant" stance and accused the commission of "appeasement"—rhetoric intended to equate domestic racism with Nazi-era ideology.[22] As one housing activist pointedly noted, "We've got the best housing laws on the books and the worst commission" because it "fails to function as a law enforcement agency."[23] The riots of the 1960s, pressure from an aggrieved minority middle class forced into new suburban ghettos, and growing militancy in the black and white communities highlighted the comparative weakness of the commission. The commission had done nothing to change the trend.[24] Rockefeller also sent mixed signals. He tolerated but did not vigorously intervene to aid state commissioner of education James E. Allen's forceful attack on "de facto classroom segregation" in Malverne on Long Island, disappointing activists. Racists, on the other hand, viewed his support of any integration as traitorous. In 1966 Rockefeller was "greeted in Nassau by hooting parents who opposed Allen's Malverne order." The governor lamely claimed that he "had no jurisdiction" as he ran to his meeting.[25]

Rockefeller, under pressure from mainstream activists, appointed a study group in 1967. In its report issued in 1968, the group recommended that the commission would be more effective as a state agency with one central and stronger commissioner. As such, it would command more respect, have a more robust budget, and become an accepted state service. The governor, following their advice, and with his eye on developments in fair housing in the nation's capital, created the New York State Division of Human Rights—a state agency that remains in place today.[26] The number of regional field offices was reduced from 14 to 7 to focus on urban areas with the most cases: New York City, Long Island, White Plains, Albany, Buffalo, Rochester, and Syracuse. Regional directors would ideally place a "greater emphasis on enforcement, rather than conciliation." The commission was also empowered to stop rental or sale of units during investigations so that realtors could not "run the clock" and rent or sell a unit to whites during the proceedings.[27] Robert Magnum, who had been serving as head of the commission, and who had been frustrated by his weakness, was tapped to lead the new division. He was a New York lawyer and a former director of the Northeast OEO [Office of Equal Opportunity], an agency of the War on Poverty, who openly linked housing discrimination to "violence we have been seeing in the cities."[28]

The results of the division's efforts, even with these enhancements, remained mixed and much debated. Housing complaints filed and investigated by SCAD went from 308 (1955–1959) to 1,680 (1960–1964) and then between 500 and 800 annually between 1965 and 1972. The total number of housing complaints filed by 1972 was 7,272. But of closed complaints in 1972 in housing just 114 out of 503 cases resulted in a hearing or settlement, 247 were dismissed with no probable cause, and 142 were withdrawn. The number of financial awards for housing discrimination increased during the 1960s, but the fines remained small for such a lucrative business. The state could force compensatory or settlement payments, but activists did not consider these large or frequent enough to change the behavior of offenders. Between 1945 and 1974, the state had levied just $132,000 in housing fines (for 444 cases decided in favor of complainants), a total that compared poorly to $1.238 million for 1,202 cases related to employment. Unlike employment cases, the courts could not levy punitive damages on housing cases, even though these might have scared many more realtors and developers.[29] Courts even reversed a one-year real estate license revocation issued by Secretary of State John Lomenzo as "too severe" for the crime.[30] In creating the division, Rockefeller had failed to confront the real estate industry head on. The federal Fair Housing Act (Title VIII of the Civil Rights Act of 1968) was far more powerful, although its complexity, and lack of money for enforcement, presented its own set of problems for activists.[31]

The division seemed weakest where it was most needed: the suburban landscapes with the high-performing schools, low crime, and newest housing. The Urban League in 1969 believed that "the Fair Housing Laws are not being enforced in Westchester and the result is frustration and rage on the part of many Negroes here." The division still relied on conciliation, dismissing many charges, and was reluctant to penalize or fine violators.[32] An Urban League official in Westchester found that "by the time the state makes its findings, the person gives up or finds another place to live. Usually it's back in the ghetto." Only a few of the most affluent minority parties seemed to hold on long enough to win their cases. Activist frustration was reflected in their growing preference for local antidiscrimination laws, a growing number of which some liberal suburbs had passed. Activists had come to believe that "local ordinances are often more effective than state and Federal laws" because the enforcement process was less bureaucratic. The mere threat of public, local enforcement was scarier for local realtors than a long, dragged-out process at the state level. Even Robert Magnum had come to prefer local laws because they reflected the "feeling of our town" rather than outside interference. It is not clear that these local rules were any more effective in the long term.[33]

The state division, in part because of the weakness of its powers in the housing sphere, and in part because the state continued to pass strong human rights laws in many additional areas, focused on employment and other cases rather than housing during the 1970s. By 1977, housing was just 6 percent of the commission's work, whereas employment discrimination alone counted for 89 percent. People seemed more concerned about jobs than housing during tough times in the 1970s, to be sure, but the lack of credibility on housing after decades of rhetoric was a problem with those who might seek redress for discrimination. Most cases continued to be settled without penalties of any kind.[34] Cutbacks during the financial crisis undermined the division further by creating growing case backlogs. By 1977 the staff for the whole division had shrunk to 190 from a more robust 277 in 1970.[35] The number of housing complaints to the division shrunk to about 300 per year after 1975 and maintained this level until the mid-1980s, when there was another spike.[36]

Suburban communities thus continued to divide along even starker racial lines, raising questions about the ability of the suburban frontier to deliver the good life for upwardly mobile minority families. Between 1970 and 1980, four out of five new black residents in Nassau moved into areas that were already majority black. The hamlet of Roosevelt had become 90 percent black and Hempstead Village was 57 percent black, while countywide the black percentage was just 7 percent.[37] In 1984 Paul Davidoff believed that "a wall of segregation still characterizes housing in the region, both public and private." Lawyer and fair housing advocate Richard Bellman said, "In today's real-estate market, industry people who practice discrimination consider a $500 damage award to be a joke. . . . When they get caught, what they face is a slap on the hand." Federal fines won under the Housing Act of 1968 were more serious, but they entailed higher legal costs to mount a challenge.[38] New York had never revoked a real estate broker license by 1989 and only a few had ever been suspended.[39]

Not much has changed. In 2005, researchers found that 84 percent of whites on Long Island lived in all-white neighborhoods.[40] In minority suburbs, appreciation of housing is slower, schools more segregated, school performance lower, poverty higher, and crime more elevated than in most white suburbs. Suburban ghettos, even if often majority working/middle class rather than poor, are a reality in the New York region and many others despite decades of legal challenges made possible by local, state, and federal law. Rockefeller and other state legislators had made laws, but they were not strong enough to guarantee the prosperity of many minority families or turn back the clock on residential segregation.

The States and Discrimination

The 1960s were the watershed for state antidiscrimination rules. A standout was California's Rumford Act of 1963. The act, according to historian Herbert Ruffin, was the result of sustained pressure and protest from civil rights activists, who received support from white liberals, Democratic state legislators, and Governor Brown. Proponents believed fair housing rules would help address the plight and growing anger of minority families trapped in the state's ghettos. Echoing the political challenges in New York, however, the bill exempted single-family homes and multifamily units of four units or less to placate opponents in the state legislature. The act as passed still covered two-thirds of the state's total housing.[41]

The California Real Estate Association, bolstered by widespread segregationist sentiment statewide, immediately launched a push for voter rescission under the banner of Proposition 14. Enemies used advertising "attacking the Rumford Act with the intent to confuse and arouse racial fears and distrust among white homeowners and small real estate investors by using such references as 'property rights,' 'forced housing,' and other slurs." Governor Brown called the proposition "the initiative to promote bigotry" but defenders of Rumford failed to organize a successful resistance. It is not clear that they would have prevailed even with more money and better organization. State voters, including both Democrats and Republicans, overwhelmingly approved Proposition 14 in 1964, with suburbanites voting three to one to kill the Rumford Act. The state supreme court in 1966, however, quickly threw out Proposition 14 for violating the Fourteenth Amendment. Rumford was superseded, but not replaced, by the federal Fair Housing Act of 1968. Many African American middle-class families, aided by these laws, found new homes in the state's cities and towns. In the years that followed, however, white flight often undid integration.[42]

By 1970 more than half the American states had developed fair housing laws, most of these in the North and West. Only one state south of the Mason Dixon line, the border state of Kentucky, had created similar regulations. The Fair Housing Act of 1968 largely superseded these state laws, but in states like New York, the state laws remained important to many activists because of the legal and administrative machinery put in place.[43] Some states also pursued antiredlining policies, of varying efficacy. Many state leaders began to realize that when lenders refused to write mortgages in racially mixed urban areas they potentially destabilized the property markets of entire metropolitan areas. California, Colorado, Connecticut, Michigan, Missouri, New Jersey, New York, and Utah adopted "disclosure measures by statute and regulation." California, Michigan, New Jersey, and Utah banned loans "which consider discriminatory factors such as racial or ethnic characteristics of the neighborhood."[44]

The high-profile housing integration efforts of this era have made a difference to many families, but they have failed to reset the racial lines of American metropolitan areas. Most regions still have sharply divided "dual housing markets" with unequal schools, tax bases, and property values. The various integrationist efforts also contributed to a multidecade backlash "by those who felt powerless to resist what they see as government-sponsored 'human engineering.'" The fight to stall suburban subsidized housing and defang aggressive enforcement of fair housing laws has been widely tolerated, and sometimes encouraged, nationally.[45] Northern whites have claimed that they were powerless and innocent in the face of more powerful social patterns creating and reinforcing segregation. Given the broader context of white hostility and dominance at the ballot box even in urbanized states, it is remarkable that any laws passed in the first place.

The failure of states to overcome ingrained social segregation reflects some of the perils of state participation in public policy. The statewide voter base will in nearly every state be whiter and wealthier than any single urban center or individual minority suburbs. Whites have more housing options and will simply leave a neighborhood en masse at a certain point in integration. Ethnic groups accepted into dominant categories of society, like Jewish and Asian families, have proven to be unreliable allies for fair housing despite the hideous discrimination that once blocked their paths to the best housing and schools. When state officials, pressured by civil rights activists, occasionally pushed hard on social and racial boundaries, their constituents and representatives found every way to avoid enforcing of laws. States have the legal right to enforce fair housing and were pioneers in doing so, but they have lacked the political will to police the bad actors.

13

The Urban Consequences of Deinstitutionalization

State governments broke down the walls between rural mental asylums and urban communities during the postwar years. In so doing, state mental health administrators ran an enormous social experiment with profound and enduring urban housing consequences. Most deinstitutionalized patients experienced substantial improvements in their quality of life, as almost anything was better than the nightmarish situation they had escaped, but thousands of other exiled patients ended up in poorly run nursing homes, jails, homeless shelters, halfway houses, and even on the streets. Because so many of the deinstitutionalized population found their way to cities, or remained in the general population under outpatient care, a new housing crisis related to mental illness quickly emerged.

The central flaw in the postwar deinstitutionalization process was that its advocates did not take seriously enough the role that asylums played in *housing* people, despite the often poor and inhumane conditions. By not fully understanding the shelter dimension of institutionalization, and what it meant to remove shelter for the mentally ill, senile, or addicted as a human right, officials dramatically changed the lives of these people and the nature of city life. Elected officials were forced to confront a large, semipermanent, and often disruptive mentally ill or addicted homeless population in city centers. The states solved a public relations problem—detention of a vulnerable population against its will in unsavory mental hospitals—while creating decades of challenges for city leaders, many patients, and their families.

The origins of mental hospitals augured an uncertain future. The first wards were in cities, often attached to hospitals, and most were dreadful places for both those with special needs and those suffering from various mental disorders. Nineteenth-century reformers convinced state governments by the second half of the century to take a role in caring for the mentally ill and those with special needs. States in the late nineteenth century thus began to relocate the patients to asylums in the countryside, where they would experience the benefits of farm schools. Indeed, contact with animals, fresh air, and sunshine had a positive effect on the patients.

The rise of big cities generated ever more potential patients, as life was hard, addiction widespread, and family breakdown common. The cynical desire of city leaders to dump senile and poor patients onto the state overwhelmed the scale and management ability of once progressive farm schools. They frequently became large, impersonal institutions more notable for horrifying conditions, lobotomies, electroshock treatment, and resident exploitation than green pastures. States across the nation had taken responsibility for the mentally ill and handicapped, but they and the citizens they represented refused to devote adequate financial resources to maintain a high quality of life for the mentally ill within these institutions.

Governor Rockefeller called these institutions "mammoth human warehouses where the sheer size and cavernous architecture make it nearly impossible to maintain human dignity or to carry out an effective therapeutic process." Sixteen of these hospitals in New York in the early 1960s held more than 3,000 patients each, and some 40 percent were overcrowded. These "huge institutions of thousands of beds designed for minimal staffing" reflected "a hopeless therapeutic outlook." The only people happy with these institutions were the many small town employees who enjoyed steady work from staffing these massive places.[1] Sadly, large-scale mental hospitals like these had become typical across the country by World War II. By many accounts, their patients were vulnerable, segregated, and mistreated. For most Americans, out of sight was out of mind.

During World War II, screening for the draft highlighted the large numbers of Americans with mental illness in the general population. The execution of the mentally ill and those with special needs by the Nazis played a role in self-searching by Americans into their nation's treatment of the mentally ill and developmentally delayed. Congress spurred the reform process by creating the National Mental Health Act in 1946, which funded research and community services.[2] With federal support, states began to reform mental health research and treatment after World War II. By 1948 every American state and territory supported a designated mental health authority.[3] The Joint Committee on Mental Illness and Health in 1961 called for facilities with a maximum of 1,000 patients "situated closer to cities" and recommended that mental hospitals "shift their emphasis from custody to therapy." Federal officials encouraged community-oriented treatment by providing subsidies, mostly seed money, for new community-based facilities, beginning most notably with the Community Mental Health Centers Construction Act (1963).[4]

California is given credit for pioneering a new approach to mental health during the postwar decade, but most American states pursued reforms. By the 1950s, too, the psychiatric profession made progress on drug treatments and talk therapy that promised more liberty for the mentally ill. The introduction of tranquilizers in 1955 and antidepressants a few years later made most patients appear and act more "normal." To keep them in dehumanizing settings and situations would no longer suffice. Their living spaces, for the first time in a long time, came to be viewed as "an important tool in their treatment and rehabilitation." The visual quality of television and magazine reporting in the postwar period likely contributed to less tolerance for squalid conditions that were once more easily hidden from sight in the countryside.[5]

The first phase of this changing environment was greater freedom within institutions nationally. In 1960, for instance, locked wards and windows in many hospitals in New York State gave way to open wards that allowed patients freer movement to treatment, recreation, and other daily activities. Patients living on open wards in New York increased from 6,268 in 1957 to 36,552 in 1960. This transition within the state hospitals represented a critical step in offering patients a new standard of living. They were still prisoners, however, who in most cases had not committed any actual crimes.[6]

The Rockefeller-era mental health program (both outpatient and residential services), costing in the hundreds of millions, openly rejected the antiquated model of rural isolation and even open wards. Instead, new facilities were to be "located on a geographical-population basis" disproportionately benefiting cities—from where most of the patients had been culled. Community integration was paramount: "Mental hospitals and institutions for the retarded should be located close to the people they serve—no more than an hour's travel from home by the means of travel that the families use." Treatment could include familiar environments and opportunities for education and employment and would include "families and community workers as much as possible." These smaller facilities, "located near cities where patients" lived, allowed patients "to come and go at will" from their homes. New rehabilitation centers emphasizing "normal living" included opportunities for education, job training, and recreation. The 1962 plan called for new 1,000-bed centers for the mentally ill in Albany, Syracuse, Brooklyn, and Staten Island that would be both smaller and closer to patients' homes. These were complemented by six new 200-unit complexes in New York City and other urban areas statewide.[7] Community mental health facilities, serving 85 percent of the state's population, offered group therapy and outpatient clinics. Six of these opened in Nassau County's fast-growing suburban communities.[8] The growth in urban facilities was swift: between 1959 and 1968, the state added 61 mental health facilities.[9] By 1982, the mental hygiene program had created 137 facilities at 56 centers.[10]

The participation of the HFA in financing these programs, approved in 1965, was crucial to creating so many facilities for the new therapeutic approach: "We had to have facilities in urban centers so people could get to them conveniently" despite "local objections." To soothe neighbors, architects were asked to create buildings that "fit in with the environment."[11] The new design ethos remains appealing in the renderings and photos. The Capital District Psychiatric Center in Albany was cited as a facility that does "not stand out as an institution" in its neighborhood.[12] Designers of the Middletown Rehabilitation Center rejected the "State institutional heritage from the Nineteenth Century," the creepy Edwardian complexes from which the public recoiled. Middletown was defined instead by one- and two-story buildings that wrapped around spacious, tree-filled courtyards. A new children's complex at Willowbrook Hospital (1965) featured "skylighted recreation rooms" where "children who once sat around dull and unresponsive to their surroundings are laughing and talking." The architecture for rehabilitation centers, built to serve special needs people, also stressed activity, openness, integration with the site, courtyards or other public spaces, large windows, and a campus feeling.[13]

FIGURE 43. Creative design for a new era of mental health treatment. New York State Mental Hygiene Facilities Improvement Fund, Report to the Governor, 1968. New York State Archives, courtesy of the Rockefeller Archive Center.

Leading avant-garde and establishment architects, most of them based in New York City, dominated the roster of design firms, many with overlapping commitments at the State University Construction Fund. The mental health program, as with SUNY expansion, thus spread contemporary architectural ideas to the suburbs and upstate. Among the firms of record were familiar names, including Marcel Breuer, M. Paul Friedberg, William Lescaze, Pomerance and Breines, Prentice and Chan, SOM, and Perkins and Will.[14]

A distinct program, with potentially powerful urban impacts, was the goal of creating a new generation of halfway houses "for residents of State schools who appear ready to return to the community." The pressure for deinstitutionalization generated demand for suitable community homes for those who could not live with their families or support themselves independently. Rather than building expensive new homes or anonymous urban institutional settings, the administrators aimed to convert multifamily buildings in declining urban areas into halfway houses. The halfway houses represented another form of state investment in declining cities, even though halfway houses were not always warmly greeted by neighbors. By the late 1960s, there were houses in operation in Kingston, White Plains, Herkimer, Poughkeepsie, Rochester, Rome, and Syracuse. At Scardefield House in Kingston, for instance, 17 women found shelter in an older home that blended in with its neighbors.[15]

Long-Term Consequences

Despite an unprecedented program of construction and reorganization, the Rockefeller administration was unable to control the negative media narrative surrounding deinstitutionalization. The chaos generated by termination of the old system paralleled the situation in many other states. New York state senator William Smith remembered that "the paint had hardly dried on our new mental hygiene buildings when the courts made the concept of deinstitutionalization the new game plan," requiring a full-court push for many more "community based facilities."[16] New York had moved much more slowly than other states in cutting resident patient numbers, in part because the directors of older mental health hospitals were under local political pressure to maintain these hospitals, no matter how sordid, because of the many jobs they supported in small towns.

The state hired Dr. Alan Miller in 1966 to accelerate the process. He created multidisciplinary teams and pushed a rapid decline in residential patients from 78,000 to 36,000 in a matter of years. Tens of thousands of additional patients shifted to outpatient services. The emphasis was now on short-term treatment and community discharge, and the state moved many of the senile, aged population to nursing homes. Many of the patients discharged from state mental hospitals in this period did not, however, experience the hoped-for improvements. The rise in homelessness after deinstitutionalization is well known, but even those with roofs over their heads were suffering because the administration had not created enough replacement "small community facilities." Some "14,000 were living in New York City in proprietary nursing homes or single-room occupancy hotels." Fast-buck operators created or opened nursing homes for these patients, and the conditions were often unpleasant. What had been a state responsibility was becoming a new challenge for the city's leaders.[17]

Some city leaders began to accuse the state of "'dumping' patients into foster homes and local hospitals." The governor and his administrators responded that the most serious patients remained in residential care, new facilities were opening quickly, better screening had reduced unnecessary hospitalization, and many pharmaceutical alternatives reduced the need for confinement. Rockefeller responded to a Queens politician that "contrary to what you have heard or read, state hospitals are not discharging large numbers of so-called 'chronic patients.'" He offered an impassioned defense of the new model: "I deeply resent any attempts to raise the specter of the so-called 'dangerous mental patients' for the purpose of arousing public opposition to the more humane and more effective openness and freedom that mark modern psychiatric care and treatment in enlightened societies around the world."[18]

Better treatment, despite a spirited defense, opened administrators to a wide range of criticism in the early 1970s. The growing number of small mental hospitals and treatment centers, usually requiring more staff and professionals per patient compared to the old institutional model, proved expensive to operate. Fiscal conservatives in legislative hearings in 1971 examined "small new hospitals which were created by separation from an existing hospital. Despite protests from the directors of two such hospitals that their programs were progressive, useful, and economical, the impression was promoted that these hospitals are unnecessary and 'redundant,' and may even have led to a lower quality of care."[19] Shutting down a section of a state hospital also often failed to yield significant saving, as "mental hospitals or State schools are total communities. In addition to psychiatric, medical, and occupational therapy, they must provide for sleeping, feeding and recreational facilities, administrative offices" if they were to remain open at any level.[20] Quality outpatient care, treating a more extensive range of new diagnoses with often expensive drugs, also cost more money than expected.

Rockefeller's progressive program, stretching over a decade of earnest effort, was widely endorsed by the mental health community, but its many successes were quickly forgotten because he had left in place remnant institutions with poor conditions. Willowbrook State School's main sections, for instance, were revealed in 1972 to be understaffed, overcrowded, poorly run, too big, and inhumane in the early 1970s. Images of these places, "hazardous to the health, safety, and sanity of the residents," received extensive play in the newspapers and media. The courts, because of a class action lawsuit, ordered the state to remedy conditions by adding staff, ending isolation, making necessary repairs, and more.[21]

State mental health leaders tried to shift attention to their plans to divide the Willowbrook patients across the five boroughs and to the declining size of the residential population there. Between 1963 and 1973, for instance, the residential population at Willowbrook declined from 6,300 to 4,500 patients. The damage to the state program's reputation seemed unsalvageable. Even a study council appointed by Rockefeller agreed that the conditions there and at the other state schools should be addressed immediately.[22]

Rockefeller defended deinstitutionalization but admitted, "We're now about a year and a half behind in our master plan of building thousand-bed hospitals." He explained that while the community mental health programs had been for "younger, less disabled" patients who "tended to be more middle class," the residential population of state institutions was still in place because they were "sadder, poorer, more disabled and more unsavory." Dealing with their needs would certainly take more time and money than anticipated—and likely much more than the public wanted to spend. Economies possible in vast asylums were difficult to reproduce in the public/private partnerships that succeeded them. Nursing homes, for instance, were very pricey. Outpatient drug and alcohol treatment was as well. The poor conditions at mental health institutions cast a cloud over Rockefeller's reform program.[23] His successor, Governor Carey, would sign a consent decree in 1975 agreeing to major improvements in the remaining state institutions.[24]

The setbacks in the deinstitutionalization program, including clear signs of a growing crisis in homelessness among the mentally ill, did not stop the process after Rockefeller left the frame. Governor Mario Cuomo, for instance, took credit in 1994 for continuing the deinstitutionalization process, increasing community residence beds (single-room occupancy hotels, supportive housing, halfway houses) from 3,000 to 11,000 between 1983 and 1993, raising community health funds, and reducing the number of admissions to state hospitals to just 15,655 in 1993 from 24,188 in 1983. Total adult inpatients fell in that period from 22,000 to only 10,500. There were now more patients in residential treatment community homes and apartments than in institutions.[25]

The public failures overshadowed the quiet success of aspects of deinstitutionalization. Officials who planned deinstitutionalization when cities were emptying out could not have predicted the tightening of urban housing markets since the 1980s: the massive loss of single-room occupancy hotels in New York City, the stagnation or loss of large-scale federal housing programs, and fewer than hoped opportunities for halfway houses due to neighborhood resistance. These factors, when combined with chronic unemployment of the deinstitutionalized population, created a highly visible homeless problem for New York City. Although only a portion of homelessness was the result of deinstitutionalization alone, the high-profile street life of the mentally ill, who often resisted entering shelters, was the dominant image of the results from changing the treatment model. The mentally ill had now become just another urban problem that shelters, public housing, and other stressed elements of the city infrastructure were asked to absorb with little additional funding. New York's affluent suburbs, as in other areas of low-cost housing, also failed to do their part to house the mentally ill homeless.[26]

American States and Deinstitutionalization

New York State's mental health efforts, and the mixed results for cities, aligned with the postwar revolution in mental health treatment in most states. California was a leader in rethinking policies on a large, urban scale. Mental health treatment there in the mid-1950s "shifted away from the big, custodial type of state hospitals to more responsive community health centers." Administrators also began "to operate regional centers for the retarded." California adopted an admired public/private outpatient service model as an alternative to hospitalization. By 1969, there were only 13,363 patients left in California state mental hospitals, thus allowing patients to remain "in the mainstream of their communities."[27] The small number of patients left in mental hospitals was linked to "increased use of tranquilizing drugs, better staffing, improved finances, facilities, and equipment." Halfway houses for community living were also important.[28]

The demise of the institutional model nationally received another push from a series of judicial decisions sharply limiting "commitment" during the 1970s. Experts, however, quickly diagnosed a "revolving door" of treatment: "From 1955 to 1980, the number of patients in state mental hospitals decreased from 559,000 to 150,000. But the number of admissions increased from 178,000 in 1955 to 375,000 in 1975," almost half of which were readmissions. Many of the discharged patients could not maintain themselves in the community at large as the various supports, including housing, provided were insufficient.[29]

States remained deeply involved in mental health services in the 1970s, but the focus had changed. While "the programs managed by the 54 state and territorial mental health agencies mark the network as the largest public health system in the free world," the large and impersonal hospitals were either gone or much smaller. Nationally, state officials had subdivided 180 of 316 large state hospitals into a unit system based largely on geographical origin. The combined systems were treating record numbers, 1.693 million people in 1971, which spoke to growing breadth of treatment. Nearly everywhere the administrators emphasized "ambulatory treatment and care at the community level" rather than "institutionalized treatment of the mentally disordered." The amount of money pumped into the system had also increased, with the help of Medicaid, indicating that states were not simply running from the problem. The total spent rose from \$832 million in 1956 (\$7.6 billion in 2018 dollars) to \$3.2 billion (\$19.6 billion in 2018 dollars) in 1971. The federal/state partnership was the key feature.[30]

In most states, the cost of mental health treatment expanded even as the residential numbers declined—confusing many legislators and the public who had hoped for cost savings with deinstitutionalization. States, however, usually still had to pay to maintain senile patients in expensive private nursing homes; most expanded their facilities for the young and mentally retarded, and state therapists began addressing alcohol and narcotic addiction as a disease rather than a moral failing. Some state hospitals often remained open despite many fewer patients.[31] One national study in the 1970s found that despite the new emphasis on community mental health, "80 percent of the money allocated to the mentally ill was still going toward the cost of state institutions."[32]

The failure to link mental health funding to patients rather than institutions would have long-term, mostly negative, consequences once states shuttered most of the large institutions. What began nationally with high hopes, deep investments, and new design thinking quickly devolved into an impossibly wide mandate and chaotic devolution of treatment to urban regions without the necessary controls or funding. New York may have been aggressive during the Rockefeller years, but it and other states failed to meet the ambitious goals in the Community Mental Health Act of 1963; by 2018, states had built only 750 of 1,500 planned community mental health facilities.[33] States also failed to sustain funding that would have compensated for the loss of institutional treatment. Medicaid now provides more to support these services nationally than state general revenues, a relatively recent shift in responsibility that reflects lagging state support. Funding of mental health service that is provided to patients also varies dramatically across state lines. Northern and western states like California still spend far more per capita and in absolute totals than southern states on these necessary services.[34] This disparity in funding by states raises questions about the reliance on federalism for such a crucial social service because the nation's fastest-growing urban regions, such as those around Atlanta, are receiving next to nothing in state help for mental health treatment. Are these areas mentally healthier or are states simply leaving the problems generated by untreated mental illness to local government, the federal government, or other states?[35]

The vulnerable mentally ill are also poorly served in the affordable housing field. States now rely primarily on a few federal housing programs to help them meet the enormous and complex housing need of clients. State funds remain a crucial but collectively small element in this housing mix (figure 44). The rise of today's small state-sponsored "supportive housing" network, with mental health services on site, reflects the continuing need for supervision and domestic structure for many of the mentally ill and drug/alcohol addicted. By almost all accounts, the combination of these state and federal housing subsidies has not been sufficient.[36]

City leaders find themselves with few good options when it comes to the mentally ill homeless. Among the "solutions" pursued are to criminalize homelessness, force the vulnerable into shelters, and maintain the revolving door of short-term treatment. As states have generously funded incarceration (45 states reported a combined $43 billion on prisons in 2015), it now seems inevitable that jails would come to be viewed as structured "shelter" by city officials desperate for any solution. New York State in 2015, for instance, spent approximately $69,000 per person annually for its 53,000 prison inmates, for a total of $3.6 billion, about equal to all state mental health funding. Among the services prisons now provide, beyond controlled shelter and meals, are "higher levels of specialized health care for a growing population with significant levels of physical and mental health concerns." Approximately 40 percent of the Riker's Island inmate population, for instance, suffered from mental health issues in 2014. It is hard to imagine that many of these people would not be better off spending time and receiving treatment in modernized, humane, long-term mental health institutions rather than a prison. Similar percentages of urban prisoners with mental illness have been identified nationally.[37]

These shortcomings in urban mental health raise questions about the validity of the extreme and rushed approach to deinstitutionalization in the 1960s and 1970s. The default use of prisons for controlling the mentally ill is

Housing Support Program Funding Sourcess	States Using Funding Sources	Housing Units Provided	States Reporting Number of Housing Units Provided
Fedral Housing Development Sources			
HUD Section 811/202	37	71,060	15
HUD Home Funds	35	3,456	9
Contunuum of Care Homeless Funds	39	5986	13
Community Development Block Grant	35	5046	11
Rural Development	22	4043	4
Low - Income Housing Tax Credits	36	6618	8
Housing Opportunities for People with AIDS	25	265	5
SAMHSA Mental Health Block Grant	13	79	4
State Housing Development Sources			
State Housing Trust Funds	19	5,326	9
State General Obligation Bond Financing	12	471	3
State General Revenue Bond Financing	14	108	1
State Mental Health Capital Funds	11	5,513	7
State Housing Tax Credits	16	2,243	5
Federal Tenant Subsidies			
HUD Section 8 Certificates/Vouchers	38	66,246	8
Shelter Plus Care	36	7676	9
HOME Tenant- Based Rental Subsidies	26	1866	5
Housing Opportunities for People with AIDS	25	2363	3
PATH Homeless Funds	29	461	3
State Tenant Subsidies			
State Housing Agency Rent Subsidies	22	11,104	3
State Mental Health Section 8 Bridge Funds	18	1,158	1

FIGURE 44. Sources of housing funding used by State Mental Health Agencies in 2009. Chart by Minna Ninova, 2018.

even more disturbing. A more logical transition to the new treatment model in the postwar years might have provided time to develop adequate support services and housing rather than simply shutting down institutions, medicating patients, and subsidizing an incomplete system of halfway houses and nursing homes. States dramatically impacted urban fortunes in the succeeding decades, and not necessarily for the better.

The Environment

14

Cities of Sludge: The Urban Water Crisis

Toxic waterways had the potential to undermine the hard-won satisfactions of the postwar good life. Streams and rivers full of sewage and industrial sludge and poisoned aquifers threatened municipal water supplies. Filthy water in rivers, streams, lakes, and harbors frequently spoiled the enjoyment of backyards, beaches, and waterfront parks. The federal government until the 1960s had weakly regulated water pollution, leaving states to make fundamental decisions about the funding, location, scale, and quality of water treatment.

Many states, in response to public demand for a cleaner environment in the 1950s, began to set standards and aid in the development of water treatment facilities and new sewers.[1] The pace of state-level water regulation picked up enough that by 1958 it was possible for experts on state policy to claim that "action to improve state administration, control, and development of water resources" was widespread. Many states also worked with local governments to find and protect new water supplies to meet the demand of growing cities and suburbs. States like New York and California in the 1960s pioneered stringent new regulations demanded by an increasingly sensitive and aware public, but the federal government also stepped up the pressure on all states in the mid-1960s.[2]

The result of states entering municipal water treatment in earnest during the late 1960s, combined with escalating federal standards, was a realization that the costs were going to exceed what could be wrung from state revenues, local taxes, or bond sales. States made crucial and early decisions on water treatment and enforcement, and continue to serve today in a prominent funding and regulatory role, but they gladly passed many of the mounting bills and dangerous politics of imposing higher national standards on to the federal government in the early 1970s. That they were willing to accept

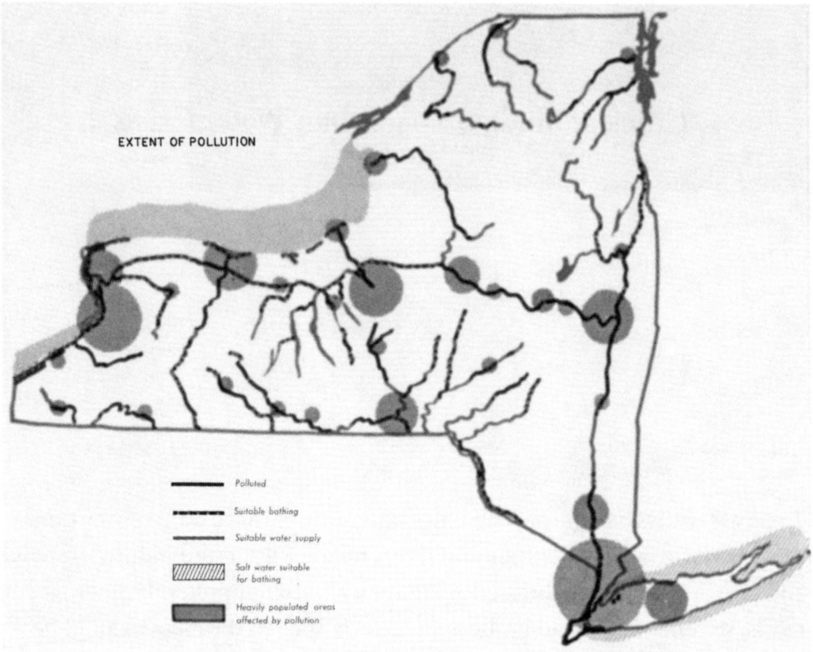

FIGURE 45. Illustrating the relationship between poor water quality and urban development. "Pure Waters: A Program to Rescue New York State's Water From Pollution," 1964. New York State Archives, courtesy of the Rockefeller Archive Center.

EPA superiority on local quality-of-life issues, when cities and states fiercely guarded local control in so many other areas, speaks to the desperation of state and local leaders.

New York State provides a clear window into the ups and downs of state engagement in water quality. As with many other dimensions of state power in urban affairs, New York's massive size and early efforts conceal its representative experience. Nearly all the problems that New York faced—spiraling costs, local resistance, and changing federal standards—were shared by other state governments. So even though New York committed unprecedented funds to the fight for clean water during the 1960s, the tremendous scale of the problems and costs were proportional to other states. State officials in New York joined with their colleagues to demand Washington set standards and open the treasury to fund the achievement of those goals.

New York's Dirty Water Business

New York City by the turn of the century was a global leader in water supply by tapping, with state permission, vast quantities of clean water for the city in Westchester County and, later, the distant Catskills. As early as 1904, New York State's Water Supply Commission also demanded plans from all the state's cities for securing adequate future water supplies. The commission slowly began to examine water quality and sewer discharge. But city leaders across the state paid precious little attention to the resulting filth generated by urban mass consumption of water.

One of the worst offenders was the city that had done the best in securing an abundant and clean supply. In the early 1960s, the city of New York was still dumping 500 million gallons of raw sewage into waterways *per day*. This dumping was terrible for health and real estate. The addition of luxurious waterfront residential districts like Battery Park City and Waterside in Manhattan during the 1960s would fail if the surrounding water remained disgusting. Out in the suburbs, green lawns hid terrible pollution below the surface. Many subdivisions lacked connection to sanitary systems because developers discovered regulatory loopholes that allowed them to use septic or other inadequate disposal methods. The private sector cannot be blamed for taking liberties with water quality. Local governments showed more enthusiasm for suburban growth and industrial expansion than very expensive sewers. Many local officials believed that sewers were county or state responsibilities and preferred to shift blame, even when it was clear that the county and state officials were doing nothing in the field.[3]

The state's Water Pollution Control Act of 1949 had laid the groundwork for the study of the state's water quality but lacked significant enforcement provisions. The act, for instance, relied primarily on voluntary action by industrial polluters who had shaped the law to begin with. The legislation also failed to provide the cash required to convince local governments, often content to send their filthy water downstream, to start expensive water treatment projects. A 1960 study by the Office for Local Government, estimating a price tag of $1 billion to create a statewide system sewage treatment program, spooked many legislators. The price of relying on local government, however, was mounting quality-of-life challenges, including groundwater contamination on Long Island. In Westchester County, septic systems undermined the quality of New York's water supply in the original Croton water system. New York City was, by volume, the worst violator of all, fouling its surrounding waters daily and making its waterfronts dangerous and unattractive.[4]

New York State under Rockefeller entered the water treatment field because local government and private interests had manifestly failed to deal with new quality of life expectations of the public. To ignore water quality was becoming a political liability.[5] The state Department of Health, with the state Attorney General's Office, aggressively challenged water pollution violations both by local governments and private businesses (including suburban developers) during this period, in the courts if necessary, thus forcing them to plan for and develop water treatment where none had existed before.[6]

In 1962, Rockefeller's administration began a 10-year program, funded initially at $120 million ($989 million in 2017 dollars), to help local governments study, expand, and operate sewerage treatment facilities. The modest program addressed both the needs of older cities like New York and Buffalo and fast-growing suburbs in Nassau County. Rockefeller, in a familiar refrain, criticized federal "discrimination" against "heavily populated urban areas" such as New York State. The state was set to receive just $5 million of an annual $100 million national program because the federal government had set a cost ceiling on new plants at just $600,000. A typical big-city treatment plant, however, might cost as much as $100 million. The federal program favored small towns and new suburban communities.[7] State officials in 1964, for instance, believed there existed a need for "approximately 800 new or enlarged treatment plants" statewide, and of that, "641 represent areas without both sewers and treatment" where 5.2 million people resided. The water crisis was a metropolitan-scale problem.[8]

Rockefeller aimed in 1964–1965 to address urban needs on the necessary level by gaining approval from voters for a massive $1.7 billion ($13.654 billion in 2017 dollars) Pure Waters Bond program. Rockefeller acknowledged that "the tide of urbanization and population growth that has swept the nation has tremendously increased the demand for water," which in turn created a new scale of disposal issues.[9] A statewide drought in 1965, which threatened water supplies for New York City and the rest of the state, helped build broad public support. The Pure Waters Bond initiative focused on water treatment in cities and towns where failures to clean water were most evident to the public—and where cleanups would be most noticeable. The bond's emphasis on municipal water treatment rather than on industrial pollution also made it business friendly. Factory owners, for instance, were given generous tax breaks to build their treatment plants. Rockefeller's bond programs rejected water conservation measures and a notion of water as a finite resource; instead, the bonds were part of a growth-oriented plan to ensure "enough useable water to meet our accelerating needs in this urban age." Abundant clean water statewide would encourage higher property values, add more construction jobs, and generate higher tax revenues. By this logic, environmentalism was a broad movement including "farmers, housewives, sportsmen, workers, businessmen, children—all want pure waters."[10]

Rockefeller's strong support, the hard work of his staff, and the growing public consciousness favoring environmental improvements in the urban environment carried the bond issue to passage in 1965 with a four-to-one margin of victory. From the bond issue came a Pure Waters Authority with the funds for loans and related training. The program was risky, however, because it required that local governments pay just 10 percent of the construction costs for their systems. This generosity removed a stumbling block to local participation but probably weakened cost controls at the local level, as elected officials had so little responsibility for cost overruns. The state agreed to cover 60 percent of the total cost and even decided to "prefinance" another 30 percent based upon the belief that the federal government would eventually step in to pick up the tab.[11]

Rockefeller pressured the federal government in a widely publicized letter to President Lyndon Johnson in early 1965 asking for $500 million ($3.9 billion in 2017 dollars) in federal funds to complement the state's planned treatment program. The federal program, he said, was "woefully inadequate" where "the need for pollution control action is greatest—the urban states." Federal funds were promised, in part because the federal government was already demanding that New York clean up the polluted Hudson. Rockefeller took that promise seriously.[12] The combined pressure from many states resulted in changes to the federal rules in 1966 to cover up to 55 percent of project costs, up from 30 percent. The federal portion would rise again in the 1960s in tandem with much higher national standards.[13]

Rapid improvements were possible in an environment so degraded. By 1969, the combined state/local/federal program had delivered 117 operating treatment plants, 83 were under construction, and 139 were in preconstruction. The Pure Waters Authority coordinated the projects and established 116 monitoring stations to make sure that the treatment systems functioned correctly. Private companies qualified for tax credits if they built integrated waste treatment plants. Reflecting the fact that the system did not outright ban toxic operations, 62 factories had operating treatment plants, and another 198 were in design. Real progress appeared to be under way.[14]

The Real Price of Clean Water

The strains in the water treatment program quickly became apparent in New York, just as they did in other states. To build systems to address the tremendous scale of urban needs began to come in at cost levels far beyond anything the Rockefeller administration had predicted. By 1969, for instance, the total anticipated cost of the state program had risen to $2.8 billion ($18.99 billion in 2017 dollars) as inflation, new federal standards, and higher volumes of pollutants from industries began to flood the plants, necessitating even more treatment. The federal government had, however, provided only about 7 percent of the costs of these plants despite promises to fund a greater percentage of the costs.[15]

In 1970 Rockefeller created the Department of Environmental Conservation (DEC) with comprehensive responsibility for water and air quality control as well as solid waste, water supply, land management, and conservation. Creation of state departments of natural or environmental resources was typical in this period in response to federal pressure for a "comprehensive environmental department or agency" that could be a more responsible partner on a variety and growing number of state and federal laws.[16] Rockefeller chose Henry Diamond—a veteran of his campaigns, a respected environmentalist, and confidant and counsel of his brother Laurance—to lead the DEC.[17] Diamond immediately targeted 197 firms for investigation on mercury discharge and forced or gained agreements with large companies such as Allied Chemical (at two plants), Olin Mathieson, and Hooker.[18] The DEC also banned or restricted many pesticides and more closely monitored air pollution.[19] State enforcement increased in the 1980s and played an essential role in toxic chemical controls, the Love Canal response, and the acid rain crisis of the 1980s and 1990s.[20]

The scale and cost of the treatment plants in New York City and elsewhere spiraled upwards in the 1970s to meet state and federal standards. By 1970 New York City had received just 16 grants for a total of $278 million from New York State.[21] These subsidies were deep, but the actual costs of the plants far exceeded the program grants. The state contributed to the construction of the vast Newtown Creek Sewage Treatment Plan (32 acres) that moved the needle on the treatment of total city sewerage from 60 to 80 percent, thus allowing for the closure of 83 direct sewer outfalls to open waterways. The state covered just $30 million of a $170 million project; most of the plant had to be funded out of city capital funds.[22]

The nearly two-decade saga of the North River Wastewater Treatment Plant reflects the deep challenge of building treatment megaprojects. On the Upper West Side, to stem the flow of untreated waste into the Hudson and Harlem Rivers, the state in 1967 provided $66 million in direct grants, the federal government promised $64 million (which the state prefinanced), and the city budget covered the remainder of the estimated $219 million construction budget.[23] The projected cost of the 30-acre North River Plant, however, rose to $780 million in the early 1970s. Construction finally started in 1972, and the city blew through the first completion target of 1977. By 1982, after many delays and a consent decree (1979) the city signed with the federal government for its violation of the Clean Water Act, the cost of the continuing construction project had risen to approximately $1.1 billion. The federal government eventually provided 75 percent of the cost, with the state providing just 15 percent and the city 10 percent. The plant only began partial operations in 1986.[24]

The Pure Waters program also generated backlash from smaller towns that lacked New York City's comparatively deep pockets and appetite for debt. The small town of Adams near Syracuse, for instance, was up in arms because "the state has ordered Adams to build a complete sewage system, including a modern treatment plant." The town fathers had been content with septic systems because most of the polluted water flowed downstream. The mayor screamed, "I'm not going to sign any papers to bankrupt this village!" and "State aid, baloney." Not only would a sewage treatment plan have been required, but expensive intercepting sewers would be needed to get the waste to the plant.[25] The Onondaga County legislature also rejected a $48 million bond for improvement of a sewer plant. DEC commissioner Diamond held back money and approval for new sewers until the county legislature approved the bond. Many fast-growing suburbs, like Suffolk County, quietly continued to allow growth of septic tank suburbs during this era rather than face the real cost of clean water. Developers were left to their own devices, which usually meant as little treatment as possible.[26]

The higher than expected costs of developing treatment plants and sewers led to a call for prioritization by the state health commissioner in 1969, which was interpreted as a sign of "growing pessimism among state officials that the goal of clean waters can be met in the foreseeable future."[27] Rockefeller's promise that the state's water would be pollution free by 1972 was starting to look like his ambitious promises for the Long Island Rail Road. Like other state projects that missed their mark regarding scale and cost, Rockefeller shifted blame to federal officials for their failure to meet their promised share. He promised, however, that the Hudson would be pure "even if we don't get a nickel of federal aid" but wisely moved the deadline for a clean Hudson to 1972.[28] He now thought that the cost of pure water in the state might be as high as $3 billion and called for a federal program of $30 billion ($192 billion in 2017 dollars).[29] By fall of 1970, Rockefeller thought that it would cost $4.2 billion ($26.9 billion in 2017 dollars) just to clean up New York State's waters.[30] The rising costs can in part be linked to the governor's addressing newly identified challenges such as detergents, mercury, and industrial sludge.[31]

Wins and Losses

The showpiece for environmental improvement was the changed situation of the Hudson River—the state's largest river and one of its most degraded. As early as 1973, however, "almost all fishermen, marine biologists, environmentalists and government officials" agreed "that the river is cleaner now than it has been in recent years." Fish were returning, and some areas even had safe swimming conditions.[32] Henry Diamond explained that this "payoff" was the result of devoting "$1.4 billion since 1965 to cleaning up the Hudson." Along the Hudson or its tributaries, there were now 17 municipal plants operating, 12 in construction, and 33 at the design stage. The river was cleaner than it had been since the nineteen century, even accounting for pollution still flowing in at high rates, invisible pollutants such as PCBs, Con Edison cooling towers at Indian Point (1963) killing fish en masse, and the North River Plant in Manhattan being years from opening.[33]

The improvements were felt statewide because of the administration's wise focus on municipal treatment, where tangible improvements would be quickly delivered to large numbers of people. By 1973, the state had placed 317 plants in operation and another 40 were under development. The state was still waiting, however, for full federal payoffs for prefinancing of $1.3 billion by 1973, having received a paltry 13 percent of the 55 percent promised from the federal government.[34]

A massive increase in federal funding for treatment in the 1970s made good on promises, but plenty of challenges remained. The available subsidy programs, for instance, lacked sufficient funds to deal with the combined storm drainage / sewer problem in New York City. In 1970, 300 million gallons of untreated sewage still flowed into the surrounding waterways daily. On very rainy days, moreover, the city's combined storm/sewer drains dumped even more.[35] The enormous cost of separating the system could not be covered then or now in any combination of local/state/federal funds. Even today, heavy downpours often lead to direct dumping of sewer water into surrounding water bodies (ca. 20 billion gallons per year), despite billions more spent on water treatment since the Rockefeller era. The water is clear enough to allow massive waterfront development and new parks, but it is not necessarily as clean as it could be.

The relatively slow pace of implementation proved excellent for unregulated suburban development. Developers and builders remained aggressive throughout this time even when their subdivisions lacked adequate local treatment plants or connections to town or city sewers. Replacement of suburban septic systems with sewers is now extraordinarily expensive, leaving substandard systems in service even when they contribute to the loss of ground and surface water quality (as on Long Island). Today, three-quarters of homes in Suffolk County are still on septic systems or tanks, posing a significant risk to groundwater supplies and the environmental quality of Long Island Sound. To hook up just 12,000 homes in Suffolk County to sewer lines and treatment plants will cost an estimated $388 million. The scale and cost of the problem come into perspective when one considers that there are currently 360,000 homes on septic systems in Suffolk County. Allowing for growth of this kind has emerged as a significant flaw in postwar infrastructure planning in New York and many other states.[36]

Rockefeller, it should be noted, also sent mixed message about water quality that likely muddied the waters. Like many governors, he remained solidly in favor of rising living standards and the polluting energy generation that lifestyle now required. Environmentalists in 1968 beat back a massive nuclear plant on the Hudson at Easton near Saratoga planned by Niagara Mohawk and supported by Rockefeller.[37] Opponents of a Con Edison backup power plant at Storm King, which would have used pumped water to generate power during peak periods, spent years fighting the plan. In frustration, they finally went over Rockefeller's head to federal officials.[38] Con Edison only canceled the plant, after years of protest and litigation, in 1980.[39]

The Rockefeller administration in fact remained tone deaf, and even hostile, to the broader ecological and countercultural movement. One of Rockefeller's allies complained in the late 1960s that the "Clear Water Program" initiated by folksinger Pete Seeger "has focused national attention on the problem of the Hudson River" while "the State's efforts have gone virtually unmentioned." Seeger and friends, gifted publicists, sailed the Hudson River in a restored sloop to highlight the need for cleaner water, "thus preempting . . . public attention and our $1 billion bond issue for cleaning up all the waterways in the State."[40] Threading the needle of so many different environmental groups, while remaining progrowth, was a challenge for governors like Rockefeller. The difficulties they faced help explain their eagerness to shift the burden as much as possible to the federal government.

American States and Water Regulation

States like New York and California deserve credit for trying to raise and meet clean water standards with limited federal support. California, for instance, had already progressively extended state control over water resources, water quality, and discharge of pollution, culminating in the Porter-Cologne Act (1969), considered by some to be a partial model for the federal Clean Water

Act (CWA).[41] In general, however, states and local government simply lacked the funding and political support to meet public demand or rising federal standards. The federal government consistently failed to provide adequate funding to the states or local governments in the 1950s or 1960s despite raising the regulatory bar. According to author Martin Melosi, "A survey of the Conference of State Sanitary Engineers in 1965 indicated that new sewage-treatment plants or enlargements and additional facilities were essential in 5,277 communities."[42]

The growing social consciousness surrounding pollution, Earth Day celebrations that began in 1970, and determined efforts of leaders such as Senator Edwin Muskie proved transformative at the federal level in the early 1970s. The federal assumption of regulatory power was based not only on its own failures to deliver necessary funds to meet stated standards but also on the "interstate spillovers of pollution; the poor performance of states as environmental regulators; and interstate competitiveness effects arising from differing environmental standards."[43] The passage of the CWA in 1972 reflected the reality that even after decades of new plant construction, in most areas of the country "industrial wastewater was generally left untreated, fisheries vanished, and sewage discharges grew at startling rates. Without federal assistance, state-run pollution control programs failed."[44]

Congress, through the CWA, planned to "restore and maintain the chemical, physical, and biological integrity of the Nation's waters."[45] Congress optimistically hoped to end "the discharge of pollutants into the navigable waters . . . by 1985" and establish "water quality which provides for the protection and propagation of fish, shellfish, and wildlife and provides for recreation in and on the water" by 1983.[46] The 1972 act even required secondary treatment at all municipal sewage plants by 1977, a much higher standard for water released back into nature than existed in most states. The EPA stepped up its regulation of industrial polluters and set strict deadlines, legal actions, and fines, with the help of most states, for meeting standards. The EPA in 1977 gained a key role in drinking water monitoring, with a strong expectation of state participation in setting and maintaining standards.[47]

State actions under the CWA have been debated for decades. The level of federal enforcement and regulation changed dramatically after 1972. For some, it was a "massive exercise of Federal authority and Federal investment." State and local officials participated in administrative procedures, but "both the ground rules and the final decisions are federally determined."[48] Other scholars give states more credit, viewing the pioneering work of some states, and their continuing activism today, as "'engines' of environmental regulation." Most scholars take a nuanced approach, viewing the post-1972 settlement of responsibility concerning a "cooperative federalism" as having both strengths and weaknesses, depending upon the water pollution issues and state involved.[49]

What distinguished federal rules was attempting to apply standards pioneered in activist states like New York and California to conservative states like Mississippi and Alabama. In California, for instance, in 1972, "in most cases discharges of waste are subject to state permits at the present time. So what we are really doing is instituting a new national permit system—not necessarily a new system of pollution control." The states with the highest standards retained significant control: "The law gives clear direction that states with acceptable programs need not give way to an EPA-administered federal program and EPA has indicated a desire to have as many state approved programs as possible so that day-to-day decision making and permit issuance will largely be the responsibility of the state."[50]

Tension has developed in the succeeding decades between the EPA and state leaders that prefer a laissez-faire approach. States can decide, for instance, to use federal water quality standards as a minimum rather than maximum, depending upon their political outlook. States looking for a higher quality environmental standard will use the federal standards as minimums, while a state seeking a business-friendly environment might use them as maximums. The actual enforcement of the rules also relies on state environmental offices: "Practically, the federal government cannot implement federal standards without the resources, expertise, information, and political support of state and local officials." Gutting a state environmental agency is an effective way to avoid state or federal rules. Where there is no monitoring, there can be few reported violations.[51]

Federal water-related lawmaking in the 1970s extended far beyond the CWA. Among the federal laws influencing states are the Marine Protection, Research, and Sanctuaries Act (1972); the Coastal Zone Management Act (1972); the Endangered Species Act (1973); the Safe Drinking Water Act (1974), the amended Clean Water Act (1977); and the Toxic Substances Control Act (1976).[52] Some states have also continued to innovate. California and Washington successfully fought for a reduction in copper in vehicle brakes, which was a significant water pollutant. New York State has recently banned fracking as a potential threat to water quality even though many more states have allowed extensive mining activities.[53]

The federal legislation eventually provided substantial funds to help urbanized states meet high standards. Between 1973 and 1977, for instance, the EPA offered a total of $28 billion to water pollution control efforts nationally. The federal government paid up to 75 percent of the planning and construction costs for treatment plants. Even such generosity, and many billions more since the 1970s, has improved water quality in the United States but has not been sufficient to meet the ambitious goals of the CWA in all areas. Many local and state governments either lack funding or are resistant to providing even their smaller shares (and sometimes those shares, in absolute terms, are not so little). For many single-family homes lacking treatment, the costs of extending sewer lines are often prohibitive.

Depending upon one's point of view, this state/local/federal water partnership proved relatively successful (the nation's surface waters have generally improved), moderately successful (much progress made but many challenges remain), a programmatic failure (business and cities can avoid severe penalties), or a waste of money (regulations kill jobs, cost too much to taxpayers, etc.). The pioneering role of states in the postwar years, and their continuing role today, redefined expectations of environmental quality for city and suburban residents.

15

Parks for City People

Postwar American states built on a proud national tradition of urban park planning. Regional park systems originated in the late nineteenth and early twentieth century with the Olmsteds and similar landscape visionaries, whose efforts inspired city parks, parkways, urban park systems, and state-enabled metropolitan park systems for the likes of Boston, Chicago, Minneapolis, and Cleveland (figure 46). The number of state parks, at a further remove from cities but still often serving the needs of urbanites, also rose modestly before the postwar decades. California's state park system, for instance, expanded after 1927 thanks to voter-approved bonds. The natural beauty in 77 parks (300,000 acres), preserved and made accessible according to a careful plan by Fredrick Law Olmsted Jr., drew millions of visitors annually by the late 1930s.[1]

Many postwar suburbanites or politicians did not, at first, show much concern for parks—or developers would have provided more of them. The front yards and backyards offered in new subdivisions, after all, represented a revolutionary increase in desirable, informal, private urban outdoor space. Kids could even safely camp out in the backyard. For urban dwellers accustomed to tenements, jammed two and three flats on tiny lots, or apartment houses, the lawns and patios on the crabgrass frontier were a revelation. As the novelty of tightly packed subdivisions wore off, or simply because they had the money and means to travel, suburbanites explored natural areas further afield for camping, hiking, skiing, swimming, and snowmobiling. The introduction of the two-day weekend, higher family income, highways, millions more cars, and camping trailers brought Americans in record numbers to state and federal parks. The mass popularity of outdoor recreation created pressure on politicians for state park acquisition and new regulations.[2]

One environmental response was a new era of state park development

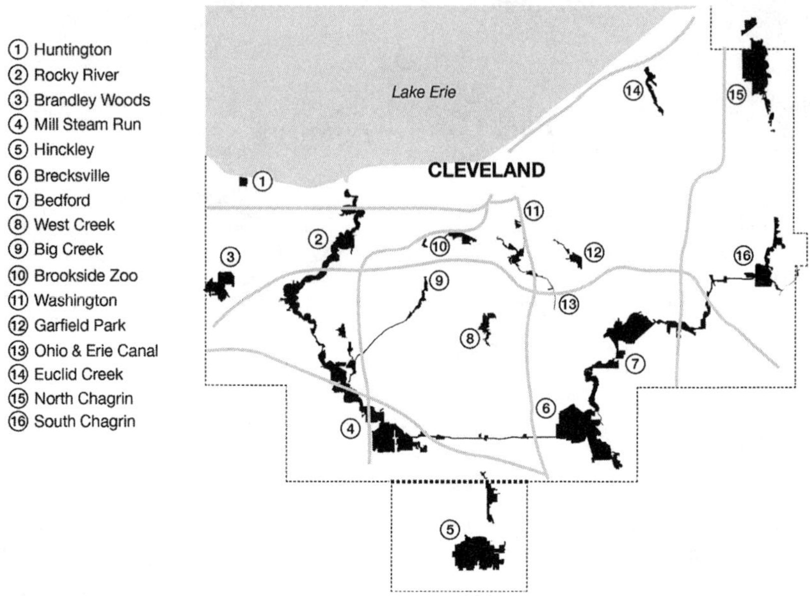

FIGURE 46. Cleveland metropolitan parks, now 23,000 acres in 18 parks, got their start with state legislation in 1917. Map by Minna Ninova, 2018.

and regulation. It was difficult for suburbanites to restrict the growth of the subdivision next door, out of a sense of fairness to the latecomers, young families, or developers, but the same could not be said of more distant rural areas. Conservation would offer the metropolitan citizen "open space, forest, cropland, and stream valleys that will keep something of nature close to urban life."[3] Ecology mattered to some of the most motivated state advocates, and to some portion of the mass public, but the present and future enjoyment of natural areas was paramount.[4]

New York State consistently pursued park development on a grand scale. Yet the growing interest of state residents in park visits, mostly by car, reflected typical national patterns, as did the emphasis on recreation for day users from nearby cities. The willingness of urban voters in New York during the Rockefeller years to purchase land, and even override local governments in the pursuit of recreational and natural beauty, parallels the extraordinary efforts of many states during this time.

New York's Regional Park Tradition

New York State had been active, and a national leader, in park development since the nineteenth century. Philanthropists and politicians expanded the park system in response to "the destruction of natural resources" by the industrial, urban system. By the early twentieth century, the state park system included both large, accessible parks near major cities and the more remote Adirondack and Catskill parks. New York's state park system was much more advanced than those of other states by the early twentieth century because of the combination of great natural beauty, rapid urbanization, and an emerging tradition of progressive state action. By certain standards, however, even this leading park system was a "hodgepodge" and would be quickly overwhelmed by "inexpensive, mass-produced automobiles" in the 1920s.[5]

Robert Moses redesigned the park system for the auto age at city, suburban, and rural scales. The state legislature, with Governor Al Smith's support, accepted Moses's plan for what became the State Council of Parks (SCP) in 1924. The key aim of the SCP, aside from creating another fiefdom for Moses, "was not simply to buy and protect places of scenic beauty but was to make such places accessible for recreation." Moses linked landscaped parkways to new or expanded parks in and around the state's major cities. In his 40-year term leading the SCP (1924–1963), Long Island State Park Commission (1924–1963), and New York City Department of Parks (1934–1960), Robert Moses consistently emphasized active recreation in parks, auto access by parkways, and ample parking lots for arriving vacationers.[6]

State parks and parkways, aided by crucial land and donations from wealthy New Yorkers, helped shape the patterns of urban growth, recreation, and transportation for the New York metropolitan region during the interwar years. Moses's creation of Jones Beach in 1926 and the renovation and expansion of New York City parks during the New Deal is famous. Long Island was Moses's focus because it had "half the State's population sitting next to a sparsely populated island." With the creation of numerous bridges and tunnels linking Manhattan and Long Island and the later extension of grade-separated parkways, suburban development overran private farms and many lush estates. Large parks added to Long Island by Moses and philanthropists included Heckscher State Park (1929) and Sunken Meadow State Park (1928). Residents of the Hudson Valley, along its urbanizing shores, benefited from an expanding "chain" of parks helped along by generous donations by wealthy families, including the Rockefellers.[7] Growing metropolitan areas upstate also benefited from the Moses program. A string of parkways and parks protected Niagara Falls and offered scenic drives and recreation for residents of the urbanized Buffalo/Niagara region. Lovely parks around Rochester included beaches and river valleys.

Moses made maximum use of New Deal works programs during the Great Depression in both the city and state parks program. By 1949, the state was still a national leader, boasting 78 state parks and 160 miles of parkways.[8] Yet Moses's obsessive focus in the postwar era on housing, highways, bridges, power generation, and urban redevelopment—and the lack of federal dollars for park programs—appears to have diverted his attention from a statewide urban parks program on a scale to meet exploding demand. When Rockefeller arrived on the scene in 1959, the increasingly mobile and affluent public had swamped state park facilities. Moses had envisioned a car society and addressed the needs of that public for decades, but he lacked the resources or state support to keep pace. New York City's political leaders also failed to provide sufficient funds to maintain high standards in the many parks and athletic facilities created by Moses and his team during the New Deal.

Fast-growing suburbs around the state's many cities often lacked adequate open and recreational spaces. On the lush hills of Long Island's North Shore, for instance, the wealthy could afford large lots and dense plantings to maintain a shaded environment characteristic of older suburbs. Mass suburbs such as Levittown that sprouted in the middle of the island, by contrast, usually lost whatever trees and natural landscapes survived through centuries of farming. The new residents planted trees, yards, and gardens but were unable to compensate for lost natural landscapes on limited family budgets. Public parks in new suburbs that did exist were usually barebones ball fields or playgrounds grudgingly provided by a developer.[9]

The Rockefeller Park Era

On a tour of Jones Beach with Robert Moses in 1959, Governor Rockefeller announced a three-part park expansion program including immediate, five-year, and population-based plans.[10] Rockefeller directed Commissioner of Conservation Harold Wilm, in cooperation with Robert Moses, to survey recreational facilities and needs. Their study revealed that the state, like most at the time, lagged in providing an adequate recreational environment for its growing metropolitan areas: "Many areas, particularly in the vicinity of our large cities, will be solidly occupied with dwellings, business, and industrial structures, unless we soon take steps to assure recreational space." They discovered that state parks lacked the necessary facilities not only for "the needs of our present population (16,500,000)" but millions more expected. Robert Moses, in his message in the report, believed that the challenge of suburban growth meant "there is no substitute for public ownership of strategic and basic recreational lands." The report's images contrasted the placid and manicured landscapes of state parks with polluted landscapes and crowded or otherwise tacky private recreational facilities. Moses and Wilm called for

FIGURE 47. The tragedy of the commons solved by state parks. State of New York Conservation Department, *Now or Never: A Bold Program for Outdoor Recreation*, 1960. New York State Archives, courtesy of the Rockefeller Archive Center.

many more miles of streams for fishing, more boat-launching sites, expanded wilderness lands, preserved wetlands, and new ski slopes. Facilities like these, they believed, might not deliver the quiet contemplation or ecological purity of nature enthusiasts, but they would offer a fun and healthy outing for the state's growing urban populations.[11]

The governor, at the urging of Laurance Rockefeller and bolstered by the Moses/Wilm report, asked the legislature in 1959 for a $75 million bond plan ($641 million in 2018 dollars) to be voted on in 1960. The program passed by a wide margin because it included funding for both state parks and city/town parks both upstate and downstate.[12] Voters approved another bond issue of $25 million in 1962. Bond packages with something for everyone statewide reflected a winning strategy to which Rockefeller would return many times. Many other states also sold bonds in this period to fund park expansions.

Rockefeller suggested that Moses step down as chairman of the State Council of Parks in 1962 to make space for his brother, Laurance Rockefeller. While nepotistic, it was in other respects a well-earned promotion for Laurance, an acknowledged giant in the field of conservation. Moses at 73 peevishly resigned from his five state park posts (SCP, Long Island State Park Commission, Jones Beach Parkway Authority, Bethpage Park Authority) and as head of the New York Power Authority. Moses had already given up his title as New York park commissioner in 1960. That Rockefeller accepted his resignation came as a surprise to Moses, who had made a career out of threatening resignation when failing to get his way. Rockefeller praised Moses, as he showed him the door, for "development of our present magnificent park system," acknowledging that "no state has a better foundation upon which to build." And there is no reason to think that Rockefeller was not offering genuine praise for Moses. Much of Nelson and his brother Laurance's subsequent program simply built on Moses's precedents. The family and Moses had also worked well together for decades on mutually beneficial projects, including the United Nations and Lincoln Center.[13] As a sign of good feeling, the state renamed several parks and parkways statewide in honor of Moses.[14]

Laurance Rockefeller became the new chairman of the State Council of Parks in 1963. Laurance, like his brother, made a point of linking park development to the future quality of metropolitan life. The state park system, "designed primarily to provide day use facilities for New York's major urban centers,"[15] had to adjust to the postwar reality that "most of the state's current growth takes place in suburban areas surrounding central areas. Open space is rapidly disappearing in these areas." The state aggressively expanded suburban parks for both suburbanites and nearby city dwellers.[16] Newbold Morris, the New York City Parks commissioner, had turned up the pressure on the state when he called for the city to buy up land and build parks in the suburbs. It was, he said, "easier for a resident of the Bronx to travel behind the Iron Curtain than it is for his children to swim in certain Westchester County Pools."[17] Voters did their part to enhance the number, size, and usefulness of state parks by approving additional and substantial bonds for parks in 1966 and 1972.[18]

Reflecting his understanding of the role of parks, Laurance changed the name of the State Council of Parks to the State Council of Parks and Outdoor Recreation. A 1966 bond issue, with the help of federal and local funds, would buy or build 40 safe harbor refuges, 150 boat launching sites, 35 beaches, 25 swimming pools, 20 golf courses, 10,000 campsites, and 500 miles of trails. The funds to repay bonds would come from user fees on recreation, "a carryover from the public authority approach by the Governor to avoid direct state debts."[19] Under Laurance's leadership, the State Parks added thousands of miles of snowmobile and hiking trails in the Adirondacks and encouraged expansions of Catskill and Adirondack ski resorts. Active facilities like these were popular with the affluent urban population out for day trips and fun on the slopes. Many environmentalists, however, questioned the wisdom of adding attractions like ski slopes and accessible paths to fragile alpine landscapes—more people crowded roads, recreational facilities added development pressure for hotels and second homes, and many activities directly disturbed flora and fauna.[20]

Suburban and exurban districts benefited from the programs more than city residents because addition and enlargement of state parks was easier on the suburban frontier than in cities. Governor Rockefeller expanded the state park system between 1962 and 1973 from 102 to 139 state parks, most of them answering needs for metropolitan-area parks. On Long Island, where there were still undeveloped lands and large estates threatened by tax bills, the council scored significant additions to meet the needs of millions of anticipated Nassau and Suffolk residents. The council acquired Caumsett State Park, Connetquot State Park, Brookhaven State Park, and Planting Fields Arboretum—all of them stunning and large properties. Up on the Hudson, subject to suburban development and recreation pressures similar to those on Long Island, the council secured impressive landscapes such as 7,000 acre Minnewaska State Park (in partnership with the Nature Conservancy) on the west side of the Hudson. Administrators even turned the former Croton aqueduct on the east side into the Old Croton Aqueduct Trail, a wooded walkway linking a series of suburban river towns.[21]

Suburbanites appeared to be disproportionately benefiting from state park programs even though they already lived with more greenery in their surroundings than most city residents. Laurance thus created two new state park regional commissions, for the Capital District (serving Albany) and New York City. The New York City commission would "concentrate on recreation and cultural activities in distressed neighborhoods" as part of an "emphatic move to bring State Parks closer to people's daily lives."[22] The council, however, had limited success in New York City, despite promises to do more, because of the cost, complexity, and lack of local political support for greater state intervention. The Roberto Clemente State Park reflects what the state could have accomplished on a grander scale. With three pools, community space, 25 acres of ball fields, picnic areas, and riverfront promenade, the park opened in 1973 between the banks of the Harlem River and Metro-North tracks in the Bronx. The nearby neighborhood up the hill was undergoing dramatic racial change, from white to a minority majority, and administrators optimistically thought that the new park would have a "stabilizing effect" on the neighborhood and attract kids off the streets.[23]

Laurance Rockefeller tried to compensate for urban park development failures by committing resources to bring city residents by bus to new and old state parks. The Outdoor Recreation Planning Program Bureau of the New York State Council of Parks thus planned special events for city dwellers and arranged subsidized transportation so that even the poor in cities might benefit from the growing state park system.[24] The bus program's development in 1968 coincided with the long hot summers that had led to disturbances in many city neighborhoods. The busing program's growth does not, therefore, appear to be a coincidence. The riots and other manifestations of urban unrest were on the mind of the governor during these years. The bus routes delivered "inner city youths" to Long Island state parks, where they would pass "the day in organized sports or in arts and crafts" rather than fighting each other or the police in city neighborhoods. The program subsequently expanded to urban neighborhoods in Buffalo, Rochester, Syracuse, and the Capital District. In 1973, for instance, 2,475 buses brought 167,000 city people to parks to "enjoy the cool, roomy greenness of a State Park."[25] The busing program operated in 8 of 11 New York park regions in 1974 with those in the Taconic, Palisades, Long Island, and New York City, serving 60.6 percent of participants. Bus visitors were never more than a small fraction of total state park visitors, however.[26]

New York's expansive park program had the intended positive effect on urban access during the 1960s and 1970s, with millions of additional visitors.[27] In 1976, for instance, 62.4 percent of state park users were from urbanized areas downstate, with additional strong representation from the surroundings of Rochester, Buffalo, and Albany. The "largest group of State park visitors, 28.9 percent, came from New York Metropolitan Area's 'inner ring counties.'" The park regions most popular with the public—Long Island, Niagara Frontier, and Palisades—handled "70 percent of park visitations primarily because of proximity to large urban centers." Upstate metropolitan residents dominated upstate campgrounds, including those in the Adirondacks. Users of parks and campgrounds had one thing in common upstate or downstate: they were higher income than average New York State residents—they had the time, automobiles, and money to access the outdoors. Park expansion, like many other state initiatives, primarily benefited the prosperous.[28]

The state park enterprise in New York remains enormous and is heavily promoted by Governor Andrew Cuomo's administration with massive blue and white signs up and down the state's highways. State parks near New York City are frequently packed by immigrant and minority families during the summer months, enjoying elaborate cookouts, swimming, and socializing. About 60 million annual visitors statewide enjoy a system with 5,000 buildings, 28 golf courses, 36 swimming pools, 63 beaches, 27 marinas, 18 nature centers, 8,355 campsites, 104 dams, and 604 bridges. Its $329 million capital/operating budget and 1,736 permanent employees make it a crucial upstate employer. Jones Beach alone attracts twice as many visitors as Yellowstone. New York's extensive parks have fallen into such a state of disrepair, however, that a nonprofit organization (the Alliance for New York State Parks, 2010) is now devoted to raising private money and lobbying for additional public funding.[29]

New York City has quietly benefited from state park initiatives since the 1960s, including carefully designed, extensively programmed, and well-maintained waterfront parks. In New York City, Governor Mario Cuomo took credit for the celebrated Riverbank State Park (1993), constructed on top of the North River sewer treatment plant in Harlem, complete with pools, gyms, fields, and "easily accessible to tens of thousands of low-income residents who live in Upper Manhattan." The park was developed to answer widespread criticism of the siting of the plant in a minority neighborhood.[30] The state also played a leading role in the Hudson River Park Trust (1998) and the many parks and Esplanade (1986–1996) of Battery Park City. Because these parks are required to generate revenue for operations, they have robust programs and amenities that make them quite popular. The high quality achieved reflects the state's potential to improve urban quality of life.

American State Parks

American state park managers accomplished a great deal with very little. By 1948, there were 1,650 state parks nationally, with an impressive 4,703,000 acres. Subtract Adirondack lands, however, and the totals were less impressive, as roughly *half* of all those acres were in that single New York park. These hard-used state parks, a fraction of the total acreage in federal parks and forests, hosted 105 million visitors in 1948. The federal government rapidly added land to state parks in the postwar era, and nearly all states pursued allied expansion programs through purchases or donations. States grew parks "to counterbalance the trend toward greater congestion and increased stresses incidental to modern living conditions." In other words, many viewed park experiences as a bulwark against urbanization.[31]

In California, for instance, state park usage rose rapidly in the late 1950s, responding to the higher mobility and affluence of urban residents. The most significant growth came in day use, illustrating the popularity of "day trips" for city dwellers. The state added 235 new park spaces just between 1956 and 1959.[32] The state developed a widely admired scenic roads program for its car-crazy urbanites that was adopted as a model in other states.[33] California, with the help of voter-approved bonds, significantly expanded beach access with new state parks, including campsites and picnic and day-use areas that helped create the state's democratic image of coastal living. The success of these parks likely drew even more Americans to the state—and created more pressure on the parks.[34]

Wisconsin also dramatically expanded state park quality and capacity in the postwar years due to urban pressures. Chicagoans and many Wisconsin residents decamped in all seasons to the state's countryside for skiing, boating, hiking, swimming, snowmobiling, hunting, fishing, camping, resort living, and second-home retreats. In both 1961 (under Governor Gaylord Nelson) and 1969 (under Governor Warren Knowles) voters approved land purchase programs to be used for a mix of state programs in recreation and conservation; purchases by 1981 had added 460,000 acres to state control. By 1979, the long-term benefits were already obvious: "Wisconsin had sixty-three state parks, nine state forests, and nine state trails, with a combined acreage of 531,000, which together attracted some 12 million visitors." Most of the use was "concentrated in the southeast, near the metropolitan populations of Chicago, Milwaukee, and Madison" despite vast national forests and state parks farther north.[35]

Many states borrowed to build additional parks. Bond programs for park development passed in Louisiana, New Jersey, Minnesota, Michigan, New Hampshire, Nebraska, Tennessee, Indiana, and Massachusetts in the early 1960s, reflecting the widespread and growing demand.[36] The federal government remained an essential partner in state park activities. The federal government's Land and Water Conservation Fund Act of 1964 provided grants to states for their expansion of parks and outdoor recreation. Early winners were New Mexico, New York, Maine, Minnesota, and Virginia.[37] Federal matching funds encouraged significant state and local investments in conservation and recreation, much of it with an urban focus: "Recent projects ranged from providing a series of spray pools in Chicago to development of a public beach in Hawaii . . . to acquisition of land for a playground in Seattle, Washington." Particularly popular with the public were parks adjacent to lakes and shorelines as well as swimming pools. New Jersey joined New York in busing city kids to parks.[38]

The number of state parks, resulting from the combined state and federal activism, increased to 3,600 (including a mix of state parks, recreation areas, historic sites, etc.) by 1980. State parks remained deeply subsidized by state government despite some fees. In 1978, for instance, 60 percent of park operating costs still came from state general revenues. Legislatures were predictably pursuing "financial self-sufficiency for their state park systems," and more than half of the parks were operating entirely from fees they generated, but to drive prices too high would, in some people's opinion, have alienated the broad public that had become accustomed to reasonable costs.[39]

Some park advocates, however, believed higher fees were the missing ingredient in building better park facilities. Marion Clawson, a leading park expert, made a colorful case:

> To me, there is something highly incongruous in seeing a family pull into the camping area of a state park, with auto and camping trailer whose original cost was at least $5000, and to have them pay a camping fee of less than $2 for inadequately improved and inadequately maintained park facilities—all on the excuse that people cannot afford to pay more or will not do so. If we are to see a healthy development of private outdoor recreation facilities, then subsidized competition from public facilities must be reduced.[40]

There is indeed something jarring about the prosperity of most campers and the basic facilities on offer, even today, in most parks. State parks by the 1970s were roughly one-fifth in total size compared to the national park system, but they hosted twice as many visitors.[41] This intensive use resulted from the fact that "state parks are easily accessible to virtually every American." The urban pattern was a crucial dimension of the story: "Parks near population centers are experiencing even greater use as the more remote parks are dropping in popularity."[42] The range of activities in parks had widened to suit the diversity of tastes of city visitors with increasingly sophisticated and expensive tastes. Among the innovations were art parks, dune buggy parks, living history sites, outdoor adventure parks, and rock climbers' parks.[43]

There is no longer the sense of crisis surrounding the size and condition of state parks, even though many are still crowded and rough around the edges. The remarkable growth in urban populations in the West, for instance, has been accommodated in the vast federal park and forest systems (and some state parks) on the edge of sprawling Sunbelt metropolitan areas. Parks in many states have also expanded thanks to the purchases and donations arranged through private land conservancy organizations. Many extensive state park systems, in areas of declining population like the Northeast, are perhaps less crowded today than feared because population growth was slower than expected.[44]

In part this adequacy can also be attributed to changing habits. Americans went wild for camping and hiking in the postwar decades, but since this boom leisure tastes have diversified. The arrival of low-cost jet travel opened a world of destinations here and abroad for the suburban middle class. The number of hotel and motel rooms, and now home or apartment sharing, has skyrocketed, offering much more comfort than is to be found in a pup tent. Backyard and community pools, private subdivision parks, second homes, RV parks, private campgrounds, commercial waterparks, ski destinations, cruise ships, and huge amusement parks are further diversions that involve less mosquito repellent and roughing it. Americans today also spend far more time on electronic diversions than outdoors. State parks remain important to millions of families thanks to the postwar park expansion era, but outdoor recreation is just one of many options in contemporary America.

16

Regional Recreational Planning

The line between recreation facilities, state parks, and regional planning blurred in many American states during the 1960s and 1970s. Preserving the recreational quality of areas many urbanites treasured sometimes required more than just a larger, new, or better-designed state park. In the Adirondacks, the Vermont ski hills, or along the nation's eastern and western shorelines, states explored the boundaries of government control over private landholding by creating new land-use classifications, adding permit requirements in fragile areas, and securing additional public lands.

State leaders and local property rights advocates discovered that courts stood behind enhanced state control of private lands if new laws clearly served the public interest. Statewide public support for control remained robust despite the lack of enthusiasm for regional planning around cities and the frequent rural objections to these plans. These recreational landscapes had such spectacular scenery or ecology that preserving them was often a matter of state pride. Many tourism-related business owners also understood the necessity of protecting "the golden goose" of natural beauty.

Excitement in the 1960s and 1970s built among urban environmental elites for what was prematurely called a "land use revolution." The *Times* in 1973 reported that "nearly all states have moved into land regulation of some sort." The more modest outcome in the long term was that certain states successfully revolutionized land use in areas of tremendous scenic and recreational value. The process by which private land in these states changed into publicly owned or managed assets, by redefining human and natural resources there as irreplaceable or precious, could be more widely imitated elsewhere.[1]

The Adirondacks Rediscovered

The Rockefeller administration's imposition of zoning and growth controls over millions of acres of *private* lands within the Adirondacks Park became known as "one of the first battles in the new front line of the environment—land use."[2] The Adirondacks' enduring land-use rules exemplify the approach of American states in this creative era of conservation. The combined power of distant urbanites, environmentalists, and interested local parties, in the name of high-quality recreation and conservation, overwhelmed local opposition to planning. A powerful local backlash, like prodevelopment forces fighting state environmental controls elsewhere, has also grown in the Adirondacks since the 1970s.[3]

The nineteenth-century environmentalists who created the Adirondack Park pioneered the American notion of landscape preservation by including both natural preserves and human activity within a park boundary. The creation of the park began early when the New York state government in the 1860s started buying up tax-delinquent land in the area. The Commission on State Parks (1873) called for a park to protect the region, but nothing was done for another decade, allowing for more logging that was barely affected by the state's purchase program (as the state had a policy of reselling some of the forests to lumber companies). The New York State Forest Preserve, created in 1885 in response to the "mercenary wastage" by an entirely unregulated forestry industry, aimed to protect the state lands in the Adirondack region (and secondarily in the Catskills) by designating them as "forever wild," thus permanently removing them from the commodity market. The state, in 1892, then drew a "Blue Line" around both these expanding forest preserves and a much larger area of privately owned tracts to create the beginning of what is today's Adirondack Park, then encompassing 2.8 million acres in total.

The integration of existing towns and private lands within a park boundary defined the Adirondacks. The combination of natural and human landscapes in and around a park would become typical in the national parks and forests, but New York State in this early period did not establish any rules for the private lands within the expanding park boundaries. The state continued buying up former timberlands in the twentieth century and expanded the Blue Line (park boundary line) in 1912, 1931, 1956, and 1972 to protect new public forest preserve areas outside the line and to recognize the rebounding forests on former industrial and agricultural lands outside the original line.

The "Great Camps" of the robber barons and rustic resorts within the Blue Line created broad awareness of the region's unique beauty. The state Conservation Department in the twentieth century managed the public for-

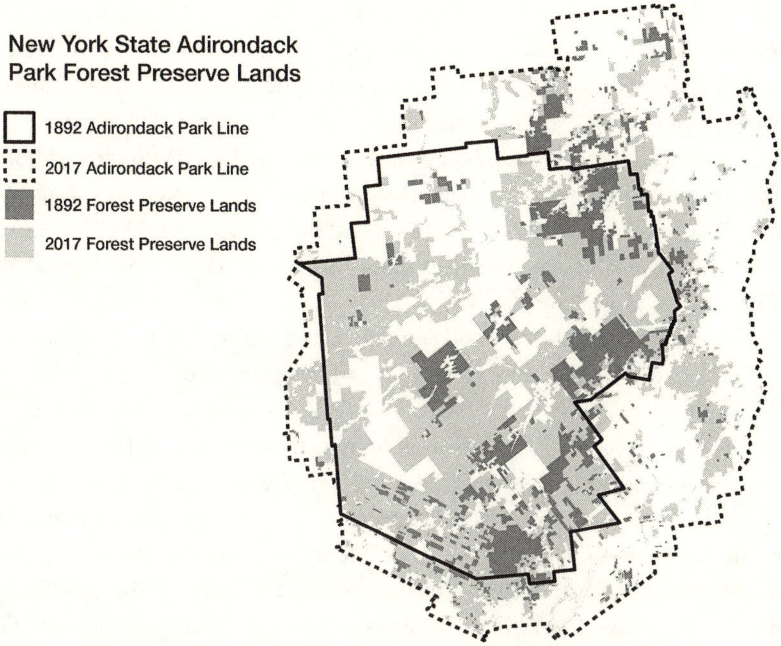

FIGURE 48. The expanding Adirondack Park borders. Map by Minna Ninova, 2018.

est preserves, slowly expanding the recreational opportunities, and sometimes allowing salvage logging—thus testing the notion of the idea of "forever wild" and infuriating conservationists. In the 1960s, roughly 60 percent of the approximately six million acres within the Blue Line remained in private hands. Landowners and the small villages scattered throughout the region did as they pleased, including conducting large-scale lumber and mining operations.

Most environmentalists, therefore, considered the park to be a fiction outside the forest preserves because so many towns lacked any zoning or regulations, and it was only "to the credit of their individual and corporate owners that many of these lands still retain[ed]their pristine quality" in the twentieth century.[4] The cold, the mosquitoes, twisting narrow roads, and the distance from surrounding cities protected the park from mass tourism for the first half of the twentieth century. Except for the growing summer colonies around Lake George and a few other lakes and the small towns that served seasonal visitors and lumber companies, millions of Adirondack private lands remained relatively undeveloped at midcentury.[5]

Adirondacks agriculture declined for much of the twentieth century as the short growing season and limited fertility proved no match for farms further west. Adirondack industries entered an extended period of decline as the iron and timber industries either exhausted their resources or failed to modernize in pace with the national economy. As farming, industry, and timber retreated, open fields or hillsides returned to second- and third-growth forests that to most visitors were indistinguishable from the remaining virgin forests in the state's forest preserves. Many wealthy families retained their vast holdings, primarily undeveloped, even as the popularity of the Great Camps declined in the twentieth century. Workers in the Civilian Conservation Corps during the Great Depression added rustic campsites that increased the accessibility of the natural areas.

The growing middle class and expanded leisure hours of Americans in the postwar era created pressure on such a vast, mountainous, and wooded refuge. Environmentalists may have wanted "no new roads, no new ski centers, no state-owned cabins for public use, no selective cutting," but state government responded to the growing popularity of the Adirondacks in the postwar era by expanding recreational elements such as campgrounds, footpaths, and ski lifts within the forest preserves. These additional elements were made possible by legal decisions and constitutional amendments.[6] By 1966, for instance, visitors spent 1.5 million evenings camping in the forest preserve.[7] The overnight guests and many day trippers damaged alpine plants, dropped litter on high peaks, recklessly hunted and fished, overburdened septic systems, and raced deep into the forest on belching, smoky motorboats, seaplanes, and snowmobiles. Many families enjoyed ice cream cones and cotton candy in tacky amusement parks or commercialized villages like Lake George.[8] In 1960 Rockefeller created the Adirondack Mountain Authority to expand the Gore and Whiteface ski areas with new lifts and runs to make "New York a major skiing center." He also took credit for increasing the number of Adirondack campsites.[9]

The Rockefeller administration set in motion the new Adirondacks land rush in the 1960s not only through new ski slopes but with new highways. The administration's promotion of the Northway (1959), a limited-access federally funded highway on the park's eastern edge, was the catalyst for second-home development. Environmentalists in the 1950s had proposed to the Harriman administration a less destructive and intrusive highway route along Lake Champlain. Both Harriman and his successor, Rockefeller, pursued the cheaper and easier path through the higher lands of the preserve. The highway destroyed just 400 acres of the reserve but introduced interstate noise and pollution along the entire eastern edge of the park.[10] This high-speed expressway, which eventually connected to the New York State Thruway, opened "up the least densely populated counties of the state to the densely populated 'megalopolis,' now only four or five hours away by car."[11]

The administration may have aimed to rationalize summer traffic on the region's "winding, congested, and over-commercialized highways" but the Northway inspired demand as urbanites sped past former bottlenecks and penetrated deep into the heart of the Adirondacks. An expanding middle class now dreamed of possessing a second home on acres of cheap forest land, a luxury formerly the province of the wealthy. Perhaps 50 million urbanites were within driving distance of the park. Environmentalists worried that this affluence and mobility could create "second home cities of ten, twenty or thirty thousand population in wild forested areas." Only 20 of 89 towns within the Adirondacks had comprehensive plans, "and most of these are patterned after urban and suburban models that allow small lots and enormous population potentials." The Rockefeller administration feared that "most Adirondack towns are now wide open to the kind of haphazard, large-scale, high-intensity development that has destroyed so much of our finest landscapes elsewhere (e.g., southern Vermont, Lake Tahoe in California, the Poconos in Pennsylvania, etc.)."[12]

The administration and environmentalists, in this case, did not seem to be exaggerating about the scale of the threat. In the years leading up to the creation of the Adirondack Park Agency, private developers would reveal alternative scenarios of development that helped gain passage of more aggressive land-use regulations. The Horizon Corporation, for instance, in 1972 would buy 23,345 acres of Adirondack Park for home development in the northwestern areas of the park.[13] The Ton-Da-Lay development near Tupper Lake also proposed to add 20,000 people to a town of just 5,000. Ton-Da-Lay's developer planned to include "resorts, shops, restaurants, and an audio-visual museum of the Adirondacks" it was destroying, in addition to thousands of home sites. The developer claimed that only about 3,000 of the parcel's 18,500 acres would be developed, but state officials were alarmed.[14] The vulnerability of the area to large subdivisions and resorts is also reflected in the fact that half of the private land was owned by just 626 companies or individuals (comprising an area of 1,963,000 acres). The opportunities for large-scale resort development were obvious.[15]

Striking the Right Regulatory Notes

The Rockefeller administration had scored mixed success in addressing broader environmental controls in the Adirondacks during the 1960s. Robert Moses had since the 1940s expressed his belief that the Adirondack forest preserves should be more recreation friendly. In 1961, he predictably opposed a bill for the creation of Adirondacks and Catskills wilderness areas because to do so would make them attractive only to "imitation Indians and amateur mountaineers." Moses envisioned expanding recreational opportunities in the Adirondacks, with only one-quarter of the forest preserves forever wild. New recreation "areas close to large urban and suburban communities, suitable for family outings and extended vacations"[16] would boost accessibility and usage. The state commissioner of conservation accused Moses of "moving in a field in which he is unfamiliar" and asserted that his approach reflected a "metropolitan" way of thinking incompatible with forest lands. Moses failed in rezoning the Adirondacks for recreation, but neither did the Rockefeller administration succeed in creating more wilderness areas in 1961.[17] More promising was the success of the Lake George Park Commission (1962), which "assisted in having four communities zoned strictly for residential uses. It has also set up standards for outdoor signs, banning the oversize, garish and spectacular variety."[18]

The creation of the Fire Island National Seashore to stop Moses and Rockefeller's road plan was a sign of the changing mood in the state concerning recreational and natural lands. Road opponents in 1964 succeeded in establishing the Fire Island National Seashore Act in 1964. It provided "a framework intended to allow limited private development along with the preservation of natural resources and public recreational opportunities." The act also gave the secretary of interior unprecedented powers over private property and land regulations.[19] A proposal by Laurance Rockefeller in 1967, however, to transform the Adirondack forest preserves into a National Park overreached.[20] Conservation Commissioner Kilburn rejected the idea as a threat to timber and long-term visitors[21] and the "wealthy owners of secluded summer homes and ski lodges were outraged. . . . Humbler year-round residents of the Adirondacks saw their lives and land falling into the clutches of federal bureaucrats. The scheme was publicly pummeled to death."[22] Even the Adirondack Mountain Club believed that protection under the "Forever Wild" designation was superior to National Park status.[23]

The governor and his brother, to whom Nelson remained loyal throughout, continued to push for regulatory control of the Adirondacks. Rockefeller turned to experts, much as he had in other initiatives, to figure out the way forward on the Adirondacks in 1968 when he created the Temporary Study Commission on the Adirondacks. Rockefeller appointed both environmentalists and substantial businesspeople, including some from the region and others from downstate. Among the members were Harold Hochschild, a devoted Adirondack seasonal resident and the former head of American Metal Company (a world leader in the production of molybdenum for steel production) and Peter Paine Jr. of New York City, an influential lawyer, environmentalist, and a large Adirondacks landowner, whose grandfather Augustus Paine Jr. had operated a paper plant in the Adirondacks. Big money, despite conservationist leanings, added heft to the proceedings.[24]

The Temporary Study Commission set the tone for its report in a few short sentences (in a document that included 40,000 words and 181 recommendations): "The Adirondack Park . . . faces an imminent crisis of unregulated development." To meet the challenge, the commission called for the creation of an "independent, bipartisan Adirondack Park Agency" to devise a comprehensive plan "for all public and private Park land." The Adirondack Park Agency (APA) would not only make the plan but would also be "empowered to regulate the use and development of such land." Despite such unprecedented powers, the commission claimed that "local government would retain their land use control powers" within their existing boundaries, while the agency's plans and enforcement would only address regional and state land development issues (and those local issues crossing into that boundary). Year-round park residents would also be guaranteed three of seven seats on the board controlling the APA. The state would mount an aggressive program of easement purchase of private lands that would be less intrusive than outright purchase or condemnation, and localities would be reimbursed for lands lost to conservation. The commission, while calling for limits on dams, endorsed logging to maintain a "viable forest industry."[25]

The public forest preserves, by then shifted to the DEC, would also have to be reorganized dramatically. A formerly undifferentiated forest preserve was now divided into four main categories: (1) wilderness; (2) primitive; (3) wild forest; and (4) campsites, boat launches, ski areas, and memorial highways. The commission called for a halt to aggressive recreational public land development, recommending instead that "the guiding recreational principle . . . should be that only public outdoor recreation consistent with the wild forest environment should be encouraged." New recreation on public lands would be developed at the fringe of the park, and park managers would rely on private recreation sites, such as campgrounds, for additions.[26]

Public Lands versus Private Lands

Having achieved his goal of securing expert endorsement of conservation and regional zoning, Rockefeller put significant political capital into realizing the report's recommendations. In 1971 the administration introduced the legislation for the creation of a state agency for the Adirondacks to implement the proposals of the Temporary Study Commission. A small group of mostly northern state assemblymen opposed the law, yet the assembly still approved the state agency by a vote of 123 to 24. Such a lopsided victory reflects the power of metropolitan areas, upstate and down, over the small towns and rural areas in New York. The new Adirondack Park Agency, as a compromise, included four full-time Adirondack residents out of seven members. The new agency, per the legislation, was given the power to create a master plan for private and public lands to be delivered by June 1, 1973.[27]

The environmentalists controlled the first phase of APA activities, the preparation of a State Land Master Plan, which was approved in 1972.[28] With Robert Moses out of the picture and a growing environmental consciousness nationwide, the APA encountered little resistance to redefining roughly half of the forest preserves as wilderness areas. Wilderness on this scale required a "rolling back of civilization" on 1 million of the 2.3 million acres of public forest preserves. A rollback would include "the erasure of truck, Jeep and snowmobile trails and the dismantling of such things as fire towers, tent platforms, and telephone lines." The wilderness areas were to become a space where "man himself is a visitor who does not remain." Except for some rustic campsites, the report called for most recreational facilities on private lands. Hiking trails would remain, but many roads would not.[29]

The DEC closed 700 lakes and ponds in 1973 to motorboats and aircraft now included in wilderness areas. The redefinition of lake use challenged recreational fishing and hunting in more remote areas, as, according to its critics, "pilots have to cancel reservations, and will be economically hard-hit in the future, as will the related tourist and sportsmen facilities." The plan, some claimed, also "discriminates against the elderly, disabled or anyone else who cannot hike this rugged terrain."[30] The APA denied aircraft use on an additional 17 lakes and ponds in 1974, thus defying an influential state official from the area, Assemblyman Glenn H. Harris.[31] By 1977 the state DEC, which managed the forest reserves, was still removing human structures from wilderness area, including forest fire towers, boat docks, truck trails, and some lean-tos.[32]

The plans for regulation of private lands proved more controversial despite the commission's attempt to claim that local land decisions would remain in local hands. The APA's rooting of the Land Use and Development Master Plan in scientific and ecological data was intended to provide a broader justification for the powerful regulations. The plan required "the collection and analysis of a vast amount of data" about soils, slopes, elevations, plant life, etc. The ecologists, scientists, and officials studied scenic vistas, historic sites, and rivers within the park boundaries. They considered precedents such as land-use controls in Hawaii, Wisconsin, Vermont, Massachusetts, Lake Tahoe, and the San Francisco Bay area. They consulted with the authors of the seminal federal report *The Quiet Revolution in Land Use Controls.* They also visited southern Vermont "to view firsthand the benefits and liabilities of the large-scale recreational and second home development taking place" there. Wary of calling their work "revolutionary," they made many statements about the need to integrate human and natural activity: "The needs and desires of the Park's permanent, seasonal and transient populations can be satisfactorily met only if the private lands of the parks are devoted to a diversity of land uses and activities." Their plan, they claimed, was only a framework that would require refinement by locals.[33]

The plan had many radical elements despite the protestation. The APA broke all the private land into just six land-use categories, with sharply contrasting levels of development allowed. While existing hamlets and industrial areas had no restrictions beyond those set by local government, all other types (moderate intensity, low intensity, rural use, and resource management) had defined, and low, density levels and uses set by the APA. The APA also proposed to retain the power to review all projects in any location within the park boundaries if they might negatively affect the park. The APA could also review special uses where no local land-use plan existed (which was true of many towns that lacked zoning at this point).

At the same time, there was plenty for private landowners to like. The APA did not specify minimum lot sizes because the planners wanted to discourage a formulaic approach to land development. Such flexible lot size rules also gave developers the chance to cluster homes and needed infrastructure in one part of a large parcel where very low densities were required. The plan was also appropriately deferential to local governments, provided they developed local land-use regulations. Nonconforming uses were grandfathered for nearly everything but junkyards; owners of lots at the time of the plan could still build a single home on their lots, and shoreline restrictions, where values were highest, were loose. The plan, in sum, aimed to "preserve the pattern of settlement characterized by urban centers surrounded by rural areas" rather than upend it entirely. Without environmentally sensitive planning, the APA believed that "the Adirondack Park could, by the end of this century, be subdivided out of existence."[34]

During this planning process, and despite the APA's and Rockefeller administration's attempts, both real and rhetorical, to stress mixing of man and nature, the local opposition within the park boundaries grew. It was clear to local officials that the proposal constituted a "radical" plan, as it imposed a "park wide zoning code administered by the Park Agency."[35] A Republican state legislator from Plattsburg reported that "local governments and residents are very concerned about the far-reaching consequences of this

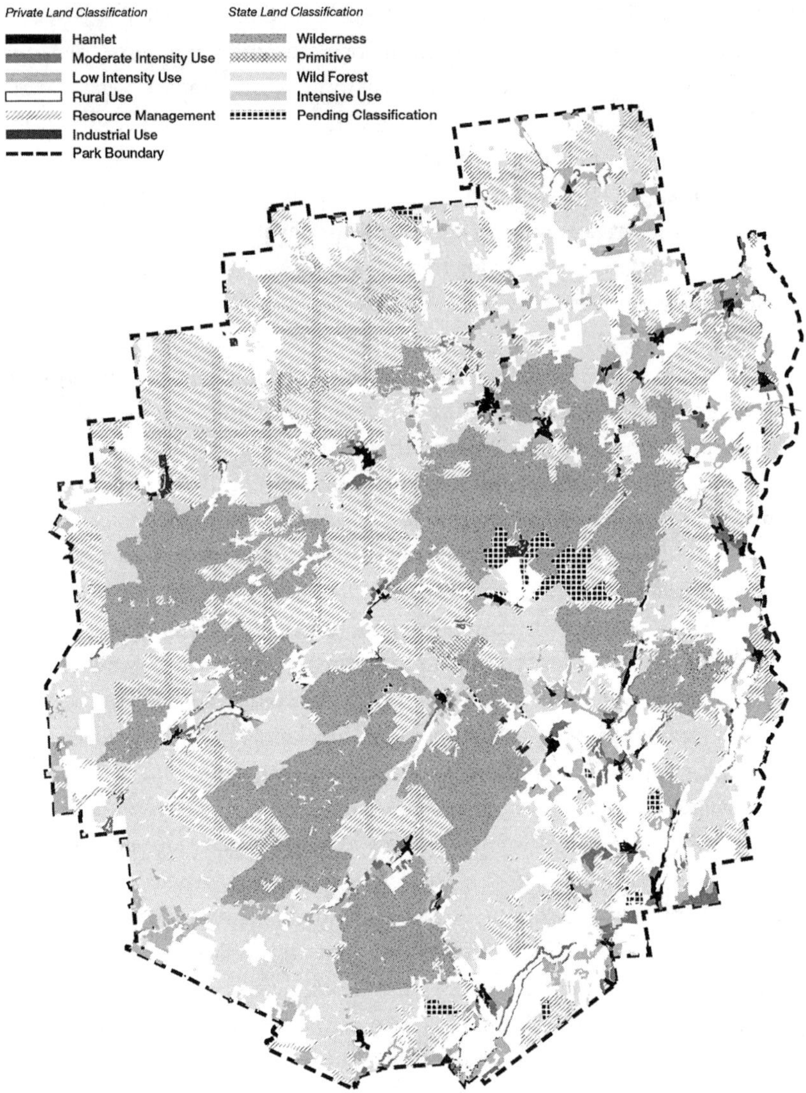

FIGURE 49. The Rockefeller administration zoned a vast region in the name of recreation and conservation. Map by Minna Ninova, 2018.

agency."[36] Some Adirondack politicians felt "the creation of the Adirondack Park Agency at the request of Governor Rockefeller has usurped the powers of local government as well as the right of a private landowner to use his property as he sees fit." A town supervisor in Newcomb was indignant over outside interference because "we feel we're as well qualified to decide what to do with our property as the professionals."[37] Quite a few opponents attempted to label the plan as elitist because "the density of development would allow only the rich, who could afford large landholdings, to enjoy the area."[38]

Public review and comment began in late 1972, and the APA officials sat through hours of public hearings, including testimony by 436 private individuals and 200 local government officials. The APA members claimed that they made approximately 500 changes to the draft plan because of these comments. Opponents, however, argued that the density rules would stifle development, erode the tax base, reduce property values, supersede existing local zoning, and encourage growth in the wrong places and that it was full of loopholes that would favor the rich who alone could afford substantial properties.[39] Environmentalists were also dissatisfied. Citizens to Save the Adirondack Park, for instance, thought that there were too many loopholes that would allow for massive development. Many environmentalists felt that the plan did too little to preserve shorelines.[40]

The Rockefeller administration in 1973, despite the local opposition and after many changes, sent the master plan to the legislature. The state supreme court struck down a legal challenge by 61 of 89 Adirondack towns. The governor also vetoed a legislative attempt by opponents to delay the plan.[41] The final plan for legislative consideration, after more negotiation, allowed for a maximum population of 2 million people in the park as opposed to the 1.2 million population target in the original plan. As there were only about 100,000 full-time residents of the park at the time, the program can hardly be called antigrowth. Most of this growth would take place within existing developed areas rather than on the vast undeveloped or wilderness parcels. The plan, to accommodate this density, allowed for "dramatic increase in density of development allowed along shorelines" and provided no "performance standards" or "use zoning."[42] Hamlets that already had zoning ordinances by July 1, 1971, controlled growth within their corporate limits. Large projects within these towns were, however, subject to APA review if they even threatened to alter the park's environment. Time was provided for some communities to create their zoning rules; those that lacked them would be directly controlled by the APA until they had rules in place.[43]

The giveaways on development in towns and shorelines compensated for the radical controls across the other private lands. The original proposal called for 53 percent of the land to allow just one building per 64 acres. In the final version, a compromise, the ratio rose only to one building per 42 acres. Another 32 percent of land allowed only one building per 8.5 acres. In sum, 85 percent of Adirondacks land required lot sizes that were greater than large-scale development plans under consideration at the time. The private-land-use plan reflected many compromises yet remained unacceptable to many local leaders and residents; nor was the plan entirely to the liking of many environmentalists, who ultimately supported it.[44] The state assembly approved the bill 117–12 and the senate by 53–12 on May 15, 1973. Urban recreation and environmental interests had won.[45]

The urban dimension of the changes was high on Rockefeller's list of justifications for continuing to support the bill despite so much blowback: "The Adirondacks are now within an easy day's drive for millions of metropolitan area residents who need relief and change from their crowded, noisy, high-pressure environments. The public lands of the Adirondacks will increasingly serve this urgent need."[46] Rockefeller also looked beyond New York with one eye on national politics. He claimed that land-use planning was "a Number One environmental priority facing our nation and, with the signing of the bill, the Adirondack Park becomes the largest area in the country to come under comprehensive land-use control."[47] The size of the Adirondacks, larger than either Vermont or Hawaii, made his point valid despite the hyperbole. He pointed out that "we have established regional planning for the Adirondacks before, rather than after, serious damage is done."[48]

Backlash and State Supremacy

The APA's new powers, beginning in 1970, met challenges similar to those experienced in other states. The local opposition managed to keep the agency staff small in comparison to its many and complex responsibilities. Adirondack residents upset by the new rules sometimes staged protests and sported bumper stickers that read "Abolish the APA." Nevertheless, environmentalists began making major decisions about the future of the park. Henry Diamond set a hard line by rejecting the Ton-Da-Lay project in August 1973. The plan had projected 300 homes per square mile, while the APA only allowed 17 per square mile. Even though the town of Altamont had approved the project under its zoning, environmentalists believed that the local government was too weak to resist big developers.[49] Diamond justified the rejection with a telling New York metaphor: "The concept of 20,000 residents—a community the size of Stuyvesant Town—set upon this fragile landscape shocks the environmental conscience."[50]

The Horizon developer sued New York for making its plan for 6,955 houses impossible; APA land-use controls allowed only 1,608 homes on the 24,000 acres. The developer claimed to be surprised by "such severely limiting controls" when it had paid $100 an acre, but the courts rejected the suit and affirmed the right of the state to regulate the region's environmental quality, including private land controls.[51] The APA also rejected a massive development near Lake Placid in 1977 of 1,300 acres for 340 homes because the APA plan allowed only about 30 under the new zoning.[52]

The APA's aggressive actions encouraged local towns to determine their own zoning plans. In fact, 50 out of 92 Adirondack local governments developed local zoning. Many of these towns simply adopted a model code provided by the APA. Those towns that refused to create zoning left land regulation of all types by default to the APA (charged with handling zoning in the absence of local zoning). The APA, unfortunately, was often slow to process paperwork, as it had just 30 overworked staff members. Delays could have been avoided had towns been more cooperative and had the state fully funded the APA.[53]

Locals and business interests since the 1970s have sued the state multiple times to push back these rules, but their lawyers have failed to convince the courts that the state and the APA did not have the right to regulate the park's private lands. They have discovered what Rockefeller and his team, and other governors already knew: the state originates and reserves powers over local government. The APA has "been very successful in these lawsuits, and courts have upheld Agency Determinations that have gone beyond the literal wording of the APLUDP [Adirondack Park Land Use and Development Plan] . . . when the exercise of the Agency's power was necessary to achieve the purposes of the Act." The bar remains high for changes to the forest preserve. By 2009, the APA Act had been amended just nine times through required state constitutional processes, primarily to accommodate new recreational facilities such as expanded ski runs in the forest preserve that urbanites desired.[54] This stability illustrates, to APA defenders, that "despite the often-vocal criticism of the APA, the APA Act has seen few amendments and produced surprisingly few public court cases. The act's stability and the agency's success in court . . . demonstrate the act's successful balancing of use, development, and preservation." It also illustrates the power of American states, should they use it, to create policies that overrule local government.[55]

Year-round residents, and their representatives, frustrated in the courts, have used their influence to weaken the APA's administrative powers. The appointment of Bob Flacke as chairman of the APA, despite his stated opposition to Rockefeller's plans, by Governor Carey weakened enforcement of the rules and cleared the way for major development projects, including the Lake Placid Hilton, a prison, and power lines. He and other local representatives welcomed an increase in subdivision activity in the 1980s (between 1967 and 1987, builders added 19,000 houses within the park boundaries). He and his allies also openly resisted the work of Mario Cuomo's Twenty-First Century Commission, which recommended enhanced land regulations, more public land purchases, and a moratorium on shoreline development for one year. The negative reaction likely contributed to the statewide defeat of both a $1.3 billion environmental bond and Governor Cuomo in a close reelection campaign. Local governments ultimately won the right to veto the use of state money for land acquisitions within their boundaries. Towns and villages have organized their lobbying groups, including the Adirondack Association of Towns and Villages (1992). Towns over the decades have demanded the APA be more development friendly, that the state provide more funds to localities to make up for growing tax-exempt nature reserves, and that the APA continue to permit motorized sports vehicles like snowmobiles and ATVs. They have reasonably sought more money for sewers and other expensive infrastructure to minimize the impact of growth. The rapid rise in housing costs within the parks is another sore point for residents. Many believe that the land regulations favor the wealthy, who are more easily able to build freely on large lots. Market appreciation driven by urban profits has worsened the situation.[56]

Local unhappiness is more than matched by environmentalists disappointed by the progrowth, hands-off compromises built into the APA structure. "You have an agency serving about 15 million people who live for the most part in sterile urban—or even more sterile suburban—sprawl, who want the park preserved, and you have about 150,000 permanent residents—let's say they're 100 percent opposed—who want that wonderful life, that 'development' and 'growth' that transforms natural areas into sterile ones."[57] Environmentalists believe that the areas outside the state-controlled districts are often environmentally compromised and undermine the quality of the park. The act is silent, for instance, on "remediation" on private lands, including "removal of utility lines from roadsides; clean-up of abandoned and derelict buildings; screening of junkyards, gravel pits, electric substations, state and local highway departments . . . and all manner of unsightly uses."[58]

Shoreline development has emerged as a flashpoint: "In some popular areas, where the shoreline has been developed about as far as the plan permits, the houses are moving up the slopes. Mountainsides that for generations have presented forested slopes of unbroken green to canoeists, hikers, and motorists are now becoming pockmarked with opulent palaces of ostentation." Warren County, within the orbit of Saratoga and Albany, is developing a cabin version of suburban sprawl, "where moderately priced homes in previously undeveloped wood lots are becoming de facto subdivisions." Development is causing water quality issues as septic systems leak into many ponds.[59] Environmentalists remain opposed to motorized sports in the park and are concerned that not enough effort has been given to prevent acidification of lakes, among many issues.[60]

The APA, despite these many challenges, set in motion the creation of a continuously forested area second only in the United States, outside Alaska, to that in northern Maine. By 1994, for instance, public lands had reached 2.7 million acres due to "the most aggressive program for public acquisition of scenic and sensitive lands in a hundred years" by the Mario Cuomo administration. Additional easements and purchases have raised the public land totals higher. The strict restrictions on land development also made it easier to negotiate conservation easements and donations of land from private owners. One public/private effort in 2004, for instance, preserved 250,000 acres held by International Paper.[61]

The regulations put in place during the Rockefeller era remain in place today, leaving hundreds of thousands of acres in a natural state that otherwise might have become home sites and larger subdivisions. The power of the state in the Adirondacks is illustrated in a recent advertiser newspaper, *Homes and Lands of the Adirondacks.* Many lakefront properties are expensive, costing a million dollars or more, despite limited acreage, but quite a few properties with vast holdings are comparatively cheap. A property at Long Lake of 4,383 acres, including 3,220 managed timber acres, can be purchased for just $4.38 million. This low price, and others like it, reflect the partial decommodification of recreational lands in the Adirondacks.

American States and Regional Recreational Planning

New York's efforts to protect the Adirondacks paralleled those in states with recreation-rich hinterlands. The generally positive outcome of these initiatives contrasts with the lackluster results from regional planning described in chapter 5. A blend of state pride, self-interest on the part of vacationers, environmental activism, and key business support sustained these different initiatives.

Hawaii, experiencing tremendous development pressure from tourism and urban development, was an early leader in this field. The war years and better air service created "a population explosion and resulting demand for housing. . . . Real estate was in demand. . . . Sprawling semiurban communities mushroomed. Ferro-concrete buildings—we call them high rises here—started to impinge on our vistas of Diamond Head." A remarkable 92,000 lots had been platted for development by 1964.[62] In response to loss of agricultural land and scenic beauty, Hawaii's state planning department worked with the transportation department to develop the *General State Plan for Hawaii, 1960–1980* (1961). The plan examined "physical conditions, existing land use, a plan for land use and subdivision, population distribution," etc. and made recommendations to the legislature.[63]

Hawaii's state government classified all land on the islands for urban, rural, agricultural, or conservation uses. To build anything within 1,000 yards of the ocean required a permit from a regional commission. State officials faced significant resistance from landowners to reclassification of their lands and "'everything hit the fan' soon after the passage of the law." Developers went on the attack, and opponents tried to gut the law in 1965 by giving county commissioners more power. The response of state leaders was to add exceptions and an appeal process for those landowners who could make a strong case that the classification was unfair. The law survived these challenges, and its success has been essential to preserving agriculture and the state's tourist gems.[64]

One of the most dramatic assertions of state government over scenic lands took place along Oregon's stunning coastline. In 1913, Progressive Era state leadership had established public access to 320 miles of beaches by declaring the coastline, the "wet sand" areas, a public highway. State leaders in 1947 recognized the scenic character of the holding when it declared the highway a "recreation area." As the decades passed and beach vacation homes and hotels proliferated thanks to new state highways and postwar affluence, property owners along the beachfronts started building ever closer to the ocean. The state had purchased some coastal lands as parks, but "by 1967, 112 miles of dry sands on the coast had been taken over by private owners." Some went so far as to fence off beaches, including wet sands, as private.[65]

The state highway department in 1967, with Governor Tom McCall's support, proposed "state ownership of all the beach, from the wet sands to the vegetation line above the dry sands," the so-called Beach Bill. Coast property owners fought back. Governor McCall stood against the "encroachment of crass commercialism" and aroused public sentiment through his connection to media. He helicoptered onto beaches, with surveyors in tow, to demonstrate the value of extending state control of beaches high up onto dry land. In the final Beach Bill, a compromise measure designed to placate property owners who feared losing their properties to eminent domain, lawmakers gave "the state the power to zone any beach it did not own, and to outlaw any development or construction not allowed by the state Highway Commission." Most observers consider this extension of state power essential to preserving the coast's great beauty.[66]

Vermont, emerging as a favorite urban getaway for skiing and second homes, was losing rustic charm due to unregulated tourism. The multiplication of private ski resorts in Vermont during the postwar years was limited, it seemed, only by the ability to string up lifts and cut down trees to build ski runs on formerly wooded mountainsides. Many of these ski resorts failed, lacking the steady weather or amenities to compete, but not before taking their toll on the environment. Others, like the popular Killington resort, were growing so fast that they came to include miles of runs through multiple mountain passes. Unlike the old ski resorts built near railroad stops, the new resorts and second homes were accessible primarily by cars streaming into the emerging interstate system. The speed of that highway system made the slopes closer than they had ever been to the eastern megalopolis.

Vermont's Environmental Control Act (1970), known today as Act 250, was the result of recommendations by Republican governor Deanne Davis's Commission on Environmental Control. The act divided the state into regional districts with the power to review all but the smallest developments, farming, and forestry. The 10 categories of projects requiring review include those above 2,500 feet (most ski development projects), construction of 10 or more units within five miles of each other, new subdivisions of 10 or more units, new roads, expansion of older facilities, and any project involving more than 10 acres. The state thus made a point of regulating large-scale ski resorts and the lucrative second-home business that supported them. New projects were to be assessed based on impact on air and water quality, scenic landscapes, soil erosion, traffic, and existing plans. Act 250 took effect and remains in effect today. The combination of the act's provisions, with the state's influential antibillboard law (1968), helped preserve the state's natural beauty although it did not entirely tame second-home developments. A statewide land development plan prepared as part of Act 250, with echoes of the private land maps created for the Adirondacks and Hawaii, would have divided all the state's land into urban, village, and natural resource classifications. The plan failed to gain support from the state legislature during the 1970s, however, reflecting typical difficulties extending planning beyond critical recreational areas.[67]

Legislators in California during the 1960s made many essential innovations in land use, including approval of the widely admired Tahoe Regional Planning Agency, but they initially resisted protecting the accessible coastal areas. A massive tide of recreationally oriented development catering to affluent urbanites threatened to flood a unique landscape with motels, shopping strips, and second homes. Voters approved a ballot initiative to create the Coastal Zone Conservation Act (1972), racing past a state legislature that had dragged its feet for years despite tremendous public pressure. Environmental historian Adam Rome offers his view of the change in popular mood that led to this landmark law: "The Santa Barbara oil spill, the construction of second-home subdivisions and high-rise apartments on bluffs overlooking the water, the increasing number of proposals for power plants . . . all contributed to popular support for state action." The initiative, which empowered the creation of a California Coastal Plan, was endorsed by the state legislature in 1976 in the Coastal Act. The law resulted in "regional and state commissions with extraordinary power to oversee development along the coast."[68]

The legislation included the Coastal Commission, the State Coastal Conservancy, and the San Francisco Bay Conservation and Development Commission.[69] The Coastal Commission gained the right to regulate development, and to override local land use and zoning, within designated areas adjoining the coast. The agency was not shy about using its powers, and its actions have often been as individually controversial as those taken by the APA. Nearly all local governments within the coastal regulation zone have developed plans that meet the commission's standards. Collectively, the coastal regulatory efforts "have protected and restored thousands of acres of sensitive coastal resources and maintained and opened up access to and along hundreds of miles of shoreline through planning and regulation of development, land acquisition and conservation, and funding of restoration and public access projects." The California Coastal Conservancy, for instance, has spent about $1.5 billion of state general revenues on programs to acquire and protect coastlands for public use.[70]

Coastal protection proved popular nationally. The federal government encouraged broader adoption of state plans through the Coastal Zone Management Act (1972). California's various rules and agencies were approved for the federal program in 1978 as part of the California Coastal Management Program. By 1980, 15 states had created federally approved coastal management zones. A national land-use law may have failed in 1975, but the "Clean Air Act, the Clean Waters Act, and the Endangered Species Act all gave federal agencies new power to regulate land use," in partnership with states, often in areas of high scenic or recreation beauty.[71] These laws have not prevented all additional coastal and mountain development deplored by environmentalists, and states pursue enforcement at various levels, but they have created a regulatory framework to force a debate and sometimes stop or limit the worst attacks on natural recreational resources.

Americans can today travel with confidence to many protected state areas in the United States and enjoy a quality, protected natural environment for either recreation or contemplation. The negative trend line in states was changed by a combination of local, state, and federal actions. The difference between those areas designated for preservation and those without this protection is often stark. Urban areas were the source of both the problem (overdevelopment) and of the solution (land preservation and regulation). Limited development in fragile areas has revealed new benefits in a time of climate change. Less developed coastlines and river valleys are better suited to rising tides and stronger rain storms than densely developed coasts in areas like New Jersey and Florida. As a result, the stories of state regulation for recreation can be a source of inspiration for today's leaders searching for long-term solutions for vulnerable areas. If landscapes, including valuable private lands, can be regulated for their recreational value to urban people, there is hope for additional conservation plans in areas of scenic beauty.

Postscript

State government remains both indispensable and invisible to most Americans. Even as families barrel down state highways, enroll their sons and daughters at state universities, recover in state-sponsored teaching hospitals, cheer at state-financed stadiums, ride a state-run metro rail line, or gaze serenely upon a preserved state park landscape, they rarely connect the dots between these vital places and the state policies underwriting them.

A booming, urbanized Sunbelt region such as North Carolina's Raleigh-Durham is attractive not only for moderate-cost suburban homes but because of the benefits that come from substantial, long-term state programs. The sprawling metropolis has gone "from Tobacco Road to global prominence" in just a few decades. State government has been a force behind the high-technology Research Triangle Park, the commodious and extensive state highways, the relatively clean environment, two powerful public research universities (University of North Carolina and North Carolina State University), the state-sponsored PNC basketball arena, the recession-proof state capital district in Raleigh, and the many accessible state parks in the metropolitan area and the nearby mountains and along the Outer Banks.[1]

State government has been an essential urban catalyst not only in North Carolina but in other Sunbelt states like Georgia, Texas, Arizona, and Florida. State leaders in those states, of both parties, have developed a potent blend of business-friendly regulation, progrowth land policies, federal subsidies, and sustained state government investments in universities, state parks, highways, basic mass transit, economic development, and urban redevelopment. Sunbelt cities thrive, like their counterparts in the North and West, in no small measure due to activist state government. Sustained state policy in urban affairs has delivered measurable benefits.[2]

In the coming years, if party conflict and antigovernment ideology continue to dominate in Washington, urban Americans will depend even more deeply on state government for improvements in their living standards. Cautious optimism about what states can accomplish, based upon on the programs described in these pages, is warranted. The number and political diversity of states have already enabled creative and controversial extensions of state power. Governors and state legislatures, mostly in response to urban pressures or needs, have pioneered same-sex marriage, greenhouse gas controls, marijuana legalization, supportive housing, free higher education, socialized health care, gun control, high-speed rail, charter schools, driverless cars, and more. These state initiatives have already had an impact both on urbanized areas and national debates about the proper role of government in managing and enhancing the American standard of living.[3]

Some states are stepping up in part because American cities are changing faster than the speed of national politics and debates. Politicians in Washington, compared to their colleagues in Beijing or Brussels, spend remarkably little money on national programs with metropolitan areas directly in mind. Urban areas benefit disproportionately from only a few federal policies, such as Medicaid and urban mass transit, and many of these are under threat. While Washington fiddles, the megaregions of the United States that produce most of the nation's gross domestic product are being whipsawed by global trends in transportation, housing, technology, culture, morals, and migration.

Business and civic leaders need new rules, guidance, and support in the short term for initiatives that transcend city and county lines. Most city governments lack the funds or powers for transformative changes; and most suburbs refuse to participate or contribute to voluntary metropolitan programs. State governments, by contrast, still have the power to develop and implement expensive regional urban policies. State programs can move from concept to reality quickly; results can be studied and programs adjusted. A single state can take a bigger risk because the impact of program failure is limited by state lines. Successful programs can be widely imitated by other states if their value is demonstrated.

The differences among the states will likely widen in the years to come. Not all states will be able or willing to pay for the infrastructure and programs that support competitive globalized cities. Some state experiments will fail and others will flourish. Even more pronounced dissimilarity will likely be the result of contemporary federalism. States like New York and California still appear determined to imitate European-style social democratic welfare states, while others, with equal passion, pursue lightly regulating laissez-faire policies. At some point this unevenness among states will build pressure for national consistency, leading to interstate compacts and new federal programs to level the playing field. Until that day arrives, however, American states will remain competitive, distinct, and unequal laboratories of urban affairs.

Acknowledgments

Writing Nelson Rockefeller more deeply into urban and planning history was an unexpected byproduct of relocating to the picturesque village of Tarrytown, New York. The Rockefeller family built a massive estate there over a century ago, and their philanthropy has been an essential element of life in the surrounding towns and New York City ever since.

Tucked away behind gates on the estate is the Rockefeller Archive Center where, aided by friendly and efficient archivists, I came to realize that Nelson Rockefeller was more than just a serial philanderer, a big-spending governor, a failed presidential candidate, and the man responsible for the punitive Rockefeller Drug Laws. As I dug in the archives, it became clear that Rockefeller was one of the most underestimated figures in the history of modern New York's redevelopment. His efforts were also exemplary of a new role for states in American civic life.

The Rockefeller landscape surrounding the town helped in the creation of this manuscript in both practical and spiritual ways. I turned over many ideas during hikes on the pastoral Rockefeller preserve, the legacy of the family estate now mostly a state park. The library at Westchester County's SUNY Purchase, one of Nelson Rockefeller's most ambitious campus plans, boasts an excellent collection in urban history and state policy. Two hours north in Albany, dramatically bookending one end of the grandiose Nelson A. Rockefeller Empire State Plaza, the New York State Library and Archive provided many critical documents of the era.

Daily journeys to Manhattan on the Metro-North commuter railroad, the legacy of the New York Central lines saved and much improved by Governor Rockefeller's MTA, drove home the legacy further. As the trains head south to the city, the stunning view to the right is of the Palisades State Park, a visionary interstate conservation project made possible in no small measure by the Rockefeller clan. A visual history of the governor's housing program unfolds out the train window from Yonkers to Manhattan, including apartment towers thrown up under the Mitchell-Lama, Urban Development Corporation, and state public housing programs. The train even briefly runs alongside Roberto Clemente State Park in the Bronx, the remnant of Laurance Rockefeller's idealistic and mostly unrealized plan to create a new generation of city parks during the urban crisis.

The subways that run from Grand Central to the New York Institute of Technology (NYIT) campus at Columbus Circle are still fairly dependable because of the MTA Rockefeller and William Ronan created in the 1960s. Near my office and classrooms are other Rockefeller family projects, including Rockefeller Center, the Museum of Modern Art, and Lincoln Center. The physical presence of these places helped keep the project vital.

My colleagues at NYIT, which in the 1970s was a recipient of a donation by Laurance Rockefeller for the NYIT College of Osteopathic Medicine, tolerated my research and defense of the liberal arts. NYIT administration provided tremendous support through two internal grants that aided the photographic and map program designed by expert designer Minna Ninova.

My thanks go to my colleagues Ellen Katz, Susanna Case, Richard Greenwald, Jonathan Soffer, Richard Pizer, Matthias Altwicker, Nader Vossoughian, Farzhana Ghandi, Adam Tanaka, Daniel Quigley, Reginald Jasmin, and Irene Wynn. I am also indebted to Jameson Doig, Mark Rose, Carol Lamberg, and Jon Teaford, who all provided early critiques of the draft manuscript. The anonymous reviewers offered crucial guidance. Thanks as well to the many scholars and reporters who have documented the different dimensions of state government during the past century. Discussions with thousands of students in my classes since 2000 have provided opportunities to take the pulse of contemporary American urban life. Leanne and Roxie Bloom will hopefully believe the final product justifies living with an anxious writer.

Timothy Mennel, executive editor at the University of Chicago Press, strongly encouraged me to think about the book project in the broadest national terms. He was right to push for a book that places Nelson Rockefeller within the story of emerging patterns of state urban policy. Even Tim owes something to the Rockefellers, of course. John D. Rockefeller Sr. transformed the University of Chicago into one of the premier educational institutions in the nation, a distinction it retains to this day.

Notes

Chapter One

1. The literature on the suburbs is now large, including, but not limited to, Lila Corwin Berman, *Metropolitan Jews: Politics, Race, and Religion in Postwar Detroit* (Chicago: University of Chicago Press, 2015); Lizabeth Cohen, *A Consumer's Republic: The Politics of Mass Consumption in Postwar America* (New York: Vintage, 2002); David Freund, *Colored Property: State Politics and White Racial Politics in Suburban America* (Chicago: University of Chicago Press, 2007); Jeffrey Hardwick, *Mall Maker: Victor Gruen* (Philadelphia: University of Pennsylvania Press, 2004); Barbara Kelly, *Expanding the American Dream: Building and Rebuilding Levittown* (Albany: SUNY Press, 1993); Kenneth T. Jackson, *Crabgrass Frontier: The Suburbanization of the United States* (New York: Oxford University Press, 1985); Kevin Kruse, *White Flight: Atlanta and the Making of Modern Conservatism* (Princeton, NJ: Princeton University Press, 2007); Kevin M. Kruse and Thomas J. Sugrue, eds., *The New Suburban History* (Chicago: University of Chicago Press, 2006); Mathew Lassiter, *The Suburban Majority: Suburban Politics in the Sunbelt South* (Princeton, NJ: Princeton University Press, 2006); Richard W. Longstreth, *City Center to Regional Mall: Architecture, the Automobile, and Retailing in Los Angeles, 1920–1950* (Cambridge, MA: MIT Press, 1997); Lisa McGirr, *Suburban Warriors: The Origins of the New American Right* (Princeton, NJ: Princeton University Press, 2001); Becky Nicolaides, *My Blue Heaven: Life and Politics in the Working Class Suburbs of Los Angeles, 1920–1965* (Chicago: University of Chicago Press, 2002); John Stilgoe, *Borderland: Origins of the American Suburb, 1820–1939* (New Haven, CT: Yale University Press, 1990); Thomas Sugrue, *The Origins of the Urban Crisis: Race and Inequality in Postwar Detroit* (Princeton, NJ: Princeton University Press, 1996); Andrew Wiese, *Places of Their Own: African American Suburbanization in the Twentieth Century* (Chicago: University of Chicago Press, 2004). My research on planned suburbs informs this analysis as well, including the summaries of the suburban critique. See Nicholas Dagen Bloom, *Suburban Alchemy: 1960s New Towns and the Transformation of the American Dream* (Columbus: Ohio State University Press, 2001), and Bloom, *Merchant of Illusion: James Rouse, America's Salesman of the Businessman's Utopia* (Columbus: Ohio State University Press, 2003).

2. John C. Bollens and Henry Schmandt, *The Metropolis: Its People, Politics and Economic Life* (New York: Harper and Row, 1975), 12–13. "Urban" was defined as a city or incorporated area with a minimum population of 2,500, a dated standard, but one that influenced policy discussions of the time. Today, for instance, the Census Bureau defines urban areas, for pur-

poses of funding, as places with population greater than 50,000. It is challenging to use terminology consistently for a book stretching over so many time periods, regions, and settings. I use the term "urban" in this book in the sense of all nonagricultural communities and often vary its use with "metropolitan" to indicate policies affecting both urban and suburban areas. I use "city" or "center city" for activities within traditional municipal boundaries. "Central business district" and "downtown" are used to describe civic, business, and cultural centers of cities.

3. John Kenneth Galbraith, *The Affluent Society* (New York: Houghton Mifflin, 1998), 187.

4. William Whyte, *The Organization Man* (New York: Doubleday, 1956); John Keats, *The Crack in the Picture Window* (Boston: Houghton Mifflin, 1956); ; Jane Jacobs, *The Death and Life of Great American Cities* (New York: Vintage, 1961); Martin Stavars, *Megalopolis* (Cambridge, MA: MIT Press, 1961); Peter Blake, *God's Own Junkyard: The Planned Deterioration of America's Landscape* (New York: Holt, Rinehart and Winston, 1964).

5. David Brandon, Office of Planning Coordination, "Planning for Development in New York State," January 1970, Nelson A. Rockefeller Gubernatorial Records (NAR GUB), Hugh Morrow, Series 21 (FA242), Box 14, Folder 153, 5.

6. Neal Peirce, *The Megastates of America: People, Politics, and Power in the Ten Great States* (New York: Norton, 1972), 98–99.

7. Robert Connery and Gerald Benjamin, *Rockefeller of New York: Executive Power in the Statehouse* (Ithaca, NY: Cornell University Press, 1979), 244.

8. Peirce, *The Megastates of America*, 419.

9. "News Conference by the Governor Concerning Legislation to Meet the Problems of the Core Areas of the Cities," Red Room, State Capitol, Albany, 27 February 1968, NAR GUB, *Public Papers of Nelson Rockefeller, 1968* (Albany: State of New York, n.d.), 949.

10. Address reprinted in *Proceedings of the Local Government Workshop, June 12–13, 1961*, NAR GUB, William J. Ronan, Series 29 (FA371), Box 23, Folder 272.

11. "State-Urban Relations," National Governors Conference Report, *State Government: The Journal of State Affairs* (published by the Council of State Governments)51, no. 1 (Winter 1968): 32.

12. Mel Scott, *American City Planning* (Berkeley: University of California Press, 1971), 587–588. See also Steven Conn, *Americans against the City: Anti-Urbanism in the Twentieth Century* (Oxford: Oxford, 2014), 13.

13. Council of State Governments, *Book of the States, 1972–1973* (Chicago: Council of State Governments, 1972), 19:445; Eleanor Brilliant, *The Urban Development Corporation: Private Interests and Public Authority* (Lexington, MA: Lexington Books, 1975) also provides a nice summary of these issues, 35–37.

14. Peirce, *The Megastates of America*, 53.

15. Jon C. Teaford, *The Rise of the States: Evolution of American State Government* (Baltimore: Johns Hopkins University Press, 2002), 159.

16. See Gerald E. Frug and David J. Barron, *City Bound: How States Stifle Urban Innovation* (Ithaca, NY: Cornell University Press, 2008) for the widespread view that state government is an impediment to a higher urban quality of life. While it is true that states could do more for cities, it is equally true that the actions they have taken since World War II are unprecedented and transformative. Frug and Barron also acknowledge, even if they dislike the fact, that states retain the fundamental power to control the destiny of cities.

17. John R. Logan and Harvey L. Molotch, *Urban Fortunes: The Political Economy of Place* (Berkeley: University of California Press, 1987).

18. "A Summary of the Proposals Made by Rockefeller," *New York Times*, 13 February 1969, 30.

19. Council of State Governments, *Book of the States, 1960–1961* (Chicago: Council of State Governments, 1960), 13:271–272.

20. Council of State Governments, *Book of the States, 1980–1981* (Chicago: Council of State Governments, 1980), 8:623–632.

21. Dan Pilcher, "State Aid to Cities: Hard Times Ahead," *State Legislatures* 6, no. 6 (June 1980): 4–13. For a detailed discussion of variation in local funding, see Frug and Barron, *City Bound*, 53–121.

22. See, for instance, Steven Fraser and Gary Gerstle, eds., *The Rise and Fall of the New Deal Order, 1930–1980* (Princeton, NJ: Princeton University Press, 1989).

23. "A Summary of the Proposals Made by Rockefeller." See also Peirce, *The Megastates of America*, 38.

24. "Revitalizing Our Cities," 25 July, no year, NAR GUB, Rockefeller Family, RG4, Series S-6, Box B3, Folder 17, 1–3.

25. Dan Pilcher, "General Revenue Sharing," *State Legislatures*, 6, no. 1 (January 1980): 6–15. On the rise of the Sunbelt and the role of federal spending, see Roger W. Lotchin, *Fortress California, 1910–1961: From Warfare to Welfare* (Urbana: University of Illinois Press, 1992); and Bruce Schulman, *From Cotton Belt to Sunbelt: Federal Policy, Economic Development, and the Transformation of the South, 1938–1990* (New York: Oxford University Press, 1991).

26. A summary of the program, including Rockefeller's critical role in its passage, is provided in James M. Cannon, "Federal Revenue-Sharing: Born 1972. Died 1986. R.I.P.," *New York Times*, 10 October 1986, https://www.nytimes.com/1986/10/10/opinion/federal-revenue-sharing-born-1972-died-1986-rip.html; see also Connery and Benjamin, *Rockefeller of New York*, 210–212.

27. Council of State Governments, *Book of the States, 1960–61*, 13:417. See also Scott, *American City Planning*, 635.

28. Council of State Governments, *Book of the States, 1960–61*, 13:417–421. Estimate on urban affairs departments from Scott, *American City Planning*, 635.

29. Council of State Governments, *Book of the States, 1980–81*, transportation stats, 8:383–401.

30. Council of State Governments, *Book of the States, 1950–1951*, (Chicago: Council of State Governments, 1950), 8:293.

31. Council of State Governments, *Book of the States, 1970–1971* (Chicago: Council of State Governments, 1970), 8:308–322.

32. Council of State Governments, *Book of the States, 1980–81*, 8:366–382.

33. Council of State Governments, *Book of the States, 1960–61*, 13:417–421.

34. Council of State Governments, *Book of the States, 1972–73*, 19:446–451.

35. Geneva Overholser, "The States and the Housing Crunch," *State Legislature* 7, no. 4 (April 1981): 4–10.

36. Corianne Payton Scally, "States, Housing and Innovation: The Role of State Housing Finance Agencies" (PhD diss., Rutgers University, 2007), 11.

37. *Book of the States*, 1960–61, 13; 419.

38. Council of State Governments, *Book of the States, 1962–1963* (Chicago: Council of State Governments, 1962), 14:364.

39. Gerrit-Jan Knaap, Zorica Nedovic-Budic, and Armando Carbonell, eds., *Planning for States and Nation-States in the U.S. and Europe* (Cambridge, MA: Lincoln Institute of Land Policy, 2015), 8.

Chapter Two

1. Those looking for a comprehensive list of all Rockefeller's policies, or his mastery of the legislative process, will need to look elsewhere. See Richard Norton Smith, *On His Own Terms: A Life of Nelson Rockefeller* (New York: Random House, 2014).

2. The many books on the Rockefeller family and their projects include Suzanne Loebl, *America's Medicis: The Rockefellers and Their Astonishing Cultural Legacy* (New York: Harper, 2010); Robert Dalzell, *The House the Rockefellers Built: A Tale of Money, Taste, and Power in Twentieth-Century America* (New York: Henry Holt, 2008); and Ron Chernow, *Titan: The Life of John D. Rockefeller, Sr.* (New York: Vintage, 2004). On Nelson Rockefeller, see Smith, *On His Own Terms*; Cary Reich, *The Life of Nelson Rockefeller* (New York: Doubleday, 1996); and Joseph Persico, *The Imperial Rockefeller: A Biography of Nelson Rockefeller* (New York: Simon and Schuster, 1982).

3. Governor Nelson Rockefeller, Address to the Thirtieth Anniversary Conference, Regional Plan Association, Inc., Hotel Roosevelt, New York City, 7 October 1959, *Public Papers of Nelson A. Rockefeller, Fifty-Third Governor of the State of New York* (Albany: State of New York, 1959), 1124.

4. Peirce, *The Megastates of America*, 50–52. Reapportionment described in Robert Pecorella and Jeffrey Stonecash, eds., *Governing New York State*, 5th ed. (Albany: SUNY Press, 2006), 154.

5. On the history of authorities, see Robert A. Caro, *The Power Broker: Robert Moses and the Fall of New York* (New York: Knopf, 1974); Jameson W. Doig, *Empire on the Hudson: Entrepreneurial Vision and Political Power at the Port of New York Authority* (New York: Columbia University Press, 2002); Nicholas Dagen Bloom, *Public Housing That Worked: New York in the Twentieth Century* (Philadelphia: University of Pennsylvania Press, 2008); Bloom, *Metropolitan Airport: JFK International and Modern New York* (Philadelphia: University of Pennsylvania Press, 2015); Louise Dyble, *Paying the Toll: Local Power, Regional Politics, and the Golden Gate Bridge* (Philadelphia: University of Pennsylvania Press, 2011); and Gail Radford, *The Rise of the Public Authority: Statebuilding and Economic Development in Twentieth-Century America* (Chicago: University of Chicago Press, 2013).

6. Persico, *The Imperial Rockefeller*, 209–210.

7. NAR to Barbara DeBevoise, 17 April 1970, NAR GUB, Public Relations, Series 27.1 (FA369), Box 2, Folder 46.

8. Nick Thimmesch, "Rocky Seems Stronger Than Ever," *Newsday*, 8 December 1970, 2B.

9. On urban renewal at the time, see James Q. Wilson, ed., *Urban Renewal: The Record and the Controversy* (Cambridge, MA: Joint Center for Urban Studies, 1966); Jeanne Lowe, *Cities in a Race with Time: Progress and Poverty in America's Renewing Cities* (New York: Random House, 1967); Edmund Bacon, *Design of Cities* (New York: Viking, 1867); Mumford, *The Highway and the City*; Herbert J. Gans, *The Urban Villagers: Group and Class in the Life of Italian-Americans* (New York: Free Press, 1962); Martin Anderson, *Federal Bulldozer: A Critical Analysis of Urban Renewal, 1949–1962* (Cambridge, MA: Joint Center for Urban Studies, 1966); and Caro, *The Power Broker*. Urban renewal is a rich area of scholarship. See Sam Zipp, *Manhattan Projects: The Rise and Fall of Urban Renewal in Cold War New York* (New York: Oxford University Press, 2010); Elihu Rubin, *Insuring the City: The Prudential Center and the Postwar Urban Landscape* (New Haven, CT: Yale University Press, 2012); Logan and Molotch, *Urban Fortunes*; John Mollenkopf, *The Contested City* (Princeton, NJ: Princeton University Press, 1983); Alison Isenberg, *Downtown America: A History of the Place and the People Who Made It* (Chicago: University of Chicago Press, 2004); Alexander Garvin, *The American City: What Works, What Doesn't* (New

York: McGraw Hill, 2013); Arnold Hirsch, *Making the Second Ghetto: Race and Housing in Chicago, 1940–1960* (Chicago: University of Chicago Press, 1998); Hilary Ballon and Kenneth T. Jackson, *Robert Moses and the Modern City: The Transformation of New York* (New York: Norton, 2007); Thomas H. O'Connor, *Building a New Boston: Politics and Urban Renewal* (Boston: Northeastern University Press, 1993); Lawrence Kennedy, *Planning the City upon a Hill: Boston since 1630* (Amherst: University of Massachusetts Press, 1994); John F. Bauman, *Public Housing, Race, and Renewal: Urban Planning in Philadelphia, 1920–1974* (Philadelphia: Temple University Press, 1987); Mark Gelfand, *A Nation of Cities: The Federal Government and Urban America, 1933–1965* (New York: Oxford University Press, 1975); and Joel Schwartz, *The New York Approach: Robert Moses, Urban Liberals, and Redevelopment of the Inner City* (Columbus: Ohio State University Press, 1993).

10. Frank Lynn, "The Rockefeller Years," *Newsday*, 15 April 1969, 10.

11. Connery and Benjamin, *Rockefeller of New York*, 218–219.

12. "Rockefeller's Fifteen Years as Governor Reflect Achievement, Growth, and Controversy," New York Times, 12 December 1973, 53.

13. John Allan, "State to Step Up Selling of Bonds," *New York Times*, 9 April 1967, 135.

14. Douglas Dales, "Governor Backs Financing Plans," *New York Times*, 16 July 1963, 19. For a clear description of the various financial tools used by Rockefeller, see Connery and Benjamin, *Rockefeller of New York*, chapter 6.

15. "Rockefeller's Fifteen Years"; "Excerpts from the Message by Governor Rockefeller," New York Times, 7 January 1971, 26. Percentage of school aid per dollar from Peirce, *The Megastates of America*, 36; payroll totals also from Peirce, *The Megastates of America*, 86.

16. Lynn, "The Rockefeller Years."

17. "Rockefeller's Fifteen Years"; "Excerpts from the Message by Governor Rockefeller." Percentage of school aid per dollar from Peirce, *The Megastates of America*, 36; payroll totals also from Peirce, *The Megastates of America*, 86.

18. Connery and Benjamin, *Rockefeller of New York*, 250.

19. "Rockefeller's Fifteen Years"; "Excerpts from the Message by Governor Rockefeller." Proportion of individual versus corporate taxes is from Connery and Benjamin, *Rockefeller of New York*, 193–194. Consistently high taxes in New York in the post-Rockefeller years are also documented in Pecorella and Stonecash, *Governing New York State*, 253–254.

20. Lynn, "The Rockefeller Years."

21. Frank Lynn, "Less Liberal and More Liberal," *Newsday*, 20 January 1970, 3B.

22. Connery and Benjamin, *Rockefeller of New York*, 1012.

23. John Hamilton, "Rockefeller Revisited," *New York Times*, 20 September 1971, 25; "Governor's Letter on City's Fiscal Crisis," *New York Times*, 25 April 1971, 69.

24. Mario Cuomo, *The New York Idea: An Experiment in Democracy* (New York: Crown, 1994), 3.

25. There are many books on planning in the New York region, including Caro, *The Power Broker*; Ballon and Jackson, *Robert Moses and the Modern City*; Gelfand, *Nation of Cities*; Schwartz, *The New York Approach*; Sam Zipp, *Manhattan Projects*; Doig, *Empire on the Hudson*; and Robert A. M. Stern, Thomas Mellins, and David Fishman, *New York 1960: Architecture and Urbanism between the Second World War and the Bicentennial* (New York: Evergreen, 1997).

26. Data from New York State, "About the Mitchell-Lama Housing Program," http://www.nyshcr.org/programs/mitchell-lama/, last updated 1 April 2015.

27. Peirce, *The Megastates of America*, 94.

28. Connery and Benjamin, *Rockefeller of New York*, 201.

29. Frug and Barron, *City Bound*, 85. See, for instance, the description of the city's corporate and personal income tax in this proposed legislation: New York State Assembly, Memorandum in Support of Legislation, http://assembly.state.ny.us/leg/?default_fld=&bn=A7464&term=2017&Memo=Y.

30. The complex accounting of New York State versus New York City spending is explored in Rockefeller Institute, "Giving and Getting: Regional Distribution of Revenue and Spending in the New York State Budget, Fiscal Year 2009–10," December 2011, http://www.rockinst.org/pdf/nys_government/2011-12-Giving_and_Getting.pdf.

31. Rachel Silberstein, "10 Key Takeaways for New York City from the New State Budget," *Gotham Gazette*, 12 April 2017, http://www.gothamgazette.com/state/6867-10-key-takeaways-for-new-york-city-from-the-new-state-budget; "Five Year Financial Plan Revenues and Expenditures," June 2017, http://www1.nyc.gov/assets/omb/downloads/pdf/fp6-17.pdf.

Chapter Three

1. Jon C. Teaford, *The Unheralded Triumph: City Government in America, 1870–1900* (Baltimore: Johns Hopkins University Press, 1984), 83–84. See also Morton Keller, *Affairs of State: Public Life in Late Nineteenth-Century America* (Cambridge, MA: Harvard University Press, 1977).

2. Among the relevant works shaping the analysis on planning history here are Christine Boyer, *Dreaming the Rational City: The Myth of American City Planning* (Cambridge, MA: MIT Press, 1983); Robert Fogelson, *The Fragmented Metropolis: Los Angeles, 1850–1930* (Berkeley: University of California Press, 1967); Bernard J. Frieden and Lynne Sagalyn, *Downtown, Inc.: How American Rebuilds Its Cities* (Cambridge, MA: MIT Press, 1989); Peter Hall, *Cities of Tomorrow: An Intellectual History of Urban Planning and Design in the Twentieth Century* (London: Basil Blackwell, 1988); Hirsch, *Making the Second Ghetto*; Roger Lotchin, *The Martial Metropolis: U.S. Cities in War and Peace* (New York: Praeger, 1984); Lotchin, *Fortress California, 1910–1961*; Jon C. Teaford, *The Rough Road to Renaissance: Urban Revitalization in America, 1940–1985* (Baltimore: Johns Hopkins University Press, 1990); Teaford, *The Unheralded Triumph*; Mary Corbin Sies and Christopher Silver, eds., *Planning the Twentieth-Century American City* (Baltimore: Johns Hopkins University Press, 1996).

3. A fine summary is provided by Alexander Von Hoffman, "A Study in Contradictions: The Origins and Legacy of the Housing Act of 1949," *Housing Policy Debate* 11, no. 2 (2000):299–326; Sara Stevens, *Developing Expertise: Architecture and Real Estate in Metropolitan America* (New Haven, CT: Yale University Press, 2016); and Bloom, *Merchant of Illusion*.

4. Scott, *American City Planning*, 500–501.

5. William Slayton, "Urban Redevelopment Legislation in the States," in Council of State Governments, *Book of the States, 1950–51*, 8:394–397.

6. Council of State Governments, *Book of the States, 1962–63*, 14:156–59. Eisenhower statement from *Facts on File Yearbook, 1960* (New York: Facts on File, 1961), 20:21.

7. Council of State Governments, *Book of the States, 1962–63*, 14:156–59.

8. Council of State Governments, *Book of the States, 1970–71*, 18:445

9. Michael Danielson and Jameson Doig, *New York: The Politics of Urban Regional Development* (Berkeley: University of California Press, 1982), 46. See Stern, Mellins, and Fishman, *New York 1960*, for a comprehensive list.

10. New York State Division of Housing and Community Renewal, "Action for Housing," April 1, 1968-March 31, 1969, New York State Library.

11. Hugh Pomeroy, director, Westchester County Department of Planning, "Planning and Land Use Controls," address reprinted in *Proceedings of the Local Government Workshop, June 5–8, 1960*, NAR GUB, William J. Ronan, Series 29 (FA371), Box 23, Folder 271, 42.

12. Brilliant, *The Urban Development Corporation*, 18.

13. "News Conference by the Governor Concerning Legislation," 944–945.

14. "News Conference by the Governor Concerning Legislation," 945.

15. "News Conference by the Governor Concerning Legislation," 943–967.

16. "News Conference by the Governor Concerning Legislation," 951.

17. T. Norman Hurd and Gerald Benjamin, eds., *Rockefeller in Retrospect: The Governor's New York Legacy*, (Albany: Nelson Rockefeller Institute of Government, 1984), 207–208.

18. John Sibley, "Rockefeller Plan for Slums Voted," *New York Times*, 10 April 1968, 1.

19. "News Conference by the Governor Concerning Legislation," 959.

20. David Bird, "Governor's Plans on Slums Backed," *New York Times*, 15 March 1968, 27.

21. Ada Louise Huxtable, "Albany's Threat to New York's Planning," *New York Times*, 22 May 1968, 46.

22. "UDC in 72: A Mini-Report," NAR GUB, Press Office, Series 25.3 (FA368), Box 75, Folder 1710, 17–33. See also UDC Annual Report 1971, New York State Archives, Box: UDC Annual Reports, 38–39.

23. Lynne Sagalyn, *Times Square Roulette: Remaking the City Icon* (Cambridge: MIT Press, 2003), 72–73. Figures on Javits from Javits Center, http://www.javitscenter.com/about/.

24. Paul Goldberg, "Architecture View; Battery Park City Is a Triumph of Urban Design," *New York Times*, 31 August 1986, https://www.nytimes.com/1986/08/31/arts/architecture-view-battery-park-city-is-a-triumph-of-urban-design.html; Edward Schumacher, "Carey and Koch Accept New Battery Park City Plan," *New York Times*, 9 November 1979, https://www.nytimes.com/1979/11/09/archives/carey-and-koch-accept-new-battery-park-city-plan-part-of-a.html; Frederique Krupa, "Battery Park City: Luring Back the Upper-Middle Class," 1993, http://www.simple-is-beautiful.org/fredek/bpc.html; Frank P. Russell, "Battery Park City: An American Dream of Urbanism," in B. C. Lightner and W. F. E. Preiser, eds., *Design Review: Practice and Critical Issues* (New York : Van Nostrand Reinhold, 1993), https://www.uc.edu/cdc/urban_database/food_resources/frank-article-02.pdf.

25. Sagalyn, *Times Square Roulette*, 78.

26. Western New York Economic Development Council, *Buffalo Niagara's Strategic Plan for Prosperity*, January 2017, https://buffalobillion.ny.gov/sites/default/files/images/BuffaloBillion2_BookREDUCEDforREDCSinglesFeb23.pdf.

27. Detailed plans of various ESDC projects can be found at Empire State Development, https://esd.ny.gov/.

28. Boston Planning & Development Agency, http://www.bostonplans.org/about-us/timeline.

29. Alan Altshuler and David Luberoff, *Mega-Projects: The Changing Politics of Urban Public Investment* (Washington, DC: Brookings Institution and Lincoln Land Institute, 2003) 20.

30. Jared S. Hopkins, "Tax Dollars Still Paying Off Renovations on White Sox Stadium," *Chicago Tribune*, 23 May 2016, http://www.chicagotribune.com/news/ct-sox-cell-funding-isfa-met-20160521-story.html.

31. Sports & Exhibition Authority, "Regional Destination Financing Plan," last updated 31 December 2013, http://www.pgh-sea.com/StadiumAuthority.htm.

32. Maryland Stadium Authority, "The Mission and Vision Statement," http://www

.mdstad.com/about/the-mission-and-vision-statement; Baltimore Convention Center fact sheet, http://www.bccenter.org/index.php?target=65.

33. Maryland Stadium Authority, "The Mission and Vision Statement."

34. Heywood Sanders, *Convention Center Follies: Politics, Power, and Public Investment in American Cities* (Philadelphia: University of Pennsylvania Press, 2014), 74–75.

35. McCormick Place, "History," http://www.mccormickplace.com/about-us/history.php.

36. Las Vegas Convention and Visitors Authority, "Mission & Purpose," http://www.lvcva.com/who-we-are/mission-and-purpose/.

37. Peter Eisenger, *The Rise of the Entrepreneurial State: State and Local Economic Development Policy in the United States* (Madison: University of Wisconsin Press, 1988), 6, 9, 56, 60, 182–191.

38. Enterprise Florida, "Why Florida?," https://www.enterpriseflorida.com/why-florida/.

39. Norton Francis, "What Do State Economic Development Agencies Do?," Urban Institute, Economic Development Strategies Information Brief 6, July 2016, https://www.urban.org/sites/default/files/publication/83141/2000880-What-Do-State-Economic-Development-Agencies-Do.pdf, 3, 1.

40. William Rohe, *The Research Triangle: From Tobacco Road to Global Prominence* (Philadelphia: University of Pennsylvania Press, 2011); Research Triangle Park, "The Transformative Impact of the Research Triangle Park—A Case Study," 15 February 2018, https://www.rtp.org/transformative-impact-research-triangle-park-case-study/.

41. Battelle Technology Partnership Practice, *Driving Regional Innovation and Growth: The 2012 Survey of North American University Research Parks*, https://aurp.memberclicks.net/assets/documents/aurp_batelllereportv2.pdf. Impact figures, 18–19; Arizona quotation, 19; "Live-work-play," 4.

42. Altshuler and Luberoff, *Mega-Projects*, 63.

Chapter Four

1. Council of State Governments, *Book of the States, 1960–61*, 13:159.

2. Council of State Governments, *Book of the States, 1980–81*, 8:266–268. Contemporary figures from "States with Most Government Employees: Totals and Per Capita Rates," *Governing: The States and Localities*, http://www.governing.com/gov-data/public-workforce-salaries/states-most-government-workers-public-employees-by-job-type.html.

3. US Census Bureau, "2012 Census of Governments: Employment Summary Report," 6 March 2014, https://www2.census.gov/govs/apes/2012_summary_report.pdf.

4. Paul Grondahl, *Mayor Erastus Corning: Albany Icon, Albany Enigma* (Albany: Washington Park, 1997), 457.

5. Hurd and Benjamin, *Rockefeller in Retrospect*, 213.

6. Peirce, *The Megastates of America*, 34.

7. William Kennedy, *O Albany! An Urban Tapestry* (New York: Penguin, 1983), 305–324. See also Paul Groth, *Living Downtown: The History of Residential Hotels in the United States* (Berkeley: University of California Press, 1999).

8. Grondahl, *Mayor Erastus Corning*, 460.

9. Samuel Bleeker, *The Politics of Architecture: A Perspective on Nelson A. Rockefeller* (New York: Rutledge Press and Nelson Rockefeller Collection, 1981), 198.

10. Hurd and Benjamin, *Rockefeller in Retrospect*, 214. The full story is recounted in Grondahl, *Mayor Erastus Corning*, chapter 13.

11. Bleeker, *The Politics of Architecture*, 201.

12. "Mall Buildings Rising in Albany," *New York Times*, 2 December 1969, 31.

13. "Mall Buildings Rising in Albany."

14. Kennedy, *O Albany!*, 317.

15. Bill Kovach, "South Mall Cost Put at Possibly over $1 Billion," *New York Times*, 17 December 1969, 66.

16. Hurd and Benjamin, *Rockefeller in Retrospect*, 214.

17. Linda Greenhouse, "Albany Malls Space Inadequate," *New York Times*, 26 January 1975, 41.

18. Kennedy, *O Albany!*, 305–324.

19. Loebl, *America's Medicis*, 277.

20. See City of Albany, NY, Commission on Public-Private Budgetary Cooperation, *Preliminary Report: Non-Profit Revenue Assessment*, Fall 2013, http://www.albanyny.gov/Libraries/Economic_Development/Albany_Public-Private_Budgetary_Cooperation_Final_Report_12-3-13.sflb.ashx.

21. Florida Department of Management Services, "Capitol Complex Information," http://www.dms.myflorida.com/business_operations/real_estate_development_and_management/facilities_management/building_information/capitol_complex_information. See also Lilly Rockwell, "The Decision-Making Process 40 Years Ago That Led to the Modern Capitol Building," *Tallahassee Magazine*, March–April 2011, http://www.tallahasseemagazine.com/March-April-2011/Floridas-Tower-of-Power/.

22. Steven Avella, *Sacramento: Indomitable City* (Charleston, SC: Arcadia, 2003), 127–129.

23. State of New Jersey, Capital City Redevelopment Corporation, "About CCRC," http://web.njeda.com/ccrc/page.aspx?id=2457.

24. Maryland Department of General Services, "Facility Operations and Maintenance," http://dgs.maryland.gov/pages/FOM/index.aspx.

25. State of Texas, *2016 Texas Capitol Complex Master Plan*, http://www.tfc.state.tx.us/divisions/commissionadmin/tools/2015-10-06_TexasCapitolComplexMasterPlan_PROPOSED.pdf.

26. James Baldwin, "Fifth Avenue, Uptown," *Esquire*, 18 October 2007, https://www.esquire.com/news-politics/a3638/fifth-avenue-uptown.

27. "Proposed Building in Harlem Scored," *New York Times*, 8 December 1966, 57.

28. James Gaynor, "State Support for City Housing," *New York Times*, 16 July 1968, 38.

29. William Robbins, "Harlem Building to Take Three Years," *New York Times*, 16 October 1966, 80.

30. Robbins, "Harlem Building to Take Three Years."

31. John Silvera, position paper, 20 August 1969, NAR GUB, Hugh Morrow, Series 21 (FA242), Box 20, Folder 209, 5.

32. Ada Louise Huxtable, "The State Office Building Dilemma," *New York Times*, 2 November 1969, D32.

33. Brian Goldstein, *The Roots of Urban Renaissance: Gentrification and the Struggle over Harlem* (Cambridge, MA: Harvard University Press, 2017).

34. NAR, "A Modern Federalism for an Urban America," draft manuscript for Modulus, 13 March 1969, NAR GUB, Public Relations, Series 27.1 (FA369), Box 2, Folder 33.

35. Silvera, position paper, 7.

36. John D. Silvera to Thelma Goodrich, president United Insurance Brokers Association, 17 October 1969, NAR GUB, Hugh Morrow, Series 21, Box 20, Folder 209.

37. "If You're against the Harlem Civic Center," advertisement, *Manhattan Tribune*, 11 October 1969; United Insurance Brokers Association, ca. 1969, NAR GUB, Hugh Morrow, Series 21 (FA242), Box 20, Folder 209, 3.

38. Maryland Department of General Services, "Facility Operations and Maintenance."

39. Texas Facilities Commission, "TFC State Building Inventory & Leases" (map), http://www.tfc.state.tx.us/divisions/facilities/prog/leasing/mapil.html.

Chapter Five

1. Scott, *American City Planning*, 457–458.

2. Danielson and Doig, *New York*, 51.

3. Danielson and Doig, *New York*, 75.

4. Brandon, "Planning for Development in New York State," 14.

5. New York State Builders Association, "About NYBSA," https://nysba.com/about/about-nysba.

6. Robert Moses, "From the Bridge," *Newsday*, 6 August 1966, 4W; "Tax and Transit Reforms Urged for L.I. by Moses," *New York Times*, 16 October 1960, 1.

7. Brandon, "Planning for Development in New York State, 8.

8. Pomeroy, "Planning and Land Use Controls," 40.

9. Office of Planning Coordination, New York State Development Plan, January 1971, NAR GUB, Hugh Morrow, Series 21.1 (FA242), Box 36, Folder 371, 7.

10. Brandon, "Planning for Development in New York State."

11. Governor's Statement on Intergovernmental Relations, NYC, 10 June 1963, NAR GUB, Hugh Morrow, Series 21.1 (FA242), Box 20, Folder 205, 3.

12. Press release, 31 January 1971, NAR GUB, Hugh Morrow, Series 21.1 (FA242), Box 36, Folder 371.

13. Office of Planning Coordination, New York State Development Plan, 7, 88.

14. Office of Planning Coordination, New York State Development Plan. See also Brilliant, *The Urban Development Corporation*, 50.

15. "Accord Reached on Tristate Plan," *New York Times*, 10 March 1965, 43.

16. Governor's Statement on Intergovernmental Relations, 6.

17. "Rockefeller on the Issues: Transportation," September 1963, transcript of speech, 5 October 1961, in Reno, Nevada, NAR GUB, Issue Books, Series 17 (FA363), Box 20, Folder 117, 88. See also Ronald Maiorana, "Rockefeller Urges U.S. Agency to Meet Transportation Crisis," *New York Times*, 16 June 1963, 43.

18. Peter Kihss, "A $10 Billion Transit Plan," *New York Times*, 19 May 1966, 1.

19. State of New York Temporary Commission on the Powers of Local Government (Wagner Commission), Robert F. Wagner, chairman, *Part A: New York City Functional Study Background Papers (1971–1972)*, NAR GUB, Press Office, Series 25.3 (FA368), Box 75, no folder, 409.

20. Danielson and Doig, *New York*, 143. See also Gerald Benjamin and Richard Nathan, *Regionalism and Realism: A Study of Governments in the New York Metropolitan Area* (Washington, DC: Brookings Institution, 2001), 25–26.

21. New York State Commission on the Preservation of Agricultural Land, report, 1 January 1968, NAR GUB, Press Office, Series 25.3 (FA368), Box 2, Folder 1543.

22. Robert O'Neil, WCBS Management Opinion, transcript, 1970, NAR GUB, Hugh Morrow, Series 21.1 (FA242), Box 14, Folder 153.

23. New York Department of Environmental Conservation, "State Land Acreage by Classification," https://www.dec.ny.gov/lands/59645.html.

24. New York State Department of Agriculture and Markets, "Agricultural Districts Law: A Current Summary," https://www.agriculture.ny.gov/ap/agservices/dis8/Summary-AgrDistrict-Law.pdf.

25. Land Trust Alliance, "What You Can Do," https://www.landtrustalliance.org/what-you-can-do/conserve-your-land/questions.

26. Persico, *The Imperial Rockefeller*, 165.

27. Council of State Governments, *Book of the States, 1960–61*, 13:414–415.

28. Council of State Governments, *Book of the States, 1966–1967* (Chicago: Council of State Governments, 1966), 16:428–431.

29. Council of State Governments, *Book of the States, 1972–73*, 19:445.

30. Council of State Governments, *Book of the States, 1966–67*, 16: 431.

31. Scott, *American City Planning*, 453.

32. Council of State Governments, *Book of the States, 1964–1965* (Chicago: Council of State Governments, 1964), 15: 485.

33. Carlton Wade Basmajian, *Atlanta Unbound: Enabling Sprawl through Policy and Planning* (Philadelphia: Temple University Press, 2013), 11.

34. Scott, *American City Planning*, 505.

35. Adam Rome, *The Bulldozer in the Countryside: Suburban Sprawl and the Rise of American Environmentalism* (Cambridge: Cambridge University Press, 2001), 227.

36. Knaap, Nedovic-Budic, and Carbonell, *Planning for States and Nation States*, 131–188.

37. Peirce, *The Megastates of America*, 209.

38. Knaap, Nedovic-Budic, and Carbonell, *Planning for States and Nation States*, 53–82, 76.

39. Knaap, Nedovic-Budic, and Carbonell, *Planning for States and Nation States*, 76.

40. Scott Beyer, "Portland's Urban Growth Boundary: A Driver of Suburban Sprawl," *Fortune*, 29 March 2017, https://www.forbes.com/sites/scottbeyer/2017/03/29/portlands-urban-growth-boundary-a-driver-of-suburban-sprawl/#48f8417d6964.

41. Scott, *American City Planning*, 557–558. Williamson Act description from California Department of Conservation, "Land Conservation (Williamson) Act: Questions and Answers," http://www.conservation.ca.gov/dlrp/lca/basic_contract_provisions/Pages/LCA_QandA.aspx#what%20is%20the%20california%20land%20conservation%20%28williamson%29%20act.

42. Knaap, Nedovic-Budic, and Carbonell, *Planning for States and Nation States*, 104.

43. Knaap, Nedovic-Budic, and Carbonell, *Planning for States and Nation States*, 42–43.

44. Knaap, Nedovic-Budic, and Carbonell, *Planning for States and Nation States*, 189–226.

45. Knaap, Nedovic-Budic, and Carbonell, *Planning for States and Nation States*, 45.

46. Knaap, Nedovic-Budic, and Carbonell, *Planning for States and Nation States*, 97–123.

47. Christina Rosan, *Governing the Fragmented Metropolis: Planning for Regional Sustainability* (Philadelphia: University of Pennsylvania Press, 2016), 59–98.

48. See Robert Bruegmann, *Sprawl: A Compact History* (Chicago: University of Chicago Press, 2005).

Chapter Six

1. Charles Grutzner, "Crises in Urban Transit Studied by U.S. Agencies," *New York Times*, 10 April 1961, 1.

2. The state created the Massachusetts Bay Transportation Authority (MBTA) in 1964 (replacing the Metropolitan Transit Authority, 1947).

3. William Reid, address reprinted in *Proceedings of the Local Government Workshop, June 12–13, 1961*, NAR GUB, William J. Ronan, Series 29 (FA371), Box 23, Folder 272, 121.

4. William Reid, address reprinted in *Proceedings*. Commuter percentages from Danielson and Doig, *New York*, 213.

5. State of New York Temporary Commission on the Powers of Local Government (Wagner Commission), *Part A*, 14.

6. Benjamin and Nathan, *Regionalism and Realism*, 29.

7. David Andelman, "It Seems to Be a Heck of a Way to Run a Railroad," *New York Times*, 30 March 1980, E6.

8. Clayton Knowles, "Agreement on Transit," *New York Times*, 6 January 1964, 22.

9. Frank Prial, "Financing of Transit Is Complex," *New York Times*, 28 December 1971, 57.

10. "Bus Gains Exceed Subway's Losses," *New York Times*, 4 December 1961, 31. See also Tony Schwartz, "The Subway: City's Lifeline for 75 Years," *New York Times*, 4 April 1980, B1.

11. Benjamin and Nathan, *Regionalism and Realism*, 137.

12. Clayton Knowles, "The Commuter Problem: What Can Be Done?" *New York Times*, 22 February 1959, E6.

13. Knowles, "The Commuter Problem."

14. "Rockefeller on the Issues: Transportation," September 1963, transcript of speech on 5 October 1961, in Reno, Nevada, NAR GUB, Issue Books, Series 17 (FA363), Box 20, Folder 117.

15. Edwin Michaelian, "The Inter-relationship between Urban Development and Transportation," address reprinted in *Proceedings of the Local Government Workshop, June 12–13, 1961*, NAR GUB, William J. Ronan, Series 29 (FA371), Box 23, Folder 272, 126.

16. "Moses Spans the RRs for 'Whining, Crying,'" *Newsday*, 26 May 1960, 4.

17. Long Island Association of Commerce and Industry, transcript of proceedings, Garden City, NY, 7 August 1969, NAR GUB, Hugh Morrow, Series 21.1 (FA242), Box 47, Folder 494. See also Danielson and Doig, *New York*, 216; and Douglas Dales, "Governor Names 5 to Study LIRR," *New York Times*, 19 September 1964, 1.

18. "Tax and Transit Reforms Urged."

19. Clayton Knowles, "Rockefeller Asking Speed," *New York Times*, 29 January 1959, 1.

20. Clayton Knowles, "Bleak Year on the Rails," *New York Times*, 8 January 1960, 17. See also Danielson and Doig, *New York*, 216–218.

21. Leo Egan, "Rockefeller Presses Bills," *New York Times*, 21 March 1959, 1.

22. Leo Egan, "Rail Aid and Rent Control Voted in Albany Wind-Up," *New York Times*, 26 March 1959, 1.

23. "Tax and Transit Reforms Urged."

24. Phil Sanborne, "How Will LIRR Find Cure for Its Fiscal Headache?," *Newsday*, 6 January 1961, 7.

25. Dick Zander, "Nassau Drawing Bill on LIRR Fate," *Newsday*, 12 November 1963, 5.

26. Michaelian, "The Inter-relationship."

27. Warren Weaver, "State to Survey New Haven Woes," *New York Times*, 7 December 1961, 45.

28. Knowles, "Bleak Year on the Rails."

29. "Central Sprucing Commuter Cars," *New York Times*, 8 May 1959, 28; Douglas Dales, "End of Commuting Called Rail Goal," *New York Times*, 11 June 1959, 35; "New Haven Closes Commuter Division," *New York Times*, 1 July 1959, 23.

30. Peirce, *The Megastates of America*, 31.

31. "Rockefeller Sees Tax Relief," *New York Times*, 18 February 1959, 35.

32. Warren Weaver, "President Signs Transit-Aid Bill," *New York Times*, 10 July 1964, 31.

33. Excerpts of remarks by Governor Nelson Rockefeller at fundraiser in Connecticut, 26 June 1963, NAR GUB, Rockefeller Family, R64, Series S-6, Box 3, Folder 17, 1–2.

34. "The State and Commuters," editorial, *New York Times*, 16 March 1959, 30; Douglas Dales, "Governor Signs Rail Bonds Bill to Permit Buying of New Cars," *New York Times*, 7 April 1962, 13.

35. "Governor Signs Subway-Car Bill," *New York Times*, 24 April 1962, 39.

36. Governor's Statement on Intergovernmental Relations, NYC, 10 June 1963, NAR GUB, Hugh Morrow, Series 21.1 (FA242), Box 20, Folder 205.

37. State of New York Temporary Commission on the Powers of Local Government (Wagner Commission), *Part A*, 194–197.

38. Warren Weaver, "Merged Line Asks Commuter Grants," *New York Times*, 30 April 1966, 28.

39. Brandon, "Planning for Development in New York State," 20.

40. State of New York Temporary Commission on the Powers of Local Government (Wagner Commission), *Part A*, 152.

41. John Devlin, "Traffic in Transit Tokens," *New York Times*, 17 January 1964, 87.

42. John Sibley, "New Law Lets Transit Authority Build 63rd Street Tunnel," *New York Times*, 22 July 1965, 33.

43. State of New York Temporary Commission on the Powers of Local Government (Wagner Commission), *Part A*, 199.

44. Richard Witkin, "Leaders Support Rockefeller Plan," *New York Times*, 27 February 1965, 1.

45. Charles Grutzner, "Rockefeller Urges State to Buy LIRR," *New York Times*, 26 February 1965, 1.

46. Long Island Association of Commerce and Industry, transcript of proceedings, 5.

47. Peter Kihss, "Roads Jammed 6.5 Hours," *New York Times*, 7 January 1966, 1. See also John A. Jakle and Keith A. Sculle, *Lots of Parking: Land Use in a Car Culture* (Charlottesville: University of Virginia Press, 2004).

48. Grutzner, "Crises in Urban Transit."

49. "Commerce Group Favors Rail Aid," *New York Times*, 28 April 1965, 47.

50. Peter Kihss, "Gain in Transit Held Vital Here," *New York Times*, 20 March 1967, 1.

51. "News Conference re Report to Governor Nelson Rockefeller by Metropolitan Commuter Transportation Authority," 28 February 1968, NAR GUB, Press Office, Series 25.3 (FA368), Box 69, Folder 1525, 3–4.

52. Richard Witkin, "Legislature Gets Rail Agency Bill," *New York Times*, 12 May 1965, 39.

53. Connery and Benjamin, *Rockefeller of New York*, 274.

54. MCTA, *1966-67 Annual Report*, New York State Library, 21–23.

55. New York State Metropolitan Commuter Transportation Authority, *First Annual Report*, 31 March 1966, 1. See also Emanuel Perlmutter, "LIRR Will Run in Queens Tunnel," *New York Times*, 28 April 1966, 1; Witkin, "Leaders Support Rockefeller Plan." Connery and Benjamin in *Rockefeller of New York* provide a comprehensive overview of the growing power of suburban Republicans in New York State during the1960s. See pp. 77–108.

56. Perlmutter, "LIRR Will Run in Queens Tunnel."

57. "Work on LIRR Started by State," *New York Times*, 31 August 1966, 45.

58. MTA, *1972 Annual Report*, "The Ten Year Program at the Halfway Mark," New York State Library, 19–20. See also "Commuter Lines at Crisis Point," *New York Times*, 28 July 1969, 1.

59. Martin Arnold, "State Gives City $100 Million Aid," *New York Times*, 19 January 1966, 30. See also "Taxes the View from Upstate," *New York Times*, 12 June 1966, 208.

60. "Transit Takeover Is Urged by Speno," *New York Times*, 18 January 1966, 10. Deficit figure from Warren Weaver, "Senator William Proposes," *New York Times*, 7 January 1966, 18.

61. Peter Kihss, "$2.6 Billion Plan," *New York Times*, 29 November 1965, 1.

62. Sydney Schanberg, "Albany Aid Seen on Transit 'Czar,'" *New York Times*, 11 February 1966, 29.

63. Arnold Lubasch, "Bank Will Fight Transit Merger," *New York Times*, 13 March 1966, 73.

64. John Callahan, "Moses Scores a Transit Merger as Unworkable," *New York Times*, 22 January 1967, 78.

65. Joseph Ingraham, "Moses Says Triborough Projects Will Absorb Surpluses Until '69," *New York Times*, 31 March 1967, 40. See also "Moses Refuses to Play Santa," *Newsday*, 8 January 1966, 13; and "Gov's Transit Plan Draws Moses' Ire," *Newsday*, 23 January 1967, 7.

66. Richard Madden, "Moses Condemns Fund Plan," *New York Times*, 14 June 1967, 41.

67. Frank Prial, "Nelson and David Rockefeller Reported Principal," *New York Times*, 10 October 1974, 34.

68. State of New York Temporary Commission on the Powers of Local Government (Wagner Commission), *Part A*. Reference to a public holding company in *MCTA, 1966–67 Annual Report*, New York State Library, 7.

69. State of New York Temporary Commission on the Powers of Local Government (Wagner Commission), *Part A*. Metro-North offers limited service on the east side of the Hudson in Orange and Rockland counties in partnership with NJ Transit.

70. "Triborough Agency Doubled Revenues in 4-Year Period," *New York Times*, 2 September 1974, 34.

71. "Bridge Authority Had a 1974 Surplus," *New York Times*, 2 April 1975, 20.

72. Benjamin and Nathan, *Regionalism and Realism*, 138.

73. Sydney Schanberg, "Transit Power Shift," *New York Times*, 24 March 1967, 31.

74. "Rockefeller Aids 8 Subway Routes," *New York Times*, 29 May 1969, 78. Figures on MTA from MTA, *1968 Annual Report*, New York State Library, 8.

75. Unfortunately, many of these areas lacked subway connections. Peirce, *The Megastates of America*, 124.

76. Kihss, "$2.6 Billion Plan."

77. MCTA, "Metropolitan Transportation: A Program for Action," February 1968, NAR GUB, Press Office, Series 25.3 (FA368), Box 69, Folder 1525, 2–3.

78. Edward Burks, "2d Avenue Subway," *New York Times*, 24 May 1969, 1.

79. MCTA, Metropolitan Transportation.

80. MTA, *1969 Annual Report*, New York State Library, 19.

81. MTA, *1970 Annual Report*, New York State Library, 37.

82. Danielson and Doig, *New York*, 236–237. See also *MTA Annual Report*, 1971, New York State Library, 3–9.

83. Dick Zander, "Peddling the Bond Issue," *Newsday*, 16 September 1973, 25.

84. Edward Hershey, "Concerning the Bond Issue," *Newsday*, 4 November 1971, 62.

85. William Farrell, "Governor Says Kheel Plan Plays Politics on Bond Issue," *New York Times*, 30 September 1971, 95.

86. William Farrell, "Governor Links Bond Issue to City Fares," *New York Times*, 24 September 1971, 28.

87. Francis Clines, "Gov. Asking 3.5 Billion Bonds for Transit Plan," *New York Times*, 21 July 1973, 57. See also Francis Clines, "Legislators Place Cost above $3.5 Billion," *New York Times*, 27 July 1973, 65.

88. E. J. Dionne, "Carey Proposes $797 Million Plan," *New York Times*, 15 May 1979, A1.

89. Peirce, *The Megastates of America*, 32.

90. Robert Lindsey, "U.S. Seeks Vast Aid for Mass Transit," *New York Times*, 10 May 1969, 1.

91. MTA, *1971 Annual Report*, New York State Library, 4.

92. Edward Burks, "Ronan Warns of 70% Commuter Fair Rise by 75," *New York Times*, 12 July 1973, 78.

93. Frank Prial, "Ronin Leaving MTA with a Lot of Believers," *New York Times*, 27 April 1974, 33.

94. MTA, *1972 Annual Report*, 16.

95. Robert Lindsey, "MTA Seeking $1 Billion," *New York Times*, 11 October 1970, 86; "Nixon Signs Transit Bill, Terming It a 'Landmark,'" *New York Times*, 16 October 1970, 54.

96. MTA, *1972 Annual Report*, 16.

97. Prial, "Ronan Leaving MTA."

98. Ralph Blumenthal, "New US Aid Formula for Transit Is Urged," *New York Times*, 29 January 1977, 23.

99. Martin Tolchin, "Transit Meeting with Rockefeller Declined by Nixon," *New York Times*, 30 November 1973, 77.

100. Robert Lindsey, "The Subway Prospect," *New York Times*, 12 October 1973, 45.

101. Edward Burks, "MTA Receives $87.5 Million Aid," *New York Times*, 20 May 1975, I74.

102. Robert Lindsey, "Plight of Public Transportation Systems Mounts," *New York Times*, 30 December 1974, 39.

103. Paul Montgomery, "Rockefeller Considers Ousting Head of LIRR," *New York Times*, 26 July 1969, 51.

104. "Commuter Survey Touches Nerves," *New York Times*, 18 August 1968, 30.

105. MTA, *1969 Annual Report*, 27.

106. Roy Silver, "Long Island Railroad Is Blamed for Family Woes," *New York Times*, 13 February 1970, 37.

107. Long Island Association of Commerce and Industry, transcript of proceedings, 47.

108. "Ronan Tempers LIRR Optimism," *New York Times*, 9 August 1969, 29.

109. Roy Silver, "LIRR Derailed," *New York Times*, 26 September 1969, 92.

110. Long Island Association of Commerce and Industry, transcript of proceedings, 17–21.

111. Hugh Morrow to NAR, 19 September 1969, NAR GUB, Hugh Morrow, Series 21.1 (FA242), Box 47, Folder 494.

112. Ronald Maiorana to the Governor, 29 September 1969, NAR GUB, Hugh Morrow, Series 21.1 (FA242), Box 47, Folder 494.

113. WCBS editorial, 7 October 1969, NAR GUB, Hugh Morrow, Series 21.1 (FA242), Box 47, Folder 494.

114. Zander, "Peddling the Bond Issue," 25.

115. Martin Arnold, "Riders Less Enthusiastic," *New York Times*, 8 October 1969, 1.

116. "Summary of the Nassau-Suffolk Comprehensive Development Plan, July 1879," *Newsday*, 13 July 1970, 1S.

117. MTA, *1970 Annual Report*, 15–16.

118. Summary statistics from multiple MTA, Annual Reports (1971–1973), New York State Library.

119. Frank Prial, "LIRR's 'Bright New Era' Is in Peril," *New York Times*, 18 December 1972, 1, 65.

120. Frank Prial, "Governor Calls Strike on LIRR 'Unconscionable,'" *New York Times*, 7 December 1972, 109.

121. Frank Prial, "Fare Rise Plan," *New York Times*, 18 January 1972, 36.

122. Edward Burks, "Riders Applaud LIRR Improvements," *New York Times*, 3 June 1974, 1.

123. Frank Prial, "Planning Group Endorses Transportation Bond Issue," *New York Times*, 28 October 1971, 82.

124. David Andelman, "World Survey Finds City Lagging," *New York Times*, 29 July 1970, 21.

125. Richard Phalon, "Ronan Admits Subway Service," *New York Times*, 18 September 1969, 55.

126. Lindsey, "The Subway Prospect."

127. Damon Stetson, "Study Says New York Transit Pay Outpaces Raises in Private Sector," *New York Times*, 16 January 1978, D4.

128. Peter Kihss, "Second Avenue Line," *New York Times*, 5 March 1969, 49.

129. Edward Burks, "Second Avenue Subway Is Delayed," *New York Times*, 1 November 1974, 84.

130. MTA, *1972 Annual Report*, 37.

131. Andrew Malcolm, "Work Begins on 752 Subway Cars," *New York Times*, 25 September 1972, 75.

132. Richard Witkin, "Transit and Politics," *New York Times*, 6 February 1970, 18.

133. Peirce, *The Megastates of America*, 32, 82.

134. Andelman, "Heck of a Way to Run a Railroad."

135. *MTA Annual Report*, 1972, 9–12.

136. Malcolm, "Work Begins on 752 Subway Cars." See also *MTA Annual Report*, 1972, New York State Library, 37–44.

137. MTA, *1975 Annual Report*, New York State Library, 6–7; Maurice Carroll, "City Will Air Condition All Its Transit," *New York Times*, 29 January 1973, 33.

138. MTA, *1973 Annual Report*, New York State Library, 1–22; Grace Lichtenstein, "New Funds Unlikely to Alter New York's View on Subway," *New York Times*, 8 May 1978, 17.

139. Martin Tolchin, "U.S. Study Decries City's New Trains," *New York Times*, 13 March 1976, 24.

140. Tolchin, "U.S. Study Decries City's New Trains."

141. MTA, *1988 Annual Report*, New York State Library, 1–10.

142. MTA, *1968 Annual Report*, 32.

143. MTA, *1972 Annual Report*, 9–12.

144. MTA, *1970 Annual Report*, 18.

145. John McQuiston, "Subway Holdups Laid to 11 Youths," *New York Times*, 2 December 1974, 69.

146. Frank Prial, "Subway Graffiti Here Called Epidemic," *New York Times*, 11 February 1972, 39.

147. Deidre Carmody, "Subway Crimes Rise 26%," *New York Times*, 10 October 1973, 99.

148. Douglas Robinson, "Goldberg Urges Transit Subsidy," *New York Times*, 30 May 1970, 13.

149. Will Lissner, "MTA Is Assailed," *New York Times*, 7 February 1970, 27.

150. Richard Phalon, "Assembly Approves Transit Loan Bill," *New York Times*, 19 February 1970, 94.

151. William F. Buckley Jr., "The Subway Shell Game," *Newsday*, 10 January 1970, 15.

152. Edward Burks, "Subways Lose Riders but Are on Time More," *New York Times*, 8 October 1973, 69.

153. Edward Burks, "Subway Ridership Lowest since '18," *New York Times*, 6 April 1975, 1.

154. Burks, "Subway Ridership Lowest since '18."

155. Edward Burks, "3-Year MTA Program Seeks to Rewin Riders," *New York Times*, 20 October 1975, 1.

156. Burks, "Subway Ridership Lowest since '18."

157. MTA, *1972 Annual Report*, 16; MTA, *1985 Annual Report*, 1985, New York State Library, 25.

158. Frank Prial, "Financing of Transit Authority Is Complex," 28 December 1971, *New York Times*, 57.

159. Edward Burks, "Second Avenue Subway Faces New Delay," *New York Times*, 14 December 1974, 61.

160. *MTA Annual Report*, 1974, New York State Library, 16.

161. Ethan Eldon, "Our Subways: Worthy of a Second Dante," *New York Times*, 2 July 1976, 22.

162. Lichtenstein, "New Funds Unlikely to Alter New York's View."

163. *MTA Annual Report*, 1985, 45.

164. Danielson and Doig, *New York*, 208.

165. The negotiations are detailed in Richard Ravitch, *So Much to Do: A Full Life of Business, Politics, and Confronting Fiscal Crisis* (New York: Public Affairs, 2014), chapter 6. See also Ralph Blumenthal, "Rail Line Spending Expected," *New York Times*, 22 November 1981, 1.

166. MTA, *1988 Annual Report*, 1–15.

167. Benjamin and Nathan, *Regionalism and Realism*, 149.

168. MTA Network, "Public Transportation for the New York Region," http://web.mta.info/mta/network.htm.

169. MTA, *1988 Annual Report*, 1–10.

170. Ari Goldman, "Accord Is Reached on MTA Operation," *New York Times*, 9 August 1982, A1.

171. MTA, *1988 Annual Report*, 1–2, 8–9.

172. Benjamin and Nathan, *Regionalism and Realism*, 147–148, 153.

173. Jonathan Mahler, "The Case for the Subway," *New York Times Magazine*, 3 January 2018, https://www.nytimes.com/2018/01/03/magazine/subway-new-york-city-public-transportation-wealth-inequality.html.

174. Office of the New York State Comptroller, "DiNapoli: MTA Financial Outlook Improved," 16 September 2016, http://osc.state.ny.us/press/releases/sept16/092816.htm; Martin Z. Braun, "MTA's Rising Debt and Payroll Cost Take Toll on Bond Rating," *Bloomberg*, 12 March 2018, https://www.bloomberg.com/news/articles/2018-03-12/mta-s-rising-debt-and-payroll-costs-take-toll-on-credit-rating.

175. Council of State Governments, *Book of the States, 1966–67*, 16:308–309.

176. Council of State Governments, *Book of the States, 1970–71*, 18:331–332.

177. Council of State Governments, *Book of the States, 1966–67*, 16:310–311.

178. Council of State Governments, *Book of the States, 1974–1975* (Chicago: Council of State Governments, 1974), 20:353–354.

179. Julian Weiss, "Public Transit: On Track at Last," *State Legislatures* 6, no. 6 (June 1980): 14–19.

180. Council of State Governments, *Book of the States, 1966–67*, 16:307.

181. Council of State Governments, *Book of the States, 1980–81*, transportation stats, 8: 383–401.

182. Council of State Governments, *Book of the States, 1973–1974* (Chicago: Council of State Governments, 1973), 20:353–354.

183. Altshuler and Luberoff, *Mega-Projects*, 192.

184. Altshuler and Luberoff, *Mega-Projects*, 209–211, 214, 217.

185. Federal Transit Administration, "Improving Public Transportation for America's Communities," https://www.transit.dot.gov/about-fta.

186. Peirce, *The Megastates of America*, 207–208.

187. Peirce, *The Megastates of America*, 207–208, 175–176.

188. Kihss, "$2.6 Billion Plan."

189. Peirce, *The Megastates of America*, 643.

190. Peirce, *The Megastates of America*, 642–644.

191. Robert Lindsey, "A Rapid Transit System of the Future," *New York Times*, 13 August 1972, 1.

192. Weiss, "Public Transit."

193. Peter Hall, *Great Planning Disasters* (Berkeley: University of California Press, 1982), 120, 123.

194. Altshuler and Luberoff, Mega-Projects, 192.

195. Council of State Governments, *Book of the States, 1973–74*, 20:353–354.

196. Robert Ashe, "Opinion: MARTA Ready to Help Region Get Around," *Atlanta Journal-Constitution*, 10 March 2018, https://www.myajc.com/news/opinion/opinion-marta-ready-help-region-get-around/faZ4MQi3di7cgwzLU88pAM/; "Atlanta Weighing Transit Expansion," *New York Times*, 13 August 1989, https://www.nytimes.com/1989/08/13/us/atlanta-weighing-transit-expansion.html; "Mass Transit Fare Raised in Atlanta to Expand System," *New York Times*, 24 June 2000, http://www.nytimes.com/2000/06/24/us/mass-transit-fare-raised-in-Atlanta-to-expand-system.html; vehicle miles traveled figures from Atlanta Regional Commission, "2014 Transportation Fact Book," http://documents.atlantaregional.com/transportation/TFB_2014_v17.pdf.

197. Council of State Governments, *Book of the States, 1973–74*, 20:353–354.

198. Weiss, "Public Transit."

199. Eric Jaffe, "2 Notes of Caution on America's 'Record' Mass Transit Year," *Citylab*, 10 March 2015, https://www.citylab.com/transportation/2015/03/2-notes-of-caution-on-americas-record-mass-transit-year/387349/.

200. Minneapolis–St. Paul Metropolitan Council, *Travel Behavior: The 2010 MSP Region Travel Behavior Inventory (TBI) Report Home Interview Survey*, October 2013, https://metrocouncil.org/Transportation/Publications-And-Resources/Travel-Behavior-Inventory.aspx. Today's commuter percentage from Shared-Use Mobility Center, *Twin Cities Shared Mobility Action Plan*, http://sharedusemobilitycenter.org/wp-content/uploads/2017/10/SUMC_TWINCITIES_Web_Final.pdf.

Chapter Seven

1. Council of State Governments, *Book of the States, 1948–1949* (Chicago: Council of State Governments, 1948), 7:334.

2. Owen D. Gutfreund, *20th Century Sprawl: Highways and the Reshaping of the American*

Landscape (New York: Oxford University Press, 2004), 29–31. See also Mark H. Rose and Raymond A. Mohl, *Interstate: Politics and Policy since 1939*, 3rd ed. (Knoxville: University of Tennessee Press, 2012), 8.

3. Council of State Governments, *Book of the States, 1948–49*, 7:335.

4. Council of State Governments, *Book of the States, 1950–51*, 8:310.

5. Rose and Mohl, *Interstate*, 22.

6. Council of State Governments, *Book of the States, 1950–51*, 8:309–311.

7. Council of State Governments, *Book of the States, 1952–1953* (Chicago: Council of State Governments, 1952), 9:269–270.

8. Council of State Governments, *Book of the States, 1954–1955* (Chicago: Council of State Governments, 1954), 10:266.

9. Scott, *American City Planning*, 536–537. Owen Gutfreund, in *20th Century Sprawl*, discusses the federal failure to act on the 1944 plan for interstates, the financial problems faced by states in funding their portions, and an urban/rural split that defined the federal formulas. See also Rose and Mohl, *Interstate*, 31.

10. Rose and Mohl, *Interstate*, 161.

11. Council of State Governments, *Book of the States, 1962–63*, 14:334–337.

12. Danielson and Doig, *New York*, 178–179.

13. Alexander Garvin, *The Planning Game: Lessons from Great Cities* (New York: Norton, 2013). See also Jameson Doig, "Regional Conflict in the New York Metropolis: The Legend of Robert Moses and the Power of the Port Authority," *Urban Studies* 27 (1990): 201–232; Owen Gutfreund, "Rebuilding New York in the Auto Age: Robert Moses and His Highways," in *Robert Moses and the Modern City: The Transformation of New York*, ed. Hilary Ballon and Kenneth T. Jackson (New York: Norton, 2007).

14. J. Burch McMorran, superintendent, New York Department of Public Works, address reprinted in *Proceedings of the Local Government Workshop, June 5–8, 1960*, NAR GUB, William J. Ronan, Series 29 (FA371), Box 23, Folder 271, 31.

15. "The Rockefeller Republican Record," ca. 1964, NAR GUB, Public Relations, Series 27.1 (FA369), Box 2, Folder 103. On highways, see Rose and Mohl, *Interstate*.

16. Connery and Benjamin, *Rockefeller of New York*, 253, 274.

17. "The Rockefeller Republican Record," 9.

18. Danielson and Doig, *New York*, 200.

19. "A New LIRR: Report to Rocky," *Newsday*, 26 February 1965, 40.

20. Byron Porterfield, "Expressway Link Is Opened on Long Island," *New York Times*, 16 August 1962, 29.

21. "Expressway Opened in Suffolk for 1st Time," *Newsday*, 16 August 1962, 34.

22. New York Department of Transportation, "Region 10 at a Glance," https://www.dot.ny.gov/regional-offices/region10/general-info.

23. Joseph F. C. DiMento and Cliff Ellis, *Changing Lanes: Visions and Histories of Urban Freeways* (Cambridge, MA: MIT Press, 2013), 180. Much more on Syracuse and other urban highway programs is presented in chapter 6, 143–208.

24. Leo Egan, "Governor Shuns Rail Aid Report," *New York Times*, 31 March 1960, 1.

25. Long Island Association of Commerce and Industry, transcript of proceedings, 49.

26. William Blair, "Bill Urges Park for Fire Island," *New York Times*, 26 April 1963, 37; Dolores Alexander and Paul Leventhal, "Moses Has Enemies at Both Ends of Bridge," *Newsday*, 17 February 1965, 21; Robert Caro, "Moses Shelves His Bill on Bridge for a Year," *Newsday*, 19 March 1965, 4.

27. "Developing and Managing Water Resources of New York State," 20 December 1967, NAR GUB, Press Office, Series 25.3 (FA368), Box 2, Folder 1532.

28. Council of State Governments, *Book of the States, 1974–75* (Chicago: Council of State Governments, 1974), 20:350–355.

29. Council of State Governments, *Book of the States, 1964–65*, 15:353–357. Reference to 37,000 people comes from Rose and Mohl, *Interstate*, 96.

30. Gutfreund, *20th Century Sprawl*, chapters 2 and 3.

31. Council of State Governments, *Book of the States, 1966–67*, 16:307–313.

32. Council of State Governments, *Book of the States, 1974–75*, 20:350–355.

33. Lois Friedland, "The Rundown, Worn Out, Underfunded Highway Blues," *State Legislatures* 6, no. 3 (March 1980): 15.

34. Council of State Governments, *Book of the States, 1980–81*, 23:383–388.

35. Greg Dierkers and Justin Mattingly, *How States and Territories Fund Transportation: An Overview of Traditional and Nontraditional Strategies* (National Governors Association Center for Best Practices, 2009), https://www.nga.org/files/live/sites/NGA/files/pdf/0907TRANSPORTATIONSTRATEGIES.PDF. Quotation from ASCE from "2017 Infrastructure Report Card," https://www.infrastructurereportcard.org/wp-content/uploads/2017/01/Roads-Final.pdf.

36. Transportation & Climate Initiative, "Summary of Policy Options in State Climate Action Plans," http://www.georgetownclimate.org/files/report/TCI-SummaryofPolicyOptionsinClimateAction(1).PDF.

Chapter Eight

1. Council of State Governments, *Book of the States, 1950–51*, 8:293.

2. Council of State Governments, *Book of the States, 1970–71*, 8:308–322.

3. Council of State Governments, *Book of the States, 1966–67*, 16:294–295.

4. Council of State Governments, *Book of the States, 1968–1969* (Chicago: Council of State Governments, 1968), 17:293.

5. Council of State Governments, *Book of the States, 1966–67*, 16:292, 298.

6. Council of State Governments, *Book of the States, 1980–81*, 8:369–370, 374.

7. Eisenger, *The Rise of the Entrepreneurial State*, 266–289.

8. John B. Clark, Bruce Leslie, and Kenneth P. O'Brien, eds., *SUNY at Sixty: The Promise of the State University of New York* (Albany: SUNY Press, 2010), 18–19.

9. Michael Fabricant and Stephen Brier, *Austerity Blues: Fighting for the Soul of Public Higher Education* (Baltimore: Johns Hopkins University Press, 2016), 53.

10. Clark, Leslie, and O'Brien, *SUNY at Sixty*, 24.

11. Clark, Leslie, and O'Brien, *SUNY at Sixty*, 24.

12. Fabricant and Brier, *Austerity Blues*, 45.

13. Clark, Leslie, and O'Brien, *SUNY at Sixty*, 14.

14. NAR, message to the legislature, 31 January 1961, NAR GUB, Public Relations, Series 27.1 (FA369), Box 2, Folder 70.

15. "Why Not a Central State Campus on LI?," *Newsday*, 29 October 1962, 9C; Martin Buskin, "The Leadership Vacuum," *Newsday*, 18 February 1964, 1C.

16. SUNY, Capital Construction Report, December 1949, NAR GUB, Issue Books, Series 17 (FA363), Box 43, Folder 493, 4.

17. SUNY, "Accent on Higher Education: Activities and Accomplishments of the New York

State Education Department," 1960–1961, Albany, NAR GUB, Issue Books, Series 17 (FA363), Box 45, Folder 499.

18. SUNY, "Accent on Higher Education."

19. SUNY, Capital Construction Report.

20. Bill Becker, "Growth Is a Factor," *New York Times*, 22 July 1962, 87. See also Margaret O'Mara, *Cities of Knowledge: Cold War Science and the Search for the Next Silicon Valley* (Princeton, NJ: Princeton University Press, 2005); Rebecca Lowen, *Creating the Cold War University: The Transformation of Stanford* (Berkeley: University of California Press, 1997); Roger Geiger, *Research and Relevant Knowledge: American Research Universities since World War II* (New York: Oxford University Press, 1993); and Stuart Leslie, *The Cold War and American Science: The Military Industrial Complex at MIT and Stanford* (New York: Columbia University Press, 1993).

21. Herman Wells, chancellor, Indiana University, and Academy for Educational Development, "The Legislature and Higher Education in New York State," report to the legislature's consultant on higher education, 10 December 1964, NAR GUB, William J. Ronan, Series 29 (FA371), Box 46, Folder 529, 11–16.

22. NAR, message to the legislature, 31 January 1961, 12–13. See also O'Mara, *Cities of Knowledge.*

23. SUNY, "The Master Plan," Nelson A. Rockefeller gubernatorial records, William Ronan, Series 29 (FA731), Subseries 2, Box 43, Folder 496; Fabricant and Brier, *Austerity Blues*, 75.

24. Hurd and Benjamin, *Rockefeller in Retrospect*, 22.

25. "State University of New York and Your Children," NAR GUB, Hugh Morrow, Series 21 (FA242), Box 12, Folder 125.

26. SUNY, "The Master Plan," 12.

27. "Report Relative to Meeting the Increasing Demand for Higher Education in New York State—The Heald Report," 15 November 1960, *Public Papers of Nelson A. Rockefeller*, 1272, 1294.

28. "The Heald Report," 1282.

29. Teaford, *The Rise of the States*, 180–181.

30. Connery and Benjamin, *Rockefeller of New York*, 307–323.

31. Hurd and Benjamin, *Rockefeller in Retrospect*, 109.

32. "The Heald Report," 1282.

33. Hurd and Benjamin, *Rockefeller in Retrospect*, 106.

34. Pecorella and Stonecash, *Governing New York State*, 294.

35. SUNY, "The Master Plan." See also SUNY, "Accent on Higher Education," 1960–1961, NAR GUB, Issue Books, Series 17 (FA363), Box 45, Folder 499.

36. "College Population Explosion Hits LI," *Newsday*, 11 August 1964, 20M.

37. Gene Maeroff, "Rejections by State University Set a Record," *New York Times*, 24 June 1971, 29.

38. Clark, Leslie, and O'Brien, *SUNY at Sixty*, 146.

39. Peirce, *The Megastates of America*, 28.

40. SUNY, "The Master Plan." See also SUNY, "Accent on Higher Education."

41. Martin Buskin, "SUNY's Quarter-Century," *Newsday*, 6 December 1973, 1A.

42. "Why Not a Central State Campus on LI?"

43. Wells and Academy for Educational Development, "The Legislature and Higher Education in New York State," 11–16.

44. Buskin, "SUNY's Quarter-Century."

45. Hurd and Benjamin, *Rockefeller in Retrospect*, 114.

46. Connery and Benjamin, *Rockefeller of New York*, 207.

47. Hurd and Benjamin, *Rockefeller in Retrospect*, 106.

48. SUNY, report to NAR, summer 1973, NAR GUB, Departmental Reports, Series 28 (FA370), Box 4, Folder 86.

49. Hurd and Benjamin, *Rockefeller in Retrospect*, 113.

50. "Agency Appraisal Report: SUNY," 1970, NAR GUB, Departmental Reports, Series 28 (FA370), Box 4, Folder 86.

51. M. A. Farber, "Albany Is Seeking the Nation's Best," *New York Times*, 11 January 1967, 29.

52. "Gould Cites Change," *Newsday*, 23 May 1966, 11C.

53. Samuel Gould, "Perils and Promise of College for All," *New York Times*, 12 January 1970, 87.

54. John Allan, "Colleges Speed Bond Sales," *New York Times*, 21 August 1966, 127.

55. "Rockefeller's Fifteen Years."

56. Anthony Adinolfi to John Fitzgerald, 26 October 1970, NYSA, Series 15422-82A, Box 10, Folder: Ernest Boyer Correspondence.

57. *New York State Housing Finance Agency Annual Report, 1966*, New York State Library Digital Collections, 2.

58. "A State Construction Fund: Management for Quality," Architectural Record, January 1971, 55–56.

59. Mildred Schmertz, "Building Types Study: An Analysis of Excellence," Architectural Record, January 1971, 105.

60. SUCF, *Annual Report, 1994–95*, 2–10, New York State Library Digital Collections.

61. Bleeker, *The Politics of Architecture*, 143.

62. Bleeker, *The Politics of Architecture*, 137.

63. Paul Venable Turner, (Cambridge, MA: MIT Press, 1984), 276–291.

64. Hurd and Benjamin, *Rockefeller in Retrospect*, 95.

65. Hurd and Benjamin, *Rockefeller in Retrospect*, 100.

66. "Buffalo Is Not Dogpatch," editorial, *Buffalo Evening News*, 1 April 1961.

67. Address by George A. Dudley, "1962–1970 . . . Years of Challenge and New York's Answer," New York Association of Architects, 20 October 1963, NYSA, Series 15422-82A, Box 2, 1–8; Anthony Adinolfi to E. Stevens, 5 March 1963, NYSA, Series 15422-82A, Box 2, 1–2; Anthony Adinolfi, "Total Professional Service," *AIA Journal* 43, no.6 (June 1965): 61–64.

68. Museum of Modern Art (MOMA), *Architecture for the Arts: The State University of New York College at Purchase* (New York: MOMA, 1971), 5.

69. Schmertz, "Building Types Study," 105.

70. Schmertz, "Building Types Study,"110.

71. Dudley, "1962–1970 . . . Years of Challenge," 4.

72. Norman Klein, Draft #2, 13 June 1963, NYSA, Series 15422-82A, Box 2, 2.

73. Pranay Gupte, "Ban on Group Living Is Spreading," *New York Times*, 7 April 1974, 97.

74. David Smiley, *Pedestrian Modern: Shopping and American Architecture, 1925–1926* (Minneapolis: University of Minnesota Press, 2013).

75. "A State Construction Fund," 55.

76. Hurd and Benjamin, *Rockefeller in Retrospect*, 100.

77. Hurd and Benjamin, *Rockefeller in Retrospect*, 100.

78. Hurd and Benjamin, *Rockefeller in Retrospect*, 100.

79. David Andelman, "Growth of Stony Brook," *New York Times*, 28 March 1971, BQ86.

80. Jerry Parker, "Blacks on Campus," *Newsday*, 16 December 1967, 10W.

81. "Poor in State U's Plan," *Newsday*, 24 September 1968, 15.

82. M. S. Handler, "State U. Expecting 195,000 to Enroll," *New York Times*, 6 September 1970, 50.

83. William Farrell, "Governor Presses Student-Aid Plan," *New York Times*, 9 March 1970, 25.

84. SUNY, "SUNY Fast Facts," https://www.suny.edu/about/fast-facts/.

85. David Andelman, "Stony Brook Starts Recruiting Blacks and Women for Faculty," *New York Times*, 7 April 1972, 30.

86. Thomas Johnson, "Bias Is Charged in State University Hiring," *New York Times*, 17 June 1971, 37.

87. Johnson, "Bias Is Charged."

88. "State U. Is Accused of Bias in its Hiring," *New York Times*, 12 November 1976, 28.

89. Data from State University of New York, https://www.suny.edu/media/suny/content-assets/documents/institutional-research/Diversity-Data-Brief-Aug2015.pdf.

90. Ernest Boyer, "Higher Education: Breaking Up the Youth Ghetto," address to American Association for Higher Education, Chicago, IL, 13 March 1974, NYSA, Series 15422-82, Box 8, Folder: Ernest Boyer, 5.

91. Gene Maeroff, "End of Building Program," *New York Times*, 9 August 1972, 29.

92. Ernest Boyer, "College," *Newsday*, 20 January 1972, 61.

93. Alice Murray, "'College for Poor' Shifting Policies," *New York Times*, 14 October 1973, 109.

94. Fred Hechinger, "Where Should You Put a University?" *New York Times*, 31 December 1967, 99.

95. Bleeker, *The Politics of Architecture*, 166–169. The "social justice theme" was the president's preference as detailed in Anthony Adinolfi to Ernest Boyer, 9 September 1970, NYSA, Series 15422-82A, Box 10, Folder: Ernest Boyer Correspondence.

96. Irvin Molotsky, "Long Island College Builds New Image," *New York Times*, 13 April 1979, B1.

97. State University of New York, https://www.suny.edu/media/suny/content-assets/documents/institutional-research/Diversity-Data-Brief-Aug2015.pdf, 17.

98. Bernard Weinraub, "British Open a College for Dropouts," *New York Times*, 12 January 1971, 37.

99. News release, 28 September 1971, NAR GUB, Hugh Morrow, Series 21.1 (FA242), Box 13, Folder 138, 6, 66, 5.

100. Damon Stetson, "State University to Open a Labor College in City," *New York Times*, 9 September 1971, 39.

101. Will Lissner, "University and City," *New York Times*, 19 February 1967, 179.

102. Anthony Adinolfi to Ernest Boyer, 8 January 1971, NYSA, Series 15422-82A, Box 10, Folder: Ernest Boyer Correspondence.

103. Peter Kihss, "State Starts Plans," *New York Times*, 4 August 1969, 1; UDC Annual Report 1970, NYSA, Box: UDC Annual Reports, 56.

104. Schmertz, "Building Types Study," 127. See also UDC Annual Report 1971, 40.

105. Hurd and Benjamin, *Rockefeller in Retrospect*, 219.

106. Harold Faber, "State Ends Community College Expansion," *New York Times*, 18 September 1974, 37.

107. Judith Cummins, "State University Raises Tuition," *New York Times*, 25 March 1976, 77.

108. Ada Louise Huxtable, "Some Awful Building Truths," *New York Times*, 16 April 1972, D21.

109. Iver Peterson, "Stony Brook's Growing Pains," *New York Times*, 16 January 1977, 390.

110. News release, 28 September 1971, NAR GUB, Hugh Morrow, Series 21.1 (FA242), Box 13, Folder 138.

111. Oscar Langford to Frank Fordham, 3 December 1976, NYSA, Series 15422-82, Box 2, Folder: Audit Report on University Space Management, 1–5.

112. Clark, Leslie, and O'Brien, *SUNY at Sixty*, 177, 182–183.

113. Clark, Leslie, and O'Brien, *SUNY at Sixty*, 176.

114. Clark, Leslie, and O'Brien, *SUNY at Sixty*, 182.

115. Linda Greenhouse, "Bond Issue Sold Out," *New York Times*, 17 September 1976, 45.

116. Ari Goldman, "Itinerary of State U. Chancellor," *New York Times*, 3 April 1978, 35.

117. Samuel Weiss, "SUNY Plant Needs a Physical," *New York Times*, 11 November 1979, EDUC26.

118. Hurd and Benjamin, *Rockefeller in Retrospect*, 116.

119. Cuomo, *The New York Idea*, 65.

120. Cuomo, *The New York Idea*, 64.

121. Pecorella and Stonecash, *Governing New York State*, 314.

122. Data from SUNY, "SUNY Fast Facts."

123. Nelson A. Rockefeller Institute of Government and University of Buffalo Regional Institute, *How SUNY Matters: Economic Impacts of the State University of New York*, June 2011, http://rockinst.org/wp-content/uploads/2018/02/2011-06-01-How_SUNY_Matters.pdf, 1–41.

124. Nelson A. Rockefeller Institute of Government and University of Buffalo Regional Institute, *How SUNY Matters*, 45–47, 86.

125. Eisenger, *The Rise of the Entrepreneurial State*, 182–191.

126. Nelson A. Rockefeller Institute of Government and University of Buffalo Regional Institute, *How SUNY Matters*.

127. Pecorella and Stonecash, *Governing New York State*, 295.

128. Nelson A. Rockefeller Institute of Government and University of Buffalo Regional Institute, *How SUNY Matters*, 5.

129. Clark, Leslie, and O'Brien, *SUNY at Sixty*, 142.

130. Clark, Leslie, and O'Brien, *SUNY at Sixty*, 50. On the corruption issues, see Liz Young, "Loss of Alain Kaloyeros Has Stalled Nanotech Growth in Albany, Authors of Report Say," *Albany Business Review*, 2 May 2018, https://www.bizjournals.com/albany/news/2018/05/02/loss-of-alain-kaloyeros-has-stalled-nanotech.html.

131. Clark, Leslie, and O'Brien, *SUNY at Sixty*, 30.

132. Turner, *Campus*, 267.

133. University of California San Francisco, "Economic and Fiscal Impact," https://www.ucsf.edu/about/economic-impact-report#the-2010-report.

134. Peirce, *The Megastates of America*, 569, 604–611.

135. Peirce, *The Megastates of America*, 205.

136. Peirce, *The Megastates of America*, 310.

137. "Number of State-Supported Junior Colleges Rising," *New York Times*, 9 April 1963, 37.

138. Teaford, *The Rise of the States*, 183.

139. Michelle Nickerson and Darren Dochuck, eds., *Sunbelt Rising: The Politics of Space, Place, and Region* (Philadelphia: University of Pennsylvania Press, 2011), 50–51.

140. American Academy of Arts & Sciences, *Public Research Universities: Changes in State Funding*, 2015, https://www.amacad.org/multimedia/pdfs/publications/researchpapersmonographs/PublicResearchUniv_ChangesInStateFunding.pdf.

141. Economic statistics from Greg Bump, "UW–Madison's Economic Impact to Wisconsin

$15 Billion Annually, Study Says," 14 April 2015, University of Wisconsin–Madison, http://news.wisc.edu/uw-madisons-economic-impact-to-wisconsin-15-billion-annually-study-says/.

142. Ethnic breakdown from Office of the Registrar, University of Wisconsin–Madison, https://registrar.wisc.edu/wp-content/uploads/sites/36/2018/02/report-enrollment-2018spring.pdf, 2, table 2.

143. University of Wisconsin–Madison, *Budget in Brief: Budget Report 2016–2017*, https://budget.wisc.edu/content/uploads/2016/11/Budget-Brief-2016–17.pdf. Total nonresident numbers from Office of the Registrar, University of Wisconsin–Madison, https://registrar.wisc.edu/wp-content/uploads/sites/36/2018/02/report-enrollment-2018spring.pdf, 2, table 2.

144. Economic Modeling Specialists International, "Fact Sheet: Demonstrating the Economic Value of North Carolina State University to Wake County and the State of North Carolina," https://www.ncsu.edu/content/uploads/2015/03/NC-State-Wake-County-impact.pdf.

145. "Analysis Finds UNC–Chapel Hill and UNC Health Care Medical Center Contribute over $7 Billion to North Carolina Economy," *University of North Carolina at Chapel Hill News*, 18 February 2015, http://uncnews.unc.edu/2015/02/18/analysis-finds-unc-chapel-hill-unc-health-care-medical-center-contribute-7-billion-north-carolina-economy/.

Chapter Nine

1. Fabricant and Brier, *Austerity Blues*, 55.

2. CUNY, University History, "The Birth of a Modern University," http://www2.cuny.edu/about/administration/chancellor/university-history/.

3. Robert Terte, "A Free University Proposed for City," *New York Times*, 24 January 1961, 17.

4. "A City University Is Sought in Bill," *New York Times*, 23 December 1960, 17

5. Edward Fiske, "After 8 years of Open Admissions City College Still Debates Effect," *New York Times*, 19 June 1978, NJ13.

6. Fabricant and Brier, *Austerity Blues*, 66–67.

7. Fred Hechinger, "New University Issue: The City and the State," *New York Times*, 21 November 1965, 9.

8. Robert Terte, "Report to State Senate Assails Free Tuition," *New York Times*, 21 November 1964, 30.

9. Fabricant and Brier, *Austerity Blues*, 69.

10. "Gov. Urges Special Colleges," *New York Times*, 16 January 1966, 76.

11. Fabricant and Brier, *Austerity Blues*, 68–80.

12. Leonard Buder, "City University Maps Big Expansion," *New York Times*, 3 July 1966, 36.

13. An excellent compendium on urban renewal in Newark past and present is available at Rutgers University Libraries, "The Newark Experience: Decline, Development and Renewal," https://libguides.rutgers.edu/c.php?g=336802&p=2272421. See also Julia Rabig, *The Fixers: Devolution, Development, and Civil Society in Newark, 1960–1990* (Chicago: University of Chicago Press, 2016); Mark Krasovic, *The Newark Frontier: Community Action in the Great Society* (Chicago: University of Chicago Press, 2016).

14. Fred Hechinger, "The City University Is Offered Aid by Governor," *New York Times*, 6 March 1966, 39.

15. Fabricant and Brier, *Austerity Blues*, 68–80.

16. Thomas Brady, "City College Agreement Reached," *New York Times*, 3 May 1969, 23.

17. Albert Bowker, "City U. Faces Up to the Urban Realities," *New York Times*, 12 January 1970, 82.

18. Gene Maeroff, "Effects of Open Admission Stir New Dispute at City University," *New York Times*, 7 June 1974, 73. Bronx Community College figures from Gene Maeroff, "This Side of Paradise," *New York Times*, 27 May 1973, 202.

19. M. A. Farber, "Many from City Apply to State University," *New York Times*, 22 February 1970, 63.

20. Michael Harrington, "Keep Open Admissions Open," *New York Times*, 2 November 1975, 261.

21. "Panel Urges City Keep University," *New York Times*, 11 April 1972, 30.

22. Leonard Buder, "On Open Admissions," *New York Times*, 11 July 1969, 38.

23. Harrington, "Keep Open Admissions Open."

24. M. S. Handler, "City U. Open Enrollment Plan Ready," *New York Times*, 28 December 1969, 58.

25. The area-to-student ratio at CUNY was 95 square feet per person, compared with 183 square feet per person at SUNY and 329 square feet per person at private schools in New York State. Carter Horsley, "CUNY Casts Wide Rental Net," *New York Times*, 9 September 1973, 443.

26. Barbara Thatcher, "Free Tuition as Public Policy," *New York Times*, 26 December 1975, 31.

27. Wolfgang Saxon, "City University," *New York Times*, 31 May 1976, 21.

28. Robert Reno, "Regents Urge Tuition at City U," *Newsday*, 12 December 1975, 7.

29. Edward Fiske, "Tuition Imposed at City University," *New York Times*, 2 June 1976, 1.

30. Fabricant and Brier, *Austerity Blues*, 88.

31. CUNY, "CUNY's 2015–2016 State Operating Budget Priorities," http://www.supportcuny.org/site/DocServer/Gold_sheet_2015_revised_1-30-15_nocrops.pdf?docID=462.

32. Spending data from State of New York, *FY 2018 Executive Budget Briefing Book*, https://www.budget.ny.gov/pubs/archive/fy18archive/exec/fy1718littlebook/HigherEducation.pdf; New York State Education Department, "Higher Ed in NY," http://www.highered.nysed.gov/ocue/he/structureofhe.html, last updated 17 January 2017; Vivian Yee, "Cuomo to Continue Shrinking State's Share of CUNY's Costs," *New York Times*, 14 January 2016, A23.

33. Pecorella and Stonecash, *Governing New York State*, 12–13, 109, 295.

34. Outcalt, Guenther, Rode and Bonebrake Architects, Cleveland, Cleveland State University Master Plan, 1966, April 1966, 2; Michael Schwartz Library, "Cleveland State University: A Brief History," http://www.clevelandmemory.org/csu/.

35. "America's Top Colleges: Cleveland State University," *Forbes*, 2017, https://www.forbes.com/colleges/cleveland-state-university/.

36. See O'Mara, *Cities of Knowledge*; Judith Rodin, *The University and Urban Revival: Out of the Ivory Tower and into the Streets* (Philadelphia: University of Pennsylvania Press, 2007); special section on Health Care and Urban Revitalization, Jared Day, ed., *Journal of Urban History* 42, no. 2 (March 2016); David Perry and Wim Wiewel, *The University as Urban Developer: Case Studies and Analysis* (Armonk, NY: M. E. Sharpe, 2005).

37. University of Maryland BioPark website, http://www.umbiopark.com/. Student demographics from University of Maryland Baltimore, "UMB Fast Facts," http://www.umaryland.edu/about-umb/umb-fast-facts/. City demographics from Baltimore city government, "Baltimore City Demographics at a Glance," http://planning.baltimorecity.gov/sites/default/files/2a_City%20Profile%20-%203.30.16_0.pdf.

38. Center for Strategic Economic Research, "Economic Impacts of the University of California, Los Angeles," 12 July 2013, http://www.ucla.edu/economic-impact/pdf/ucla-economic-impact-report-2013.pdf.

39. University of California San Francisco, "Economic and Fiscal Impact."

40. Georgia Tech, "Creating the Next . . . Economic Impact," http://www.gatech.edu/creating-next/economic-impact; University of Alabama at Birmingham, "UAB Annual Impact on the Alabama Economy," https://www.uab.edu/impact/.

Chapter Ten

1. Alexander von Hoffman, "The Origins of American Housing Reform," Joint Center for Housing Studies, Harvard University, 5 August 1998, https://www.innovations.harvard.edu/sites/default/files/von_hoffman_w98-2.pdf, 25.

2. Council of State Governments, *Book of the States, 1960–61*, 13:417–421.

3. Council of State Governments, *Book of the States, 1950–51*, 8:390.

4. Council of State Governments, *Book of the States, 1962–63*, 14:458, summary of data from 456–459.

5. New York Committee on Slum Clearance, *Slum Clearance Progress: Title I, NYC* (1957), Columbia University Library.

6. Joseph P. McMurray, "The People Decide for Housing," 1955–1958, Executive Department, McMurray Commissioner of Housing, NAR GUB, William J. Ronan, Series 29 (FA371), Box 11, Folder 127, 11.

7. McMurray, "The People Decide for Housing."

8. Department of Audit and Control, Audit Report on Financial and Operating Practices of NYSHA, Report no. NY 3-67, 1964, NYSA, Series 12309, 17–18, 26.

9. McMurray, "The People Decide for Housing," 39.

10. John Callahan, "Rockefeller Acts to Add to Housing," *New York Times*, 22 March 1959, R1. See also Furman Center, "State of New York City's Subsidized Housing: 2011," http://furmancenter.org/files/publications/SHIPReportFinal.pdf.

11. Press release, 19 October 1961, Governor's Office, NAR GUB, Hugh Morrow, Series 21.1 (FA242), Box 22, Folder 229, 1.

12. NAR, message to the legislature, 18 March 1959, NAR GUB, Record 15, Series 29, Box 2, Folder 9, 1.

13. John B. Callahan, "Governor to Spur Housing Projects," *New York Times*, 29 March 1959, R1.

14. New York State Housing Finance Agency Annual Report, 1963–64, New York State Library Digital Collections, 6.

15. Hurd and Benjamin, *Rockefeller in Retrospect*, 85.

16. Connery and Benjamin, *Rockefeller of New York*, 261.

17. Hurd and Benjamin, *Rockefeller in Retrospect*, 200.

18. Persico, *The Imperial Rockefeller*, 162.

19. "A Year of Innovation and Growth," *Annual Report 1960–1961*, New York State Division of Housing and Community Renewal, NAR GUB, William J. Ronan, Series 29 (FA371), Box 11, Folder 129.

20. New York State Housing Finance Agency Annual Report, 1961–1962, New York State Library Digital Collections, 2.

21. Department of Audit and Control, "Audit Report on Financial and Operating Practices of NYSHA," 17–18, NYSA, Series 12309-97, 20–21; Legislative Commission on Expenditure Review, "Preliminary and Confidential: Middle-Income Housing in New York," 25 January 1966, NYSA, Series 12309-97, Box 22, 1–34.

22. Connery and Benjamin, *Rockefeller of New York*, 261.

23. Furman Center, "State of New York City's Subsidized Housing," 35.

24. *New York State Division of Housing and Community Renewal Annual Report*, 1960–1961, NAR GUB, Series 29, Box 11, Folder 128, 11.

25. Study Committee for Urban Middle Income Housing, "Space for Urban Living: A Plan of Action to Provide Urban Homes for Middle-Income Families Utilizing Air Rights Over Public Facilities," 1961, NAR GUB, Hugh Morrow, Series 21.1 (FA242), Box 22, Folder 229, 8–13.

26. Press release, 19 October 1961, Governor's Office, NAR GUB, Hugh Morrow, Series 21.1 (FA242), Box 22, Folder 229, 2.

27. Newbold Morris to James Gaynor, 22 November 1961, NAR GUB, Hugh Morrow, Series 21.1 (FA242), Box 22, Folder 229.

28. Statement of James Gaynor, New York City, 27 September 1967, NYSA, Series 12309, 4.

29. Edith Asbury, "Logue Proposes a Town," *New York Times*, 22 July 1971,1.

30. Charles Urstadt, "Should Taxes Pay for Good Design?," *Cooperator*, November 1971, 7.

31. Square footage from Furman Center, "State of New York City's Subsidized Housing."

32. Connery and Benjamin, *Rockefeller of New York*, 261.

33. Charles Urstadt, "For City Housing, Build on Big Scale," *New York Times*, 26 November 1972, R1.

34. New York State Division of Housing and Community Renewal, Agency Appraisal Report, 15 July 1970, NAR GUB, Departmental Reports, Series 28 (FA370), Box 2, Folder 47.

35. New York State Division of Housing and Community Renewal, "The Urban Frontier," 1 April 1966–31 March 1967, Annual Report, NAR GUB, Press Office, Series 25.3 (FA368), Box 69, Folder 1522.

36. New York State Division of Housing and Community Renewal, Agency Appraisal Report, 10.

37. New York State Division of Housing and Community Renewal, Agency Appraisal Report, 12.

38. Urstadt, "For City Housing."

39. Charles Urstadt, speech to Annual Housing Conference of the UHF, New York City, 22 March 1969, NYSA, Series 12309.

40. New York State Division of Housing and Community Renewal, "Action for Housing," 31 March 1969, NAR GUB, Record 15, Series 3, Box 70, Folder 1586.

41. New York State Division of Housing and Community Renewal, "The Urban Frontier."

42. New York State Housing Finance Agency Annual Report, 1964–1965, 15.

43. New York State Division of Housing and Community Renewal, "The Urban Frontier," 6–12.

44. Urstadt, "For City Housing."

45. Charles Urstadt to Nelson Rockefeller, Operations and Status Report #10, 10 July 1972, NYSA, Series 12309.

46. Legislative Commission on Expenditure Review, "Preliminary and Confidential." 37.

47. R. Allen Hays, *The Federal Government and Urban Housing: Ideology and Change in Public Policy* (Albany: SUNY Press, 1995), chapters 4 and 5. A HUD-sponsored study in 2000, for instance, found that 37 percent of the residents in the LIHTC projects studied relied upon Section 8: US Department of Housing and Urban Development, *Assessment of the Economic and Social Characteristics of LIHTC Residents and Neighborhoods: Final Report*, August 2000, https://www.huduser.gov/publications/PDF/lihtc.pdf.

48. Bleeker, *The Politics of Architecture*, 126–127.

49. Urstadt to Rockefeller, Operations and Status Report #10.

50. Charles Urstadt to Norman Hurd, 21 March 1971, NAR GUB, Departmental Reports, Series 28 (FA370), Box 2, Folder 47. See also Lee Goodwin to Albert Hinkle, 30 May 1973, NYSA, Series 12309, Folder: Program Analysis and Review.

51. Murray Schumach, "Co-op City: A Symptom of Mitchell-Lama Ills," *New York Times*, 18 June 1975, 38.

52. Legislative Commission on Expenditure Review, "Preliminary and Confidential," 1–34.

53. Fred Hecht to Charles Urstadt, 14 March 1972, Division of Housing and Community Renewal, NYSA, Series 12309, Folder: Surcharges.

54. Mrs. Claire Rudnick to Lee Goodwin, 15 September 1973, NYSA, Series 12309, Folder: Surcharges.

55. Daniel Rose, "Point of View," *New York Times*, 5 October 1975, 291.

56. "Lessons to Be Learned from U.D.C.'s Collapse," *New York Times*, 9 November 1975, E8.

57. Charles Urstadt to Norman Hurd, 21 March 1971, NAR GUB, Departmental Reports, Series 28 (FA370), Box 2, Folder 47, 2.

58. *Housing Finance Agency Annual Report 1973*, New York State Library Digital Collections, 3.

59. Legislative Commission on Expenditure Review, "Preliminary and Confidential," 76–78.

60. Ravitch, *So Much to Do*, 112–113.

61. New York State Housing Finance Agency, "Policy Review Paper of the New York State Housing Finance Agency," 1982, New York State Library, 3, 9, 13, 20, 22, 26.

62. *New York State Housing Finance Agency, Annual Report*, 1977, New York State Library Digital Collections, 2; *New York State Housing Finance Agency, Annual Report*, 1978, New York State Library Digital Collections, 4, 5.

63. Furman Center, "State of New York City's Subsidized Housing," 35.

64. Robert Alden, "Point of View," *New York Times*, 8 February 1970, 282.

65. Bleeker, *The Politics of Architecture*, 126–127.

66. Hurd and Benjamin, *Rockefeller in Retrospect*, 207–208.

67. Council of State Governments, *Book of the States, 1973–74*, 20:443–447.

68. "UDC in 72: A Mini-Report," NAR GUB, Press Office, Series 25.3 (FA368), Box 75, Folder 1710, 8.

69. Brilliant, *The Urban Development Corporation*, 68.

70. "UDC in 72," 48.

71. "UDC in 72," 70.

72. "UDC in 72," 8.

73. "Urban Agreement Reached," *New York Times*, 22 May 1969, 1.

74. "UDC in 72," 71.

75. "UDC in 72," 77. See also UDC Annual Report 1973, 38–43, NYSA, Box: UDC Annual Reports.

76. Paul Goldberger, "UDC's Architecture Has Raised Public Standard," *New York Times*, 3 March 1975, 43.

77. UDC Annual Report 1973, 36.

78. Allan Talbot, "Rules on Subsidies Spur Housing Segregation," *New York Times*, 4 August 1974, 274.

79. Arthur Gordon, "The Viability of the Urban Development Corporation," State of New York Department of Audit and Control, 1979, New York State Library Digital Collections, 3.

80. George Sternlieb, "A Housing Shortage No Longer the Issue," *New York Times*, 13 July 1975, 212.

81. Hurd and Benjamin, *Rockefeller in Retrospect*, 208–209.

82. "UDC in 72," 8.

83. Edith Asbury, "Federal Freeze Imperils Housing Projects in Area," *New York Times*, 4 February 1973, 1.

84. Joseph Fried, "Urban Development Unit Curbed," *New York Times*, 6 October 1974, 1.

85. Linda Greenhouse, "Expert Criticizes UDC's Operation," *New York Times*, 16 October 1975, 31.

86. "Carey Asks $178 million in Loan," *New York Times*, 24 January 1975, 61.

87. Linda Greenhouse, "$90 Million Aid for UDC Voted," *New York Times*, 5 March 1975, 1.

88. The complicated story of the bailout is described in far greater detail in Ravitch, *So Much to Do*, 45–70. See also Linda Greenhouse, "Banks Refuse Carey Plea," *New York Times*, 25 February 1975, 1.

89. Greenhouse, "$90 Million Aid."

90. Linda Greenhouse, "Big Banks to Lend UDC $140 Million," *New York Times*, 27 March 1975, 1.

91. Linda Greenhouse, "Legislature Votes UDC $228 Million," *New York Times*, 1 May 1975, 1.

92. Edith Asbury, "Chairman Reports UDC Is Doing Well," *New York Times*, 20 November 1975, 44.

93. Linda Greenhouse, "After Five Months, the Crisis Mooted UDC," *New York Times*, 24 July 1975, 26.

94. Gordon, "Viability of Urban Development Corporation," 7, 11–12.

95. Gordon, "Viability of Urban Development Corporation," 8, 10.

96. For an overview of New York's role in shaping the new paradigm, see Nicholas Dagen Bloom and Mathew Lasner, *Affordable Housing in New York: The People, Places, and Policies That Transformed a City* (Princeton, NJ: Princeton University Press, 2015).

97. Cuomo, *The New York Idea*, 141–144.

98. Percentage of state contribution to city from Abigail Savitch-Lew, "Cuomo and De Blasio: Political Foes . . . but Affordable Housing Partners?," citylimits.org, https://citylimits.org/2018/03/16/cuomo-and-de-blasio-political-foes-but-affordable-housing-partners/.

99. Frug and Barron, *City Bound*, 118. See also Roberta Gold, *When Tenants Claimed the City: The Struggle for Citizenship in New York City Housing* (Urbana: University of Illinois Press, 2014).

100. Council of State Governments, *Book of the States, 1972–73*, 19:446.

101. Council of State Governments, *Book of the States, 1973–74*, 20:443–447.

102. Council of State Governments, *Book of the States, 1970–71*, 18:445.

103. Council of State Governments, *Book of the States, 1973–74*, 20:444.

104. Council of State Governments, *Book of the States, 1980–81*, 8:486.

105. Geneva Overholser, "The States and the Housing Crunch," *State Legislatures* 7, no. 4 (April 1981): 4–10.

106. Scally, "States, Housing and Innovation," 11. See also Moulton, "Access and Sustainability for First Time Homebuyers: The Evolving Role of State Housing Finance Agencies," Harvard University Joint Center for Housing Studies, October 2013, http://www.jchs.harvard.edu/sites/jchs.harvard.edu/files/hbtl-10.pdf.

107. Scally, "States, Housing and Innovation," 11. See also Stephanie Moulton, "Access and Sustainability."

108. Florida Housing Finance Corporation, *Creating Inclusive Communities in Florida*,

https://www.floridahousing.org/docs/default-source/press/newsroom/publications/2017 nimby-book.pdf?sfvrsn=2.

109. Shimberg Center for Housing Studies, University of Florida, *2016 Rental Market Study*, July 2016, http://www.floridahousing.org/FH-ImageWebDocs/Newsroom/Publications/MarketStudies/2016/2016_Full_RMS_final.pdf, 6.

110. Corianne Payton Scally, "The Past and Future of Housing Policy Innovation: The Case of US State Housing Trust Funds," *Housing Studies* 27, no. 1 (January 2012): 129.

111. Elizabeth J. Mueller and Alex Schwartz, "Reversing the Tide: Will States and Local Governments House the Poor as Federal Direct Subsidies Decline?" *Journal of the American Planning Association* 74 (8 February 2008): 122–135, 124.

Chapter Eleven

1. Thomas Sugrue, *Sweet Land of Liberty: The Forgotten Struggle for Civil Rights in the North* (New York: Random House, 2008); Sugrue, *The Origins of the Urban Crisis*. On race and the suburbs, see Jackson, *Crabgrass Frontier*; Wiese, *Places of Their Own*; William H. Wilson, *Hamilton Park: A Planned Black Community in Dallas* (Baltimore: Johns Hopkins University Press, 1998); Kruse, *New Suburban History*; Shirley Ann Wilson Moore, *To Place Our Deeds: The African American Community in Richmond, California, 1910–1963* (Berkeley: University of California Press, 2000); Bruce D. Haynes, *Red Lines, Black Spaces: The Politics of Race and Space in a Black Middle-Class Suburb* (New Haven, CT: Yale University Press, 2001); Steven Gregory, *Black Corona: Race and the Politics of Place in an Urban Community* (Princeton, NJ: Princeton University Press, 1998); Jeff Wiltse, *Contested Waters: A Social History of Swimming Pools in America* (Chapel Hill: University of North Carolina Press, 2007); Martha Biondi, *To Stand and Fight: The Struggle for Civil Rights in Postwar New York City* (Cambridge, MA: Harvard University Press, 2003); and Peter R. Eisenstadt, *Rochdale Village: Robert Moses, 6,000 Families, and New York City's Great Experiment in Integrated Housing* (Ithaca, NY: Cornell University Press, 2010).

2. "Negro Population Growing in Suffolk," *New York Times*, 23 February 1969, 37.

3. Martin Tolchin, "The Housing Tangle," *New York Times*, 26 November 1971, 41.

4. "UDC in 72," 19.

5. Brilliant, *The Urban Development Corporation*, 16.

6. "UDC in 72," 8–19. See also UDC Annual Report 1971.

7. Peirce, *The Megastates of America*, 29.

8. See Bloom, *Public Housing That Worked*, for details on the Forest Hills issues and the broader debates about public housing decentralization.

9. Regional Plan Association, *Westchester County Supplement to the Second Regional Plan* (New York, 1971), 64.

10. Danielson and Doig, *New York*, 59.

11. On the history of the suburbs, see Dolores Hayden, *Redesigning the American Dream: The Future of Housing, Work, and Family Life* (New York: Norton, 1984); Jackson, *Crabgrass Frontier*; Robert Fishman, *Bourgeois Utopias: The Rise and Fall of Suburbia* (New York: Basic Books, 1987); Stilgoe, *Borderland*; Richard Harris, *Unplanned Suburbs: Toronto's American Tragedy, 1900 to 1950* (Baltimore: Johns Hopkins University Press, 1996); Rosalyn Baxandall and Elizabeth Ewen, *Picture Windows: How the Suburbs Happened* (New York: Basic Books, 2000); Nicolaides, *My Blue Heaven*; and Sam Bass Warner Jr., *Streetcar Suburbs: The Process of Growth in Boston, 1870–1900* (Cambridge, MA: Harvard University Press,1962).

12. Stern, Mellins, and Fishman, *New York 1960*, 1072–1088.

13. Lawrence O'Kane, "Negro Mobility on Rise in State," *New York Times*, 4 May 1961, 37. The African American count included some Asians listed as minorities, but not Puerto Ricans.

14. Danielson and Doig, *New York*, 64.

15. David Shipler, "Lawsuit to Challenge Suburban Zoning," *New York Times*, 29 June 1969, 39.

16. "UDC in 72," 26.

17. Hurd and Benjamin, *Rockefeller in Retrospect*, 210–211.

18. "Nine Town Plan Set for Westchester," *New York Times*, 13 February 1972, 422.

19. Linda Greenhouse, "Low Income State Housing Due in Rural Westchester," *New York Times*, 21 June 1972, 1.

20. "Housing Opposed in Westchester," *New York Times*, 23 July 1972, 50.

21. Brilliant, *The Urban Development Corporation*, 143.

22. Linda Greenhouse, "Suburbs Fighting State Agencies Plan," *New York Times*, 17 July 1972, 26.

23. Linda Greenhouse, "Support for Housing Projects," *New York Times*, 26 January 1973, 71.

24. Greenhouse, "Suburbs Fighting."

25. Peirce, *The Megastates of America*, 30.

26. Linda Greenhouse, "Accord Reached on Bill," *New York Times*, 20 May 1973, 28.

27. Robert Lindsey, "Experts Say Housing Programs Fail to Open Suburbs," *New York Times*, 11 November 1975, 18.

28. Peirce, *The Megastates of America*, 151.

29. Peter Siskind, "Suburban Growth and Its Discontents," in *The New Suburban History*, ed. Kevin Kruse and Thomas Sugrue (Princeton, NJ: Princeton University Press, 2006), 176–178.

30. See the chronology in David Kirp, John Dwyer, and Larry Rosenthal, *Our Town: Race, Housing, and the Soul of Suburbia* (New Brunswick, NJ: Rutgers University Press, 1997), 197–230; David O'Reilly, "With 20-Year Plan Mount Laurel writes 'New Chapter' in Long Affordable-Housing saga," *Philadelphia Inquirer*, 7 December 2016, http://www.philly.com/philly/news/20161207_With_20-year_plan__Mount_Laurel_writes__new_chapter__in_long_affordable-housing_saga.html; Knaap, Nedovic-Budic, and Carbonell, *Planning for States and Nation States*, 131–188.

31. O'Reilly, "With 20-Year Plan."

32. Knaap, Nedovic-Budic, and Carbonell, *Planning for States and Nation States*, 97–123.

33. See, for instance, Glenn Thrush, "Under Ben Carson, HUD Scales Back Fair Housing Enforcement," *New York Times*, 28 March 2018, A1.

Chapter Twelve

1. "Tuttle Is Counsel of Anti-Bias Group," *New York Times*, 8 August 1944, 20.

2. NAR, speech on receiving Human Relations Award, Urban League of Greater New York, 13 December 1962, NAR GUB, William J. Ronan, Series 29 (FA371), Box 2, Folder 12.

3. *New York State Committee against Discrimination Annual Report 1959*, NAR GUB, William J. Ronan, Series 29 (FA371), Box 19, Folder 201, 27.

4. Richard Wiebe to William Ronan, 22 April 1963, NAR GUB, Departmental Reports, Series 28 (FA370), Box 2, Folder 47, 1, 3.

5. Wiebe to Ronan, 22 April 1963.

6. "Forest Hills: A Bridge?," *Cooperator* (UHF), December 1971, 4.

7. Council of State Governments, *Book of the States, 1960–61*, 13:417–421.

8. *New York State Committee against Discrimination Annual Report 1959*, 23–26.

9. Leonard Buder, "City's Million Negroes Still Face Color Barrier," *New York Times*, 13 March 1962, 1.

10. NAR, speech on receiving Human Relations Award, 1–3.

11. Farnsworth Fowle, "Rockefeller Gives Sermon in Harlem on Civil Rights," *New York Times*, 29 January 1962, 1.

12. "SCAD Ruling on Long Island," *New York Times*, 22 December 1961, 19.

13. John Stevens, "Negro Wins Right to a Lease in Rye," *New York Times*, 14 July 1962, 8.

14. "2 State Agencies Fight Realty Bias," *New York Times*, 12 August 1962, 81.

15. Douglas Dales, "Governor Signs Bill Extending Ban on Housing Discrimination," *New York Times*, 23 April 1963, 1.

16. "Housing Powers of State Upheld," *New York Times*, 3 November 1963, 64.

17. "Rights Suit Wins House for Negro," *New York Times*, 10 April 1964, 20.

18. "Rights Suit Wins House for Negro."

19. Martin Gansberg, "State Human Rights Unit," *New York Times*, 2 October 1967, 1.

20. Merrill Folsom, "Abolition Urged for Rights Unit," *New York Times*, 25 May 1968, 31.

21. Samuel Kaplan, "Rights Unit Slack on Housing," *New York Times*, 3 June 1965, 23.

22. Homer Bigart, "NAACP to Back Agency Revision," *New York Times*, 7 February 1967, 28.

23. "Rockefeller Urged to End Human Rights Commission," *New York Times*, 4 March 1967, 22.

24. Buder, "City's Million Negroes."

25. Dick Zander, "The Richest Legacy: Second," *Newsday*, 17 April 1969, 10.

26. Folsom, "Abolition Urged for Rights Unit."

27. "State to Revise Its Rights Group," *New York Times*, 26 June 1967, 33.

28. Edward Burks, "Magnum Pledges a Busy Time," *New York Times*, 1 August 1967, 18.

29. *New York State Division of Human Rights, Annual Report, 1972*, NAR GUB, Press Office, Series 25.3 (FA368), Box 75, Folder 1707. Figures for awards from *New York State Division of Human Rights, Annual Report, 1974*, New York State Library Digital Collections, table 6.

30. Dick Zander, "The Rockefeller Years," *Newsday*, 18 April 1969, 10.

31. Scott, *American City Planning*, 632.

32. Nancy Moran, "State Held Lax on Fair Housing," *New York Times*, 22 November 1969, 34.

33. Agis Salpukas, "Local Laws Are Curbing Bias in Housing," *New York Times*, 21 September 1969, 82.

34. Carter Horsely, "Are Cooperatives as Exclusive as They Were? No and Yes," *New York Times*, 4 September 1977, 160.

35. E. J. Dionne Jr., "Rights Division Says Low Budget Hampers Its Enforcement Laws," *New York Times*, 5 March 1978, 47.

36. *New York State Division of Human Rights, Annual Report, 1988*, New York State Library Digital Collections, 6.

37. Michael Winerip, "Lines That Divide Towns and Races," *New York Times*, 22 December 1985, E7.

38. George Goodman, "Housing Bias Pervasive," *New York Times*, 20 May 1984, R7.

39. Alan Finder, "Blacks Remain Shut Out of Housing in White Areas," *New York Times*, 13 March 1989, B1.

40. John Rather, "Nassau and Suffolk Address Housing Bias," *New York Times*, 12 February 2006, L110.

41. Summarized from narrative in Herbert Ruffin, *Uninvited Neighbors: African Americans in Silicon Valley, 1769–1990* (Norman: University of Oklahoma Press, 2014), chapter 5, 92–121.

42. Ruffin, *Uninvited Neighbors*, 117. See also Daniel Martinez HoSang, "Racial Liberalism and the Rise of the Sunbelt West: The Defeat of Fair Housing on the 1964 California Ballot," in Nickerson and Dochuck, *Sunbelt Rising*, 188–213.

43. Council of State Governments, *Book of the States, 1970–71*, 18:445

44. Council of State Governments, *Book of the States, 1980–81*, 8:488.

45. Tolchin, "The Housing Tangle." See also Bloom, *Suburban Alchemy*.

Chapter Thirteen

1. Draft press release, ca. 1963–1964, NAR GUB, Hugh Morrow, Series 21 (FA242), Box 20, Folder 215, 3.

2. Council of State Governments, *Book of the States, 1950–51*, 8:326.

3. Council of State Governments, *Book of the States, 1950–51*, 8:326.

4. Zander, "The Rockefeller Years."

5. New York State Health and Mental Hygiene Facilities Improvement Corporation, Report to the Governor, 1969, NAR GUB, Series 3, Box 70, Folder 1584.

6. 17th Annual Report of the Department of Mental Hygiene, Year Ending March 31, 1958, NAR GUB, Series 29, Box 14, Folder 165.

7. Draft press release, ca. 1963–1964, 3.

8. 17th Annual Report of the Department of Mental Hygiene.

9. Zander, "The Rockefeller Years."

10. New York State Housing Finance Agency, "Policy Review Paper of the New York State Housing Finance Agency," 1982, New York State Library, 40.

11. Hurd and Benjamin, *Rockefeller in Retrospect*, 103–104.

12. Hurd and Benjamin, *Rockefeller in Retrospect*, 103–104.

13. New York State Health and Mental Hygiene Facilities Improvement Corporation, Report to the Governor, 1969, 4–12.

14. New York State Health and Mental Hygiene Facilities Improvement Corporation, Report to the Governor, 1969.

15. "1968 Highlights, New York State Department of Mental Hygiene," NAR GUB, Hugh Morrow, Series 21 (FA242), Box 20, Folder 215, 16.

16. Hurd and Benjamin, *Rockefeller in Retrospect*, 34–36, 46.

17. Connery and Benjamin, *Rockefeller of New York*, 173.

18. Nelson Rockefeller to Matthew Troy (councilman, Queens), 22 January 1973, NAR GUB, Hugh Morrow, Series 21 (FA242), Box 21, Folder 220, 2–3.

19. Dr. Alan Miller to Robert Douglass and Hugh Morrow, 26 July 1971, NAR GUB, Hugh Morrow, Series 21 (FA242), Box 20, Folder 214, 2–3.

20. New York State Mental Hygiene Facilities Improvement Fund, Report to the Governor, 1968, NAR GUB, Record 15, Series 3, Box 70, Folder 1558, 2.

21. Dr. Miller to Mr. Wolfe, 12 April 1973, Highlights of Memorandum by Federal District Judge Orrin Judd on the Class Action Suit Involving Willowbrook State School, NAR GUB, Hugh Morrow, Series 21 (FA242), Box 21, Folder 220, 6.

22. Press release, Willowbrook Report, 28 February 1973, NAR GUB, Hugh Morrow, Series 21 (FA242), Box 21, Folder 220.

23. Hurd and Benjamin, *Rockefeller in Retrospect*, 34–36.

24. Cuomo, *The New York Idea*, 133.

25. Cuomo, *The New York Idea*, 135–137.

26. Cuomo, *The New York Idea*, 135–137.

27. Peirce, *The Megastates of America*, 602.

28. Council of State Governments, *Book of the States, 1960–61*, 13:350.

29. Joyce Jennings, "Mental Health Care: The Hard Choices," *State Legislatures* 8, no. 4 (April 1982): 15.

30. Council of State Governments, *Book of the States, 1972–73*, 19:374–376.

31. Council of State Governments, *Book of the States, 1966–67*, 16:340–345.

32. Jennings, "Mental Health Care," 14.

33. *New York Times* Editorial Board, "The Crazy Talk about Bringing Back Asylums," *New York Times*, 12 June 2018, SR8.

34. US Department of Health and Human Services, Substance Abuse and Mental Health Services Administration, *Funding and Characteristics of State Mental Health Agencies, 2010*, https://www.aahd.us/wp-content/uploads/2012/12/FundingStateMentalHealthAgencies2010.pdf.

35. Kaiser Family Foundation, "State Mental Health Agency (SMHA) Per Capita Mental Health Services Expenditures," https://www.kff.org/other/state-indicator/smha-expenditures-per-capita/?currentTimeframe=0&sortModel=%7B%22colId%22:%22Location%22,%22sort%22:%22asc%22%7D. See also "Mental Health Spending: State Agency Totals," *Governing: The States and Localities*, http://www.governing.com/gov-data/health/mental-health-spending-by-state.html.

36. US Department of Health and Human Services, Substance Abuse and Mental Health Services Administration, *Funding and Characteristics of State Mental Health Agencies, 2010.*

37. Vera, "Prison Spending in 2015," https://www.vera.org/publications/price-of-prisons-2015-state-spending-trends/price-of-prisons-2015-state-spending-trends/price-of-prisons-2015-state-spending-trends-prison-spending; Michael Winerip and Michael Schwirtz, "For Mentally Ill Patients at Rikers Island, a Cycle of Jail and Hospitals," *New York Times*, 10 April 2015, https://www.nytimes.com/2015/04/12/nyregion/for-mentally-ill-inmates-at-rikers-a-cycle-of-jail-and-hospitals.html?mcubz=1. See also Alisa Roth, *Insane: America's Criminal Treatment of the Insane* (New York: Basic Books, 2018) for percentages from other cities.

Chapter Fourteen

1. "Rockefeller Backs Democrats' Plan," *New York Times*, 20 April 1959, 17.

2. Council of State Governments, *Book of the States, 1970–71*, 18:464–467.

3. Ronald Sullivan, "The Mighty, Dirty Hudson," *New York Times*, 21 February 1965, E5.

4. Connery and Benjamin, *Rockefeller of New York*, 328–367.

5. "Environmental Plan for New York State: Preliminary Plan," New York State DEC, ca. 1973, NAR GUB, Hugh Morrow, Series 21.1 (FA242), Box 14, Folder 150.

6. Mr. Macharg to Mr. Reilly, New York State Department of Health, 16 July 1964, NYSA, Series A1122-80, Box 1, Folder: Pure Waters; New York State Department of Health, memo, Haberer to Regional Health Directors, 19 February 1963, NYSA, Series A1122-80, Box 1, Folder: Pure Waters.

7. "State Aid Begins on Sewage Today," *New York Times*, 1 July 1962, 40.

8. Dr. Thompson to Mr. Kendrick, "Aid for Sewerage Construction," 4 August 1964, State of New York Health Department, NYSA, Box 1, Folder: Pure Waters, Series A1122-80.

9. "Governor Asks U.S. for Pollution Aid," *New York Times*, 24 February 1965, 33.

10. NAR to Barbara DeBevoise, 9.

11. NAR, "A Livable Environment," statement, ca. 1969, NAR GUB, Public Relations, Series 27.1 (FA369), Box 2, Folder 44.

12. "Governor Asks U.S. for Half-Billion Aid," *New York Times*, 4 January 1965, 31.

13. NAR, "A Livable Environment."

14. NAR, "A Livable Environment."

15. A. G. Marshall to Hugh Morrow, 15 October 1969, NAR GUB, Hugh Morrow, Series 21 (FA242), Box 15, Folder 158.

16. Council of State Governments, *Book of the States, 1972–73*, 19:464–473.

17. Linda Charlton, "Environmental Watchdog for State," *New York Times*, 24 April 1970.

18. Henry Diamond to Nelson Rockefeller, 17 August 1970, NAR GUB, Record 15, Series 21, Box 14, Folder 140.

19. "Pollution Bond Issue," *Sunday Times Union*, 12 March 1972.

20. Cuomo, *The New York Idea*, 209–217.

21. "City Gets Funds for Clean Water," *New York Times*, 22 April 1970, 72.

22. David Bird, "Governor Lauds Big Sewage Plant," *New York Times*, 25 July 1967, 37.

23. Sydney Schanberg, "State Gives $130 Million to City," *New York Times*, 19 September 1967, 53.

24. Harold Faber, "Hudson River Getting Cleaner," *New York Times*, 29 September 1973, 1, 29; Suzanne Daley, "New York City Seeking to Cut Size of Sewage Plant on the Hudson," *New York Times*, 4 September 1982, 1, 25; Barbara Basler, "Delay Plagued Sewage Plant on Hudson Started Up," *New York Times*, 31 December 1985, 17, 18.

25. David Bird, "Sewer Costs Imperiling State Pure Water Drive," *New York Times*, 11 March 1969, 39.

26. Peter Kihss, "Gains Reported on Environment," *New York Times*, 11 October 1970, 44.

27. "State Explains Lag in Pollution," *New York Times*, 26 October 1969, 50.

28. "State Explains Lag in Pollution."

29. David Bird, "Rockefeller Calls Nixon Plan on Water Pollution Inadequate," *New York Times*, 30 January 1970, 22.

30. William Farrell, "$4.2 Billion Is Needed to Clear State's Waters," *New York Times*, 20 August 1970, 27.

31. Clayton Knowles, "Rockefeller Plans Action on Water," *New York Times*, 3 September 1970, 27.

32. Faber, "Hudson River Getting Cleaner."

33. Faber, "Hudson River Getting Cleaner."

34. Connery and Benjamin, *Rockefeller of New York*, 343–344.

35. Peter Kihss, "Good Future Seen for Hudson River," *New York Times*, 25 May 1970, 36.

36. "Suffolk Will Use $388M in Grants to Extend Sewers to 12,000 South Shore Homes," *Newsday*, updated 12 September 2015, http://www.newsday.com/long-island/suffolk/suffolk-will-use-388m-in-grants-to-extend-sewers-to-12-000-south-shore-homes-1.10837378; CBS New York, "Suffolk County Program Offers to Replace Septic Tanks That Leak Nitrogen," 29 March 2017, http://newyork.cbslocal.com/2017/03/29/suffolk-county-septic-tanks/.

37. "Atom Power Plant Dropped Upstate," *New York Times*, 9 August 1968, 26.

38. Frank Adams, "Who Should Protect the Hudson Valley," *New York Times*, 2 August 1965, 28. See also Robert Caro, "Hudson Hysteria," *Newsday*, 2 July 1966, 11W.

39. Ralph Blumenthal, "New Phase Due in Hudson Valley," *New York Times*, 18 September 1966; "Governor Scores Report by Udall," *New York Times*, 9 October 1966, 43.

40. Robert R. Douglass to Hugh Morrow, 20 October 1969, NAR GUB, Hugh Morrow, Series 21 (FA242), Box 15, Folder 158.

41. Alexandra Dunn and Chandos Culleen, "Engines of Environmental Innovation: Reflections on the Role of States in the U.S. Regulatory System," *Pace Environmental Law Review* 32 (Spring 2015): 436.

42. Martin Melosi, *The Sanitary City: Urban Infrastructure in America from Colonial Times to the Present* (Baltimore: John Hopkins University Press, 2000), 331–332.

43. Dunn and Culleen, "Engines of Environmental Innovation," 440. See also J. G. Speth, "Environmental Critique (The 1972 Federal Water Pollution Control Act: Problems and Prospects After One Year)," *Natural Resources Lawyer* 7, no. 2 (Spring 1974): 249–256.

44. Cathleen Day, "Down by the Chesapeake Bay: Cooperative Federalism, Judicial Intervention, and the Boundary between State Land Use and Federal Environmental Law," *Energy Law Journal* 38 (2017): 254–255.

45. Day, "Down by the Chesapeake Bay."

46. Dunn and Culleen, "Engines of Environmental Innovation," 6.

47. Council of State Governments, *Book of the States, 1972–73*, 19:464–473.

48. Harvey Lieber and Bruce Rosinoff, "Evaluating the State's Role in Water Pollution Control 24 Billion Dollar Program in 1972," *Real Estate Economics* 1, no. 2 (June 1973): 76.

49. Dunn and Culleen, "Engines of Environmental Innovation," 442.

50. Ronald B. Robie, "State Viewpoint: The Federal Water Pollution Control Act and the States: Love in Bloom or Marriage on the Rocks," *Natural Resources Lawyer* 7, no. 2 (Spring 1974): 231–232.

51. Day, "Down by the Chesapeake Bay," 255.

52. Council of State Governments, *Book of the States, 1972–73*, 19:464–473.

53. Dunn and Culleen, "Engines of Environmental Innovation," 449.

Chapter Fifteen

1. Teaford, *The Rise of the States*, 116–117. Extensive references on the history of American tourism and a good overview essay are provided in Nicholas Dagen Bloom and J. Mark Souther, *American Tourism: Constructing a National Tradition* (Chicago: Center for American Places at Columbia College, 2012).

2. Marion Clawson, "State Governments and Outdoor Recreation," *State Government: The Journal of State Affairs* 4 (Autumn 1967): 216–223.

3. NAR to DeBevoise, 1–2.

4. On modern environmentalism and its relationship to affluence and the suburbs, see Rome, *The Bulldozer in the Countryside*; Ted Steinberg, *American Green: The Obsessive Quest for the Perfect Lawn* (New York: Basic Books, 1999); and Christopher Sellers, *Crabgrass Crucible: Suburban Nature and the Rise of Environmentalism in Twentieth-Century America* (Chapel Hill: University of North Carolina Press, 2012).

5. *Fifty Years: New York State Parks, 1924–1974* (Albany: Natural Heritage Trust, 1975), accessed through New York State Library Digital Collections, 15.

6. Teaford, *The Rise of the States*, 115.

7. *Fifty Years*, 19, 27.

8. *Fifty Years*, 36.

9. Sellers, *Crabgrass Crucible.*

10. Leo Egan, "Rockefeller Plans Big Park Program," *New York Times*, 21 August 1959, 1.

11. State of New York Conservation Department, "Now or Never: A Bold New Program for Outdoor Recreation," 1960, NAR GUB, William J. Ronan, Series 29 (FA371), Box 10, Folder 108. See also Charles Grutzner, "State Aims to Expand Parklands," *New York Times*, 22 May 1960, XX1.

12. State of New York Conservation Department, "Now or Never."

13. "Text of Statements by Moses and Rockefeller," *New York Times*, 1 December 1962, 13. See also Harvey Aronson, "Many See Loss to State in Moses' Resignation," *Newsday*, 1 December 1962, 3.

14. Robert Maver, "4 Parkways, Parks Renamed after Him," *Newsday*, 28 June 1963, 15.

15. "The Next Step: Building for Outdoor Recreation," 1965, NAR GUB, Hugh Morrow, Series 21.1 (FA242), Box 40, Folder 424, 9.

16. "The Next Step," 15.

17. Alice Murray, "NYers would Overrun LI Parks: Moses," *Newsday*, 14 July 1960.

18. *Fifty Years*, 1–52.

19. "Governor Signs Major Park Bill," *New York Times*, 4 July 1965, 36.

20. Laurance Rockefeller, New York State Council of Parks, 1968 Annual Report, 27 March 1969, 2.

21. *Fifty Years*, 42, 47.

22. *Fifty Years*, 40.

23. Farnsworth Fowle, "Site of First State Park in City Is Being Cleared," *New York Times*, 9 April 1971, 62.

24. Fowle, "Site of First State Park."

25. *Fifty Years*, 43–45.

26. Legislative Commission on Expenditure Review, "State Parks and Recreation Program," program audit, 47.

27. *Fifty Years*, 47.

28. Legislative Commission on Expenditure Review, "State Parks and Recreation Program."

29. New York State Council of Parks, Recreation and Historic Preservation, *2012 Annual Report*, https://parks.ny.gov/state-council/documents/2012StateCouncilAnnualReport.pdf, 7.

30. Cuomo, *The New York Idea*, 206.

31. Council of State Governments, *Book of the States, 1950–51*, 8:420.

32. Council of State Governments, *Book of the States, 1960–61*, 13:452–54.

33. Peirce, *The Megastates of America*, 643.

34. Council of State Governments, *Book of the States, 1962–63*, 14:486–489; Freeman Tilden, *The State Parks, Their Meaning in American Life* (New York: Knopf, 1962).

35. William F. Thompson, *Continuity and Change, 1940–1965: History of Wisconsin* (Madison: Wisconsin Historical Society, 1998, 2013), 304.

36. Council of State Governments, *Book of the States, 1962–63*, 14:486–489.

37. Council of State Governments, *Book of the States, 1966–67*, 16:439–442.

38. Council of State Governments, *Book of the States, 1970–71*, 18:467.

39. Council of State Governments, *Book of the States, 1980–81*, 8:520.

40. Clawson, "State Governments and Outdoor Recreation," 222.

41. Council of State Governments, *Book of the States, 1980–81,* 8:518.

42. Council of State Governments, *Book of the States, 1980–81,* 8:518.

43. Council of State Governments, *Book of the States, 1980–81,* 8:519.

44. Lisa Foderaro, "Conservation Group Keeps Buying Land, Helping State Parks Grow," *New York Times,* 15 November 2013, A15.

Chapter Sixteen

1. Gladwin Hill, "Public Control Growing in a Land Use Revolution," *New York Times,* 3 September 1973, 35.

2. "Landmark Fight over Land Use," *New York Times,* 20 May 1973, 213.

3. Jerry Jenkins, *The Adirondack Atlas: A Geographic Portrait of the Adirondack Park* (Syracuse, NY: Syracuse University Press, Adirondack Museum, 2004), 29.

4. Adirondack Park Agency, "Adirondack Park: Planning for Its Future," undated, NYSA, Record #18880-94, Box 5, Folder 29, 1.

5. Bayard Webster, "'Taming' of Adirondacks Feared," *New York Times,* 21 December 1970, 37.

6. Lithgow Osborne, "Great Adirondack Forest Preserve Is Now 75," *New York Times,* 7 August 1960, X21.

7. Cecil Heacox, "New York State's Most Valuable Possession," *New York Times,* 30 April 1967, 426.

8. Webster, "'Taming' of Adirondacks Feared."

9. "The Rockefeller Republican Record," ca. 1964, NAR GUB, Public Relations, Series 27.1 (FA369), Box 2, Folder 103; "Ski Center Bill Signed," *New York Times,* 30 April 1960, 17–19.

10. John Oakes, "Conservation: Saving the Wild," *New York Times,* 12 October 1958, XX17.

11. Robert Hall, "Price of Progress," *New York Times,* 8 May 1966, XX3.

12. Dick Beamish to Hugh Morrow, 8 May 1973, NAR GUB, Hugh Morrow, Series 21 (FA242), Box 13, Folder 150, 3.

13. David Bird, "Adirondacks Development Stirs Major Ecology Fight," *New York Times,* 23 May 1972, 43.

14. David Bird, "Key Decision Near on Adirondacks Development," *New York Times,* 8 November 1972, 51.

15. William Farrell, "Bill Creating Adirondacks Unit Stalled," *New York Times,* 2 June 1971, 45.

16. "Moses Assails Bill on Forest Preserve," *New York Times,* 22 September 1961, 29.

17. "Moses Criticized on Forest Plans," *New York Times,* 30 September 1961, 27.

18. David Johnson and Associates, "Welcome to Lake George," reprint, 1968, NAR GUB, Press Office, Series 25.3 (FA368), Box 2, Folder 1546, 2, 5–6.

19. Knaap, Nedovic-Budic, and Carbonell, *Planning for States and Nation States,* 31.

20. "Adirondack Study Awaits Chairman," *New York Times,* 29 September 1968, 32.

21. State of New York, Conservation Department, "The Adirondacks: New York's Forest Preserve and a Proposed National Park," 1967, NAR GUB, Press Office, Series 25.3 (FA368), Box 2, Folder 1538.

22. Persico, *The Imperial Rockefeller,* 48.

23. Adirondack Mountain Club, Inc., Statement of Position on the July 27, 1967, Proposal

for an Adirondack Mountains National Park, 30 October 1967, New York State Library Digital Collections, 1–3.

24. "Adirondack Study Awaits Chairman."

25. "Brief Summary of the Final Report of the Governor's Temporary Study Commission on the Future of the Adirondacks," 17 December 1970, NAR GUB, Hugh Morrow, Series 21.1 (FA242), Box 14, Folder 153, 1–6.

26. "Brief Summary of the Final Report of the Governor's Temporary Study Commission," 1–6.

27. William Farrell, "Assembly Backs Control of Adirondack Park Land," *New York Times*, 8 June 1971, 21.

28. Hugh Morrow to Dick Beamish, 8 May 1973, NAR GUB, Record 15, Series 21, Box 14, Folder 150.

29. David Bird, "Adirondack Plan Offered by State," *New York Times*, 9 May 1972, 30.

30. Glenn Harris, majority whip, to Nelson Rockefeller, 30 July 1973, NAR GUB, Record 15, Series 21, Box 14, Folder 150.

31. Harold Faber, "Adirondack Wilderness Is Focus," *New York Times*, 23 August 1976, 25.

32. Harold Faber, "State Removing Man-Made Structures," *New York Times*, 2 January 1977, 29.

33. "Private Land Use and Development," 1972 draft, NYSA, Record #18880-94, Box 4, Folder 10, 11–12.

34. Dick Beamish to Hugh Morrow, 8 May 1973, NAR GUB, Hugh Morrow, Series 21 (FA242), Box 13, Folder 150, 2.

35. Jenkins, *The Adirondack Atlas*, 28.

36. Farrell, "Bill Creating Adirondacks Unit Stalled."

37. William Farrell, "Adirondack State Park Residents Await Development Agency," *New York Times*, 24 August 1971, 39.

38. David Bird, "Adirondack Park Agency Meets Opposition," *New York Times*, 9 January 1973, 42.

39. Office of Legislative Research, "Adirondack Park Private Land Use and Development Plan," 30 March 1973, NAR GUB, Hugh Morrow, Series 21.1 (FA242), Box 14, Folder 150.

40. John Darnton, "Governor Approves Plan for the Adirondacks," *New York Times*, 26 July 1972, 74.

41. "Modified Plan for Adirondacks," *New York Times*, 6 March 1973, 44.

42. William F. Porter, Jon D. Erickson, and Ross S. Whaley, eds., *The Great Experiment in Conservation: Voices from the Adirondack Park* (Syracuse, NY: Syracuse University Press, 2009), 231.

43. M. A. Farber, "Adirondacks Compromise Is Reached," *New York Times*, 9 May 1973, 33.

44. Farber, "Adirondacks Compromise Is Reached."

45. Alfonso Narvez, "Legislature Passes Bill on Development of the Adirondacks," *New York Times*, 15 May 1973, 81.

46. NAR, statement on the signing of Adirondack Park Bill, 22 May 1973, NAR GUB, Hugh Morrow, Series 21.1 (FA242), Box 13, Folder 150.

47. M. A. Farber, "Governor Signs Adirondack Park Bill," *New York Times*, 23 May 1973, 22.

48. "Governor's Press Release on Signing of Bill," 22 May 1973, NYSA, Record #18880-94, Box 5, Folder 30.

49. David Bird, "Environmental Chief Bars Adirondack Home Project," *New York Times*, 2 August 1973, 73.

50. "Commissioner Says 'No' to Ton-Da-Lay Project," *New York State Environment* 3 (1 September 1972): 1.

51. David Bird, "Suit Challenges Adirondack Plan," *New York Times*, 12 December 1974, 21.

52. "Park Agency Rejects a Proposal," *New York Times*, 20 February 1977, 33.

53. Frances Clines, "Adirondacks Weight Land-Use Law Impact," *New York Times*, 6 November 1973, 41.

54. Porter, Erickson, and Whaley, *The Great Experiment in Conservation*, 223.

55. Porter, Erickson, and Whaley, *The Great Experiment in Conservation*, 225.

56. Porter, Erickson, and Whaley, *The Great Experiment in Conservation*, 394–397.

57. Porter, Erickson, and Whaley, *The Great Experiment in Conservation*, 278.

58. Porter, Erickson, and Whaley, *The Great Experiment in Conservation*, 267.

59. Porter, Erickson, and Whaley, *The Great Experiment in Conservation*, 266–267, 356–357.

60. Porter, Erickson, and Whaley, *The Great Experiment in Conservation*, 358–369.

61. Cuomo, *The New York Idea*, 209.

62. Myron Thompson, "Hawaii's State Land Use Law," *State Government* (Spring 1966): 98.

63. Council of State Governments, *Book of the States, 1962–63*, 14:451–453.

64. Thompson, "Hawaii's State Land Use Law," 99.

65. Brent Walth, *Fire at Eden's Gate: Tom McCall and the Oregon Story* (Portland: Oregon Historical Society, 2003), 186.

66. Walth, *Fire at Eden's Gate*, 189–191.

67. See John S. Banta, "The Adirondack Park Land Use and Development Plan and Vermont's Act 250 after Forty Years," *John Marshall Law Review* 45, no. 2, (2012): 417–421; State of Vermont, Natural Resources Board, "History of Act 250," http://nrb.vermont.gov/act250-program/history; Peirce, *The Megastates of America*, 227; and Barry Cullingworth, *The Political Culture of Planning: American Land Use Planning in Comparative Perspective* (New York: Routledge, 1993), chapter 11.

68. Rome, *The Bulldozer in the Countryside*, 228–229.

69. Jefferson Decker, "Pacific Views: Property Rights, the Regulatory State, and American Conservatism," *Journal of Policy History* 28, no. 4 (2016): 654–679.

70. Charles Lester, "CZM in California: Successes and Challenges Ahead," *Coastal Management* 41, no. 3 (May 2013): 219–244.

71. Rome, *The Bulldozer in the Countryside*, 247.

Postscript

1. See Rohe, *The Research Triangle.*

2. See, for instance, David Goldfield, *Cotton Fields and Skyscrapers: Southern City and Region* (Baltimore: Johns Hopkins University Press, 1989).

3. A recent overview of state and climate change action can be found at Transportation & Climate Initiative of the Northeast and Mid-Atlantic States, "Summary of Policy Options in State Climate Action Plans," http://www.georgetownclimate.org/files/report/TCI-SummaryofPolicyOptionsinClimateAction(1).PDF.

Index

Page numbers in *italics* indicate figures.